Fodor's EXPLORING

Scotland

FODOR'S TRAVEL PUBLICATIONS, INC.

NEW YORK • TORONTO • LONDON • SYDNEY • AUCKLAND

WWW.FODORS.COM

Copyright © The Automobile Association 1999
Maps copyright © The Automobile Association 1999

All rights reserved under International and Pan-American Copyright conventions. Distributed by Random House, Inc., New York. No maps, illustrations, or other portions of this book may be reproduced in any form without written permission from the publishers.

Published in the United States by Fodor's Travel Publications, Inc.
Published in the United Kingdom by A.A. Publishing.

Fodor's and Fodor's Exploring Guides are registered trademarks of Fodor's Travel Publications, Inc.

ISBN 0–679–00276–6
Third Edition

Fodor's Exploring Scotland

Author: **Gilbert Summers**
Revision Verifier: **Gilbert Summers**
Joint Series Editor: **Josephine Perry**
Original Copy Editor: **Barbara Fuller**
Original Photography: **Steve Day, Eric Ellington, Marius Alexander and Ken Patterson**
Cartography: **The Automobile Association**
Cover Design: **Tigist Getachew, Fabrizio La Rocca**
Front Cover Top Photograph: **Automobile Association**
Front Cover Silhouette: **Catherine Karnow**

Special Sales
Fodor's Travel Publications are available at special discounts for bulk purchases (100 copies or more) for sales promotions or premiums. Special editions, including personalized covers, excerpts of existing guides, and corporate imprints can be created in large quantities for special needs. For more information, contact your local bookseller or write to Special Marketing, Fodor's Travel Publications, 201 East 50th Street, New York, NY 10022. Inquiries from Canada should be directed to your local Canadian bookseller or sent to Random House of Canada Ltd., Marketing Department, 2775 Matheson Blvd. East, Mississauga, Ontario L4W 4P7.

Printed and bound in Italy by Printer Trento srl
10 9 8 7 6 5 4 3 2 1

How to use this book

ORGANIZATION

Scotland Is, Scotland Was
Discusses aspects of life and culture in contemporary Scotland and explores significant periods in its history.

A to Z
An alphabetical listing of places to visit. The book begins with sections on Edinburgh and Glasgow, and is subsequently divided into regions. Places of interest are listed alphabetically within each section. Suggested walks, drives and Focus On articles, which provide an insight into aspects of life in Scotland, are included in each section.

Travel Facts
Contains the strictly practical information that is vital for a successful trip.

Hotels and Restaurants
Lists places to stay and places to eat alphabetically by region. Entries are graded budget, moderate or expensive.

ABOUT THE RATINGS
Most places described in this book have been given a separate rating. These are as follows:

▶▶▶   Do not miss

▶▶   Highly recommended

▶   Worth seeing

MAP REFERENCES
To make the location of a particular place easier to find, every main entry in this book is given a map reference, such as 176B3. The first number (176) indicates the page on which the map can be found, the letter (B) and the second number (3) pinpoint the square in which the main entry is located. The maps on the inside front cover and inside back cover are referred to as IFC and IBC respectively.

Contents

6

Gilbert Summers is a Scot who has spent many years living in Scotland and earning his living writing about his native land, working closely with the tourism industry. He has also produced a variety of material for many international publishers. Much to the surprise of his friends, in 1996 he became the manager of a marine aquarium in Macduff, but continues a freelance writing career in his spare time.

My Scotland by Gilbert Summers

Growing up in the northern part of a pre-motorway Scotland brought its own pleasingly skewed perceptions of the shape and form of the nation. Aberdeen was a dramatic granite city in the south; Edinburgh was an age away and only really existed as an illustration on a tin of shortbread; Skye and the west coast were fantastically exotic, and Orkney and Shetland were definitely abroad. Yet all were encompassed by "Scottishness."

Since then, distances have shrunk, both in my perception and because of improved communications. Now, travel in Scotland is measured out in manageable statistics: over five hours to the Moray Firth coast from the border near Carlisle; just an hour from Inverness to Ullapool and the ferry to the Western Isles, and less than one hour by train from Edinburgh to Glasgow. But this vague feeling of many Scotlands still clings on.

It is remarkable how little time it takes to reach widely contrasting places, and for me this is one of the best things about Scotland. If the Edinburgh Festival crowds begin to wear you down, there are high, wide and brackeny green hills close at hand in the Pentlands. Or you can lose yourself in the native Scots pinewoods that lie within easy distance of, say, Inverness airport.

As a native, I have always wondered why Scotland, with all its diversity of ancestry, landscape, and culture, drapes itself in tartan finery as an instantly recognizable symbol of Scottishness. The once despised humble cloth of the Celt has become a powerful marketing tool. Yet, this convenient stereotype hides Scotland's complex character. I have always exhorted any traveler to pull aside the tartan curtain and discover other threads of the nation's complex story, such as Picts and Vikings, or links with France and the Low Countries, or even why more Scots gave their allegiance to the government at the Battle of Culloden than joined Bonnie Prince Charlie.

And finally, Scotland is fertile ground for romantics. Hills that make the heart ache, city skylines with castles and spires, tales of heroism in the glen—you can find them all. Maybe delving too deep into Scotland's history isn't necessary. Just sit back and enjoy the sheer variety of it all!

Scotland Is

Misty glens, lochs, mountains, tartan, bagpipes, and kilts: these are the most familiar images of Scotland. How these essentially Highland aspects came to represent the whole of Scotland —Highland, Lowland, urban, and rural—is one of the oddities of the nation's history.

TARTAN Today, you can cross over the Border from England and hear bagpipes in a Southern Uplands town, eat shortbread from a tartan wrapper in the middle of Glasgow, and take in a Highland Games within easy reach of Edinburgh. All this is well before you reach the real Highlands. Scotland, at least those aspects of it dealing with tourism, embraces its kilted image wholeheartedly: tartan sells.

The glorious paradox is that if a tartan-clad Highlander had appeared in a Lowland town a few centuries ago, he would have been locked up, if not shot on sight. The Highlanders were regarded as barbarous thieves by Lowland Scots. After the crushing of the final rebellion against the Hanoverian dynasty on Culloden Moor near Inverness in 1746, the tartan was even banned by Act of

The new face of Scottish tradition?

Parliament. Tartan was associated with revolt and lawlessness. Now the kilt and its associated paraphernalia represent the whole of Scotland, Highland or Lowland, Gaelic-speaking or otherwise, to many of today's visitors.

BAGPIPES The unmistakable tones of the bagpipe or Highland war pipe form the soundtrack to the romantic image of Scotland. Perhaps originally a device for signaling across long Highland distances, the bagpipe survived partly through its use in Highland regiments, and now plays its role in many pipe bands. Most Scottish towns have at least one band, and the pipes create instant Highland atmosphere at all kinds of gatherings, from protest marches to weddings.

SCENERY As for the misty glens (valleys) and bens (high hills), a love for this landscape grew out of the cult of the picturesque embraced by the Romantic poets (William Wordsworth, strongly associated with the English Lake District, made several tours of the Highlands). Today, a taste for wild scenery is for many the main reason for visiting Scotland.

The scenery is absolutely amazing, and it is possible to see some of Scotland's most rugged places without leaving a main road. This is why the name Glen Coe appears on the destination headboard of so many tour buses. The valley provides a matchless combination of awesome scenery and chilling tale of the Highlands of old: a massacre of the local clan by a clan militia took place there in 1692. Farther west, the island of Skye makes a startling impact when the Cuillin Hills etch themselves against a blue sky.

Morning mist over Flanders Moss, from the edge of the Trossachs

With scenic grandeur like this, and the romance of kilts and other Highland paraphernalia, it is all too easy to forget the other aspects of Scotland. The country has some of the finest stretches of unspoiled coastline in Europe: on the east coast, both sheer cliffs and sandy beaches provide superb scenery. The Borders towns, with their textile traditions and strong sense of community, are full of character and do not need any dressing up in Highland costume. The Northern Isles, notably Shetland, are a world away from "Highlandry" and have a vivid Scandinavian heritage. Then there is the modern Scotland, as expressed in style-conscious Glasgow or cosmopolitan Edinburgh. Scotland can offer you ceilidhs (Highland-style evenings of song and dance) if you want them, but make the most of its wealth of other attributes as well.

❏ After the Battle of Culloden in 1746, many rebels were condemned to death by the authorities. One of these unfortunates was a Highland piper. He pleaded for mercy on the grounds that he was a musician, but the judge defined his pipes as a weapon of war and the sentence was duly carried out. ❏

Many Scottish postcards tend to perpetuate the tartan cliché

Perhaps the best-known Scottish festivity is Hogmanay—the last night of the year and its hungover aftermath. Until recent years, it was far more important than Christmas north of the border.

HOGMANAY Though none can agree on the word's origins (possibly dialect French *au geux menez,* "bring [gifts] to the beggars"), Hogmanay is still strong in Scotland. Until recent times, the night of December 31, Hogmanay Night, was the most important on the Scots calendar. Other deep-winter festivals, derived from early pagan fire rituals, survive in places, for example the swinging of fireballs, with the combustible material held in place by wire, in Stonehaven; or the "burning of the clavie," a kind of portable bonfire in a basket, at Burghead in Moray. Most famous of all is Up-Helly-Aa, a Viking celebration in Shetland, when people go guising (dressing up in costume) and enjoy various shows, including the spectacular burning of a Viking longship. Beltane or May Day festivities can also be found in a few places in modern Scotland.

Other types of event are those comparatively modern ones, such as Highland Games and agricultural shows. Highland Games are very popular in many towns, and not just

Fringe Sunday in Edinburgh's Holyrood Park—truly cosmopolitan

in their namesake region. A combination of musical, dancing, and athletic skills all happening in the same arena, often simultaneously, they are held in towns and villages throughout the Highlands and far beyond.

HIGHLAND GAMES Clan societies and other promoters of Scotland's romantic martial image claim for the games an ancient history, arguing that they were originally held so that clan chiefs could select the most talented people for their retinues. However, most seem to have originated in early Victorian times, when a resurgence of interest in things Scottish resulted in the formation of various Caledonian clubs. Games gave the members an excuse to cavort in tartan finery. Yet another explanation is that the games were trials of strength devised by bored lumberjacks, busy cutting down the Highland forests. No matter what their origins, be prepared to enjoy parachute jumps and guest appearances by TV characters as happenings in the games "tradition" as well.

RURAL EVENTS Agricultural shows are as entertaining as Highland

On the festival cavalcade

Games and serve as a showcase for Scottish agriculture. They take place throughout the Lowlands. Great meeting places for the rural communities, they embrace not just the serious business of selling agricultural machinery and livestock, but also displays of just about anything else from trick cycling to terrier racing.

❏ Like the Mod, the Borders Common Ridings have strong regional associations. These ancient celebrations of horsemanship in the Borders towns owe their origins at least in part to a need to reaffirm town boundaries in the face of frequent cross border raiding parties. Unlike Highland Games, they are definitely not held for the benefit of visitors. ❏

CULTURAL FESTIVALS The Edinburgh International Festival is the spectacular flagship of mainstream cultural events, from theater to comedy skits. In fact, the capital suffers from festival overkill in late August, partly due to the size of the Fringe, the less formal and more unruly younger brother of the "official" festival. This huge grab bag of performances spreads out of the city's halls and theaters onto the streets. Nobody could visit Edinburgh during the Fringe and possibly miss it! Also adding to the throng is the

Highland events—the hammer thrower at the Pitlochry Games

❏ The Gaels—that is, the Gaelic speakers of Celtic origin whose linguistic stronghold is in the far northwest of Scotland—have their own big cultural event for Gaeldom in the fall, the National Mod, which is sometimes rather unkindly and unjustifiably described in the press as the "Whisky Olympics." ❏

Edinburgh Military Tattoo and a range of smaller events such as the Book Festival and the Jazz Festival.

In January, rival Glasgow holds the Celtic Connections festival, a homage to Celtic music, with performers from all over the world playing and teaching at workshops for prospective players or instrument-makers. Folk festivals are also held in many places at various times of the year, two of the most notable being in Shetland: the Folk Festival in April and the Accordian and Fiddle Festival in October.

Three languages are spoken in Scotland: Gaelic, (Lowland) Scots, and English. All Gaels are bilingual. Some Lowlanders still tend to under-value their native tongue, while the adoption of broad Scots vowels by a child of English parents living in Scotland can be greeted in some homes with something near to horror.

THE FIRST LANGUAGE Gaelic was once the principal language over much of Scotland, but it has been in slow retreat for seven centuries. Today, Gaelic's stronghold is the far north and west, notably the Outer Hebrides islands. However, increased funding for Gaelic broad-casting in the early 1990s has resulted, ironically, in Gaelic being heard in parts of Scotland that have had virtually no Gaelic speakers for centuries. Gaelic enters the vocabulary of Scots and English speakers most often in anglicized or part-anglicized place-names or topographical features such as ben

LOWLAND SCOTS In its late medieval heyday, the Scots tongue, which evolved from a Northumbrian form of Anglo-Saxon, had roughly the same relationship to "English" that Dutch has to German. Today, it is diluted and impoverished by its kin-ship with "Standard English," and has the further disadvantage of non-standardized spelling. However, its rich borrowings from Norse, French, German, and Dutch can still be heard, especially in the northeast, which most linguists consider to be its heartland. Even in its densest forms it roughly follows standard English in most grammatical forms,

This Gaelic sign in Fort William literally means "a hundred thousand welcomes"

(high hill), loch (lake), strath (river valley or adjacent low-lying grass-land), glen (valley), or cairn (heap of stones). Sassenach (Englishman), slo-gan (war cry), and ceilidh (a sort of Scottish hoedown) are other Gaelic words commonly encountered. As the panel at the top shows, many places on the west coast possess only a Gaelic name.

but differs considerably in vocabu-lary and pronunciation.

TRAPS FOR THE LISTENER The lin-guistic nuances of Scotland are worth listening for. For example, there are Scots constructions using an every-day English vocabulary. "I'll see you the length of the bus stop" is all but opaque to many non-Scots, yet does not use any exclusively "Scots" words. It means "I will escort you as far as the bus stop." There are single

words that mean something different to Scots and English. "Messages" means shopping to most Scots (and French, for that matter), with the mysterious "going the messages," that is, doing the shopping, a further complication.

Dingwall in Highland Region also uses the traditional Gaelic welcome

SCOTS: A SEPARATE LANGUAGE?

Perhaps the listener will *skite* (slip) on a *creishy* (greasy) butter wrapper on a *dreich* (dull) day, accidentally *breenging into* (colliding with) the farm's *dour* (unfriendly) *orraman* (spare hand) *daundering* (walking slowly) down to the *roup* (auction)!

Language experts talk of "the great vowel shift," that is, the change in vowel qualities that took place in medieval times (and makes the works of English medieval writer Geoffrey Chaucer difficult for English speakers today). This shift did not occur in northern word forms. Thus "take" is "tak," "bowl" is "bool," "cow" is "coo," "most" is "maist" and so on in northeast Scotland today. Then listen for a scattering of surviving weak

❑ If you are a non-Scot and your car breaks down—beware. A mechanic telling you "I doubt you'll need a new engine" is giving you bad news, not good. In Scotland "I doubt" often means "I regret that..." or "I am afraid that...." ❑

Anglo-Saxon plural forms: "shoes" are "sheen," "eyes" are "een." Add Scottish constructions to the northern vocabulary and characteristic pronunciation, and it takes a brave linguist to say that Scots is just a dialect of English.

But do not worry—you will be understood everywhere, and might hear no Scots tongue at all. Bilingual Scots, in the sense of those who can still speak "dense" Lowland forms as well as English, modify their language into a near standard English (with a Scots accent, naturally) for the benefit of everyday conversation with the rest of the English-speaking world.

ENGLISH IN SCOTLAND The overheating of England's real-estate market in the mid-1980s saw many English people take advantage of the high selling prices in the south to move into rural Scotland, where property was much cheaper. It is possible to travel in many parts of the Highlands and hear no local native voices at all.

❑ The linguistic historian Billy Kay has memorably described Lowland Scots as being "a language spoken by consenting adults in private." ❑

In the Scotland of old, diet and wealth were interrelated; the same is true today. But instead of trips to the supermarket to load up the station wagon, the wealthy merchants and lairds and the powerful clan chiefs took advantage of direct trading links across the North Sea to acquire the dainty spices and French wines that went with their status.

A MEAGER DIET It is significant that Scotland's most famous dish, haggis, is an ancient folk recipe using the cheapest cuts of meat, stuffed into tripe, then boiled. In a nation with an unpredictable climate and a history of economic uncertainties, everyday Scots cooking had much to do with eking out ingredients.

Today, poverty in the bleak housing projects of deindustrialized Scotland is a factor in health statistics that no amount of tartan packaging can totally conceal. In low-income households, a dependence on cheap and convenient high-cholesterol and otherwise unbalanced foods ensure that Scotland is a poor performer in comparison with other parts of Britain; indeed, deaths through heart disease are the worst in Europe.

Paradoxically, Scotland today has numerous advantages when it comes

The Waterfront Wine Bar in Leith, near Edinburgh

to "local produce." Peterhead is Europe's largest whitefish landing port. Scottish seafood is sought out by top chefs south of the border and on the Continent. (In fact, locals grumble that the best is exported.) Aberdeen Angus beef, though eclipsed by overseas breeds in recent years, is making a comeback and still has considerable cachet. Scots farmers remind anyone who will listen that their beef is "grass-fed" on natural pastures. Meanwhile, Scottish farmed venison, with all its low-fat virtues, is widely available on restaurant menus.

THE SCOTS AS HOME BAKERS The largest soft-fruit-growing area in the European Union lies within the hinterland of Dundee, in central Scotland. With the prevailing climate just right for raspberries and their cousins, as well as strawberries, it is no coincidence that Dundee is famous for its jams. The Scots sweet

16

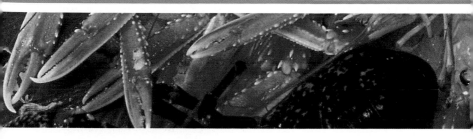

Shortbread—distinctive product and unmistakable packaging

masquerade as traditional dishes, and even the humble cup of coffee is translated into creaking mock Scots as a "tassie o bean bree." (Tassie is "cup," bree is "soup" or "brine.") There is much more to good Scottish food than "flambéing" the steak in whisky or coating the ice cream with oatmeal, and the discriminating diner will find plenty to please the hungry palate, not just an updated local tradition. Other styles, from Italian to Indian, are also well represented, notably, but not only, in the larger towns.

tooth not only sends some of its population to an early grave, but also is evident in a still sturdy tradition of home baking, including shortbread and other traditionally fattening goodies. Finally, the humble oat—until well into the present century still a staple of Lowland farmhands—has recently won new converts with the discovery of its role as a good source of soluble fiber.

EATING OUT TODAY Food lovers find a high standard of cuisine north of the border. Some restaurants advertise "Taste of Scotland" menus, which means they belong to an organization dedicated to high standards and the fresh and creative use of Scottish local produce. However, an establishment offering "Scottish" cuisine will not automatically be of the highest order. In a few places there still exists the fake Scots menu, where catered foods

---

❏ "The little Highland Mutton, when fat, is delicious, and certainly the greatest of luxuries And the small Beef, when fresh, is very sweet and succulent.... Amongst the poorer classes in Scotland, beef is eaten only at Martinmas, when a Mart or Ox is killed; and the only other butcher meat they eat throughout the year is an occasional Braxy."

Edward Burt's Letters from the North of Scotland, 1730

A "mart" is an animal, such as an ox or sheep, killed for salting for winter.
A "braxy" is a sheep that has died of braxy, an intestinal illness. ❏

To many people, especially from the more urban south, the appeal of Scotland lies in its "unspoiled" qualities: the silent hills and open skies of the northlands represent a near-mystical, changeless purity. But is the north really the untouched wilderness, a description so beloved by the writers of tourist brochures?

18

THE FATE OF SCOTLAND'S WOODLANDS

In environmental terms, the upland landscapes that cover 75 percent of Scotland have a sad story to tell of destruction and forest clearance, started originally in the Southern Uplands and the Lowlands by Bronze Age man about 3,000 years ago. The needs of agriculture meant that by the Middle Ages much of the forest south of the Highlands had gone.

Harboring wolves and brigands, the Highland forests, too, were destroyed. Charcoal made from Highland oaks was used in early iron smelting. Queen Elizabeth I of England (1558–1603) decreed that English trees should be reserved for shipbuilding, so her smelters turned to the Highlands, aided and abetted by Scottish Lowland businessmen. Until coke replaced charcoal in around 1813, Highland forests were destroyed wholesale for smelting purposes.

By 1743 the last wolf had gone, following the brown bear, reindeer, elk, boar, and beaver into oblivion. Then the great flocks of sheep—still a feature of the Highlands today—arrived, with flockmasters firing whole hillsides, eager to extend the grazings. The modern type of sporting estate seen today, encouraging red deer on an open hillside, also evolved. High populations of nibbling sheep and deer still prevent forest regeneration. In the eastern Highlands, the management of grouse on the moor involves annual burning of open hillsides, to encourage young heather growth.

When reforestation was at last tackled, much of it was at first in blocks of Sitka spruce or other alien

The Black Wood of Rannoch—a rare surviving example of Scotland's natural pine forest

species now seen throughout the Highlands, even in traditional beauty spots such as the Trossachs. Elsewhere, it is the open "hillscape"—burned and overgrazed, degraded for quick profit, and described by some ecologists as a wet desert—that is the wilderness enjoyed by millions each year.

FINDING THE REAL WILDERNESS Yet the picture is not all gloomy. Real wilderness, in the sense of an unchanged landscape (give or take a few ski resorts), lies above 2,800 feet. Meanwhile, on lower ground, there is a more sensitive attitude to forestry planting, at least in some places, and a wide range of habitats, many in the care of conservation organizations. Little chunks of high-grade landscape survive even in the Lowlands in the form of river gorge woodlands, Lowland raised bog, and also wetlands, notably at the Loch of Strathbeg in the northeast.

The oakwoods on the east side of Loch Lomond still ring with spring birdsong. An echo of the great wood of Caledon can be found in the Black Wood of Rannoch on the south shore of Loch Rannoch. Here the characteristic habitat survives: an open woodland of great-limbed pines, with an undergrowth of juniper and heather. Crossbills call in the treetops, and it is still possible to see capercaillie, the big grouse of the woods. Around Rothiemurchus on Speyside, near Aviemore, and by Loch Maree in Wester Ross, on the Beinn Eighe side, wild country can be enjoyed in a comparatively "undegraded" state.

Finally, though land misuse is undeniable, the paradox is plain: despite everything, the Highlands, with their vast stretches of open, man-made moorland, remain hauntingly beautiful.

A remnant Scots pine in Glen Falloch. Overgrazing prevents its offspring from regenerating

19

❏ The unique survival of a feudal method of land owner-ship in Scotland—10 percent of Scotland is owned by just 13 individuals—has not always worked in favor of conservation and healthy land use. The financial worth of sporting estates is partly measured in deer numbers, so the incentive exists to keep stocks at artificially high levels, to the detriment of the Highland habitat. ❏

Why do many Scots still write "Scottish" and not "British" in passports and hotel guest-register books? In 1997, the Scottish electorate threw out the only British Parliamentary party still in favor of the Union with England in its present form. For Nationalists, mild or fervent, there are interesting times ahead.

WHO FEELS BRITISH? In 1707, during the rounds of negotiations and bribes in Westminster that ended with the Union of Parliaments and the loss of Scotland's independence, the pro-posals for each day of negotiation were laid before the Scots, who were left to argue among themselves. The English Parliament continued its business. When the deal was finally concluded, nothing much had changed for

Scotland. They flourished and withered over the decades. In 1928 the forerunner of the Scottish National Party (S.N.P.) was formed. It gained 11 M.P.s by 1974 while campaigning under the slogan "It's Scotland's Oil," though these were reduced to three throughout the 1980s.

By that time, Scotland had become a Labour Party stronghold, with the ruling Conservatives' policies deeply unpopular north of the Border. A wave of well-off southerners who had capitalized on the mid-1980s property boom and were snapping up desirable property all over Scotland further increased resentment.

Before the

Saltire, symbol of Scotland

English parliamentary repre-sentatives. There were new Scots faces at Westminster, but nothing was fundamentally altered to make the English feel British. Neither do many Scots, even to this day.

By the 19th century, the Liberal Party and a succession of pressure groups had pledged themselves to Home Rule for

key general election of 1992, the media—much of it London-based and supporting the Conservative government—hyped the Nationalists' chances, seeing them as the "second force" in Scottish poli-tics. However, the S.N.P. breakthrough did not occur, though its share of the vote increased, as it did again in 1997. Over that five year period, Scotland was governed by a party with barely enough Scottish Conservative M.P.s to man the

Scottish Office in Edinburgh. They, in turn, were completely wiped out in the 1997 general election, when the Scottish people delivered their verdict on the Conservatives' pro-Unionist agenda.

THE SCANDINAVIAN MODEL

Nationalists argue that Scotland is self-sufficient in food and energy, while proportionately exporting 21 percent more for every manufacturing worker than the U.K. as a whole. Of the 11 nations that have overtaken the U.K. in terms of wealth in the last 30 years, seven are small European nations. And of those, three—Finland, Iceland and Norway—have become independent this century. Nationalists in Scotland look closely at the Scandinavian model of economic success, and point to the influence of Denmark, for example, within the E.U. with its similar population size, climate, resources, and economy. Far older than the present Union with England, they point out, is the Auld Alliance—the historical tendency for Scotland to unite with France against England. Old trading alliances with the Low Countries, too, are reminders that Scotland formerly looked to the Continent and may do so again.

The commitment of the Labour government, elected in 1997, to a Scottish Parliament has awakened the minds of many Scots—and also the media—to the possibility of going beyond this halfway measure in a way that has not been discussed in Scotland for three centuries. From a

The Vigil for a Scottish Parliament trailer, parked outside government buildings in Edinburgh

position of near hostility to the proposed Scottish Parliament the S.N.P. now seems to view it as a springboard to full independence at some point in the 21st century. Whether or not the nation of Scotland is able to grasp this particular nettle, only time will tell.

❑ Linda Colley, a professor of history at Yale University, describing Scotland's situation: "...the alienation of the Celtic fringe is not a recipe for a healthy democracy, nor for a happy and long-lasting union." ❑

Political message on a disused railroad viaduct, north of Montrose

One fact is certain: Scotland as the "Workshop of the Western World" has gone for ever, the nation's smokestack industries, dependent on coal and iron, mostly reduced to dereliction and the memories of old men.

Harvesting in Fife; agriculture now plays a lesser role in the economy

Even as late as the mid-1960s, manufacturing made up 32 percent of Scotland's G.D.P. and employed 35 percent of its workforce. By the mid-1990s, manufacturing was down to 22 percent, with only 20 percent of the workforce in this sector—below the United Kingdom average. Today, seven out of ten workers are now in the service sector and not manufacturing anything. However, Scotland is not quite yet a nation of waiters and tartan gift-shop assistants.

ELECTRONICS—THE SUNRISE INDUSTRY Silicon Glen was the apt name coined to describe the sunrise industry of electronics, which currently employs 46,000 people north of the Border. At least 38 percent of personal computers and 57 percent of workstations sold in Europe are actually built in Scotland, thanks to financial incentives for inward-bound companies, plus a skilled workforce. The view from IBM's site (where all of its monitor research and development worldwide takes place) is out to the moors of Renfrewshire. Compaq, the world's largest computer manufacturer (and recent buyer of Digital) has a substantial Scottish presence, notably at Erskine, west of Glasgow. There are many more examples from the 550 companies in this sector, many of them household names.

EXPORTS Scotland's most famous export, whisky, continues to be important, though the degree of Scottish control within the industry is limited, as most brands belong to multinationals based outside Scotland. Roughly 70,000 jobs directly or indirectly depend on it U.K.-wide, while exports per employee (totaling £2.39 billion—the equivalent of US$3.82 billion—in 1996) are six times the U.K. average. Interestingly, in spite of the product's Highland associations, 55 percent of production and 70 percent of the workforce are in the Lowlands.

Another of Scotland's famous products is textiles. This sector has had a tough time but is still worth £1.76 billion annually (approximately US$2.81 billion) to the Scottish economy. Employing 41,000 people, the industry is centered on the Borders, where one of the nation's few homegrown multinationals, Dawson International, employs around 6,000. This concentration in the south of Scotland leads to some unusual statistics: for instance, the town of Hawick (population 15,000) exports more than £110 million (US$176 million) of knitwear annually, making it one of the largest exporting centers per capita anywhere in the U.K. (All this in a town that has the dubious distinction of being the largest in Scotland not to be served by the railroad.)

BLACK GOLD FROM THE NORTH SEA

Oil has made a substantial impact on the Scottish economy since the late 1960s, turning upside-down the local economies of places like Aberdeen, often described as Scotland's oil capital, and Peterhead, a leading fishing port on the north-east coast, whose harbor of refuge found a new role in sheltering and servicing oil supply vessels. In fact, more than 45,000 jobs in Grampian depend on oil. However, some say the boom has passed, not just because the easier finds have been exploited, but also because increasing offshore automation requires fewer workers, while onshore supply bases also require fewer staff. Meanwhile, optimists point to the imminent opening up of a second exploration front in the waters west of Shetland (the so-called "Atlantic frontier"), where surveys have revealed huge accumulations of untapped oil.

OTHER SECTORS

The impact of tourism should not be overlooked. It contributes £2.4 billion (US$3.84 billion) annually to the Scottish economy and supports 177,000 jobs, including 15 percent of the Highlands and Islands workforce. Meanwhile, fishing, fish farming, agriculture, the financial industry, plus the survivors in the engineering sector (which still includes names like British Aerospace, Howden

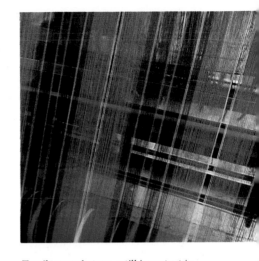

Textile manufacture—still important in the Borders' economy

23

Group, John Brown, Weir Group, and Motherwell Bridge) should continue to ensure a measure of prosperity north of the Border.

❑ Oil experts estimate the recoverable reserves in the fields west of Shetland to be 5 billion barrels—roughly equivalent to the entire North Sea production for between seven and eight years. Rigs will have to combat heavy Atlantic swell, strong winds, and twice the water depth of the North Sea in order to gain this new oily bonanza. ❑

Ravenscraig—the heavy industry of yesterday?

Scotland's position on the edge of continental Europe, bordered by sea on three sides, helps explain her unpredictable weather. The country is a battleground between the continental climate of Europe and the weather systems coming off the Atlantic Ocean.

NOT TRULY TROPICAL The Gulf Stream is often heralded as the saving grace of Scotland's weather. Much emphasized in travel brochures, this warming oceanic current reaches Scotland as the North Atlantic Drift. It hardly lends a "subtropical air" to the west coast (as is sometimes claimed in print), but it is appreciated by tender tree ferns and cabbage palms at places like Logan Botanic Garden in Galloway in the southwest, and Inverewe Garden in Wester Ross (at the same latitude as Moscow).

weather is a risk worth taking. The popular tourism area of Lochaber is one of the wettest parts and July one of the wetter months, but also one of the busiest for tourists.

When it is not raining, the sparkling colors of the hills and sea lochs of the west make some of the finest landscapes anywhere in the world. Besides, the dreaded east coast *haar*, a summer sea fog, also complicates the picture. Scottish weather is a highly localized gamble, with few rules or generalizations—except to expect the worst and then be pleasantly surprised.

> ❏ The summit of Ben Nevis has a pretty generous mean annual rainfall twice that of Fort William (4 miles away), which gets 79 inches. But if you really want to test your rain gear, visit the head of Glen Garry, which offers a spectacular 200 inches every year. ❏

Glen Coe, one of Scotland's five ski resorts

Hebridean rain, Berneray, one of the smaller Western Isles

WHERE TO FIND GOOD WEATHER
Sunshine in Scotland is most likely to be encountered away from the prevailing southwesterlies: the east coast "resorts"—Dunbar, St. Andrews, and Lossiemouth—all have encouraging statistics. The west is far wetter than the east. While Dunbar gets away with 22 inches of rainfall yearly, Inveraray on Loch Fyne enjoys 81 inches. For many visitors, wet

Scotland was

The scanty clues from "shell-middens," the garbage dumps of early man, suggest that Scotland was first colonized about 8,000 years ago, after the last Ice Age. Over the millennia, different races blended together, leaving only their grave goods, standing stones, and cairns (stone heaps) as mysterious evidence for today's archeologists. Then Celtic invaders from Europe arrived in about 500 BC with superior metal-working techniques. The Romans came and failed to subdue the northlands, finally withdrawing shortly after AD 212.

After the Romans, "Scotland" roughly comprised a British kingdom in Strathclyde and the southwest, with a capital at Dumbarton. ("Dun-Briton" means "the fort of the Britons," who had been the main Celtic tribe until pushed west by European invaders.) A Pictish confederation controlled the north. Within a couple of centuries a new wave of Celtic settlers arrived, this time from Ireland. These were the Scots who established the kingdom of Dalriada, with its center at Dunadd near Crinan in Argyll, in western Scotland.

THE SHAPE OF SCOTLAND The Angles arrived in the southeast in the 5th century. This Germanic tribe created a powerful Northumbrian kingdom, which took in the counties of East,

West, and Mid Lothian (by present-day Edinburgh). Thus, along with the three Celtic ethnic groups (Britons, Picts, and Scots), a fourth, non-Celtic power base became important.

The northern expansion of this Anglo-Saxon grouping was checked at the Battle of Nechtansmere in Angus in AD 685, when the Pictish King Brude defeated the Angles under Egfrith, one of the important events that influenced the final form of Scotland. It also shifted the power base in England south from Northumbria to around the Thames, where it has remained ever since, so the shadowy northern Picts altered the course of English history as well.

Christianity played its part in

The Stones of Stenness, Orkney

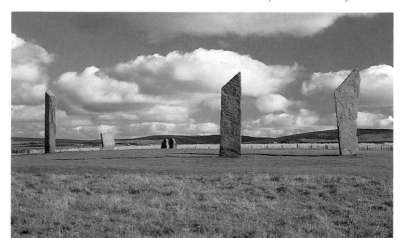

Dun Troddan Broch, Glenelg

❏ The Roman historian Tacitus records a tantalizing tidbit on Scotland's first named battle, when red-haired warriors with painted bodies were defeated by a Roman force at Mons Graupius, a site as yet unidentified. There are traces of Roman marching camps as far north as the Moray Firth (estuary), but their greatest monument is the remains of the Antonine Wall (AD 142–143), which was built across the narrow waist of Scotland. ❏

raids that Kenneth MacAlpin, King of Scots, was able to extend his kingdom north and east. He was crowned King of Scots and Picts in AD 844.

Thereafter, MacAlpin strengthened an alliance with the Britons, further extending his sway. However, only after the Battle of Carham (on the English side of the border near Coldstream) in 1025, when the Scottish King Malcolm I defeated the Northumbrians, did they give up the southeast so that the counties of Lothian became part of Scotland.

Finally, the marriage in 1070 of King Malcolm III to Margaret, a daughter of Edward the Confessor, last Anglo-Saxon king before William the Conqueror, set a pattern of inter-marriage between the royal houses of Scotland and England that would also strongly influence the fate of Scotland.

Scotland's story. A Galloway-born Briton, St. Ninian, is the first recorded native Christian. However, the later St. Columba is better known. He came from Ireland to Iona in Dalriada in AD 563 to convert the northern Picts. As the Britons were already Christian by this time, this forged closer links between the two groups.

Yet another factor was at work in shaping Scotland. The ravages of the Vikings troubled both the northern Picts and also the Scots on the western seaboard. Some say the repeated pil-laging of the Christian settlement and seat of learning at Iona set back the course of civilization for centuries. The Picts were so weakened by Norse

❏ Tacitus uses the word Picti—painted people—as well as Caledonii (hence Caledonian) to describe the northern tribes. Later, Alba (hence Alban and Albion) was the Gaelic word that described the combined Scot-Pictish kingdom north of the rivers Forth and Clyde. ❏

The Wars of Independence refer to a period in Scottish history when Scotland's right to exist as an independent nation was threatened by the expansionist aspirations of the English Plantagenet kings. But it was not quite as simple as that. Nothing between Scotland and England ever was simple.

THE ENGLISH OVERLORDS? In 12th-century Scotland, mainly in the time of King David I (ca1080–53), the Norman feudal system had taken root. David married the daughter of an English earl, gaining lands near Cambridge in southern England. In feudal terms, land meant an obligation to the overlord, in this case the English king. This bowing of the knee as an English landholder by

Bannockburn prelude—Robert Bruce kills Sir Henry de Bohun in single combat

David (and earlier kings) reinforced a view that the Scots were under English command. This was strengthened by the Treaty of Falaise in 1174, signed by King William the Lion, who, seeking territorial gains, joined a revolt by English barons against King Henry II of England. The barons were defeated; William was captured and forced to sign a treaty of allegiance, confirming the feudal overlordship of England. (Scotland later bought its "independence" back when King Richard the Lionheart needed money for a crusade.)

A TRAGIC FALL King Alexander III of Scotland ruled a comparatively peaceful kingdom until 1286, when he died after falling from his horse. Through intermarriage, King Edward I of England was the great-uncle of the heir to the Scottish throne, Margaret of Norway. Acting as arbiter, he suggested she marry his son, thus securing close union between the two kingdoms. The Scots agreed but unfortunately the Maid of Norway died, leaving 13 other claimants with varying degrees of legitimacy.

Edward seized his chance in the power struggle and demanded acknowledgment of his own claim as overlord of Scotland. The claimants complied and Edward chose John Balliol, who became a puppet king, ever after known in Scotland as "Toom Tabard"—empty coat. However, even he was pushed too far by Edward, who demanded his services against the French. Balliol sided with France and saw his army crushed at Dunbar by Edward's forces in 1296. Scotland was occupied by the English thereafter. The Scots aristocracy, spectacularly sycophantic, secured their property by meekly swearing allegiance to Edward. He then destroyed many of Scotland's own records and carried off a variety of relics, including the Stone of Destiny, which was at last returned to Scotland in November 1996.

This was the background to the campaign called the Scots Wars of Independence. In the midst of Edward's policy of dismantling Scotland's machinery of nationhood, there arose the first of her freedom fighters, William Wallace, who achieved some successes before his betrayal and death in 1305.

Stirling Castle—key to the kingdom

❏ William Wallace's most famous victory was at the Battle of Stirling Bridge in 1297, where, within sight of the English-held Stirling Castle, Wallace's men fell upon and defeated the opposing forces while they attempted to cross the narrow bridge. ❏

THE BANNOCKBURN CAMPAIGN

Then Robert Bruce saw his chance. Bruce came from an old Norman family (de Brus refers to a Normandy place-name and is often anglicized as "the Bruce"), and, like other Scots nobles, he played his part in the complex politics of English court life. His grandfather had been one of the original 13 claimants to the Scottish throne. He was crowned King of Scotland in 1307 and initiated a seven-year military campaign, which ended at the Battle of Bannockburn in 1314 with a (historically rare) Scots victory. Thereafter, though Scotland and England were certainly not at peace, Scotland won almost 400 years of independence from England.

Scotland's churchmen were unreservedly nationalist throughout the struggle. With the Pope still believing in England's right to rule Scotland, they met to prepare Scotland's most famous document, the Declaration of Arbroath, in 1320: "For so long as a hundred of us remain alive, we shall never accept subjection to the domination of the English..."

Robert Bruce, victor at Bannockburn

Mary was queen for only seven years, but she played her part in a large-scale drama involving the royal houses of Scotland, France, and England. Since her death more than 400 years ago, she has become perhaps the best-known figure in Scotland's history.

Mary, Queen of Scots (1542–1587) was at the center of political upheavals even as a small child. The Stuart monarchs of Scotland had the inconvenient habit of dying when their offspring were too young to rule. Mary's father, King James V, died a week after hearing of his daughter's birth. Within three years this led to English attacks on Scotland—the destructive episodes known as the "rough wooing." This was King Henry VIII of England's less than subtle attempt to marry off his own young son Edward to the infant Mary. To get rid of the English invaders, the Scots called on the French for help. The price for this was the removal of Mary to France in 1548 for marriage to the Dauphin, the young French prince, in order to secure a Catholic alliance against England.

SCOTLAND'S TRAGIC QUEEN On her return to Scotland in 1561, Mary was a young and beautiful widow. The Dauphin had died, still in his teens. With Scotland in the throes of the Reformation and a widening Protestant–Catholic split, Mary was, politically speaking, hot property. Politicians (Scottish and English) soon worked out that finding Mary a Protestant husband might

Mary, Queen of Scots

offer the best chance of stability. However, Mary fell for the lanky young Lord Darnley. (Mary, being very tall, may have enjoyed the novelty of being looked down on.) Though at first she described him as the "lustiest and best proportioned lang man," the marriage proved a disaster. Darnley took to tavern life in solace, finding that Mary soon excluded him from any real authority.

The murder (by Darnley and others) of her secretary and favorite, David Riccio, witnessed by Mary while six months pregnant, indicates the ruthlessness of the conspirators against her in that age of political and religious instability. The birth of a son—the future King James VI of Scotland, James I of England—and his baptism as a Catholic at Stirling Castle were cause for alarm among the Protestant factions.

30

PLOT AND COUNTERPLOT More controversy followed. The house in which Lord Darnley was convalescing after an illness suddenly blew up one night. Darnley was later found strangled in the adjacent garden, his body strangely unmarked by the explosion. Exactly what happened that night in February 1567 remains one of Scotland's great historical mysteries, but suspicion still falls on the third man in Mary's life, the earthy James Hepburn, Earl of Bothwell. Before Darnley's death, it was well known both that Mary's reconciliation with him had failed, and that she was pregnant once again. Rumors were rife at court about the possible father of her child. In any event, Mary married Bothwell after his acquittal of Lord Darnley's murder. The last Scottish scenes in the drama saw the rising of a confederacy of the Protestant Lords of the Congregation against her new liaison, which eventually led to Mary's surrender and imprisonment in Loch Leven Castle. Her pregnancy subsequently ended with stillborn twins.

A few months later, in May of 1568, she escaped from her confinement, gathered an army, and suffered defeat at Langside at the hands of the Protestant faction. Soon after the battle, she fled to England, crossing the border only 11 days after escaping from her imprisonment in Loch Leven Castle. There she remained a political pawn in the hands of Queen Elizabeth I, her cousin, who signed her death warrant in 1587.

31

Renaissance stonework on Falkland Palace, hunting lodge of the Stuarts

❑ Riccio was ugly, small, and hunched (though a fine lutenist), and it is unlikely that his role extended beyond that of musician and chief secretary to the Queen. Court gossip, however, suggested otherwise. ❑

The Union of Parliaments and Scotland's loss of independence is a live issue in a way that it has never been in England. Now, in the early days of a new Scottish Parliament, there is a strong sense north of the border that history has come full circle.

SCOTLAND'S FOREIGN VENTURE

After the Union of the Crowns in 1603, when James VI of Scotland became James I of England, Scotland shared a monarch with England but had its own Parliament. Poorly developed Scotland assumed that this would mean sharing in trade with England's burgeoning colonies. When it became clear that England intended to keep the economic benefits to herself, the Scots decided to found their own colonies. The Darien Scheme, the establishing of a settlement on the disease-ridden isthmus of Panama in 1698, proved a

Christmas in Parliament Square, on Edinburgh's Royal Mile

financial catastrophe. Fever struck the colonists, and neighboring Spanish possessions rose against them. The Scots appealed to nearby English colonies for aid. This was refused for fear of upsetting Spain.

Everything was abandoned, ruining both the Scottish aristocracy and the ordinary folk who had put up funds. By 1701, anti-English feeling was running high. There was also a crisis of succession for Scotland and England. The Scots Parliament attempted blackmail. They stated that unless Scotland gained trading rights in English markets, they would not choose the same monarch as England. Instead of favoring the Protestant Hanoverian succession,

❑ The Earl of Seafield, as Lord Chancellor instrumental in carrying forward the legislation, touched the written Act with the royal scepter (symbolizing royal assent) and consigned Scotland to history. As he handed the scepter back to a clerk, he was heard to mutter, "Now, there's an end of an auld sang." Three centuries later, with a new Scottish Parliament, he has been proved wrong. ❑

they would turn instead to the exiled Catholic Stuart dynasty. Once more for England the threat of a Scottish alliance with Catholic France presented itself.

POLITICAL HORSE-TRADING The foolish blackmail attempt caused England to retaliate with the Alien Act of 1705. This prevented Scots from holding property in England, and banned the purchase of all Scottish goods and services in England. England's parliament thus alarmed the now penniless Scots nobility, many of whom also had English properties, and also closed off Scotland's main market.

The price of peace was accepting the Hanoverian succession and the end of an independent Scottish parliament. As a trade-off, England offered access to her markets in the colonies. In addition, an English army stationed itself at Newcastle, close to the Scottish border. Discussions began in London, with the Scottish representatives aware that if agreement to England's terms was not secured, Scotland would be invaded.

BOUGHT AND SOLD FOR ENGLISH GOLD? When the final votes were taken, the nobility were heavily in favor and the popular representatives more evenly divided. This is hardly surprising. The Scottish landowners could recoup their losses after the Darien disaster, since bribes were standard parliamentary practices for moving through legislation. The Duke of Atholl was recompensed generously for not making trouble. The Duke of Argyll became a general, his brother

Archie acquired a peerage. About £20,000 ($30,000) in all was spent in buying off the Scottish aristocracy.

Later, the Scots said the deal was crooked, though the machinations were everyday parliamentary routine and only marginally less subtle than today's practices. Robert Burns wrote the song still widely sung in Scotland today:

We are bought and sold for English gold,
Such a parcel of rogues in a nation.

VOTING FOR A NEW PARLIAMENT
Shortly after taking office in May of 1997, the Labour government held a referendum in which almost three-quarters of the Scots who voted were in favor of the principle of a new Parliament. The Labour Party was eager to stress the devolution aspect, and emphasized that this would strengthen rather than weaken the U.K. Subsequently, the Scotland Bill of 1998 paved the way for the new body, which comes into being in 2000.

James Ogilvy, 1st Earl of Seafield, as portrayed by Sir John Baptiste de Medina

33

In about a century, the Jacobites went from feared political and military force to a suitable sentiment for Victorian drawing-room song. Most celebrated of all is Prince Charles Edward Stuart, the Bonnie Prince Charlie of Jacobite hagiography.

34

WHO WERE THE JACOBITES?

Decades of conflict between the monarch, the church, and the state (both in Scotland and in England) came to a head with the exile of the Catholic King James VII (II of England) in 1689.

Though opinion on the matter was divided, a Convention of Estates (political representatives who formed a decision-making committee) in Scotland eventually went along with England and accepted William of Orange, husband of Mary, the daughter of the exiled King James VII. The Scottish supporters of the exiled James were furious. Thus originated the Jacobites (from the Latin Jacobus, for James). They rallied around John Graham of Claverhouse, the "Bonnie Dundee" of later Jacobite image-building.

He led them against a government army in the Battle of Killiecrankie in 1689. Fortunately for later tourism, he chose a most scenic location in Perthshire for his side's victory and his own demise, killed by a stray bullet. The Jacobites had created their first saint, but, deprived of a figurehead, they were soon stopped in their tracks at nearby Dunkeld. There the grimly fanatical Cameronians, earlier persecuted by the Catholic faction, took their revenge.

"IT WAS A' FOR OOR RIGHTFU' KING..." (It was all for our rightful king.) It is sometimes forgotten that the exiled Stuarts were actually the rightful bloodline. This belief in the justice of their cause was instilled into James Francis, the Old Pretender, King James VII's son, as he grew up on the Continent. In turn, it was also fostered in the last Stuart king's grandson, Italian-born Charles, the Young Pretender, who as Bonnie Prince Charlie became the most famous Jacobite of all.

UPRISINGS Encouraged by Catholic France and Spain, this court in exile waited for the call, which came with an

Highlander statue on top of the Glenfinnan Monument

uprising in 1715. Its leader, John, Earl of Mar, was known even in his own lifetime as Bobbin John, from his habit of changing sides—an indication of the political complexities of the times. Mar led an army out of the hills to an inconclusive battle above Stirling on the hillslopes of Sheriffmuir. The affair had fizzled out by the time the Old Pretender "James VIII" landed on Scottish soil at Peterhead, so he did not stay long.

The 1719 rebellion was even more farcical. Spanish mercenaries were landed on the northwest coast near Dornie. They linked up with local Jacobites in Glen Shiel. Mortar fire from a detachment of government troops soon dealt with the matter. "Sgurr na Spainteach," Spaniards' Peak, in Glen Shiel, commemorates the incident. In between times, there were other plans and other invasion fleets that failed to materialize or were blown off course by storms.

THE LAST REBELLION Later, France and Britain went to war. Eager to encourage any destabilization of her island neighbor, France equipped the hot-headed, handsome Bonnie Prince Charlie and sent him off to Scotland in 1745 to raise support. After some successes, the mad escapade ended with Charles's army cut to pieces on the battlefield of Culloden. Charles was in Scotland for less than a year. The Jacobites were never a threat again. Soon the bloodshed had been sanitized and transformed into romantic notions of exiled kings across the water and a huge number of maudlin songs.

When Charles first landed on Scottish soil on Eriskay on the Outer Hebrides, the northwestern islands off mainland Scotland, he was told by the local chief to go home. He said he had come home. Only about 6,000 of the 30,000 fighting men in the Highlands rallied to his cause.

❑ King James VII was the last of the Catholic Stuart dynasty, a line that had originated in the 14th century with the grandson of Robert the Bruce. ❑

Glenfinnan, where Bonnie Prince Charlie landed on the Scottish mainland some 250 years ago on August 19, 1745

35

Far from being absorbed by the expanding greater Britain, Scotland retained its identity in the 18th century with an intellectual renaissance that tended toward a liberal-minded patriotism. It played an important role in the international movement known as the Age of Reason.

Some people label the entire period between the Union of the Crowns in 1707 and the death of the influential writer Sir Walter Scott in 1832 as the Scottish Enlightenment. However, if Scotland did have a true post-Union Golden Age, then most commentators place it within the second half of the 18th century.

EDINBURGH'S GREATNESS In its heyday, the movement was centered upon Edinburgh. The New Town was its architectural expression, but the Enlightenment embraced many other fields, from medicine to philosophy, agriculture to economics. This was the time of Edinburgh-born David Hume, one of the more influential philosophers of the Western world; of Kirkcaldy-born Adam Smith, who wrote the Wealth

Adam Smith, whose Wealth of Nations was the first masterpiece in political economy

of Nations as the cornerstone of the new science of political economy; of Edinburgh's pioneering geologist James Hutton; of chemists such as Joseph Black, discoverer of carbon dioxide; and of many more who laid the foundations of a range of modern disciplines, many of them flowering out of the seedbed of Edinburgh University.

INTELLECTUAL LIFE Edinburgh was the first university in the world to introduce a chair of English Literature, and it also led the way in important pioneering medical work. No less than three generations of Monros held the professorship in anatomy. Glasgow-born William Cullen not only established a tradition of chemical research work, but also became professor of chemistry at Edinburgh in 1756 and lectured in clinical medicine at the Royal Infirmary, exploring the links between the two disciplines.

Edinburgh between 1750 and 1790 was certainly a stimulating place to live. It was also a place where those creating the intellectual wealth were well aware of their role. They recognized that a lead in so many fields had been taken, paradoxically, by a poor nation that had so recently lost status.

Even with New Town construction under way, the sheer proximity of many families of both high and

❑ George III's chemist Amyat, commenting on the intellectual life of Edinburgh society in the 1750s, remarked: "Here I stand at what is called the Cross of Edinburgh, and can, in a few minutes, take 50 men of genius and learning by the hand." ❑

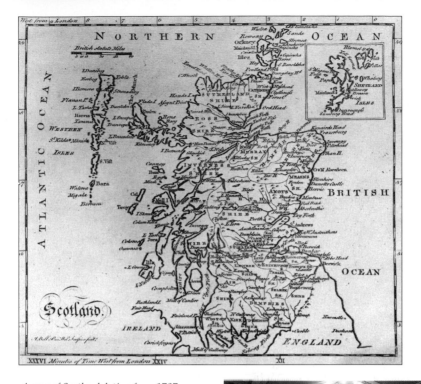

A map of Scotland dating from 1797

Royal Society of Edinburgh, founded in 1783

humble birth in the tall, cramped tenements of Edinburgh's Old Town seemed to generate a special atmosphere, a cross-fertilizing of ideas that was widely commented upon by outsiders. They noted the debating and literary societies, the interest in written essays and stimulating conversation, as well as in the concrete forms of communication, such as building roads, bridges, and canals. Referring to this ready access to scientists, engineers, and all kinds of thinkers and writers, the English visitor Amyat (chemist to King George III) wrote that the philosophers in Scotland "tell us what they know, and deliver their sentiments without disguise or reserve."

By 1789 Thomas Jefferson, traveling in Europe on political business, wrote that "no place in the world can pretend to be competition with Edinburgh." Yet half a century later, the light had dimmed. An urge for rapid political change, embodied in the French Revolution and the Romantic movement, had overwhelmed the moderation and harmony that were the goal of the greatest Enlightenment thinkers.

❑ David Hume to Elliott of Minto in 1757: "Is it not strange… that, at a time when we have lost our Princes, our Parliaments, our independent Government, even the presence of our chief Nobility, are unhappy in our accent and Pronunciation… speak a very corrupt Dialect of the Tongue… is it not strange… we shou'd really be the People most distinguish'd for literature in Europe?" ❑

The great mercantile cities of the Lowlands went about their business of making money. The powerful Highland landowners were similarly motivated. To improve their estates, they cleared their tenants from ground they had worked for centuries. Today this process might be called ethnic cleansing.

The series of evictions and forced emigration known as the Highland Clearances did not happen immediately after the defeat of the Jacobite rebel forces at Culloden in 1746. Nevertheless, after Culloden, the old-style clan chiefs were stripped of their powers. The reality of hard economics asserted itself in the poor lands of the north.

fish, and meal. Also, kelp was gathered, dried, and burned, and the ash used in the manufacture of soap and glass. This made money for landowners with coastal properties.

The landowners raised rents to increase profits and altered leases to reduce individual landholdings, in order to compel tenants to spend more time fishing or kelp-gathering.

38

An abandoned croft at Arnol, on the Isle of Lewis in the Western Isles

THE IMPROVING LANDLORDS
A program of improvements was implemented by new landowners, only some of whom were still of Highland stock, as they tried to make money from their property. The second half of the 18th century saw the founding of state-sponsored fishing stations such as Tobermory and Ullapool. The potato was first grown and soon became a staple. Better nourishment allowed the Highland population to expand.

A SHORT-LIVED PROSPERITY
Britain's wars employed Highland manpower and were also a market for Highland produce such as cattle,

Far from evicting tenants, landowners in the first decades of the 1800s—the majority of whom were absentees—actually required manpower to make money.

The slump came at the end of the Napoleonic Wars in the early 19th century, when the market for cattle collapsed. Agricultural improvements, successful in the Lowlands, just did not work on the thin, acid Highland soils. New chemical processes made kelp-gathering unnecessary, and even the fishing became unprofitable. The landowners turned to sheep to make money. Unfortunately, the tenants' farming activities—the growing of potatoes and the pasturing of cattle—conflicted with the needs of the new-style Cheviot or black-face breeds.

❏ "Much the same thing is done today by town councils who uproot people from their old, shabby, but neighborly streets and place them in ultra-modern, clinically clean, but often inhuman high-rise flats [apartments], usually against their will." Dunrobin Castle Guidebook, 1991. Dunrobin was the home of the initiators of the Sutherland Clearances. ❏

VIOLENCE IN THE GLENS The people of the glens were evicted. The violence that accompanied the policy flared up in a now infamous list of Highland place-names, of which Strathnaver on the Sutherland Estates is perhaps the best known.

In 1785, the last Earl of Sutherland's daughter, Elizabeth Gordon, married one of the richest men in England, George Granville Leveson-Gower, second Marquess of Stafford. He had made a fortune in coal and wood, and owned a vast estate in England. With his marriage came most of the northern Scottish county of Sutherland, including Dunrobin Castle.

In the program of estate improvements, nearly 5,000 Highlanders were cleared up to 1821. They were either settled on narrow coastal strips or were forced to emigrate, mostly across the Atlantic. In Strathnaver, many of the tenants were unable to salvage their belongings, because their houses were burned before their eyes. The estate factor, Patrick Sellar, was even charged with arson and homicide, as some homes were set on fire with old people still inside them. He was acquitted.

The same pattern of evictions by landowners—titled aristocrats, entrepreneurs, and industrialists—stretched from Shetland to Perthshire. Many sincerely believed it was for the best. Today, in the Highlands, with their silent glens admired by city dwellers, visitors creep reverently around the treasures in the castles of the descendants of these "improvers."

Dunrobin Castle, Golspie, Sutherland

The Scots have always been adventurers. Soldiers and merchants traveled in Europe from the very early days of the Scots nation. Then, when ships became large enough to undertake longer voyages, Scots left their homeland and became entrepreneurs and explorers, as well as simply colonists, all over the globe.

In 1297, Sir William Wallace, the Scottish freedom fighter, wrote to the senators of Lubeck and Hamburg thanking them for helping Scottish merchants, and offering safe conduct for any of their representatives at Scotland's ports. This is an early reference to Scots entrepreneurs abroad. It is estimated that Poland had 30,000 Scots living and operating in business there in the 17th century.

Dunbar acknowledges its famous son, John Muir

TO THE FOUR CORNERS OF THE GLOBE Scots were prominent in the Far East. William Jardine, born in Dumfriesshire, in southern Scotland, was an independent China trader who joined forces with James Matheson to form the Hong Kong-based Jardine Matheson of today. Its early profits were amassed in the

unsavory opium trade. Hugh Falconer and William Jamieson were early Scottish pioneers of tea plantations in India. Fraserburgh-born Thomas Glover introduced modern technology to Japan, particularly in shipbuilding. He ordered Japan's first slip dock, which in turn led to the expansion of the now multinational company Mitsubishi.

Not only was Thomas Glover a trusted adviser and personal friend of Mitsubishi's founder, Yataro Iwasaki, he also imported the first steam locomotive and the first telegraph line. Incidents in his extraordinary life are said to have inspired Puccini's opera Madame Butterfly.

The Scots turned westward as well, building Glasgow's early wealth on plantations of Virginia tobacco and Jamaican sugar. Later developments such as the Prairie Cattle Company Limited, Texas's first major joint stock venture in cattle ranching, were actually Edinburgh-based. More than half the Hudson Bay Company's senior staff were Scots. Even more significantly, at least 13 U.S. presidents claimed Scottish ancestry.

These emigrant Scots or their descendants became involved in every sphere. The son of a poor country tailor in an upcountry parish in Aberdeenshire went on to found Forbes Magazine, the still-successful financial journal. Bertie Charles Forbes (1880–1954) became a millionaire in the process. James Gordon Bennet (1795–1872) left his native Keith in Moray in the northeast, and went on to found the New York Herald. In industry, the best-known Scot is the steel magnate Andrew Carnegie from Dunfermline; his name has become a byword for philanthropy. The squalor of the

Dunfermline-born industrialist Andrew Carnegie

Glasgow slums of the early 19th century produced Allan Pinkerton, the founder of the oldest and largest private investigation agency in the world. In 1867, a young Scottish emigrant, John Muir from Dunbar, began to develop the idea of environmental conservation while walking in the Sierra Nevada. It was to lead to the founding of the conservation movement in the United States.

There were, naturally, the oddities: the Scots who suddenly popped up in unexpected places, like the businessmen who formed the African Lakes Corporation in 1878, or the Scottish lace workers in Spain who founded the first Spanish soccer team. Less surprising, perhaps, is a certain James Chisholm, who founded the first pub in Sydney, Australia, called the Thistle Tavern—presumably around the same time as another Scot, Lachlan Macquarie, brought order as the first governor of the former Australian penal colony of New South Wales.

THE HOMELAND Whatever the reason—religious persecution, lack of opportunity, forced clearance, voluntary emigration, or just a sense of adventure Scotland's people have been the country's leading export over the centuries. Small wonder the Clan Donald has over 100,000 members worldwide. For many, the call of the homeland is still strong. Libraries throughout Scotland, carrying records on microfiche formerly available only at New Register House in Edinburgh, do brisk business with genealogical inquiries.

❑ The word Scot in Polish also means a commercial traveler, and the Poles have a simile "as poor as a Scots peddler's pack." Evidently not all Scots were successful in business. ❑

The image of Scotland as a resourceful, industrial place sits uncomfortably with the more romantic notion of misty bens (hills) and glens (valleys). Yet, in times gone by, the output of heavy industry and, in particular, shipbuilding, ensured that Scottish products went around the world and that "Clyde built" (that is, a product of the many shipbuilding yards along the River Clyde) meant the very finest of its kind.

The Scottish industrial belt was formerly a diagonal corridor across the waist of Scotland, less than 30 miles wide from coast to coast. It took in the coalfields of Ayrshire and the south of Edinburgh, the Vale of Leven dyeing industries south of Loch Lomond, and Angus textile manufacturing (all now mere vestiges of their former size, if there at all). Paradoxically, it also included some of Scotland's best farmland.

THE KEY TO PROSPERITY—COAL AND IRON Among these activities, those based on locally available coal and iron had the highest profile, if only because of the effect they had on

The Clydeside birth of a Cunarder, the Queen Mary

the environment and landscape. It is arguable that the real cradle of the Industrial Revolution in Scotland lay east of Glasgow, in the Falkirk area, where the Carron Company was founded in 1760, close to iron mines.

However, by the early years of the 19th century, the easily workable blackband iron ore of Lanarkshire had been discovered. What had been the fruit garden of western Scotland was demolished in a search for this important mineral. The air of Lanarkshire filled with grime and smoke as ironworks sprang up, using local coal to fuel the furnaces. The stage was set for the Clyde area to become one of the world's greatest shipbuilding centers. Though England's River Tyne was also important, most of the developments in ship design and, in particular, marine engines and boilers, were made on the banks of the Clyde.

❑ The Carron Company's most famous product was the carronade, a short-barreled, large-bore cannon used in Britain's imperialist wars. ❑

THE SONG OF THE CLYDE Formerly, the shipyards stretched practically unbroken all the way downstream to Greenock, but these days most have long gone. Even as recently as 1929, the Clyde built 20 percent of the world's shipping. Then the so-called Clyde symphony or the "song of the Clyde" was at its height: the noise of thousands of riveters banging home the red-hot rivets that held together the locally made steel plates.

43

Sunset over the Clyde shipyards

THE ROMANCE OF SHIPS Glasgow, of course, had all kinds of other manufacturing operations, including the production of railway locomotives. Dundee and the Angus hinterland thrived on textiles, Edinburgh had her printing and publishing industries, as well as shale oil extraction to the west. Even modest Aberdeen could claim a surprisingly large engineering sector, while the Borders were well-known for textiles.

Yet only shipbuilding and the proud and graceful products that sailed the waters of the globe acquired the romance and mystique that come with the associations of distant places. Though the local coal and iron that helped build the ships have long been depleted, the hammers are not yet silent. The

❏ During World War II, the Clyde shipyards still had the capacity to build 2,000 ships, repair more than 23,000, and convert hundreds more. To put it another way, the workforce built or repaired 13 ships every day for five years. ❏

Clyde still sees the launch of large vessels—as ever, diagonally into the narrow river. But on the banks of today's Clyde there are also long stretches of landfill docks and redeveloped sites.

Only at places such as the Denny Ship Model Experiment Tank at Dumbarton (see page 140) are there echoes of the great, grimy days of the Clyde, the river that made Glasgow.

Edinburgh

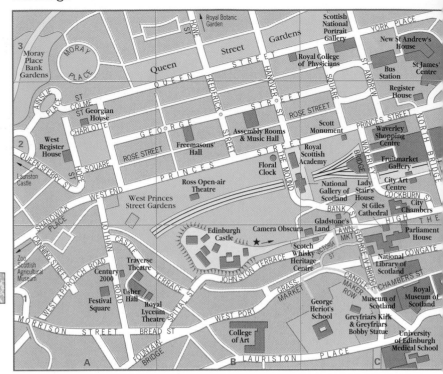

3
Moray Place Bank Gardens
MORAY PLACE
Royal Botanic Garden
HOME STREET
Queen Street Gardens
Scottish National Portrait Gallery
YORK PLACE
New St Andrew's House
St James' Centre
Bus Station
Register House
Royal College of Physicians
ST ANDREW SQUARE

AINSLIE PLACE
ST COLME ST
St Georgian House
CHARLOTTE
West Register House
QUEENSFERRY ST
HOPE SQUARE
GEORGE STREET
FREDERICK STREET
HANOVER STREET
ROSE STREET
Scott Monument
PRINCES STREET
Waverley Shopping Centre
NORTH BRIDGE
Register House
Lauriston Castle
2
Freemasons' Hall
ROSE STREET
Assembly Rooms & Music Hall
THE MOUND
Royal Scottish Academy
WAVERLEY BRIDGE
Fruitmarket Gallery
City Art Centre

PRINCES STREET
Floral Clock
National Gallery of Scotland
Lady Stair's House
COCKBURN ST
City Chambers

WEST END
Ross Open-air Theatre
West Princes Street Gardens
BANK
St Giles Cathedral
HIGH THE

SHANDWICK PLACE
Gladstone's Land
Parliament House

Zoo
Scottish Agricultural Museum
CANNING STREET
WEST APPROACH ROAD
LOTHIAN ROAD
CASTLE TERRACE
Traverse Theatre
Century 2000
SPITAL ST
Edinburgh Castle
JOHNSTON TERRACE
Camera Obscura
Scotch Whisky Heritage Centre
LAWN MKT
VICTORIA ST
GEORGE IV BRIDGE
National Library of Scotland
COWGATE
CHAMBERS ST
Royal Museum of Scotland

1
Usher Hall
Festival Square
Royal Lyceum Theatre
GRASS-MARKET
CANDLE MAKER ROW
Museum of Scotland

MORRISON STREET
BREAD ST
FOUNTAIN BRIDGE
WEST PORT
College of Art
George Heriot's School
Greyfriars Kirk & Greyfriars Bobby Statue
University of Edinburgh Medical School

LAURISTON PLACE

A
B
C

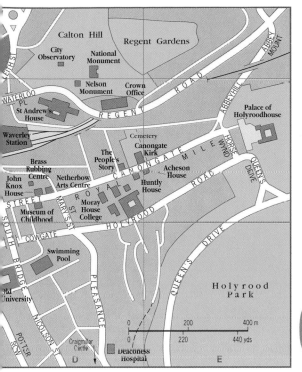

STIRRING FIRST IMPRESSION By road, only a couple of hours or less from the border with England, A68 plunges over the edge of the Southern Uplands to reveal the Lothians, Edinburgh's countryside, spread out below: the sweep of the Pentland Hills stopping short at the edge of the city; farther around, the dark profile of Arthur's Seat dominating the other, gentler rises on which Scotland's capital is built; then the long reach of the estuary known as the Firth of Forth, with just a hint of the Highlands beyond. This is the setting for one of the world's most distinguished cities, now once again to be the seat of the Scottish Parliament.

From the air, on the final approaches, the city map is plain: the castle on its high rock and the Palace of Holyroodhouse in its Royal Park act as head and tail for the backbone of the Royal Mile, which runs through the Old Town. Across the green space of Princes Street Gardens, symmetrical patterns reveal the plan of the neoclassical New Town. Moments after this port-wing view, and over the high spans of the Forth rail and road bridges, the traveler touches down.

By train, you reach the center at Waverley Station. On emerging, the skyline seems familiar: the profiles of castle and battlement, the Gothic-spired Scott Monument, and Greek-porticoed art galleries, popular postcard images, are known worldwide.

From every angle, Edinburgh strikes theatrical poses. The neoclassical collection of monuments on top of Calton Hill seems about to frame some Greek tragedy. Above the rooftops of the Royal Mile, the long, red ridge

*Edinburgh Castle domi-
nates the city skyline*

of Salisbury Crags skirts the rocks of Arthur's Seat—it could well be a painted backdrop for one of Sir Walter Scott's melodramas. At 1 PM each day a cannon cracks out, puffing blue smoke over the castle battlements. Do not be alarmed: this is not another uprising, only Edinburgh squeezing extra drama out of a time check. Edinburgh generates excitement and a sense of expectation. This is where things happen…

OLD EDINBURGH Edinburgh's **Castle Rock** dates from the last Ice Age. An eastward-grinding glacier nibbled away at its hard, volcanic plug, leaving three steep sides and a ramp running down eastward. An archeological dig in the 1990s to establish the age of settlement on the Rock found some chewed herring bones, now carbon-dated to around 800 BC.

The Castle Rock was a Dark Age stronghold, fortified by the Saxon King Edwin in the 7th century. The oldest building in Edinburgh today is the 11th-century **St. Margaret's Chapel** within the castle, named after Queen Margaret. She married King Malcolm, whose Celtic court was at Dunfermline, then the capital. As a Saxon southerner, she persuaded the court to move to the Saxon-influenced Lothians. Edinburgh became the capital thereafter.

By the 12th century, the huddle of little houses protected by the castle had spilled down the ramp—the embryonic **Royal Mile**—perhaps as far as today's Tron Kirk ("kirk" is the Scottish word for church) on the High Street. Margaret's son, King David, founded **Holyrood Abbey**, another landmark in the shaping of the old city.

The castle was sacked by King Edward I of England in 1296, and many of the nation's records destroyed. After the English withdrew, Edinburgh became a royal burgh (town; see panel) in 1329, and faced the wars and vicissitudes of Scotland's long struggle under a weak monarchy with a powerful and ambitious neighbor on her southern border. The High Kirk of St. Giles was burned in 1385 by King Richard II of England, the Royal Mile torched in 1542 during Henry VIII's "rough wooing" (see page 30).

As a means of defense, Edinburgh was a walled town. Bits of wall survive today, near St. Mary's Street and above the Grassmarket. In the main, the community remained within its high walls until the mid-18th century.

Then it crossed the marshy defensive gap, now the site of Princes Street Gardens, to found the New Town.

NEW EDINBURGH In the creative heat and spirit of optimism of the Age of Enlightenment, the city laid the foundations of the townscape of today. The first **New Town** comprises the rectangle bounded by **Charlotte** and **St. Andrew Squares** to west and east, and **Princes** and **Queen Streets** to south and north. Other development plans followed around Moray Place and, less successfully, along Royal Terrace.

The great public buildings and monuments that enhance the city environment so much today were built at the same time: the **Royal Scottish Academy** and the **National Gallery**, honey-colored, columned temples floating in garden greenery when viewed from the east; the fluted shapes of more columns of Calton Hill's unfinished National Monument, which block and change the views east along Princes Street from every angle.

Amid all this neoclassicism, the monument to Sir Walter Scott shoots out of the trees like a Gothic sky-rocket. Architecturally isolated, Scott's immortalization in sandstone plays its part in the theatrical quality of Edinburgh and has become an essential symbol of the city. Towering above Holyroodhouse, the impossible profile of **Arthur's Seat** looks like a backdrop for one of Scott's own theatrical melodramas—or an entirely appropriate setting for the cultural overkill generated annually through the Edinburgh International Festival, the Fringe, and other attendant festivals.

For all its expensive parking fines and crowds, as well as the proportion of well-meant but uninspiring productions that turn the Fringe into something of a grab bag, Edinburgh undoubtedly remains an exciting place. Away from the downtown cosmopolitan throng, life in the New Town goes on as it has for more than two centuries, below the plasterwork in elegant drawing rooms or amid the shade of the private gardens overlooked by palace-fronted façades. all in all, a curious meeting of the past and present.

SCOTLAND'S BURGHS
A Scottish burgh, a term first used in the 12th century, was a town with certain rights; when these rights were granted by the monarch, a town became a royal burgh. The rights were mainly to do with mercantile matters, such as the granting of the right to hold fairs or markets, in order to raise money for the Crown, as well as for the community itself. Characteristics of a burgh usually included a mercat (market) cross, to indicate the place of the market and the town center, as well as a tolbooth, a civic building that served as an administrative center and, very often, a courtroom and prison, too. Burghs disappeared with the local government reorganization that took place in 1975.

47

Calton Hill commands some fine views over Edinburgh—see page 49 for an example

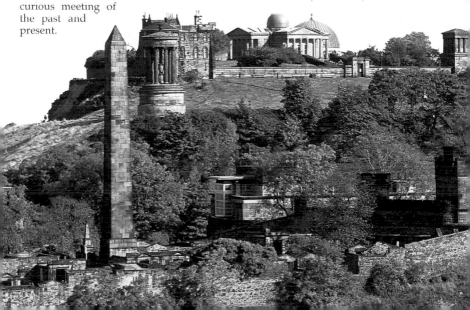

Visitors view the former Royal High School near Calton Hill

EDINBURGH'S UNFINISHED PARTHENON
The prolific architect William Playfair had a hand in many Edinburgh streets and buildings. He is also less happily associated with the National Monument, the columned façade on Calton Hill. Intended to be an exact copy of the Parthenon in Athens and a tribute to the dead of the Napoleonic Wars, it was started in 1822. Money ran out in 1829, and the work has been left unfinished ever since. It has become known as "Edinburgh's Disgrace," but it has a certain appeal even in its present state.

▶▶ Calton Hill   45D3

Robert Louis Stevenson's favorite view of Edinburgh was from this hill to the east of Princes Street. Even in Stevenson's day it carried its extraordinary neoclassical collection of buildings: the **Old Observatory** (the only surviving building by New Town planner James Craig), the **City** or **New Observatory**, the **Dugald Stuart Memorial** (loosely based on the temple of Lysicrates in ancient Athens), the unfinished **National Monument**, and the **Nelson Monument**, which ignores its neoclassical neighbors and instead is shaped like an upturned telescope. If the walk up the steps to the hilltop is too much, take the car. Look for the turnoff by the former Royal High School. The hill is open at all times.

▶ Camera Obscura   44C1

594 Castlehill
Open: Apr–Oct, Mon–Fri 9:30–6, weekends 10–6; Nov–Mar, daily 10–5. Admission charge
This building has a varied history: the lower stories were built in the 17th century, and the upper, castellated stories added in 1853, when the building first became a camera obscura. As well as panoramic projections of Edinburgh, thanks to its revolutionary design and mirrors, the center offers Edinburgh-related exhibitions.

▶ Canongate Kirk   45D2

Canongate
This church was built in 1688 for the congregation when King James VII converted the abbey church at Holyrood into a chapel for the Knights of the Thistle. Of greater interest, though, is the adjoining **graveyard**. Graves include that of Mrs. McLehose, the attractive young woman abandoned by her husband and with whom the 18th-century Scottish poet Robert Burns conducted a passionate correspondence (just that and no more, since Burns was confined to his Edinburgh lodgings with a twisted knee). She outlived him by 45 years. Also here is the grave of Robert Fergusson, the brilliant Edinburgh poet who inspired Burns, though they never met. When Burns visited, he was shocked to find Fergusson's grave unmarked, and paid for his headstone.

Itinerary

Three days in Edinburgh

DAY 1 Rampart views from Edinburgh Castle aid orientation in this simply laid-out city, and a self-guided castle tour, taking most of a morning, is worthwhile. Then go downhill, diverting for **Victoria Street** shopping. (Use the steps at West Bow.) Try, say, Jacksons on the **Royal Mile** for lunch, or head to the Kalpna by Nicholson Street, or take a chance with a pub lunch anywhere on the Mile. Visit the **Museum of Childhood**, or continue to **Huntly House**. The **Palace of Holyroodhouse** is also popular. Alternatively, go to **Calton Hill** for city views, en route to the **National Gallery** at the Mound. You should just catch it before closing.

DAY 2 Yesterday the Old Town, today the New. Start at the **National Portrait Gallery**, then go on to the **Georgian House**. In between, try Jenners on Princes Street for shopping. For lunch, choose from the many options nearby: La Lanterna on Hanover Street if on a budget, or **Martin's** on **Rose Street** if you have reservations, or a Rose Street pub. In the afternoon, explore northward through the New Town to reach the Royal Botanic Garden, then return via Stockbridge and shops. In the evening, check out Leith's choice of eating places, or, if the weather is fine, walk in the Royal Park to enjoy great views from Arthur's Seat, followed by a beer in the Sheep's Heid in Duddingston.

DAY 3 The **Waverley Market** shopping mall is useful for last-minute souvenir shopping. If you have time, revisit the Royal Mile. The **Scotch Whisky Heritage Centre,** the **Writers' Museum**, and **Gladstone's Land** are all within easy reach of the city center.

TIMEKEEPING
The firing of the 1 PM gun from the ramparts of Edinburgh Castle originated from a request by the Leith Dock Commission in 1861 to locate a time ball on top of the Nelson Monument (which was visible from the docks). Punctually every day since then (except in wartime and on Sundays), an audible signal has boomed out across the city, and simultaneously the time ball has dropped down its pole on the monument, enabling mariners of old to check their chronometers and nowadays making tourists jump visibly as they stroll along Princes Street at lunchtime.

Edinburgh Castle from Calton Hill

A ROYAL MYSTERY
In 1830, workmen discovered a tiny coffin hidden in the royal apartments in Edinburgh Castle. Within was a baby with an embroidered "J" still legible on his golden shroud. This added to rumors that Mary, Queen of Scots' own infant had died and another substituted. The prime suspect is the Countess of Mar, since the future King James VI was brought up with the Earl and Countess's own son, whom he resembled closely.

▶▶▶ Edinburgh Castle   44B1

Open: Apr–Sep, daily 9:30–5:15; Oct–Mar, daily 9:30–4:15. Admission charge

Possibly Scotland's most famous landmark, Edinburgh Castle dominates the center of the city with its silhouette of ramparts and rooftops. Almost a million visitors every year swarm over its buildings, from the 11th-century chapel to its latest addition, a restaurant with one of the finest views anywhere in the city.

Edinburgh Castle was an important royal court from at least the 11th century. Through the Middle Ages, its buildings were mainly around the highest point of the Castle Rock. King David II built the first strong defensive line across the eastern neck after 1356.

Little of the very early works survives. Today's **Great Hall** of King James IV dates from the early 16th century, but has been greatly altered. The massive **Half Moon Battery** dates in part from the latter half of the 16th century. As the castle's royal role became less important than its military one, successive waves of buildings and defenses were dictated by military needs and warfare, which severely damaged the castle on many occasions.

The castle fired its last shot in anger in 1745 at Bonnie Prince Charlie's men, who failed to take the high rock. Thereafter, as well as a barracks and administrative center, the castle also became a military prison. It still serves as a military headquarters.

Start your tour by the **Esplanade**, the mid-18th century parade ground. Beyond the Victorian gatehouse, you find yourself below the vast walls of the **Half Moon Battery** and **Forewall Battery**. The upper levels are reached beyond the **Portcullis Gate**.

Reminders of a constant military presence include the handsome **Governor's House**, dating from 1742, now the Officers' Mess, and the **New Barrack**s, whose bold blocking has dominated the skyline since the 1790s. The former hospital, to the right (beyond tiny **St. Margaret's Chapel**), is now part of the Scottish United Services Museum, a place of monosyllabic attendants and immaculate uniforms. (The main historic collection is in the Queen Anne Barracks.)

The Vaults, beside the Victorian prison, have more atmosphere. These dripping, dank corridors of naked rock have been barracks, stores, bakehouse, and, as memorably described in Robert Louis Stevenson's *St. Ives*, a prison for French soldiers (look for their graffiti). The most famous inhabitant today is the great cannon known as **Mons Meg**: she squats evilly on a spotlit plinth beside her audiovisual introduction.

Back above ground, on Crown Square, is the **Scottish National War Memorial**, an emotional ambush of gray light, tattered flags, and endless names. Opposite is the anticlimax of the **Great Hall**. Like the small room in the palace in which Mary, Queen of Scots gave birth to the James who was to rule both Scotland and England, this just fails to grab the imagination. However, also here is a very illuminating display on the story of the castle, plus

The Scottish United Services Museum, Edinburgh Castle

the **Honours of Scotland Exhibition**. This is a highlight, where you can view the oldest regalia in Europe: the Scottish crown, scepter, and sword of state. In close-up, the royal crown seems a bit like the castle itself: a little battered and frequently repaired over the centuries, yet the pride of a poor nation.

▶ City Art Centre   44C2
Market Street
Open: Mon–Sat 10–5, Sun during Festival 2–5. Admission free
The city's own art gallery is housed in a six-floor former warehouse. It stages a changing program of exhibitions, and displays the city's collection of Scottish paintings. It brings world-class exhibitions to the city, from the Chinese Warriors to the Pharaohs.

▶ Craigmillar Castle   45D1
Off A68
Open: Apr–Sep, daily 9:30–6:30; Oct–Mar, Mon–Wed and Sat 9–4:30, Sun 2–4:30, Thu 9:30–12. Admission charge
If Edinburgh Castle were not such a magnet, and if Craigmillar Castle were not situated quite so near one of Edinburgh's less salubrious housing developments, then the impressive Craigmillar would have many more visitors. In Mary, Queen of Scots' time, the imposing fortress was held by Sir Simon Preston, one of her staunchest allies. Behind the massive curtain wall, somewhere amid the 16th-century buildings, the murder of her husband, Lord Darnley, was planned (see pages 30–31).

City Art Centre

THE SCOTTISH REGALIA
On June 24, 1953, the Regalia of Scotland were taken from the castle to St. Giles Cathedral, where they were presented to Her Majesty the Queen. The galaxy of lords and earls who guarded the Honours of the Nation were dressed in ermine and grand costumes. The Queen, however, wore a simple coat and hat. Still clutching her handbag, she touched the oldest crown in Europe. The incongruity is still remembered in Scotland to this day, though in the official portrait of the event, by Stanley Cursiter, now in the Royal Collection, the handbag has been carefully painted out.

MONS MEG
This siege gun or bombard was made in Mons in the 1440s and sent by its owner, the Duke of Burgundy, to his nephew by marriage, King James II, in 1457. The gun had a firing rate of, at the most, one cannonball every 30 minutes. Though cumbersome to move over the rough roads of its day, it did take part in sieges before finally bursting while firing a salute in 1680. It was later displayed in the Tower of London, before its return to Edinburgh Castle.

Edinburgh Castle from Princes Street Gardens

Walk

A flavor of old Edinburgh

This pleasant stroll takes in attractions on the Royal Mile, before heading to the Grassmarket and a fine view of the castle. Allow two hours. *See map on page 44.*

Amid the general crush of visitors on Castlehill at the very top of the **Royal Mile**, look for the **Witch's**

Looking east down the Royal Mile in the direction of the Palace of Holyroodhouse

Well (on the wall), which recalls the last witch burned here in 1722. Nearby is **Cannonball House**, which has a cannonball embedded in the gable with a variety of explanations as to how it got there. Farther down the hill are the **Camera Obscura** (see page 48) and the **Scotch Whisky Heritage Centre** (see page 63). Continue down the hill to the traffic circle.

The Lawnmarket has numerous souvenir shops to distract you, but for a hint of old Edinburgh, turn right just after the traffic circle into the short Upper Bow. Go to the end of this truncated street and look over the railings to see Victoria Street curving down below. Now imagine the shape of the town before Victoria Street was built: Upper Bow plunged steeply down to join the lowest point of Victoria Street, called West Bow, which leads into the Grassmarket. The insignificant lane you have just come down used to be the main road into old Edinburgh from the west.

Return to the Lawnmarket on the Royal Mile. Opposite is **Gladstone's Land** (see page 54), one of a number of restored 17th-century properties in this area.

Lady Stair's House (the Writers' Museum; see page 57) is also on the north side of the street—cut through an alleyway to reach it—with **Deacon Brodie's Tavern** occupying the corner site. Deacon Brodie, a respectable locksmith by day and a villain by night, inspired Robert Louis Stevenson's story *The Strange Case of Dr. Jekyll and Mr. Hyde.*

Turn right onto George IV Bridge and right again to reach Victoria Street, which has a good selection of shops and cafés. West Bow leads into the **Grassmarket**. The right to hold regular markets here was granted by King James III in 1477. The area gained notoriety as the hanging place of common criminals, as well as Covenanter martyrs (see page 55). **St. Andrew's Cross**, railed and set into the cobbles, marks the gallows' site.

For an impressive view of the castle, cross over the Grassmarket, go halfway along, and follow The Vennel up in a series of steps to a well-preserved portion of the city wall. This is **Telfer's Wall**, 1628–1636, which now defines the boundaries of George Heriot's School beyond. From here, there is an excellent view north to the castle. Return to the Grassmarket, then bear right, passing **Mr. Wood's Fossil Shop**, which offers souvenirs with a difference (very small trilobites are a bargain). Then go up **Candlemaker Row**, where tourists risk life and limb standing in the middle of the road to photograph the statue of **Greyfriars Bobby** (see page 55) at the far end. Make your way back to the Royal Mile along George IV Bridge.

❏ Beneath Edinburgh City Chambers on the High Street, site of the former Royal Exchange, lies Mary King's Close. This narrow street was abandoned after the plague of 1645 and sealed off to prevent the disease from spreading. It was subsequently covered by the foundations of the later buildings on the High Street. The 17th-century time capsule survives today and is used for storing council documents. It can be visited on conducted tours. ❏

❏ The Old Town right up to the 18th century, and even later, was a pretty smelly place. This fact was recorded by numerous visitors. Household wastes of every description were emptied from the tall tenements into the narrow High Street with a warning cry of "gardyloo" from on high (the phrase comes from the French *gardez l'eau*—"beware, water"). This was the cause of great embarrassment to biographer James Boswell as he escorted the distinguished man of letters, Dr. Samuel Johnson, up the Royal Mile before they set off for their Hebridean Tour in 1773. The odor is also immortalized by a famous fiddle tune, somewhat ironically entitled "The Floo'ers (flowers) o' Edinburgh." ❏

The City Chambers, built as the Royal Exchange

54

*The Georgian House,
Charlotte Square*

*Greyfriars Bobby,
Edinburgh's
best-known dog*

▶ **Fruitmarket Gallery**   44C2

Market Street
Open: Tue–Sat 10–6, Sun 12–5. Admission free
Another of Edinburgh's high-profile art showcases, the Fruitmarket emphasizes contemporary art and design with a strong international flavor. Combine it with a visit to the City Art Centre opposite (see page 51).

▶▶ **Georgian House**   44A2

Charlotte Square
Open: Apr–Oct, Mon–Sat 10–5, Sun 2–5, last entry 4:30. Admission charge
In the middle of Scottish architect Robert Adam's palace-fronted block, at No. 7 Charlotte Square, the National Trust for Scotland has re-created the look of 1796, when the building was new. From the magnificent drawing room with its glittering candlesticks, to the well-scrubbed pantries and kitchen, it demonstrates the impact the New Town made on Edinburgh's wealthier residents.

▶ **Gladstone's Land**   44C2

477 Lawnmarket
Open: Mon–Sat 10–5, Sun 2–5, last entry 4:30. Admission charge
When the local merchant Thomas Gledstanes acquired the property that now bears his name in 1617, it was a typical 16th-century building that would have resembled John Knox House farther down the street (see page 57). Gledstanes modernized it by adding a stone front and stone arcading. Like so much of the Royal Mile, this

tenement was scheduled to be swept aside, but instead a purchaser presented it to the fledgling National Trust for Scotland in 1935. The Trust restored it and uncovered its by then hidden arcades, now unique in Edinburgh. Some fine painted ceilings also survive from Gledstanes's time and are set off by period room settings.

▶ **Greyfriars Kirk**   44C1

Greyfriars Place
Open: Kirk Easter–Oct, Mon–Fri 10:30–4:30, Sat 10:30–2:30; Nov–Easter, Thu 1:30–3:30. Churchyard daily. Admission free

The Covenanters Prison in Greyfriars Kirkyard

King Charles I's attempt to introduce England's Anglican service book to Scotland in 1637 was widely opposed. The following year, a large crowd gathered in the churchyard of the Greyfriars to sign the National Covenant. This important manifesto professed loyalty to the king, but warned him not to interfere in the affairs of the kirk. It can be seen to this day within the church. Thus were born the Covenanters, participants in the religious wars of the 17th century. The churchyard itself, where 1,400 Covenanters were imprisoned in 1679, is on the site of a 15th-century Franciscan friary and has many 17th-century grave monuments.

55

It was also the burial place of John Gray, the owner of Greyfriars Bobby, a dog who refused to leave his master's grave. The kindhearted graveyard attendant fed him at first. Soon the faithful terrier was a well-known phenomenon cared for by the locals. He soon adopted a local restaurant, delighting its owner, who did extra business because of the publicity. People came from long distances to see the dog arrive each lunchtime.

When a law was passed forbidding ownerless dogs, Bobby's supporters appealed to the Lord Provost, who gave the dog immunity by way of an inscribed collar. Bobby died in 1872, but the tale did not end there. A baroness erected a fountain at one end of nearby Candlemaker Row. Later still, in 1961, the story of Greyfriars Bobby was the subject of a Walt Disney movie, which explains his appeal to many visitors today. Dog artifacts are on display in Huntly House (see below).

▶▶ **Huntly House**   45D2

Canongate
Open: Mon–Sat 10–5; during Festival Sun 2–5. Admission free
This 16th-century building houses the city's museum of life over the centuries. Local silver, glass and pottery, and a host of other artifacts are all displayed in a maze of interconnecting rooms. It helps to know a little of Edinburgh's history before you visit so that, for example, the artifacts connected with King George IV's visit, or the original New Town plan signed by James Craig, are more significant.

REGISTER HOUSE
Record-keeping in Scotland has had a troubled history. King Edward I of England vindictively destroyed the country's earliest records in the 13th century. Register House was situated in the castle by the mid-16th century, and then in the Tolbooth a century later. Only in 1774 was a foundation stone laid for a custom built Register House, designed by Robert Adam, and partly financed by funds raised from the sale of estates forfeited by Jacobite lairds (see page 38). The building, at the east end of Princes Street, is still in use today, guarded by a statue of the Duke of Wellington, who defeated Napoleon at Waterloo.

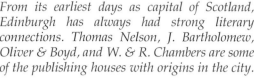

From its earliest days as capital of Scotland, Edinburgh has always had strong literary connections. Thomas Nelson, J. Bartholomew, Oliver & Boyd, and W. & R. Chambers are some of the publishing houses with origins in the city.

SCOTLAND'S POETIC GOLDEN AGE

Medieval Edinburgh was a literary place. Gavin Douglas, ca1474–1522, Dean of St. Giles, translated the Aeneid, the first translation of a Latin poet ever printed in English. William Dunbar, ca1460–1520, was a court poet whose work was in print by 1508, the earliest example of Scottish typography. Sir David Lyndsay of The Mount scandalized the courtiers with his Satyre of the Thrie Estatis in 1540. The piece returns regularly to the Edinburgh Festival.

56

Originally a wig-maker in the Grassmarket, 18th-century poet Allan Ramsay set up Britain's first circulating library, and his is the first of the "modern" names associated with literary Edinburgh. Then came Robert Fergusson, who captured the spirit of the Enlightenment in Edinburgh and inspired a later generation, among them Robert Burns.

A vibrant literary community Conspicuous in the 19th century was Sir Walter Scott, writing of "mine own romantic town" from his house on Castle Street. As a teenager, he had once met Burns at a local literary gathering. Edinburgh's literary life, with its publishers, tavern life, and buzzing creativity, attracted writers from all over the world. It was the first city to recognize the achievements of Charles Dickens by making him a citizen. Charlotte Brontë was also enthralled by the place. Her brother Branwell wrote to the influential Edinburgh-based Blackwood's Magazine asking for a job when he was 15. His letter was ignored at the time but is now in the National Library.

Edinburgh in its prime Robert Louis Stevenson, a native of Edinburgh, became one of its most famous Victorian writers. Stevenson wrote of the city not just in romantic terms, but in a style that still brings its taverns and low life alive. Scotland's most influential 20th-century poet, Hugh MacDiarmid, also had strong Edinburgh connections through a variety of publishing enterprises. British novelist Muriel Spark was educated at James Gillespie's High School for Girls, model for the Marcia Blane School in The Prime of Miss Jean Brodie.

Burns' memorabilia, The Writers' Museum

Today, it is still possible to rub shoulders with poets and writers, even moderately famous ones, in one of the city's "literary" pubs such as Milne's Bar on Hanover Street. The bohemian life survives in Edinburgh, perhaps as a reaction to the city's Calvinistic and prim outlook.

► John Knox House 45D2

45 High Street
Open: Mon–Sat 10–5 (last entry 4:30). Admission charge
Nobody seems to know if John Knox (see panel) really did live in this house on High Street. However, a folk tradition was enough to save it when demolition threatened as long ago as 1849. The late 15th-century building with its projecting second-floor gallery is a reminder of what the Royal Mile would once have looked like: narrow and lined by tenements, with their projecting floors virtually shutting out the light. The house was damaged by the English Earl of Hertford's men in 1544, when it was owned by Mariota Arres and James Mossman. Their initials are on the wall above the shop door. Mossman was the keeper of the Royal Mint to Mary, Queen of Scots, and was eventually hanged for his allegiance. Today, there is an exhibition on the lives of both Mossman and Knox within the property.

► Lady Stair's House
(The Writers' Museum) 44C2

Off Lawnmarket
Open: Mon–Sat 10–5; during Festival Sun 2–5. Admission free
This building, bearing the date 1622, was only later associated with the first Earl of Stair's widow who died in 1759. The close on which it was built was at one time the main communication between the Old Town at the Lawnmarket and the New Town. The house was given to the city in 1907, and it is now a museum of Burns, Scott, and Stevenson memorabilia.

► Lauriston Castle 44A2

Off Cramond Road South
Open: Apr–Oct, Sat–Thu 11–5; Nov–Mar, Sat–Sun 2–4.
Admission charge
Slightly removed from the main tourist thoroughfares, Lauriston Castle makes a worthwhile excursion, perhaps combined with a quiet walk along the River Cramond. Built in 1593 on the site of a tower destroyed in 1544, the castle's original owner was John Napier (1550–1617). This Scottish mathematician was the inventor of logarithms. The castle was presented to the city in 1926, and its turn-of-the-century interiors are carefully preserved.

Lauriston Castle near
Cramond

JOHN KNOX
Born at Haddington (see page 115), John Knox (1513–72), architect of the Reformation in Scotland, became filled with Lutheran reforming zeal in 1544 and was called to the ministry in 1547. He led an adventurous life, including a spell as a French galley slave, following capture at St. Andrew's Castle. He preached in England and on the Continent, as well as making his mark in Scotland, where his views were uncompromisingly antagonistic to those of Mary, Queen of Scots.

EDINBURGH'S OLDEST HOUSE
Moubrey House, next door to John Knox House, is probably even older than its more famous neighbor and can therefore claim the distinction of being Edinburgh's oldest dwelling, built by Andrew Moubrey around 1472.

►►► Museum of Childhood 45D2

High Street
Open: Mon–Sat 10–5; during Festival Sun 2–5. Admission free
If you have never really forgotten your last train set or the
day your dollhouse was packed into the attic, then the
Museum of Childhood should appeal to you. There is a
collection of older material such as Victorian dolls and
German automata, but the eerie part is the objects half recognized from one's own childhood. There, behind glass,
is that even larger construction set to which you always
aspired. If you have children, then you should consider
visiting, though the younger members may be overwhelmed by the massed ranks of historic teddies. Even
without children, this museum should be on the "must
see" list.

►► National Portrait Gallery, Scottish 44C3

Queen Street
Open: Mon–Sat 10–5, Sun 2–5. Admission free
The Scottish National Portrait Gallery was built with
much Caledonian zeal after funding was provided by
John Ritchie Findlay, who owned The Scotsman newspaper. At the gallery's opening in 1889, it was stated that
"a gallery such as this is … the highest incentive to true
patriotism we can possibly have." Since then, the images
of the famous Scots who stare down from the walls have
become part of Scotland's fabric, reproduced both in
scholarly books and on shortbread cans, so that the
viewer coming upon Nasmyth's Robert Burns may find it
quite familiar—a veritable icon of Scotland.

Take time to look at the setting of these famous Scots.
The architect Robert Rowand Anderson was an
Edinburgh native, but amid the orderly neoclassicism on
the very edge of the first phase of the New Town, he created a Gothic palace, now one of Edinburgh's few monuments to Gothic revivalism. Inside, the late Victorian
fashion for mural painting found expression in a
processional frieze of famous Scottish figures—a kind of
miniature portrait gallery in itself—with other wall-sized
scenes from Scotland's story, set between the sandstone

**A MUSEUM FOR
ADULTS?**
The founder of the
Museum of Childhood,
Patrick Murray, an
Edinburgh town councillor,
insisted it was a museum
portraying a specialized
field of social history. A
bachelor, he did not
actually like children—or
at least he pretended not
to. He formerly displayed
in the museum entrance
hall a design for a memo-
rial window to "good" King
Herod!

columns. Stained glass and Scottish heraldry make their contribution to the general ambience.

The Stewart monarchs are here, including the only portrait of Mary, Queen of Scots made in her lifetime—a small bronze bust of Mary, around age 17. Flora Macdonald, who played a role in Jacobite schemes, is also on view, as is King George IV entering Holyroodhouse in 1822. this visit of the monarch marked the rehabilitation of tartan, which is much in evidence in many other works.

Poets, painters, novelists, engineers, philosophers, and famous fiddlers are all here—and not only from distant times. Though the heyday for the medium of portraiture has gone, there are many powerful figures from nearer our own time, such as Hugh MacDiarmid, Norman MacCaig, and Muriel Spark. Some of the more recent pictures are the result of a survey that asked gallery users which natives they would most like to see on the walls. So Sean Connery has also entered this hall of fame. A visit here is an insight into the qualities of "Scottishness".

A GREAT ARCHITECT
William Henry Playfair (1789–1857) not only designed the National Gallery (which was finally completed in the same year that he died), but is also associated with many other buildings in and around the New Town, which still lend distinction to the city's profile. These include Donaldson's Hospital, St. Stephen's Church, and, on Calton Hill, the National Monument, the New Observatory, and the monument to Scottish philosopher Dugald Stuart (1753–1828).

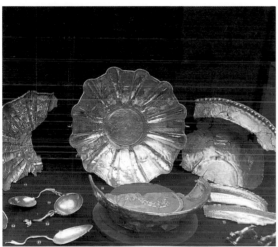

Roman treasure in the Royal Museum of Scotland collections

The Museum of Childhood, a top attraction on the Royal Mile

▶▶▶ National Gallery of Scotland   44B2

The Mound
Open: Mon–Sat 10–5, Sun 2–5. Admission free
William Playfair's National Gallery was completed in 1857 and rates among the top two or three classical designs in Edinburgh. Its sparingly ornamented length, honey-colored in the thin Edinburgh sunlight, has a simple dignity entirely in keeping with its role as a repository for Scotland's finest art.

Inside, its human scale makes it easily accessible, with no vast, intimidating halls. But when the present 19th-century-inspired display first opened in the late 1980s, controversy raged in the conservative Edinburgh art world. Against a rich red background, many of the paintings are hung very high and close together. Visit it for some of the best Old Masters in the United Kingdom outside London, for its Impressionists, and, naturally, for its Scottish paintings. There are also important collections of prints, drawings, and watercolors.

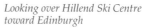

Looking over Hillend Ski Centre toward Edinburgh

Walk

From Swanston to Colinton Dell

A rural walk south of Edinburgh in the footsteps of Robert Louis Stevenson, with spectacular views back toward the city. Allow about three hours for the walk (one way).

Take a bus or car to the southern edge of the city. Bus travelers can alight at the Hillend Ski Centre on A703 and cross Lothianburn Golf Course by a path to reach the attractive little hamlet of Swanston to the west. Those with a car can take it all the way to the hamlet, where there is a parking lot.

Swanston is associated with Robert Louis Stevenson—his family had a summer cottage there—and is part of the setting for his unfinished novel *St. Ives*. The former Stevenson family home (private) is still there as described in the work: "It had something of the air of a rambling, infinitesimal cathedral... grotesquely decorated with crockets

The Hermitage of Braid, on the way from Edinburgh to Swanston

and gargoyles, ravished from some medieval church." (In real life, these were salvaged from the restoration of St. Giles.)

For a longer expedition (more than just to Swanston)—one that requires good footwear and the best part of a morning or afternoon — follow the track into the Pentland Hills south of Swanston. The objective is the broad ridge, seen to the south, of Caerketton and Allermuir Hills, two of the Pentland "tops". Alternatively, Caerketton (the rocky one) can be reached by missing Swanston entirely and going up toward the ski center at Hillend, striking upward on a path to the left of it. Either way, you join a sky-line path westward along the heathery hilltops, enjoying superb city views. Take in Capelaw Hill before descending an easy path and track to Bonaly Country Park. (There is a parking lot for those making a separate excursion.) Follow Bonaly Road down into the suburb of Colinton to reach Spylaw Park. Turning right (toward town) soon brings the walker to Colinton Parish Church above a bend in the Water of Leith, another place which Stevenson knew well; his maternal grandfather, the Reverend Dr. Lewis Balfour, was minister here. It is childhood memories of this leafy dell, with its mossy banks and river, that Stevenson recalls in his lines: "Here is the mill with the humming of thunder./Here is the weir with the wonder of foam." Buses run from Colinton back into the city center.

▶ Palace of Holyroodhouse 45E2

*Open: Apr–Oct, daily 9:30–5:15; Nov–Mar, daily 9:30– 3:45.
Admission charge*

As late as the 1890s, Robert Louis Stevenson in his Picturesque Notes on Edinburgh observed that "the Palace of Holyroodhouse has been left aside in the growth of Edinburgh, and stands gray and silent in a workman's quarter among breweries and gasworks." This was the low point in the story of what is still the official residence of the Royal Family in Scotland. The palace evolved from the guest house of the adjacent Holyrood Abbey, now a ruin.

The first palace, started by King James IV, was damaged during the English raids of 1544, part of the "rough wooing" (see page 30), though the northwest tower (or the King James V Tower—the left-hand tower on the frontage) survived the flames to be rebuilt. It contains the rooms associated with Mary, Queen of Scots.

Holyrood was ablaze again in 1650, the same year as Oliver Cromwell and his troops stayed there while occupying the north. He ordered some repair, but the main work seen today is primarily the result of a major remodeling in 1671–1680, during the reign of King Charles II. His brother, King James VII (James II of England), was sometimes in residence there.

However, it is most strongly associated with Mary, Queen of Scots (see page 30), though the site of the murder of her secretary Riccio is no longer marked with red paint but instead by a discreet plaque. After such highlights as grand receptions held by the transient Bonnie Prince Charlie and later by King George IV in his 1822 visit, it fell into decline, though Queen Victoria used it in 1850. Much restoration work this century has restored its dignity. In addition to portraits of monarchs (some of them mythical), there are tapestries and fine furniture from the royal collections. It closes to visitors and transforms itself from a tourist center to a high-security establishment whenever a member of the Royal Family comes to visit.

*Palace of Holyroodhouse
—detail of entrance gates*

THE LAW COURTS
Behind St. Giles, Parliament House, the seat of Scottish government until 1707, is now the Supreme Law Courts of Scotland. There are portraits by Sir Henry Raeburn among other artists, as well as a hammerbeam (ornate wooden-beamed) ceiling to admire.

ROYAL PORTRAITS
Jacob de Witt, a Dutchman living in Edinburgh, signed a contract with His Majesty's Cash Keeper in 1684 to deliver 110 portraits of Scottish kings within two years at £120 ($180) per year. These ran from the possibly mythical King Fergus I to the then contemporary King Charles II—so at least in one case de Witt had a likeness to work from. The painter fulfilled his contract at more than one a week, and at least 80 of the portraits can be seen today.

Palace of Holyroodhouse

THE OLD PHYSIC GARDEN

Few of the train passengers arriving at Waverley Station notice the plaque that records the site of the first public botanic garden in Edinburgh. The Old Physic Garden was in the hollow now occupied by the station and post office. The area saw many changes, not the least of which was the draining of the Nor' Loch, which once provided Edinburgh Castle's defenses to the north (in part of today's Princes Street Gardens). The partial draining of the ancient loch flooded the Old Physic Garden in 1689, and many of its precious plants were lost.

Royal Botanic Garden—an all-weather, all-year attraction

A PRESBYTERIAN PROTEST

A humble cabbage stall owner called Jenny Geddes earned her place in history on July 23, 1637. King Charles I had declared St. Giles a cathedral and had ordered the use of the Anglican service book. No sooner had the Dean of Edinburgh started this unfamiliar service to the staunchly Presbyterian congregation, than Jenny Geddes threw her prayer stool at him, screaming "Daur ye say mass in my lug! (Dare you say mass in my ear?)." More missiles followed, and a full-scale riot ensued. Her great gesture over, Jenny quietly returned to cabbage selling.

▶▶ **The People's Story**   45D2

Canongate

Open: Mon–Sat 10–5; during Festival Sun 2–5. Admission free

The People's Story is just that—a museum recording the experiences of the ordinary folk of Edinburgh from the 18th century to the present day. As such, it does not portray a sanitized view of a city in which bad housing and poor working conditions coexisted with a genteel preoccupation with middle-class respectability. It is overtly political in its cameos of the local trades and the workers who put in long hours for small rewards. The overwhelming impression is of generations of drudgery for all kinds of people, from skilled craftsmen making beer barrels for the local brewing industry, down to humble servants whose first job was to polish the steel in the grate until it shone, then light the mistress's fire to blacken it again. It certainly puts today's Royal Mile in a new light.

▶▶▶ **Royal Botanic Garden**   44B3

Inverleith Row

Open: daily Apr–Aug 9:30–7; Mar, Sep 9:30–6; Feb, Oct 9:30–5; Nov–Jan 9:30–4. Admission free

One of Edinburgh's most precious recreational assets, the garden is strollable from Princes Street via Stockbridge, though you may wish to take the bus back up the hill. It is especially suitable for children as it is dog free—though the squirrels can be persistent. In addition to its large rhododendron collection, and a magnificent rock garden (best in May), there are substantial areas under glass. The highest point of the garden has a fine view over the city.

▶▶ **Royal Museum of Scotland and Museum of Scotland**   44C1

Chambers Street

Open: Mon, Wed–Sat 10–5, Tue 10–8, Sun 12–5. Admission charge

This lofty Victorian building, with its soaring columns

and galleries, houses the national collection of scientific, natural, historical, geological, archeological, and other objects.

The adjacent new Museum of Scotland building, which was opened in late 1998, houses a collection of artifacts that relate specifically to Scotland. The museum organizes a program of special talks and lectures that it is worth checking out.

John Knox in St. Giles

▶ St. Giles: the High Kirk of Edinburgh 44C1
High Street
Open: Mon–Sat 9–5, Sun 1–5 and for services Admission free
Often called St. Giles' Cathedral, though purists argue it only achieved this status briefly, St. Giles was at one time the only church within the walls of old Edinburgh. The tower of St. Giles is one of the few remaining examples of 15th-century work to be seen on the High Street today. Much of the church has been altered and reworked over the centuries. Today's dull exterior is the result of 19th-century "restoration"; only the tower and crown escaped this gray stone. Once the venerable church even had a long arcade of booths, the "krames," leaning against the north side. These were removed in 1817, along with the "luckenbooths," other small shops that contributed to the crowded narrowness of this part of the High Street. Just to the west of the church is the site of the Old Tolbooth, also removed in 1817. Now stones mark the spot in the shape of a heart—a reference to Scott's description of the Tolbooth as the "Heart of Midlothian."

▶ Scotch Whisky Heritage Centre 44C1
354 Castlehill
Open: daily 10–5:30, last tour 5, extended hours in summer. Admission charge
The problem with whisky-making (note the Scots spelling) is that it is not in itself a visually dramatic process, much of it consisting of waiting until the enzymes do their job. The centre injects fun into the subject by taking a high-tech approach, with talking tableaux and commentary all viewed while riding along on a hollowed-out whisky barrel. Whisky's story is told from its ancient origins via prohibition to modern marketing methods.

THE OLD TOLBOOTH
It was formerly considered good luck to spit on the heart shape that marks the Old Tolbooth site beside St. Giles. This was perhaps a contemptuous gesture toward the town authorities, who used the Tolbooth as a prison.

JOHN KNOX
John Knox's statue can be seen inside St. Giles, but the fiery reformer's grave is no longer marked. He was buried in the old St. Giles churchyard, which is now covered by flagstones.

ST. GILES
St. Giles, the church, was probably founded by Benedictine followers of Giles, the saint, who brought the name from the south of France. In 1466, the Preston Aisle of the church was completed, in memory of William Preston, who had acquired the arm-bone of the saint in France. This relic disappeared around about 1577, but St. Giles' other arm-bone is still in St. Giles Church, Bruges.

The story of Scottish whisky is told on the Royal Mile

The Scottish patriot Fletcher of Saltoun wrote in 1698: "As the happy situation of London has been the principal cause of the glory and riches of England, so the bad situation of Edinburgh has been one great occasion of the poverty and uncleanliness in which the greater part of the people of Scotland live ..."

Top: an ornate ceiling inside the head office of the Royal Bank of Scotland at 36 St. Andrew Square

THE MOUND
In the great building spree that went on in 18th-century Edinburgh, somewhere had to be found for the material dug out for foundations. In the case of the Royal Exchange (today's City Chambers), the rubble became the Castle Esplanade. Meanwhile, Geordie Boyd, a local tailor, started dumping earth into the quagmire of the old Nor Loch. So did everyone else, and "Geordie Boyd's mud brig" grew and grew. Two million cartloads later, in 1830, it became The Mound, the elegant roadway linking the Old and New Towns.

An 18th-century vision Many stories of the squalor of the Old Town of Edinburgh are documented. As the more peaceful 18th century began in Scotland, improvements began within the Old Town itself. But the long-term solution was for the city's inhabitants to escape entirely from the rocky ramp running down from the castle.

George Drummond, Lord Provost of Edinburgh, had a clear vision of a new Edinburgh rising on what was then only a low ridge between the castle and the sea. A competition to design a new town was organized, which was won by a young and unknown architect, James Craig. His 1767 design shows a simple grid of streets balanced by a square at either end. This is the Princes Street to Queen Street area, with Charlotte Square and St. Andrew Square at either end.

Princes Street If you stroll along Queen Street today, you can see how it echoes Princes Street: it is built up on one side only and has gardens (still private) opposite. Down amid the hubbub and main street shopfronts on Princes Street, it is hard to believe that in Craig's original plan the area was meant to be entirely residential. He designated today's Thistle and Rose streets, lesser byways between the grand thoroughfares, as the abode and business place of tradesmen and shopkeepers. The use of the lanes behind Thistle and Rose streets to reach the back doors of the wealthier residents was a clever element in his deceptively simple plan.

Princes Street did not remain residential for long. The main tide of commercial developments began to flow from east to west by the mid-19th century. Before that, the residents whose grand drawing rooms looked out to the castle over the trees in the gardens had fought another battle. A speculator had wanted to build along the south side of Princes Street, and the indignant citizens, determined to

Period atmosphere in elegant Charlotte Square

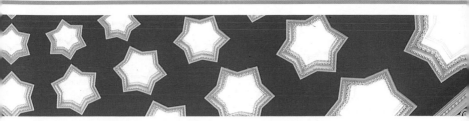

preserve their views, had to take their case to the House of Lords before the project was stopped. (The city fathers of the day were quite happy to allow the speculator to build.) Today's low-profile Waverley Market is a reminder of those far-off legal battles.

String-pulling Stand on what used to be the bare ridge, and is now George Street, about halfway along, and look up and down the street. In Craig's plan the two squares, Charlotte and St. Andrew, at either end of the view, also had churches. While the green copper dome of the former St. George's (now West Register House) is plain on the western skyline, to the east in St. Andrew Square there is a fine town house instead of a church.

A place of worship was never built there because of civic string-pulling by Sir Laurence Dundas. Rich, powerful, and

PRINCES STREET
Princes Street was to be called St. Giles Street, but King George III objected as it reminded him of the St. Giles district of London, which was notorious for its lowlife at the time. So the most famous street in Scotland became Prince's Street after the Prince Regent, before assuming its plural form in 1848.

65

onetime Commissary General of the army in Flanders, Dundas acquired the site and altered the plan to suit himself. He employed Sir William Chambers to design the magnificent façade that is seen today, and this fine townhouse is now the headquarters of the Royal Bank of Scotland. It has ornate ceilings in its main hall, well worth looking at even if you do not have an account there. The city fathers got their church eventually, built on a less satisfactory site, around the corner on George Street. This is St. Andrew's, still in use today and open to visitors.

By the end of the 19th century, the first New Town was complete, paving the way for further phases to the north, east, and west, and creating Edinburgh's unique neo-classical ambience.

The grand façades of Edinburgh's New Town

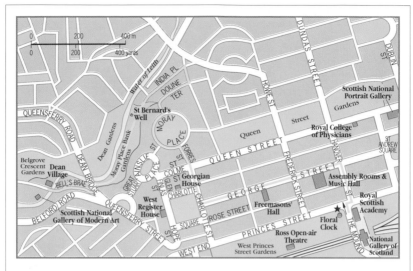

Walk

The New Town

Discover the surprisingly intact second phase of the New Town in the streets that lie north of Charlotte Square. Allow three hours.

Starting from the **Floral Clock** on Princes Street, opposite the Royal Scottish Academy, walk north to George Street, turning left at the **statue of King George IV**. Go past the **Assembly Rooms**, now a major Festival Fringe showcase, where Sir Walter Scott publicly admitted to writing the Waverley Novels during a grand dinner in 1827.

Continue down George Street to **Charlotte Square** at the west end, which balances **St. Andrew Square** at the east. The Robert Adam-designed north façade of Charlotte Square is impressively harmonious, while intrusive modern additions detract from the other three sides.

Continue downhill to **Moray Place**, typical of the New Town with its private gardens, cobbled roads, and grand façades. Leave by **Doune Terrace**. Cross the **Water of Leith** to shop in Stockbridge, otherwise turn left along undistinguished India Place. Keep going to enter the wooded valley of the Water of Leith, and go down steps by the bridge. **St. Bernard's Well**, half hidden in the greenery, is a former mineral spring in the shape of a Grecian temple with a statue of Hygeia, designed by Alexander Nasmyth in 1789.

The footpath continues to **Dean Village**. Overhead is Thomas Telford's road bridge, built in 1832. A 1643 Baxters (Bakers) "coat-of-arms" survives on the abutment of the original bridge below. Climb back to the busy streets by cobbled Bell's Brae, the former main road.

St. Bernard's Well

▶ **Scottish Agricultural Museum** 44A1

Ingliston, 7 miles west of Edinburgh
Open: Apr–Sep, daily 10–5; Oct–Mar, Mon–Fri 10–5.
Admission free, except during Royal Highland Show
This is Scotland's national farming museum,
adjacent to Scotland's premier agricultural show-
ground site. It covers all aspects of bygone rural life,
including trades associated with farming, and social
and home life in the countryside. There are good
displays of equipment and artifacts, and evocative
photographs.

▶ **Scottish National Gallery**
of Modern Art 4466

Belford Road
Open: Mon–Sat 10–5, Sun 2–5. Admission free
Housed in former school premises, an excursion here
could be made via a stretch of the Water of Leith footpath, joining it perhaps at Dean Village. Scotland's own
collection of moderns includes works by Derain,
Matisse, Picasso, Giacometti, Hockney, and Hepworth,
among many others. Scotland's own artists are not
neglected, with the Scottish colorists—Peploe, Cadell,
Fergusson, and Hunter—well represented. The gallery
also has a popular cafeteria.

An adaptation of The
Rev. Robert Walker
Skating *by Raeburn—
symbol of Edinburgh art*

▶ **(Edinburgh) Zoo** 44A1

Corstorphine Road
Open: Apr–Sep, Mon–Sat 9–6, Sun 9:30–6; Mar and Oct,
Mon–Sat 9–5, Sun 9:30–5; Nov–Feb, Mon–Sat 9–4:30, Sun
9:30–4:30. Admission charge
The zoo once suffered all the problems of financing a
traditional, wide-ranging animal collection in a time
when other leisure attractions were siphoning off visitors.
Now its collection is smaller. The sad, solitary elephant
has gone, and, along with some new and spacious enclosures, there is a very substantial animal-themed gift shop.
A few of the fairly primitive enclosures still remain—for
the tigers and some other big cats, for instance—but the
penguins and gorillas (awesome in close-up through the
glass) certainly look happy enough. Young children will
undoubtedly appreciate it, though parents may get a
backache from lifting them up to see into some of the
enclosures. Also, the zoo is built on a slope, which makes
stroller-pushing something of an endurance test. There is
a breeding program for endangered species.

PENGUINS ON PARADE
Edinburgh Zoo's "Penguin
Parade" is an old-
established institution.
The penguins are
shepherded out of their
modern, spacious enclo-
sure daily in the summer
months, and they trundle
around a grassy area
nearby. Formerly, they
were walked right out of
the zoo, but their appearance on the sidewalks
along Corstorphine Road
caused traffic accidents
as drivers were distracted.
Their perambulations
these days are less extensive.

Edinburgh

RESERVING ACCOMMODATIONS

The Edinburgh and Scotland Information Centre (see page 272) helps visitors find accommodations, though the lines can be very long. Try the advance central reservation service (tel: 0131-473 3855), but note that it cannot be used to reserve accommodations at Festival time.

Accommodations

Sit on the top deck of a bus coming in on the main road from Cameron Toll, through the district of Newington, and you can get some idea of the selection of accommodations. The hotels and guest houses are lined up as far as the eye can see—and that is just one street, though it changes its name as it heads toward The Bridges and central Edinburgh.

However, do not be misled into thinking that finding the right place to stay will be easy, since Edinburgh is a hugely popular destination. If you are visiting specifically to "do" the Edinburgh Festival, then make reservations well in advance. Otherwise, late August–early September is best avoided altogether. Finding somewhere at a reasonable rate will be much easier outside that period, and easier still out of season (November to Easter). If you do find yourself in the city during the festival and need somewhere to stay, it's worth persevering with the Edinburgh and Scotland Information Centre, 3 Princes Street (tel: 0131-557 1700), who will certainly assist. It would be misleading to suggest that finding accommodations is impossible, more that things are very busy.

HOTELS Many international chains are represented in Edinburgh, for example, the Edinburgh Sheraton, with its views of the castle, or the Hilton, down by the Water of Leith. Then there are the former railroad hotels: the grand-style Caledonian, with its sumptuous Pompadour Restaurant, and, dominating the skyline at the other end of Princes Street, the equally luxurious Balmoral. (This used to be called the North British, taking its name from the other pre-1923 railroad company that ran into Edinburgh.)

Also in the expensive bracket are the Howard Hotel on elegant Great King Street, the popular George on George Street, the Roxburghe in Charlotte Square, the Carlton Highland on North Bridge, and the King James Thistle off Princes Street at the east end.

Quality can be enjoyed without overspending. Notable for its personal service and country-club atmosphere in the city is

Echoes of the great railroad age—the Caledonian Hotel

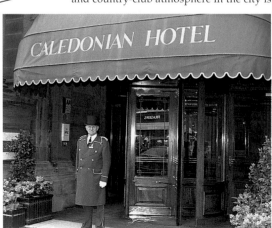

A Princes Street land-mark—the clock tower of the Balmoral Hotel at Princes Street, east end

Channings, on South Learmonth Gardens. The Malmaison, with a strong French flavour, is in a quiet location close to the waterfront in Leith, yet only 10 minutes from the city center.

GUEST HOUSES There is a wide choice of guest houses. Many can be found south of the city center: try the Thrums Private Hotel on Minto Street, Newington, for example. As a general rule, the smaller establishments tend to be some distance from the downtown area though this should not be a problem, as Edinburgh bus services are adequate. Remember, if coming by car, to inquire about parking at the establishment of your choice, since Edinburgh dishes out parking tickets without mercy after 8 AM.

In all cases, rates during the off-season period between November and Easter are cheaper, and there are often special weekend rates or other kinds of deals from the larger hotels.

HOSTELS There are two permanent Edinburgh youth hostels, at 7 Bruntsfield Crescent EH10 4EZ, tel: 0131-447 2994, and 18 Eglinton Crescent EH12 5DD, tel: 0131-337 1120; these are supplemented in summer by additional hostel accommodations using university student residences. For advance bookings, contact the District Office, 161 Warrender Park Road EH9 1EQ, tel: 0131-229 8660. All are within easy reach of the main visitor attractions.

OUT OF TOWN Another option is to choose accommodations outside the city. The Norton House Hotel and the Royal Scot are on the west side of the city, within easy reach of Edinburgh Airport. South of the city, the Roslin Glen Hotel, in the conservation village of Roslin, is close to Rosslyn Chapel with its magnificent medieval stonecarving.

PARKING
If you are bringing a car to Edinburgh, it is best to check exactly what the parking arrangements are, especially if you wish to sleep late in the morning. Parking laws are rigorously enforced after 8 am.

HISTORIC FEATURES
You might notice the extra-wide front doors in some of the city's New Town properties that are now hotels. Together with the generous hallways between inner and outer doors, these were originally built to park sedan chairs, which were borne on poles by two men. Similarly, the New Town's George Street was not built so broadly with central parking in mind, but to let a coach-and-six do an easy U-turn.

Food and drink

Edinburgh's colorful pub signs

Edinburgh sees itself as a cosmopolitan city so you'll find cuisines from around the world on offer in its restaurants. However, many establishments come and go, and chefs move around, so it is always best to take up-to-the-minute local advice if you want a meal to remember.

RESTAURANTS In addition to freestanding restaurants, the main hotels all have good restaurants, with the Grill Rooms at the Balmoral and the Sheraton hotels, and the Pompadour at the Caledonian of particular note. On the other hand, the area around the university, especially around Nicolson Street, has a number of eating places offering particularly good value. Leith, Edinburgh's seaport, is the setting for a number of enterprising restaurant developments and should not be overlooked. This is a place to head to in the evening to eat, drink, and to see and be seen in one of the trendy wine bars.

For consistent quality, Martin's on Rose Street North Lane and The Vintner's Room down in Leith are examples of well-prepared, imaginative cuisine, but it is almost unfair to single them out as the city has so many good restaurants to choose from: Atrium, Jacksons, the Malmaison Brasserie, L'Auberge, Duck's at Le Marché Noir, The Witchery by the Castle. For top quality at top prices, try Jeff Bland's cooking at No. 1 The Restaurant (in the Balmoral Hotel). If you want quality on a budget, try The Kalpna on Nicolson Street, with its reasonably priced, inspiring Indian vegetarian

70

IN THE HAGGIS SEASON...
Haggis (boiled, meat-stuffed tripe) may be Scotland's national dish, but it can be dull, dry, greasy, or gritty—though it can also be spicy and delicious. If you want to try it, you will sometimes find it on Scottish-themed restaurant menus as an appetizer.

Plenty of atmosphere at the Café Royal Oyster Bar

Scotland's sweet tooth—
Casey's candy shop

cooking; to join a cross section of the natives enjoying an evening out, try the Waterfront Wine Bar in Leith.

The only thing that is really hard to track down in Edinburgh is an easily identifiable local cuisine, though the surrounding East Lothian countryside is market-garden country, supplying plenty of local produce. The other name for Edinburgh's eastern hinterland is "Scotland's Granary," which has in turn helped develop a tradition of fine baking, though probably no more so here than in other parts of Scotland. Local food-lovers are more likely to whisper reverently about the near-legendary Valvolla and Crolla delicatessen on Haddington Place, with its authentic Italian ambience.

HEALTHY EATING Edinburgh's fairly enlightened attitude to food can be deduced from the success of Henderson's on Hanover Street. This vegetarian, organic-food self-service restaurant is not a new place capitalizing on the current trend for healthy eating. Instead, it has survived and prospered on the same site for decades—since long before the notion of health food reached the rest of high-cholesterol Scotland.

The heavyweight traditional Scottish breakfast is still available in most guest houses and bed-and-breakfast establishments, but you can skip it and linger instead over a croissant and coffee in any one of the city's numerous café bars. Home-baked cakes for afternoon tea are also easily found, and the Sheraton offers traditional Scottish shortbread, though you need not go so far upscale.

EDINBURGH ROCK CANDY

This item is the quintessential Edinburgh souvenir and is sold at any number of tourist shops, and could be the perfect gift for someone with a (very) sweet tooth. If you prefer a different sort of souvenir look for some authentic Scottish shortbread in a delicatessen or gift shop.

ROLL PLAY

An Edinburgh bakery is a good place to note the regional differences in the names for various baked goods. Muffins describe at least two types of bun. Pancakes are even more of a problem. Are they the same as crumpets, or even pikelets? Aberdeen rolls in most Edinburgh bakeries are butteries, sometimes rowies. And what exactly are Jap cakes and German biscuits? If you think this is complicated, try ordering a pound of potted hough from the butcher next door.

Ross's

EDINBURGH CASTLE ROCK

Tartan umbrellas—practical souvenirs of Edinburgh

OPEN FOR BUSINESS
Especially at the height of the season, many shops catering to visitors are open every day. Off-peak, stores in the city open late-night on Thursdays (7:30–8 PM). Supermarkets stay open late right through the week, all year round.

The elegant interior of Jenners

Shopping

MAIN SHOPPING AREAS Do not make the mistake of assuming that Edinburgh's shopping ends with Princes Street. Far from it. With the exception of Jenners, which is the city's last independently owned major store, and a very few other places, Princes Street has little more to offer than can be found on a dozen other British main streets. This is not to say that the shops are necessarily bad—just that there is not a huge choice of unique or characterful Scottish wares along its length.

Within a few moments' walk of Princes Street are two covered malls. The St. James Centre was built on the site of part of the New Town and offers an assortment of clothing retailers and the like. The Waverley Market beside the Scott Monument is much more interesting.

SCOTTISH GOODS Shopping in Edinburgh is worthwhile, but the best shops are not all in one place. The city offers a good range of Scottish products. Stores selling imported souvenirs abound along the Royal Mile, but there are high-quality outlets as well. The Edinburgh Old Town Weaving Co., at 555 Castlehill, offers a good cross section of Scottish wares made on the premises, including bagpipes and kilts. Scottish Gems, at 24 High Street, has a fine silver and gold jewelry. Judith Glue, just below St. Giles Kirk, has an excellent selection of Orkney knitwear and Scottish gifts.

SPECIALTY SHOPS Small, individual businesses still survive on Victoria Street, along with Byzantium, an interesting antiques and crafts market. A little farther on in the Grassmarket, among the odd mixture of down-and-outs and exclusive designer shops, is Mr. Wood's Fossils, which sells all kinds of fossils. Also within easy reach of Princes Street is the William Street/Stafford Street area, where

there are a number of smaller specialized fashion and gift shops, of which Studio One on Stafford Street is a long-established example.

SHOPPING OUT OF THE CENTER Farther afield, the districts of Bruntsfield and Morningside are worth a stroll along the main streets, down the high canyons of the Edinburgh tenement blocks. Stockbridge, toward the Water of Leith, is also worth a look, and only minutes from the heart of the city. Edinburgh Crystal at Penicuik,

A Royal Mile souvenir shop—tartan all the way

about half an hour away by car, runs factory tours showing the glass-blowing process and has hand-cut products. (You can also buy this selection in the city.)

BOOKSTORES Edinburgh's literary leanings are confirmed by the large number of bookstores scattered around, many of which are secondhand stores. Among new book retailers are James Thin, The Edinburgh Bookshop, and Waterstones. Many more, some with late hours, make the city a browser's paradise.

ART AND ANTIQUES Antiques shops seem to come and go, but try Bruntsfield Place or Causewayside, where they gather in clusters. It is best to ask around for up-to-the-minute information. Some antiques shops usually have a good selection of Scottish paintings, but Edinburgh is exceptionally well-endowed with specialized galleries, with excellent selections of both contemporary and antique material. The Firth Gallery on William Street specializes in living Scottish artists; the Dundas Street Gallery on Dundas Street tends toward contemporary figurative and landscape work; while Stills on Cockburn Street exhibits photography by both Scottish and international artists. For those who hunt around, bargains and high-quality work can be found in the city. If tracking them down takes you off Princes Street, then that is all the better—the real Edinburgh can be found en route.

JENNERS
The last independent store on Princes Street, Jenners has been an Edinburgh institution since 1838. It offers a good selection of items, from Edinburgh Crystal to exclusive fashions and a large toy department. This traditional department store is housed in a handsome building of 1895, with lots of baroque detail outside and a mock-Jacobean galleried interior.

Nightlife

It may not be Las Vegas, but the city of Edinburgh belies its sober and respectable image with a vibrant nightlife.

The annual flurry of Fringe posters

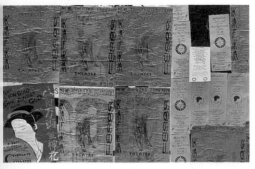

THEATER AND CONCERT HALLS The Traverse Theatre on Cambridge Street (tel: 0131-228 1404) puts on experimental material, while the Royal Lyceum Theatre on Grindley Street (tel: 0131-229 9697) stages more middle-of-the-road plays. The Kings Theatre on Leven Street (tel: 0131-229 1201) has a varied lightweight program, including variety and pantomime. The Usher Hall on Lothian Road (tel: 0131-228 1155) is the city's old-established concert hall, now sharing prestige with the Festival Theatre on Nicolson Street (tel: 0131-529 6000). The Queen's Hall on Clerk Street (tel: 0131-668 2019) is a more intimate concert setting, while The Playhouse, Greenside Place (tel: 0131-557 2692), sees a lot of big showbiz names.

74

FESTIVAL NIGHTS
Remember that Edinburgh's nightlife, like the city itself, moves up a gear in Festival time. Everywhere is crowded and full of visitors. This is the season when Edinburgh appears truly cosmopolitan.

LISTINGS
For up-to-the-minute events information in Edinburgh, try The List, available from all downtown newspaper stalls, or The Scotsman on Saturdays, whose weekend section is very strong on entertainment events throughout Scotland, but emphasizing Edinburgh. The latter is a useful place to find information on folk music in the capital.

MOVIES The independent Dominion on Newbattle Terrace in Morningside (tel: 0131-447 2660) is particularly good, while the Filmhouse on Lothian Road (tel: 0131-228 2688) is the place to see off-beat, less commercial, or foreign-language films.

OTHER KINDS OF NIGHTLIFE The city's casinos include the Stanley Berkeley on Rutland Place (tel: 0131-228 4446) and Stanley Martell on Newington Road (tel: 0131-667 7763). Both offer free membership with 24 hours' notice.

Alternatively, treat yourself to a Scottish evening, with lots of songs and dancing. Several of the downtown hotels hold these on a regular basis. Try the Carlton Highland Hotel on North Bridge (tel: 0131-556 7277) or the King James Hotel, Leith Street (tel: 0131-556 0111).

There are at least half a dozen disco clubs, offering something for fans of Techno, rave, chart sound, mainstream, and/or the gay scene, where you can dance till dawn. A couple of examples are Café Graffiti, in the former Mansfield Place Church (tel: 0131-557 8003), and Club Mercado in Market Street (tel: 0131-226 4224).

Fringe actors—an encounter at every street corner

Practicalities

AIRPORT TRANSFERS Edinburgh Airport, Edinburgh EH12 9DN (tel: 0131-333 1000) is 7 miles from the center of the city. Airport buses run at peak times every 15 minutes (every hour off-peak) between the terminal building and Waverley Bridge. The ride lasts 30 minutes (45 minutes in the rush hour) and costs roughly a quarter of the taxi fare.

ARRIVING BY TRAIN OR BUS Waverley Station could hardly be closer to the city center, and there is a taxi stand right within the station. The main bus station is at St. Andrew Square, moments away from Princes Street, along which run the principal city bus services (see below).

TOURIST INFORMATION For the main Edinburgh tourist information center, see page 272. For information about Edinburgh at the airport, check with the Tourist Information Desk (tel: 0131-333 2167).

GETTING AROUND BY BUS Edinburgh has an extensive bus network, with two main companies covering most of the routes in and around the city.

On Lothian Region Transport (L.R.T.) maroon and white buses, you pay the driver when you get on with the exact fare. L.R.T. offers a variety of unlimited travel tickets to visitors. Further information from the L.R.T. information office at 27 Hanover Street (tel: 0131-555 6363).

On S.M.T. Eastern Scottish green and cream buses, you pay the driver when you get on, and change is given. Some of these services are small buses known as Citysprinters. Further information can be obtained from The Bus Shop, St. Andrew Square Bus Station, Edinburgh (tel: 0131-663 9233).

TAXIS Black taxis are widely available within the city. There are a number of taxi stands, and taxis showing an illuminated "For Hire" sign can be hailed on the street. Black taxis cannot be picked up at Edinburgh Airport, but a fleet of other licensed cabs (usually ordinary cars) is available there.

TRAVEL TO THE AIRPORT Both main rail lines converging on Edinburgh, from Glasgow and from the north, pass the airport practically adjacent to its perimeter. So far, nobody has thought to build a station. Airport-to-city-center connections are by road, through the suburb of Corstorphine, which can get very busy at peak times, to Princes Street. Allow a good hour before check-in time if you are catching a plane.

75

If time is short, take a bus tour

Glasgow

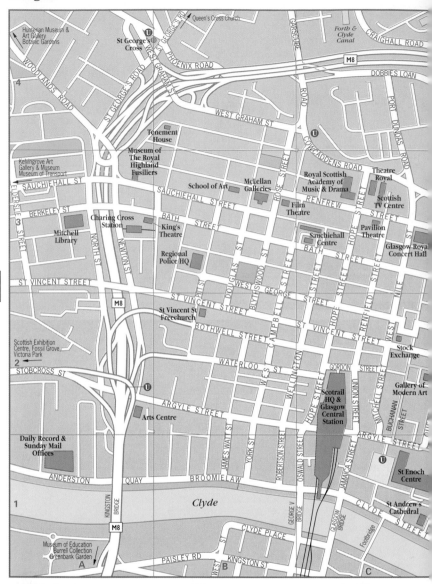

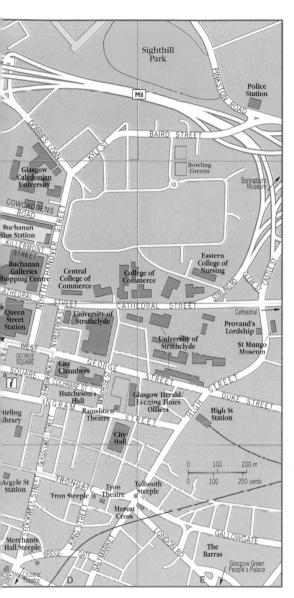

Sighthill
Park

Police
Station

M8

BAIRD STREET

Bowling
Greens

DOBBIE'S LOAN

KYLE ST

PINKSTON ROAD

Glasgow
Caledonian
University

Springburn
Museum

COWCADDENS
ROAD

NORTH HANOVER STREET

Buchanan
Bus Station

KILLERMONT
STREET

Buchanan
Galleries
Shopping Centre

Central
College of
Commerce

College of
Commerce

Eastern
College of
Nursing

STIRLING RD

GLEBE ST

CASTLE ST

CATHEDRAL

NREDRICK'S ST

Queen
Street
Station

CATHEDRAL STREET

University of
Strathclyde

University of
Strathclyde

Cathedral →

Provand's
Lordship

St Mungo
Museum

WEST
GEORGE
SQUARE

FREDERICK'S ST

City
Chambers

GEORGE

STREET

STREET

DUKE STREET

COCHRANE ST

MONTEITH ST

SQUARE

i

Stirling
Library

INGRAM

Hutcheson's
Hall

Ramshorn
Theatre

STREET

GLASSFORD STREET

Glasgow Herald/
Evening Times
Offices

HIGH ST

High St
Station

City
Hall

0   100   200 m

0   100   200 yards

Argyle St
Station

TRONGATE

Tron Steeple

Tron
Theatre

Tolbooth
Steeple

STOCKWELL STREET

KING STREET

Mercat
Cross

SALTMARKET

LONDON RD

GALLOWGATE

Merchants
Hall Steeple

BRIDGE
GATE

The
Barras

Glasgow Green
People's Palace

Citizens'
Theatre

D

E

CHANGING IMAGE Not so long ago, the idea of down-to-earth Glasgow becoming a serious challenger to Edinburgh's supremacy in the cultural and entertainment stakes would have been dismissed as impossible (especially by the complacent capital). But, throughout the 1980s, Glasgow ran a broadly based campaign to change its image. The native Glaswegians' friendliness, adaptability, and innate loyalty to their native city was harnessed to turn Glasgow into one of the most exciting places in the United Kingdom. Today, a thousand cameos of downtown Glasgow with its fine civic buildings rival the grand panorama of Edinburgh. The buoyant enthusiasm of the folk of the west make Edinburgh's

Look up for the best details on Glasgow's buildings

standoffishness seem all the more absurd. Glasgow's choice of cultural, entertainment, eating, and shopping attractions matches anything the capital can offer, except perhaps at Edinburgh Festival time. In short, Glasgow has arrived.

The story of the city is essentially one of trade, though long ago it was a religious center of some importance. St. Kentigern, also known as St. Mungo (ca518–603), is said to have built its first church on the site of the present cathedral, founding the settlement that became a royal burgh (town) in 1611. This status gave certain trading rights, though the prosperity of the city's traders grew slowly at first, their activities hindered by the shallow, silty river. Only after the Protestant Reformation, which ended Glasgow's role as a religious seat, did commerce really get under way. By 1688, the first pier had been built on the Broomielaw, on the riverside.

After the Union of 1707, the pace accelerated as it became easier to trade with the English colonies in America. Set on the western seaboard, Glasgow was well placed for this trade, and it soon began to rival the English port of Bristol in importance. In came rum, cotton, and tobacco; out went manufactured goods such as hats, shoes, and linen. One group of merchants in particular came to rival the aristocracy because of their wealth and power: Glasgow's Tobacco Lords.

"WORKSHOP OF THE WESTERN WORLD" The Glasgow talent for adaptability and resourcefulness showed itself in the way that new markets were founded after the collapse of the tobacco trade when America became independent in 1776. Using the nearby resources of coal and ironstone, Glasgow was soon a city with a heavy manufacturing

Typical Glasgow street scene: St. George's Tron Church closes off the view west down George Street

base in the throes of the Industrial Revolution. At its height it became the "Second City of the British Empire" and was the "Workshop of the Western World" throughout the 19th century. This confidence expressed itself in fine civic buildings, both in the Merchant City—that part of Glasgow lying west of the old High Street—and farther west in the streets that were built on a relentless grid, disregarding local topography. It is in this inner city that the finest architecture can be seen today.

However, the ores and the coal that formed the backbone of the heavy industry, particularly around Lanarkshire immediately to the south, gradually became depleted. Even by the early years of the 20th century, Glasgow was losing touch with the shifting patterns of the world economy. By mid-century, many of the shipyards were uncompetitive, and its locomotive works were finding it difficult to compete for orders.

Glasgow today is a postindustrial city, now emerging from a phase of urban renewal, with something of the spirit of the enterprising Victorians playing a part in the city's rebirth. Indeed, it is the 1999 U.K. City of Architecture and Design.

The city still has some problem peripheral housing projects (but then, so has Edinburgh). There are still holes in the Merchant City, a few building sites with grand plans still unfulfilled. But anyone strolling through the fashionable Italian Centre (an 18th-century warehouse conversion) or the sophisticated Princes Square (everything that a modern shopping mall ought to be, but more often than not isn't) can see that the new Glasgow has something rather special.

Medieval stained glass at the Burrell Collection (see page 81)

79

THE RIVER CLYDE
Mention the River Clyde to the locals and soon the phrase "doon the watter" (down the water/river) will be heard. This refers to the now all-but-vanished summer vacation tradition of the tolling masses in the Clydeside area, who escaped from the shipyards, foundries, engineering works, mills, and offices, on a trip by steamer down the Clyde to the playground of the lower estuary—to Rothesay, Dunoon, Helensburgh, or any one of the other Clyde resorts (see Bute, page 231).

FIT FOR FISH
Salmon returned to the River Clyde in 1983. Because of pollution, they had not been found there for the previous 120 years.

Glasgow

AN EXPLODING MYTH
One enduring Glasgow myth is that the Kelvingrove Art Gallery and Museum was built back to front, and that the architect committed suicide by jumping from the tower. It isn't, and he didn't!

▶▶ Art Gallery and Museum   76A4
Kelvingrove Park
Open: Mon–Sat 10–5, Sun 11–5. Admission free
This arresting, turn-of-the-century building in red sandstone sits in Kelvingrove Park. Often known as the Kelvingrove Art Gallery, it houses one of Britain's finest civic art collections. Within, individual galleries or wings lead off from its high, cold, and echoing central hall. French paintings of the Barbizon, Impressionist, and Post-Impressionist periods are here in plenty, as well as the old masters, with 17th-century Dutch work particularly prominent. "Home-grown" work is likewise strong, with The Glasgow Boys, a late 19th-century artistic flowering, represented by Hornel, Henry, Guthrie, Walton, and others. Also featured are works by the Scottish colorists—Peploe, Cadell, Hunter, and Fergusson.

The museum is strong on European arms and armor, with good displays of silver, pottery, glass, porcelain, and archeological and ethnographic materials. The Natural History section has an important taxidermy department.

▶ Botanic Gardens   76A4
Great Western Road
Open: daily 7–dusk. Admission free
The original botanic collection was in a physic garden of the university, which moved to its present site on Great Western Road in 1842. The centerpiece of the garden today is the magnificent Kibble Palace of 1863, a sort of glass "big top" originally built for a well-to-do Glasgow merchant named John Kibble at his Clyde coast home. He decided to give it to the city, provided he could use it for 20 years, and it was reassembled in the garden in 1871. It has been a warm and ferny refuge ever since, with its bleached statues reflected in the ponds of colorful water lilies. Exterior features include an herb garden and an arboretum. Specialties are a renowned orchid collection, and the national collection of begonias.

The 18th-century elegance of Pollok House, in whose grounds stands the Burrell Collection

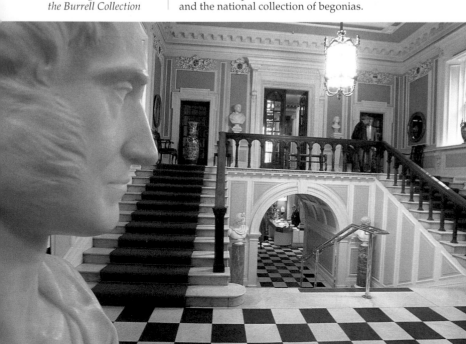

▶▶▶ Burrell Collection 76A1

Pollok Country Park, 4 miles southwest of Glasgow
Open: Mon, Wed–Sat 10–5, Sun 11–5. Admission free
Sir William Burrell was a wealthy Glasgow shipowner with a wide-ranging taste for objets d'art. He started collecting as a boy and was still acquiring pieces at the time of his death in 1958, aged 96. Even by 1901, when the city staged the Glasgow International Exhibition, Burrell was the largest single lender for the displays, which included medieval tapestries, ivories, wood and alabaster sculpture, stained glass and bronzes, Roman glass, 16th- and 18th-century Dutch, German, and Venetian table glass, plus silver, furniture, Persian rugs, and many paintings, including works by Manet, Whistler, and Monticelli. He acquired his first Degas just a little later, an indication that his eclectic tastes were already fully formed when he still had more than half a century of collecting ahead of him. In 1944, he gave the whole collection of 8,000 or so items to the city, along with almost half a million pounds ($750,000) to build a suitable home for them. As one of the conditions attached was a rural and pollution-free setting, matters languished for some years, but a site was found by 1967 and, after a competition and a 12-year building phase, the magnificent Burrell Collection opened in Glasgow's Pollok Park in 1983.

At the Art Gallery and Museum, Kelvingrove

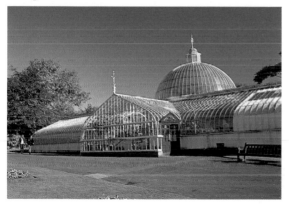

▶▶▶ Gallery of Modern Art 77D2

Royal Exchange Square
Open: Mon, Wed–Sat 10–5, Sun 11–5. Admission free
The Gallery of Modern Art (opened 1996) started life as a tobacco baron's mansion of 1780, then became a bank, an exchange or meeting and entertainment place for businessmen, then a library. It is one of Scotland's major contemporary art venues, its four floors each identified by one of the elements: fire, earth, water, and air. It displays Glasgow Museums' collection of art, craft, and design from 1950 to the present, with artists who have become internationally known since the 1980s being emphasized. Crafts and design also play an important role as an integral part of the building. The gallery has actively acquired works from beyond Scotland, for example, from Papua New Guinea and Ethiopia, and runs a wide-ranging program of temporary exhibitions, events, workshops, and performance art.

BUYING WORKS OF ART
Sir William Burrell used 28 school exercise books between 1911 and 1957 to record the purchase of each item. He bought cautiously, and though he used trusted dealers in London and Paris, he often sought a second opinion and liked to haggle over prices. Though wealthy, he was up against the even greater wealth of a number of American art magnates, such as John Paul Getty.

The Kibble Palace, Glasgow Botanic Gardens

POLLOK HOUSE
Pollok Park, the setting of the Burrell, comprised the former policies (grounds) of Pollok House, donated to the city in 1967. Nearby Pollok House, built around 1750 with later additions, now houses a further European painting collection as well as furniture, ceramics, glass, and silver.

EARLY 18TH-CENTURY GLASGOW
The writer Daniel Defoe was very impressed by Glasgow and wrote in his Tour Through the Whole Island of Great Britain: "It is a large, stately, and well-built city, standing on a plain... and the five principal streets are the fairest for breadth, and the finest built that I have ever seen in one city together." This was before rapid industrialization brought its special problems of poor housing and degradation.

▶▶ Glasgow Cathedral   77E3

Cathedral Street
Open: Apr–Sep, Mon–Sat 9:30–6, Sun 2–6; Oct–Mar, Mon–Sat 9:30–4, Sun 2–4. Also for services. Admission free
Now a little isolated from the main thrust and vigor of the modern city center, Glasgow Cathedral is one of the most ancient and historic sites in the city. The short trip eastward is well worth making and is an easy walk from the Merchant City. The site has been occupied from the early days of Christianity here, and is associated with Glasgow's patron saint, St. Kentigern, or Mungo. He founded a church here, possibly in the early 7th century. The earliest identifiable work dates from the 13th century.

There are five elements in the cathedral, which has an unusual shape: the nave, the choir, the upper and lower chapter houses, the lower church, and the Blacader Aisle. The late medieval roof, towering 99 feet above the nave, incorporates 14th-century timber, while the choir and nave are separated by a 15th-century screen or pulpitum. The unique lower church, below the choir, was a

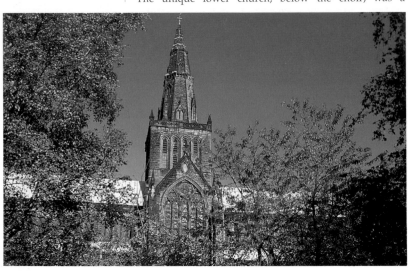

Glasgow Cathedral

13th-century extension on the sloping site and contains St. Mungo's tomb. The Blacader Aisle, where spotlights pick out the ceiling bosses (ornamental studs), is the "youngest" part of the cathedral, built by Archbishop Blacader (1483–1508). The Necropolis behind the cathedral is also worth a visit.

▶ City Chambers   77D2

George Square
Open: Mon–Fri, tours at 10:30, 2:30. Admission free
The exterior of the City Chambers is exotic enough, with its turreted, colonnaded façade in Venetian style, topped by a tower and festooned with carving. Inside, it verges on the outrageous, with a mosaic basilica of an entrance hall, marbled staircases, and galleries, epitomizing the excessive exuberance of full-blown Victoriana. The building was intended to restore confidence after the City of Glasgow Bank collapse, and was opened by Queen Victoria in 1888.

Glasgow's transformation from religious seat to commercial center resulted in the original community expanding westward from its High Street, cathedral, mercat (market) cross, and other trappings of a market town. It was this "new town," at the heart of Glasgow today, that became the Merchant City.

The growth of trade Glasgow's expansion could only be funded by trade, but the shallow, silty nature of the river at first hindered the aspirations of the traders and burgesses (borough citizens). The first pier was built on the nearby Broomielaw by 1688, and over the years the river was deepened. Gradual commercial expansion meant that the rural grazings west of High Street were required for commerce. Various manufacturing concerns, vast warehouses, and grand mansions owned by successful traders sprang up in successive waves. Expansion picked up steam in the 18th century as a planned development of gridded streets.

Glasgow became one of Europe's most important tobacco ports, with its nerve center within the Merchant City. The ships that came in with the golden leaf from Virginia sailed out again with cargoes ordered by the planters on the far side of the Atlantic. Thus the Merchant City prospered, even surviving the economic disruption of the American colonies gaining independence.

Architectural style The city developed urban characteristics unique in Scotland. Most notable of these is the compact Glasgow square, usually enclosing a church: one example is at Nelson Mandela Place, west of Queen Street Station. Another feature is the deliberate placing of prominent buildings to close off vistas.

The Victorians, with their emphasis on civic pride, brought other styles to the Merchant City. However, decline set in during the 20th century, when the 18th century warehouses sat empty and the old tobacco exchanges were outmoded. The area became a little run-down until the design-led, late 20th-century renaissance. Now the Merchant City is again the focus of innovation, though this time it is the small, specialized (and very exclusive) retailers of fine clothes, furniture, and other up-scale supplies who have brought new life to this fascinating and historic area.

Top: chimney pots are numbered for each tenement apartment

COTTON
One way the business community of the Merchant City diversified after American independence was by investing in cotton. Glasgow became second in importance only to Manchester, England, in this industry.

83

The Duke of Wellington *by Marochetti*

Walk

Glasgow city center

A walk that takes in the architectural riches, past glory, and modern regeneration of the Merchant City area. Allow two and a half hours. *See map on pages 76–77.*

Near Queen Street Station, admire the early French Gothic style of the *Glasgow Stock Exchange* (1875). Go down Queen Street, with its views across statue-filled George Square, to the **Gallery of Modern Art**, in the former Royal Exchange. Originally a grand mansion, it had a colonnaded classical façade stuck on later to enhance the view from Ingram Street.

Go through **Royal Exchange Square** (there is a good tearoom here) for the shopping delights of pedestrians-only **Buchanan Street**. The modern charms of the discreet **Princes Square** shopping development, airy yet compact, contrast with the **Argyll Arcade** beyond, built in 1827 as Scotland's first shopping arcade. The arcade

Glasgow offers the best shopping choice in Scotland

opens onto Argyle Street itself.

The shops move generally downscale the farther east you go, so, unless you intend a weekend visit to the flea market at the **Barras** farther yet to the east (see panel, page 86), turn up Candleriggs to reach the heart of the old **Merchant City**. Some 18th-century warehouses survive. The Italianate-style City Hall (1817) is still a concert hall, though only the façades of the markets remain. The Merchant City is still in the throes of regeneration: note the **Café Gandolfi** on Albion Street, around the corner, an example of the new Merchant City enterprise.

Thread through Wilson Street, past more interesting new shops on **Ingram Square** and the massive, classical, old **Sheriff Court**. Continue west to Virginia Street, named after the New World trade. **Virginia Court**, halfway along, has ancient cart ruts in its cobbles. Nearby is the former **Tobacco Exchange**, now a collection of bookshops and antique stalls. Then make your way through to **George Square**, with Robert Adam's **Trades House** (his only surviving work in Glasgow) in the near vicinity, and, to the north, **Hutchesons' Hall** on Ingram Street.

▶ Greenbank Garden 76A1

Flenders Road
Open: daily 9:30–sunset. House: Apr–Oct, Sun 2–4.
Admission charge
Greenbank is 6 miles south of town, in fairly plush
Clarkston. Set around a fine Georgian house, originally
built for a Glasgow merchant, the 12-acre policies
(grounds) include a big walled garden. Greenbank is run
as a demonstration garden, with a variety of small-scale
features. It is owned by the National Trust for Scotland.

▶▶ Hunterian Museum and Art Gallery 76A4

University Avenue and Hillhead Street
Open: Mon–Sat 9:30–5 (Mackintosh House closed 12:30–
1:30). Admission free
William Hunter (1718–1783) trained at Glasgow
University and became a famous physician in London. He
bequeathed substantial scientific collections to his parent
university, and the Hunterian opened in 1807 as
Scotland's first public museum. The emphasis is now on
geology, archeology, coins, and art. Exhibits include the
fossil of the Bearsden shark (named after a suburb of
Glasgow), as well as the city's own meteorite!

The Hunterian Art Gallery has existed as a separate (but
practically adjacent) entity since 1980. It includes European
works from Rembrandt to Sir Joshua Reynolds, as well as
Scottish 19th- and 20th-century work. The Print Gallery
exhibits works from the largest print collection in Scotland,
from Dürer to David Hockney. Also prominent is the
American-born painter James McNeill Whistler, whose
estate was made a gift in 1935. Charles Rennie Mackintosh
is well represented, too. Furniture and fittings from the
architect's home are displayed in the Mackintosh House—
a reconstruction of the principal rooms of his own home.

▶ Hutchesons' Hall 77D2

158 Ingram Street
Open: Mon–Sat 10–5. Admission free
Hutchesons' Hall was built in 1802 to a design by David
Hamilton, one of the city's most talented local architects. It
has a National Trust for Scotland visitor center and shop.

**CHARLES RENNIE
MACKINTOSH
(1868–1928)**
Mackintosh gutted the
end of the town house at
78 Southpark Avenue,
Hillhead, and refitted it in
his own unique style. It
came into the hands of
the university in 1945 and
was demolished in 1963.
Prior to demolition a
detailed survey was
carried out and much was
salvaged, ultimately to be
lovingly rebuilt almost 20
years later in the
Mackintosh section of the
Hunterian Art Gallery.

*Mackintosh's distinctive
style in the Hunterian*

St. Mungo, who now has a museum named after him

BARRAS FLEA MARKET
If it is a weekend, a visit to the People's Palace can be combined with a browse around the Barras, Glasgow's flea market. It lies within easy walking distance north of Glasgow Green.

86

GLASGOW GREEN
In the days when Glasgow was a hotbed of Communism and the struggle for workers' power, the Clydeside area orators used Glasgow Green as an important speaking platform. The authorities retaliated in the 1930s by planting flower beds in strategic positions to discourage crowds from gathering.

At the Museum of Transport

▶ St. Mungo Museum 77E3
Cathedral Square
Open: Mon, Wed–Sat 10–5, Sun 11–5. Admission free
With picture windows that reveal the skyline of the soaring cathedral and the knobbly monuments of the Necropolis, this museum of religious life and art also takes a broad overview of human ways of dealing with big issues—life, death, the hereafter—and how they are treated across the world. Salvador Dali's Christ of St. John of the Cross is here, just around the corner from a many-limbed Shiva as Nataraja, the Lord of the Dance. Dali's masterpiece is hung so high that it is best viewed from the gallery on the other side of the room. From Japanese shrines to Aboriginal paintings, the religious art and artifacts of all kinds of cultures are brought together here. A separate gallery shows material from human rites of passage—birth, marriage, and so on—more anthropological, perhaps, than religious in the usual sense. Take time to read the comments boards, where visitors are asked to write a few notes on what they think of the museum experience. Quite a few note the close relationship between religion and conflict.

▶ Museum of Education 76B1
Scotland Street
Open: Mon–Sat 10–5, Sun 2–5. Admission free
Housed in a Mackintosh building of 1904, the former Scotland Street School now pays homage to education in Scotland and gives a sense of how it felt for pupils, right down to the squeak of chalk on slate. Inside are period classrooms from various eras, and changing exhibitions.

▶▶▶ Museum of Transport 76A4
Kelvin Hall, 1 Bunhouse Road
Open: Mon, Wed–Sat 10–5, Sun 11–5. Admission free
This spacious site around the back of the Kelvin Hall holds all kinds of historic transportation exhibits. It is fun, and not just for children, with huge steam locomotives, brooding and awesome, tramcars and buses, Hillman Imps (Scotland's fairly awful last home-produced automobile), and other gleaming vehicles from past eras. The fire engines and ship models are hugely popular,

and there is also a very evocative 1938 Glasgow street scene. The Museum of Transport is just across the road from the Art Gallery and Museum at Kelvingrove.

▶▶▶ People's Palace 77E1

Glasgow Green
Open: Mon, Wed–Sat 10–5, Sun 11–5. Admission free
In the heart of the ancient park known as Glasgow Green, the People's Palace, as the name implies, is for and about the "ordinary people" of Glasgow. This late-Victorian sandstone edifice has a museum at the front and a huge, glass conservatory, known as the Winter Gardens, at the back. The latter is heated so that palms and other tender plants can flourish, and there is also a café, which makes it a popular place for idling and for posing for wedding and other photographs. To go from the clear light and bustle of the Winter Gardens, through the swing-doors to the museum, is an odd experience, a little like discovering someone's attic.

The story of the Tobacco Lords is told in the museum, together with those of the radical weavers, the temperance and Co-operative movements, and women's suffrage, alongside the ephemera of countless everyday lives, from tram tickets to wartime ration books, as well as reconstructions of typical Glasgow working-class tenement housing.

Just down the road, off the Green, is the former Templeton's Carpet Factory, another of Glasgow's exuberant examples of Victoriana, sometimes called the Doge's Palace. Multicolored brick and tile have been used to create an extraordinary Venetian-style façade (the building can only be viewed from the outside). Also on Glasgow Green, which, in spite of renewals, still has a faintly neglected air, is the Doulton Fountain, a 43-foot-high terracotta creation, formerly an exhibit at the 1888 International Exhibition at Kelvingrove.

A shopfront from the Glasgow street in the excellent Museum of Transport, where the year remains 1938

88 *Provand's Lordship, one of only two remaining medieval buildings in Glasgow*

▶ **Provand's Lordship**   77E3
High Street
Open: Mon, Wed–Sat 10–5, Sun 11–5. Admission free
Close to the cathedral is Glasgow's only other downtown medieval building, Provand's Lordship. The word "Provand" is the same as prebend, a clergyman who is paid from cathedral revenue and who officiates there. The Provand of Balornock once inhabited the house.

It was built in 1471 as a manse (minister's house) for the long-vanished hospital adjacent. With its characteristic steeply pitched roof with crow-stepped gables and armorial panels, it was, in its day, a suitably dignified residence for churchmen. Later in its long history, it had less distinguished occupants. Glasgow's hangman occupied a one-story lean-to cottage next door. Now a lone survivor, Provand's Lordship has become a city museum housing period furniture. The dark rooms, with their low doorframes, small windows, and worn steps, have a curious musty atmosphere about them (yes, the house is said to be haunted). In addition to the interesting furniture, there are displays on the many changes of use the building has undergone in its 500-year history.

▶ **Queen's Cross Church**   76C4
Garscube Road
Open: Mon–Fri 10:30–5, Sun 2:30–5. Admission free
This is the only church designed by Charles Rennie Mackintosh. Built in 1897–1899, it is now the headquarters of the Charles Rennie Mackintosh Society, with a small exhibition area, library, and shop.

▶ **(Glasgow) School of Art**   76C3
Renfrew Street
Open: tours Mon–Fri 11, 2, Sat 10:30. Closed last 2 weeks in Jun. Admission charge
This is Mackintosh's masterpiece, a work of world stature, though crowded by later developments, and is still a breathtaking design. The School of Art is sometimes described as the first and finest architectural work of the modern European movement. Here all of the Mackintosh characteristics are seen to good effect: the sinuous swirls of the forms of nature, the bold and uncluttered lines, the detailing and supreme awareness of the effect of light and shadow.

Charles Rennie Mackintosh, architect, designer, and leading exponent of art nouveau in Scotland

▶▶ **Springburn Museum**   77E4
Atlas Square
Open: Mon–Fri 10:30–5, Sat 10–4:30. Admission free
Springburn was a hamlet with a few weavers and quarrymen on the north side of Glasgow until the railroad came in 1842. Thirty years later, it was the center of a railroad empire. Most of the 27,000 Springburn folk were at one time connected with the railroad in some way. The workshops of the Caledonian and the North British Railways were here, as well as two more builders, one of them, Hyde Park, the largest in Europe. Their products were exported all over the globe. Now almost everything is gone, and the shriek of the steam dinosaurs has long been silenced. The Springburn Museum records a vanished way of life and the industrial heritage of the community.

►► The Tenement House 76B4

145 Buccleuch Street
Open: Mar–Oct, daily 2–5, last entry 4:30 Admission
charge

A young girl moved into the tenement building with her mother in 1911. They were pleased to have found such well-appointed accommodations. The young girl was a Miss Toward. She never married, and after her mother's death lived alone in the apartment until 1965. A relative who bought the apartment realized that it was a "time capsule" of Glasgow life, because Miss Toward had never thrown any thing away and had never changed the layout of her home. Here, preserved in its entirety, was a slice of tenement life from the early years of the 20th century.

The apartment has a hall and four rooms: the bedroom (reserved usually for the lodger, in Miss Toward's case); the parlor or best room, used when, for example, the minister or a kirk elder (church officer) called; the bathroom—a sure sign that this was a very well-appointed tenement for its date (it was built in 1892); and the kitchen, complete with a large black cooking range and bin for storing coal.

89

Glasgow School of Art, a
remarkable example of
Mackintosh design

THE COAL BIN
Miss Toward of the Tenement House had a kitchen coal bin that held half a ton when full, which would have been typical of its time. Pity the poor coalmen on the Glasgow tenement stairs!

FOSSIL GROVE
Among Glasgow's many green spaces, Victoria Park is notable for its Fossil Grove. This is a roofed area in which excavations have exposed the fossilized stumps and roots of trees that grew here 330 million years ago.

Accommodations

As befits Scotland's largest city and one where tourism is increasing, Glasgow has a reasonable choice of accommodations at all price levels. An increasing number of quality hotels opening up close to the center, mainly serve the business and conference market, partly because of the Scottish Exhibition Centre down by the Clyde. Another trend has been the arrival of a few smaller, intimate, town house–style establishments among the city's rows of Georgian houses. Lodging in the university residence halls should not be overlooked at the budget end of the market. The city's Tourist Information Centre (see page 272) can also organize special short stays in the city.

OUT OF TOWN It is easy to get into the countryside from Glasgow—Loch Lomond is only half an hour away—so it is also worth considering out-of-town accommodations if exploring the city. Organizations such as the Farm Holiday Bureau, National Agricultural Centre, Stoneleigh, Warwickshire, England CV8 2LZ, tel: 01203 696909, offer farmhouse accommodations in the silence of the moors and upland grazings of the Campsie Hills, for example, both of which are well within an hour's journey of the city center.

Though Glasgow does not have anything like the accommodations bottlenecks of Edinburgh, it certainly gets very busy. Remember that there are tourist information centers that can find accommodations both in Paisley and at Glasgow Airport, as well as the main downtown office.

TOP HOTELS Starting at the top end, the Glasgow Hilton has all the style and high levels of service (and, of course the prices) that you would expect from this international hotel chain. (Driving here can be tricky, though the tall

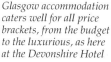

Glasgow accommodation caters well for all price brackets, from the budget to the luxurious, as here at the Devonshire Hotel

Many original features survive in the Victorian rowhouses of Devonshire Place, including stained glass in the Devonshire Hotel at No. 5

building is visible enough. The hotel thoughtfully provides a little map in order to help you find your way to the parking lot.)

The Moat House International, the Glasgow Marriott (right in the center), and the Holiday Inn Garden Court (likewise in the thick of things) are all worth considering if you are looking for the no-nonsense professionalism of the larger establishment. The Kelvin Park Lorne is moderately priced—ideal for the Art Gallery at Kelvingrove and large enough to have good facilities, yet still small enough to be friendly. (The locals' "genius for instant friendship" is most noticeable in the service industries—receptionists sometimes genuinely remember guests.)

The Devonshire Hotel, at 5 Devonshire Gardens, is a town house of deluxe standard near Great Western Road. (Not to be confused with One Devonshire Gardens, a couple of doors down, which is equally luxurious and slightly more expensive.)

Also at the top end and out of town is Cameron House Hotel and Country Club, on the banks of Loch Lomond, with superb leisure facilities. Other possibilities, if you want a country base with easy access to the heart of the city, are the areas around Balloch (at the south end of Loch Lomond), Helensburgh (a Clyde resort), and Drymen, which is to the east of the loch.

RESIDENCE HALLS For travelers on a budget, as well as a good selection of all manner of bed-and-breakfast establishments and guest houses, there are university residence halls available (see panel). Locations include Sauchiehall Street, ideal for the city-center shops, Clyde Street, a good base for the Merchant City, and Cathedral Street, and all offer reasonable value for money. Glasgow also has a large youth hostel in a good location overlooking the park, at 7/8 Park Terrace, G3 6BY, tel: 0141-332 3004.

CAMPUS LODGING
For details of Glasgow's on-campus lodging—there are at least six residence halls for Glasgow University alone—contact Glasgow University's Conference and Vacation office at 81 Great George Street, Glasgow G12 8RR (tel: 0141-330 5385), or Strathclyde University's Residence and Catering Services at 50 Richmond Street, Glasgow G1 1XP (tel: 0141-553 4148).

PACKAGE DEALS
Glasgow is now a popular destination for English-based bus companies and other operators, who offer a complete package of travel and accommodations. For more details, contact the Greater Glasgow and Clyde Valley Tourist Board (address in Travel Facts, page 272) and ask for its latest list of package tours.

Food and drink

As in any other big city, fashionable places to eat and drink in Glasgow come and go, as do chefs. You need to strike up a conversation with a local or follow current recommendations of local restaurant critics (see panel page 96). Glasgow has ambience in plenty when it comes to eating and drinking: that is all part of its downtown vibrancy and its newfound confidence—it is probably the most exciting place to be in Scotland for an evening out. The city also has a core of well-loved favorites that are easy to track down.

Glasgow seems to specialize in the kind of place that offers competent cuisine along with plenty of atmosphere, so that any minor shortcomings are easily forgiven. Another characteristic is the many pubs and restaurants that now occupy buildings originally designed for other commercial uses—you can catch yourself staring upward from your glass of beer at the fine old woodwork of a former bank, or the decorated tiles of a Victorian insurance office. There are themed places as well, which are very popular with locals and have an element of theatricality. Yet another category is the restaurant with a pub or café attached.

Scotland's patriot, William Wallace, has given his name to several pubs

ASK A CABBIE
One way of getting a really up-to-date tip on the best places to eat is to ask a taxi driver. Certainly, Glasgow is noted for its friendliness (though the same can be said about plenty of other places in Scotland). However, Glasgow's talkative cabbies definitely made an impression on the American Society of Travel Agents when it held its annual conference there in 1997. Their helpfulness was officially recognized by the Scottish Tourist Board, which awarded a commemorative plaque to the local taxi drivers' association in acknowledgment of their role as "outstanding ambassadors of tourism!"

RECOMMENDED RESTAURANTS The well-loved Ubiquitous Chip off Byres Road offers a menu that is probably as near as you can get to a local cuisine, with a pronounced Scottish flavor. Much the same can be said about the Buttery on Argyle Street, with its Victorian décor. Another favorite with a loyal clientele is the long-established Rogano in Exchange Place, which first opened its art-deco doors in 1935. Seafood is a specialty here.

A Glasgow institution for Italian cuisine is La Parmigiana on Great Western Road, which has a loyal local following for its tuna with borlotti beans, *rabbit alla cacciatore*, and other slightly out-of-the-ordinary dishes. Also hugely popular, especially with the business crowd, is Yes, on West Nile Street, where the purple and red decor provides a striking setting for an eclectic cuisine making strong use of Scottish ingredients—with a twist: try the gateau of haggis, neaps and tatties! Stravaigin, on Gibson Street, looks world-wide for its inspiration; it has a refreshingly laid-back attitude, but the quality of the cooking, in the Hanoi duck soup, Chilean *curanto*, or Mexican *estofado de lengua*, is top-notch. The café-bar/restaurant Papingo on Bath Street is a good-value venue for modern Scottish cooking: roasted vegetables with honey, garlic, and balsamic vinegar, or mussel, leek, and crab soup, for example. If you want to go all out, try the restaurant at One Devonshire Gardens for painstakingly prepared modern cuisine.

PUBS Glasgow's pubs vary, but the centrally placed ones can be very upscale. Typical of this kind is the Drum and Monkey, formerly banking premises on St. Vincent Street. It is popular with businesspeople, who have lunch in its small and intimate back room with its dark wooden pews, and has a more boisterous main hall. Not far off on West Regent Street, a similarly success-ful transformation can be seen at De Quinceys. At one time the Moorish tiles that brighten the walls of the premises looked down on to the main business hall of another banking company; now they provide an impres-sively stylish background to a scene of cheerful drinking.

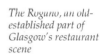

TEAROOMS Glasgow's tea-rooms have always been something of an institution. The Willow Tea Room is a sur-viving, though restored, typi-cal Mackintosh design on Sauchiehall Street. These days, tea and coffee are also served throughout the day in any of a number of bistro-style establishments. The Victoria and Albert on Buchanan Street serves tea or coffee with home-made shortbread in the morning in its bar, and the Jenny Tearoom beside the Gallery of Modern Art on Exchange Square has a reputation with the serious tea drinker.

The Rogano, an old-established part of Glasgow's restaurant scene

WILLOWY WAY
Sauchiehall Street is really *sauchie haugh street*: "sauchies" are wil-lows, and a "haugh" is a watery field. The willow reference is echoed in the Willow Tea Room on the street.

FOR SHOPPERS
Princes Square has a variety of places to eat. Try the October Café, right on the top floor, with its noticeably bright atmosphere—perhaps an effect of being so near to the glass roof.

Byres Road pub

ST. ENOCH SQUARE
Built on the site of the old
St. Enoch Station, St.
Enoch Square is now a
massive undercover shop-
ping mall, a touch better
than most 1990s malls
thanks to its interesting
architecture, with exposed
girders and pipes.
However, it is not as
upscale and intimate as
Princes Square.

Shopping

There are more shops in Glasgow than anywhere else in
Scotland. All the usual chain stores can be found, but,
thanks partly to Merchant City enterprise, there is also a
very good selection of smaller specialized outlets. Glasgow
is style- and fashion-conscious, so clothes shops proliferate,
though not all of them survive.

MAIN AREAS The main shopping streets are found from
Argyle Street northward as far as Sauchiehall Street, taking
in streets off pedestrianized Buchanan Street, northwest of
which is a grid of streets well worth exploring. The
Merchant City lies to the east of it and should be trawled
through. There is a further cluster of shops around Byres
Road to the west, which should not be overlooked. Except
for Byres Road, most of Glasgow's shops are within walking distance of Buchanan Street. The best of the new-style
malls are likewise found around Buchanan Street: Princes
Square and the Buchanan Galleries, which open directly off
it, and the St. Enoch Centre, just across Argyle Street and
less upscale in feel, but rewarding if only for its design.

OUTLETS FOR SCOTTISH GOODS If you are looking for
high-quality Scottish wares, then Geoffrey (Tailor)
Highland Crafts—quite
far along Sauchiehall
Street, but worth the
walk—is just the place
for Scottish knitwear or
tweed souvenirs or for an
entire Highland outfit.
Hector Russell, Kilt-
maker, on Renfield Street
will also oblige in much
the same market niche.
Old-established John
Smith's, Glasgow's own
bookshop, has a huge
selection of material on
Scotland and Glasgow.
Postcards home could be

*The Barras (or
Barrowland) is an essen-
tial part of the Glasgow
shopping experience—
but don't make it the
only one*

written with something exclusive picked up at the Pen
Shop in Princes Square, which is a useful shopping mall
for gifts as well as fashions, including reasonably priced
knitwear at a branch of the Jumpers chain.

DESIGNER SHOPS If you ask about designer shops in the
Merchant City, locals may well point you toward
Mademoiselle Anne in Stockwell Street, which has
women's collections. Another Merchant City treat for
(male) shoppers is Slater Menswear, famous throughout
Scotland for its huge array (the largest in the world) of suits
and casual clothing at discounted prices. If antiques are
your interest, then the Virginia Galleries are good for
browsing. The galleries comprise a number of small
antiques businesses, with prices surprisingly reasonable
considering their location. The atmospheric Argyll Arcade
(dating from 1827) offers a choice of 32 jewelry shops.
Catherine Shaw, on Gordon Street and in the Argyll
Arcade, has giftware in Charles Rennie Mackintosh style.

Jewelers are plentiful in the Argyll Arcade

Typifying the new Glasgow style is the Italian Centre, just off Ingram Street, of which the city is proud, particularly because this gathering of fashion shops includes labels seen nowhere else in the United Kingdom outside London.

FLEA MARKET If you tire of the chic shops of the Merchant City, then a trip to the Barras flea market will prove a refreshing antidote—though the market is open on weekends only. The Barras is a reminder that Glasgow has not yet become too precious in its new image. The name may have been translated into "Barrowland" in an attempt to prettify it, but it still remains a boisterous flea market in sheds and warehouses. There at least, the prospect of a real bargain flits just ahead at the next stall, and even if it remains out of reach, the market nevertheless provides great entertainment.

PADDY'S MARKET
Do not confuse the Barras with Paddy's Market, near the river. Paddy's Market gets its name from the penniless Irish immigrants of a century ago, who would literally sell the shirts off their backs, so desperate was their poverty. Something of the same air of desperation still hangs around today. This little lane of stalls belies Glasgow's upbeat new image.

95

Princes Square—modern shopping at its most sophisticated

Glasgow

Nightlife

Glasgow has a huge selection of pubs and bistros, plus a range of clubs offering musical entertainment from proper ceilidhs (not fake affairs for tourists) to new wave.

THEATERS AND CONCERT HALLS The city's cultural flagship is the Royal Concert Hall, Sauchiehall Street (tel: 0141-287 4000), the home of the Royal Scottish Orchestra, which, along with Scottish Ballet and Scottish Opera, has its headquarters in the city. The Royal Scottish Academy of Music and Drama, Stevenson Hall, Renfrew Street (tel: 0141-332 5057) presents a varied program of international performances. The Tramway, Albert Drive (tel: 0141-287 4000), is a showcase for opera, drama, and dance performances. The Tron Theatre, Trongate (tel: 0141-552 4267), offers contemporary Scottish and international theater. The Pavilion Theatre, Renfield Street (tel: 0141-332 1846), puts on variety shows, rock, and pop concerts, while the Kings Theatre, Bath Street (tel: 0141-287 4000), has drama and various popular productions. With the Citizens' Theatre, Gorbals Street (tel: 0141-429 5561), the City Hall, and the Henry Wood Hall, these are just some of the performing spaces Glasgow has to offer.

MOVIES An alternative to the regular movie theaters, the Glasgow Film Theatre, Rose Street (tel: 0141-332 6535) is an independent concern, offering new releases, classic revivals, and popular reruns.

OTHER NIGHTLIFE Some examples from the broad spectrum: Glasgow's "Grand Ole Opry," 2 Govan Road (tel: 0141-429 5396), is where locals hang out (and dress up) for the country and western music. Archaos, Queen Street (tel: 0141-204 3189) is the biggest club in Glasgow and offers an eclectic musical mix. The Arches, Midland Street (tel: 0141-221 4001) offers house, Techno, and big music names at one of the city's largest venues. Victoria's, Sauchiehall Street (tel: 0141-332 1444), is an upscale nightclub: the hunting ground of professional soccer players, off-duty air crew, and models, with several floors to suit all musical tastes. The Riverside Club, Fox Street (tel: 0141-248 3144) is the ceilidh place in town, like an upstairs barn with a tiny stage. The Renfrew Ferry, Clyde Place (tel: 0141-429 8676), looks like a floating conservatory but is actually the former Renfrew ferry: another great ceilidh place with other kinds of music as well (best to check the local papers for details). The Scotia Bar, Stockwell Street (tel: 0141-552 8681), is an old-fashioned pub with lots of impromptu performances.

The groundbreaking Citizens' Theatre, at the heart of Glasgow's art scene

Practicalities

AIRPORT TRANSFERS Glasgow Airport, Paisley PA3 2ST (tel: 0141-887 1111), is 8 miles from the center of the city, with a bus service that takes 30 minutes at a reasonable fare. These buses connect with the hourly service to downtown Edinburgh. There is also a railroad station at Paisley Gilmour Street, about 2 miles away. Metered taxis are available, with fares upward of £12 ($18) to the center. The Airport Tourist Information Centre (tel: 0141-848 4440) can reserve accommodations (see addresses page 272).

Arriving by train or bus Glasgow Central is the central train terminus for services from the south (London's Euston Station is about five hours away). Glasgow Queen Street is the terminus for services from Edinburgh (45 minutes by rail) and the north and west (Aberdeen and Fort William, for instance). Glasgow's main bus station is Buchanan Bus Station, Killermont Street.

The Drum and Monkey,
St. Vincent Street

PUBLIC TRANSPORTATION within Glasgow Glasgow is the only Scottish city with an underground (subway) network, a modernized and useful service open 6:30 AM–10:30 PM daily, with trains every six–eight minutes all day. Flat-rate tickets are on sale at all stations on the Underground, which takes the form of a large circle. For information contact St. Enoch Square Centre (tel: 0141 226 4826). This important source of travel information for Glasgow's excellent fully integrated transportation network is centrally located beside the St. Enoch Centre, and also has details of Glasgow's extensive suburban rail network.

There are many bus companies operating within the city. Several different types of multi-journey or flexible tickets are available, some combining train, bus, and Underground. The Family Day Tripper ticket, allowing travel as far afield as Loch Lomond, is good value.

Taxis Black cabs are widely available throughout the city, and main taxi stands are located at the stations. A fleet of airport taxis operates the service from the airport.

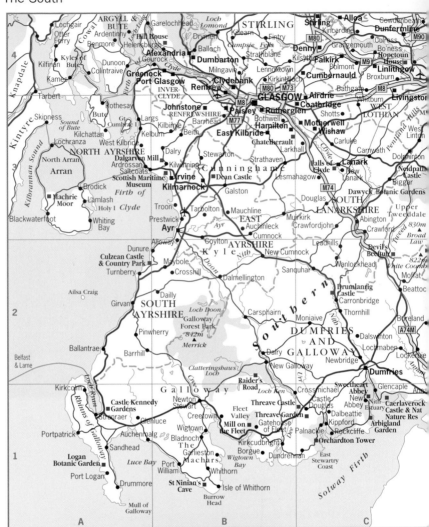

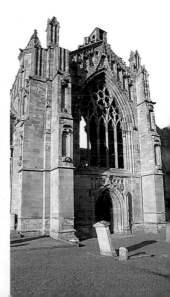

ACROSS THE BORDER Unless indulging in the souvenir
shops and tartan frolics of Gretna or Gretna Green ("Joke
Anvil Weddings Performed Here") crossing the border
from England is a low-key affair. Sometimes a piper plays
at Carter Bar, where A68 enters Scotland, but otherwise at
first sight things look much the same.

However, Scotland is distinct from England, even in its
southern sector. From the look of the money to buying
beer in pubs, a subtly altered culture is all around.
Geographers call the area the Southern Uplands—blue
waves of hills, resonant with tales of ancient skirmishes in
these fought-over lands—a dramatic sight from Carter
Bar. Farther west, in the Galloway Forest Park north of
Newton Stewart, the end of the park road is within walking distance of The Merrick, at 2,613 feet the highest
mountain in southern Scotland, with a vista of dark lochs,
birch woods, and purple slopes.

The South

100

AYRSHIRE Continuing north from Galloway, the sheep-cropped moors and conifer woods blend into Ayrshire, another area with a highly characteristic landscape. There is a lushness in the river valleys, woods, and hedgerows that is highly reminiscent of South Wales, a parallel sustained by the signs, in places, of now-vanished heavy industry, coal, and ironworks, backed by green hills. Farther north, the typical Ayrshire view is across hawthorn hedge and pasture to a long horizon dominated by the blurred profile of Arran (an island) and Kintyre (a peninsula), a setting more Highland than Lowland.

Beyond the geological edge of the Southern Uplands, and into the southern part of the central corridor across Scotland, the scenery changes again. The summery yellow grainfields of East Lothian have red-roofed villages with hills as a backdrop, or even the delightfully unexpected vista from the prehistoric site on the top of Cairnpapple Hill behind Linlithgow, with the Forth Valley spread out in front of you like a geography lesson.

In addition to fine landscapes, southern Scotland has highly individual townscapes and communities. The characteristic pastel-washed frontages and wide streets of the Galloway towns are surprising for anyone with preconceptions of dour, gray Scottish communities. No one who accidentally stumbles upon a Common Riding in one of the Borders towns can fail to notice the groundswell of loyalty to place and

Marking the border at Coldstream

Borders landscape near Galashiels

Typical river valley scenery near Walkerburn, west of Galashiels

THE RIVAL COUNTY TOWNS
After Berwick became English, Greenlaw saw its chance to become the county town of the Scottish county of Berwickshire. However, nearby Duns also wanted this status, and managed to achieve it several times. Each time it did so, little Greenlaw built another fine civic building. A 17th-century courtroom and prison, an 18th-century hotel to accommodate visiting lawyers and officials, and a 19th-century town hall all add to the fine town-scape of today's Greenlaw. It was superseded by Duns for the last time in 1903.

culture. These are mainly modern revivals of the ancient customs of marking out the boundaries of the community, as well as great celebrations of horsemanship, another Borders specialty (A Scottish Borders MP—member of parliament once requested that the date of a general election be changed so that it did not clash with the Selkirk Common Riding, which he enjoyed attending.)

LAND OF BURNS Similarly, in Ayrshire, where you cannot turn a corner without finding a signpost pointing to some aspect of the life of Robert Burns, there is a genuine and unique regard for Scotland's poet. This is not something that tourism promoters have foisted upon reluctant communities, but instead an affection for the plowman poet and pride in his achievements.

From bards to model villages by the tumbling cataracts of New Lanark, from stern Borders towers to the softness of East Lothian, from the faded Victorian resorts of the golf-mad Clyde coast to the breathtaking bird cliffs of St. Abbs, the south of Scotland offers a slice of the real Scotland without too much tartan ribbon (even if you can find a pipe band in a Borders town just as easily as farther north). In fact, the region's variety and complex character may ultimately satisfy much more than that of the weather-dominated north. It is certainly not an area to hurry through.

AYRSHIRE ELECTRIC ILLUSIONS
At a point within sight of Culzean Castle, 9 miles south of Ayr, A719 is called Croy Brae, or more familiarly, Electric Brae. Because of a particularly effective optical illusion, the road gives the impression of going downhill when it is actually going up. The site got its name as it was formerly thought that electricity had some part to play in the phenomenon, though this is not the case. Take care when traveling this road, as you are likely to encounter puzzled drivers freewheeling "uphill" to satisfy their curiosity.

THE EDINBURGH LIGHT HORSE

Sir Walter Scott was a countryman at heart, with the landowner's ideal of an ordered society where everyone knew their place. He and some friends founded the Edinburgh Light Horse, a kind of "Home Guard," in response to a threatened Napoleonic invasion in 1797. They galloped around enthusiastically, but saw little real action. However, in the troubled times when workers began to protest about working conditions, Scotland's champion did manage to threaten to saber some mill workers at Moredun Mill and take a few pot shots at dissenting miners at Cross Causeway, both in Edinburgh.

▶▶▶ **Abbotsford House**   *99D3*

Open: Jun–Sep, daily 10–5; mid-Mar–May and Oct, Mon–Sat 10–5, Sun 2–5. Admission charge

Sir Walter Scott's creation of his own version of Scotland and its heroic past is embodied in the house that was his life. Here is the door from the Old Tolbooth in Edinburgh, there is the desk made with wood from a Spanish Armada ship. Look at Rob Roy's gun, Bonnie Prince Charlie's quaich (cup), James IV's hunting bottle (did he club game with it?), the keys of Lochleven Castle, and other treasures.

▶ **Ayr**   *98B3*

A preference for a two-week stint in the Mediterranean sun instead of a traditional seashore vacation, plus the demise of traditional industries such as coal mining, have left Ayr and its hinterland facing a challenging future. Nevertheless, it is a bustling place (but take care with the parking system, which needs vouchers from local shops and garages). It makes a good base for keen golfers.

Non-golfers can pursue the life of Burns. There seem to be so many places in the vicinity in which Burnsiana are displayed that after a day or two you will recognize his handwriting from several paces off. Take your pick from the **Auld Kirk**, the church where many of Burns's contemporaries are buried, the **Twa Brigs o Ayr**, the older of

Scottish memorabilia, Abbotsford House

which is 15th century or earlier, plus a statue or two, then follow signs to Alloway.

Alloway▶ ▶, a leafy suburb of Ayr, is disturbed only by incessant tour groups from all nations on their way to the shrine of Scotland's national bard. **Burns Cottage**, with a museum adjacent (*Open* Apr–Oct, daily 9–6; Nov–Mar, Mon–Sat 10–4, Sun 12–4. *Admission charge*) is an excellent starting point. Down the road the **Tam O'Shanter Experience** has a 10-minute presentation on Burns, then the poem "Tam O'Shanter" springs to life in a three-screen theatrical event (*Open* Apr–Sep, daily 9–6; Oct–Mar, daily 9–5. *Admission charge*). Nearby, the Burns Monument's neoclassical columns rise from a clipped garden, one of many contrasts with the poet's life of poverty and struggle. Also moments away are the **Auld Brig o Doon** and **Alloway Kirk**, both immortalized in the poem "Tam o' Shanter," a tale of drunkenness and orgy in a setting now taken over by suburban respectability

Dalgarven Mill

On the Burns trail Incurable romantics will pursue the poet east to **Mauchline**, a village sitting dourly on a grassy ridge in the hinterland of hawthorn-hedged fields. There they will find **Burns House Museum** (*Open* Easter–Sep, Tue–Sat 10–4, Sun 2–4. *Admission charge*) and—even better—a breathtaking view from the **Burns Memorial Tower** just up the road. Burns signposts are everywhere. You can even follow them to the grimly workaday town of **Kilmarnock**, where in a country park stands **Dean Castle**. A rare volume, the first or Kilmarnock Edition, of Burns poetry is on display, but just as interesting are the early musical instruments and European armor collections. (*Open* castle daily 12–4 restricted winter opening; grounds daily dawn–dusk. *Admission charge*).

Elsewhere in Ayr's hinterland, **Dalgarven Mill**—the Ayrshire Museum of Countrylife and Costume, just north of Kilwinning—is in a restored water-powered flour mill (*Open* Easter–Sep, Mon–Fri 10–5, Sun 11–5; Oct–Easter, Tue–Sun 10–4. *Admission charge*). Also within easy reach of Ayr are the **Magnum Leisure Centre**, much trumpeted for its modern approach to recreation now that the traditional Clyde Coast seashore vacation is out of favor; the **Scottish Maritime Museum** (see page 117); and **Culzean Castle** (see page 110).

103

THE SOUTHERN UPLANDS FAULT
The Southern Uplands Fault, where the midland plain gives way to the high ground of southern Scotland, is most conspicuous in the east. Running into East Lothian and prominent from A68 south of Dalkeith (Midlothian), the ancient tough rocks of the Lammermuir Hills form an escarpment above the soft sandstones to the north. A convenient stopping point on A68 at Soutra Hill offers superb views back to the Pentlands, Edinburgh, the Firth of Forth, and beyond.

TOURIST INFORMATION
Ayr: Burns House, Burns Statue Square (tel: 01292-262555).

The gardens beside the Brig o Doon in Ayr

Robert Burns (1759–1796) is the best-known figure in Scottish literature, though whether for his poems or his pursuit of the lasses is perhaps another matter. Large tracts of Ayrshire and the area around Dumfries have plenty of signposted places of interest associated with his life.

SATIRICAL OBSERVATIONS
As an observer of others' follies, Burns wrote plenty of scathing and satirical observations of both people and state. A poem to the "Scotch Representatives in the House of Commons" contains the line, often quoted by the distilling industry: "Freedom and Whisky gang thegither" (go together). It also contains this observation on the Scots army regiments:

"But bring a Scotchman
frae his hill
Clap in his cheek a
Highland gill
Say, such is royal George's
will And there's the foe,
He has nae thought but how
to kill Twa at a blow."

[A gill is a measure of whisky; royal George means King George III.]

Robert Burns

Ayrshire beginnings With his farming background and his daily toil, Burns might have lived and died anonymously as just another Ayrshire farmer, struggling with poor soil and the primitive agricultural practices of the day. Instead, his immortality was assured through poetry filled with shrewd observations on human nature, with lyricism and with optimism, and above all, belief in the brotherhood of man.

His father was a farmer who moved to Ayrshire from Kincardineshire, on the east coast, and built a cottage on some land he had acquired. This "auld clay biggin" still stands, a shrine to the thousands who have flocked there since the beginning of the 19th century. Burns's father was a hard worker determined to educate his family. Robert and his brother Gilbert acquired a reasonable, if sporadic, education. Robert read avidly when he was not helping on the farm. He had committed "the sin of rhyme" by the time he was 15 years old, while on the farm of Mount Oliphant.

Poems and passion After his father's death in 1784, he and his brother rented the farm of Mossgiel near Mauchline. Robert soon gained a local reputation as a maker of rhymes (among his other vices). In a period when passion and poverty went together with fierce creativity, Burns wrote some of his best-known works. This culminated in the publication of the famed Kilmarnock Edition of *Poems, Chiefly in the Scottish Dialect* in 1786. Around the same time there were writs from Jean Armour's father, livid at his daughter's association (pregnancy, to be precise) with Burns, the poor farmer; penance in the local church (for fornication); thought of emigration—only "the feelings of a father" kept him in Scotland; and also an affair with Highland Mary, which ended in mysterious circumstances. Highland Mary (Mary Campbell) is a figure about whom very little is known. She died in October 1786, possibly after bearing him a child. Certainly, Burns felt terribly guilty about her in later years. It is said she consented to be his wife, but he was already committed to Jean Armour, whom he later married.

Through the success of the Kilmarnock Edition, Burns gained sudden fame. He was soon lionized by the literary classes of Edinburgh and welcomed as a plowman poet into genteel drawing rooms. He went along happily with the image.

The Songwriter Burns was also a maker of songs. In 1787, he started his completely unpaid contribution to James Johnson's *Scots Musical Museum*, reworking and improving many songs and fragments, a huge body of work still popular to this day. By 1788, he was back once again with Jean Armour. He married her and gave up the hopeless struggle of farming at Mossgiel, deciding instead to move to Ellisland Farm, not far from Dumfries. He took up employment with the Excise (taxation bureau), although he was still determined to succeed as a farmer. The farm at Ellisland failed in 1791.

In between his commitments to the Excise and the needs of the farm, he worked on with further volumes of *The Scots Musical Museum* as well as his own poetic

out-pourings. Illness and low spirits dogged him as the 1790s progressed. Rheumatic fever took its toll in 1795 as he struggled to maintain the output for *A Select Collection of Original Scottish Airs for the Voice*. By July 1796, at the age of 37, he was dead.

Memories of Burns The Burns "industry" followed on thereafter. The first of many biographies was published by 1797, the year after his death, and the Irvine Burns Club, started in 1826, claims to be the oldest continuously operating club of its kind. Today, his birthday (January 25) is celebrated throughout Scotland—and far beyond, wherever Scots gather—with Burns Suppers, a unique format of haggis, whisky, poetry, and song. No other British poet has achieved anywhere near the same kind of popular appeal. On Burns Night even buttoned-up Scots have a good time, with their stern Calvinistic streak temporarily obscured by the outlook that, at least for one evening,

"…man to man, the warld o'er
Shall brithers be for a' that."

Burns would certainly have approved.

(see page 48)

THE BROW WELL
Though places associated with Burns are scattered throughout Ayrshire and Galloway, perhaps the saddest lies adjacent to B725 southeast of Dumfries. The Brow Well is a rock-cut well close to the sea, and was once famed for its mineral properties. The poet, desperately ill with rheumatic fever and possibly bacterial endocarditis, visited it while sea-bathing nearby, in a last attempt to recover his health. He died three days after he returned from Brow.

Burns Cottage in Alloway, near Ayr

AE FOND KISS
The curious affair by mail (see page 48) that Burns had with Mrs. Agnes McLehose in Edinburgh resulted in a great deal of correspondence, some frigid literary exercises in neoclassical idiom, and one great, truly great, love poem and song of parting—"Ae fond kiss and then we sever," with its haunting fourth verse:
Had we never lov'd sae kindly,
Had we never lov'd sae blindly!
Never met—or never parted,
We had ne'er been broken hearted.
This was written in 1791, as "Clarinda," as Burns addressed her, was preparing to rejoin her husband in the West Indies. Burns never saw her again.

TOURIST INFORMATION
Biggar: (Easter–Oct) 155
High Street (tel: 01899-
221066).

▶ **Biggar** 98C3

The town of Biggar, equidistant from Glasgow and Edinburgh, has retained its own character and a sense of heritage. The original settlement is associated with 12th-century Flemish immigrants who arrived under the patronage of the Scottish kings. The incomers built "mottes," earthen mounds once topped with wooden castles. A motte survives behind today's High Street.

Biggar is essentially a center for a rural hinterland, and the **Corn Exchange**, with its clock tower, still dominates the wide main street, scene of former markets. **St. Mary's Kirk** dates from 1545—the last church to be built before the Reformation—and is open to view. It is a collegiate church, founded by Lord Fleming, Mary, Queen of Scots' uncle, to support teaching priests. All this can be taken in on a few minutes' walk from the main street. The town also has a puppet theater — not a common feature of Scottish towns—as well as several worthwhile museums.

Biggar Gasworks (no longer operating) is Scotland's oldest surviving rural gasworks (1839)

Gladstone Court Museum, a tribute to the energy of the local museum trust, is an indoor "street" of shops with a good selection of nostalgia-inducing artifacts (*Open* Apr–Oct, Mon–Sat 10–12:30, 2–5, Sun 2–5. *Admission charge*). The **Greenhill Covenanter's House**, downhill toward the Biggar Burn behind St. Mary's, is a 17th-century farm relocated stone by stone. It sheds some light on the Covenanting movement (see page 55) and the complexities of the Scottish religious wars by way of artifacts and displays (*Open* Easter–early Oct, daily 2–5. *Admission charge*). For a total contrast, visit **Biggar Gasworks Museum**▶ (*Open* Jun–Sep, daily 2–5. *Admission charge*). Thanks to North Sea Gas, traditional gasworks have vanished from most places, but not from Biggar. Sometimes

An old-fashioned pharmacist's shop in Gladstone Court Museum, Biggar

they fire it up, creating an olfactory trip down memory lane for some. **Moat Park Heritage Centre** tells of Biggar's early history and also focuses on geology and on embroidery, with samplers and patchwork coverlets (*Open* Easter–mid-Oct, Mon–Sat 10–5, Sun 2–5. *Admission charge*).

▶▶▶ Caerlaverock Castle and National Nature Reserve   98C1

Caerlaverock Castle is unique in Britain. No other castle builder employed this odd triangular moated design. The castle sits in its moat, massive and menacing in red sandstone, and offers another puzzle. Nobody knows who built Caerlaverock, which is of late 13th-century origin. It was taken by King Edward I of England around 1300 and regained by the Scots by 1312, only to suffer further in later Anglo–Scots conflicts. Unexpectedly for this frontier fortress, there is an ornate 17th-century range within: Nithsdale's Building, built by the Lords Maxwell. But all is scarred and ruinous—a troubled history in stone. (*Open* Apr–Sep, daily 9:30–6, Oct–Mar, Mon–Sat 9:30–4, Sun 2–4. *Admission charge*).

Caerlaverock National Nature Reserve▶▶▶ Combine a castle visit with deluxe bird-watching on the marshes: particularly good away from high summer, best of all on a calm winter's day. Among the birds here are 13,000 barnacle geese from Spitzbergen (superb views are possible of the flocks from the visitor center or from the conveniently placed hides). This is one of Scotland's major wildlife spectacles if you time it right. The reserve is open all year.

▶▶ Castle Kennedy Gardens   98A1

Open: Apr–Sep, daily 10–5. Admission charge
The Earl of Stair built these pleasure grounds. As a field marshal, instead of toiling with a wheelbarrow and shovel he used his troops to build the main landscape features. (They were supposed to be chasing Covenanters.) The result is gardening on a grand scale, with superb vistas down the monkey puzzle tree avenue, lovely woodland walks and lakes, and masses of rhododendrons in spring. May is probably the best month to visit. It is undoubtedly worth the excursion to the west of Galloway, and could easily be combined with a visit to Logan Botanic Garden (see page 120).

CASTLE REMAINS
Within Castle Kennedy Gardens is the shell of Castle Kennedy, burned down in 1716 but now lending an antique air to the parklands. The Victorian Lochinch Castle on the grounds is strictly private.

THE DEBATABLE LAND
The Debatable Land was the name given to disputed territory between England and Scotland, between the rivers Sark and Esk, not far from Carlisle, England. Grazing was its only use, as buildings were forbidden. In 1552, it was split in two and a settlement agreed.

107

Two sides of Caerlaverock Castle's triangular moat

The magnificent Adam interior of Chatelherault Lodge, near Hamilton

TOURIST INFORMATION
Castle Douglas: (Apr–Oct)
Markethill (tel: 01556-502 611).
Coldstream: (Apr–Oct)
Town Hall, High Street
(tel: 01890-882 607).

The past uniform of the famous Coldstream Guards

► **Castle Douglas** 98C1

This is a cheerful sort of place, with its busy main street at the center of a simple grid. The town's designer, Sir William Douglas, was a rich local merchant who rebuilt the old village in 1792. Now bypassed by A75, Castle Douglas has plenty of shops to make strolling worthwhile.

Adjacent Carlingwark Loch was once a source of marl, the limey clay used as fertilizer that originally made the town prosperous. To the northeast is the Motte of Urr, the largest man-made castle mound in Scotland. The former 12th-century administrative headquarters of the de Berkeleys is now an impressive green mound by the river, visible from B794.

A few minutes to the southeast of Castle Douglas, **Threave Garden►►** is the training ground for the National Trust for Scotland's gardeners. There are always fresh plantings and new ideas to see within its 64 acres. Early spring (April) has spectacular drifts of daffodils, with over 200 cultivars. Later, the peat garden—that specialty of the cool, moist, Scottish climate—is a high point. Most aspects of Scottish gardening can be seen here, from the traditional flower border to the Victorian hothouse. (*Open* daily 9:30–sunset; walled garden and greenhouses: daily 9:30–5; visitor center: Apr–Oct, daily 9:30–5:30. *Admission charge*).

Threave Castle►► (*Open* Apr–Sep, daily 9:30–6. *Admission charge*) This gaunt 14th-century tower rising out of the watery scenery on an island in the River Dee was once owned by Archibald the Grim. It is an appropriate setting for the name. The Lord of Galloway built his fortress with the intention of intimidating. Formerly the main power base of the Black Douglases, the strongest of the Scottish nobles until they overreached themselves in a conflict with King James II, Threave was successfully besieged in 1455 by the king's forces. Excavations have revealed a lot about medieval defensive buildings, as well as the most complete medieval riverside harbor in Scotland. There is a pleasant walk, though wet in places, from the farmyard parking lot to the riverside. Ring a bell for the boatman. Even when the castle is closed, the walk is worthwhile, with close-up views from the bank. Threave Wildfowl Refuge is nearby.

►► Chatelherault   98B3

The wealthy Duke of Hamilton asked William Adam to design a hunting lodge and kennels within the pleasure grounds surrounding Hamilton Palace. Chatelherault was part of one of the most ambitious landscaping works in 18th-century Britain. Nothing remains now of the 3-mile avenue, the lake, or the canalized River Clyde. Even Hamilton Palace was demolished in 1927 after most of the land was sold. Today there is only a country park— plus an $11 million restoration of Adam's one-room-deep façade, part of which is a visitor center telling the extraordinary story. It is well worth the diversion from M74. (*Open* Mon–Sat 10–5, Sun 12–5:30 (5 PM Oct–Mar). *Closed* occasional Fridays. *Admission free*).

COLDSTREAM
Birthplace of the Regiment

► Coldstream   99E3

A pleasant village just north of the border, Coldstream, like Gretna Green, once did a brisk trade in marrying elopers. This is recalled on a plaque by the little tollhouse on the Scottish side of John Smeaton's elegant 1760s bridge. Coldstream is also associated with the Guards regiment of the same name. Items from their glorious past can be seen in the Coldstream Museum (*Open* Apr–Sep, Mon–Sat 10–4, Sun 2–4; Oct, Mon–Sat 1–4. *Admission charge*).

North of the village is **The Hirsel►**, once the home of Sir Alec Douglas-Home, Lord Home of The Hirsel, who was prime minister in 1963–1964. Walks through varied habitats of woodland (with rhododendrons in spring), farm, and lake, are enjoyed by bird-watchers in particular. A craft complex and visitor center in a converted farm building sheds light on the life of a Borders country estate. (*Open* grounds daily, sunrise–sunset; museum and crafts center Mon–Fri 10–5, Sat–Sun 12–5. *Admission free, parking charge*).

THE COLDSTREAM GUARDS
The primacy of the Grenadier Guards as the senior regiment in the Guards Division of the British Army is disputed by the Coldstream Guards. Both regiments share 1660 as their official founding date. When on parade the Coldstreamers will not stand next to the Grenadiers, instead taking the left of the line. Their motto is *Nulli secundus*, second to none.

FOUND IN THE LOCH
Not only valuable marl came out of Carlingwark Loch by Castle Douglas. Among other historical artifacts, a forge was once recovered from the lakewaters. It is thought to have been used by King Edward I's forces as they passed this way during one of their forays in around 1300.

109

Threave Castle, near Castle Douglas

In 1946, the top floor of the main part of Culzean Castle was put at the disposal of General Dwight D. Eisenhower as a token of the Scottish people's gratitude for his role as Supreme Commander of the Allied Forces in Europe in World War II. It has become known as the National Guest Flat, and its story is told in the Eisenhower Room in the castle today.

▶▶ Crichton Castle   99D3

Open: Apr–Sep, daily 9:30–6. Admission charge

This forbidding, brooding castle is easily missed if you hurry along A68, intent on Edinburgh. It is worth stopping, not least because of the fine Lothians countryside in which the castle is set. Built between the late 14th and late 16th centuries, it is associated with the Earls of Bothwell. Mary, Queen of Scots was here in January 1562, attending the wedding of her half brother to Lady Janet Hepburn. The son of that marriage, the 5th Earl of Bothwell, frequently in exile, commissioned the castle's unique feature: the diamond-faceted façade of the north range. Beyond the castle a pathway leads through some pleasant scenery to Borthwick Castle (a private hotel).

▶▶▶ Culzean Castle and Country Park   98A2

Open: house Apr–Oct, daily 10:30–5:30 (last entry 5); country park daily 9:30–sunset. Admission charge

Culzean, pronounced "Kul-*ain*," is the National Trust for Scotland's most popular attraction. Set on its cliff-top perch, it has been associated with the Kennedy family since the 14th century. The present building was commissioned by the 10th Earl of Cassillis, and is one of Robert Adam's most famous designs, taking 20 years to reach completion in 1792. The structure itself, with its ornate plasterwork, oval staircase, and round drawing room, plus 570 acres of policies (grounds), came into the hands of the National Trust in 1945, to be held for all time. Now the once-private grounds swallow up more than half a million visitors every year, though fewer visit the castle itself. Stabilizing the wind- and salt-eroded sandstone of the structure and the outbuildings was only one problem for the Trust to solve. Simply running the estate is a huge operation in itself. This is conservation and countryside education on a large scale. Within the extensive policies are woodland walks, a walled garden, swan pond, deer park, and aviary, as well as a helpful ranger service, based in a reception and interpretation center.

AN ITALIAN INFLUENCE?
The unique studded façade of Crichton Castle dates from the 1580s. The Palazzo Steripinto (1501) in Sciacca, Sicily, is one possible source of inspiration, as the 5th Earl of Bothwell was in exile in southern Italy.

Culzean Castle has fine Adam architecture, extensive gardens, and superb views to Arran and to Ailsa Craig, a steep rocky island once the plug of a volcano

▶ Dalbeattie　　　　　　　　98C1

Dalbeattie presents an uncharacteristic Galloway townscape of silver granite, like a little detached chunk of Aberdeen, but its granite has brought prosperity—even the Grand Harbor of Valletta in Malta used it. The town is a good base for exploring the coastline, especially around

The beach at Yellowcraigs, Dirleton, with Fidra offshore

111

Rockcliffe and Kippford, two little communities dozing quietly by the estuary. Kippford is favored by sailing enthusiasts, Rockcliffe has more the air of a retirement haven. Farther up the Water of Urr is Palnackie, where a flounder-tramping festival is held annually in the muddy creek. Also nearby is Orchardton Tower, a 15th-century tower house unique in Scotland because it is circular.

▶▶ Dawyck Botanic Gardens　　　98C3
Open: Mar–Oct, daily 9:30–6. Admission charge
On B712 southwest of Peebles, this specialist garden of the Royal Botanic Garden in Edinburgh lies a little off the main tourist routes and as such is often overlooked. It is worth seeking out, especially in late spring and early summer when the garden is ablaze with rhododendrons. The plantings here are on a large scale, with grand conifers and shrubs, and woodland walks.

▶▶ Dirleton Castle　　　　　　99D4
Open: Apr–Sep, daily 9:30–6; Oct–Mar, Mon–Sat 9:30–4, Sun 2–4. Admission charge
Overlooking the village green of Dirleton, this ancient fortress dates back in part to the early 13th century, when its great circular towers, now overlaid with later work, were built by the Anglo–Norman de Vaux family. The strategically important castle, commanding east–west routes around the Lammermuirs, was captured by King Edward I of England in 1298. It also has a pit-prison cut from the solid rock. Left in ruins by Cromwell's troops in 1650, the castle became part of the Archerfield estate. The site lies within a much later wall, enclosing a 17th-century bowling green, ancient yews and a fine garden. This last feature is at its colorful best in high season. Historic Scotland, the organization that cares for the castle, has re-created a Victorian garden here. Combine a visit with a walk at Yellowcraigs, for fine coastal scenery. An access road is signposted just east of the castle.

A STABBING AT THE ALTAR

In assessing his chances of securing the throne of Scotland, Robert the Bruce (see page 28) had to deal with other powerful families with Scottish interests at the English court. Most historians believe that he and John Comyn (the Red Comyn) had been jointly plotting against King Edward of England, and that Comyn had let the English know about this. Bruce was warned and left England in great haste. At his meeting with Comyn at Greyfriars Kirk in Dumfries, he accused Comyn of treachery, and the fatal stabbing followed—such were the murky politics of the day. The game was now up. To return to King Edward was impossible. Bruce had to declare his intention: to win Scotland's crown.

Eyemouth, an active fishing port

Decorative tiles in a Dunbar shop

▶ Dumfries   98C2

With its old bridges, museum, and Camera Obscura, a reasonable range of shops, and plenty of Burns strands to follow, Dumfries is a pleasant rather than a breathtaking town. Known as the Queen of the South, the town is the largest center for some distance around, with a good mix of light industry, commerce, tourism, and historic sites. Now that it is bypassed by terrifyingly busy A75, the

town environment has greatly improved. The prevailing street color is the distinctive pink of the local sandstone. Dumfries grew up around the ford on the River Nith, becoming a royal burgh in the 12th century. The now-vanished Greyfriars was the scene of the stabbing of the Red Comyn by Robert the Bruce, an incident that led to the Scottish Wars of Independence (see panel). Much later, and flying in the face of Jacobite romantic myth, Dumfries wanted no dealings with Bonnie Prince Charlie, who helped himself to town funds as well as the lead off the roof of St. Michael's Church.

Like Ayr, Dumfries has capitalized on its Robert Burns connections (see pages 104–105). He moved here in 1791 to take up his post as an excise officer and now lies buried in a grand mausoleum in St. Michael's churchyard. The house in which he died is also a museum (*Open* Apr–Sep, Mon–Sat 10–5, Sun 2–5; Oct–Mar, Tue–Sat 10–1, 2–5. *Admission free*). The Globe Inn, known to Burns, is still a pub, complete with the chair he used and the window on which he scratched some radical verses.

Robert Burns Centre▶ Modern input to the Burns cult takes the form of this handsome former mill building by the River Nith. The center offers an exhibition on the Dumfries Burns connection. (*Open* Apr–Sep, Mon–Sat 10–8, Sun 2–5; Oct–Mar, Tue–Sat 10–1, 2–5. *Admission free*).

▶▶ Dunbar   99D4

Boasting high sunshine records (when the sea fog stays away) and low rainfall, Dunbar is a curious mix of traditional resort, decayed port, and elegant Georgian sea town. Down by the harbor are the shattered, eroded fragments of one of medieval Scotland's most important fortresses, which controlled an important coastal route used by the English invaders. The Scots were defeated

*Burns' Mausoleum, one
of many stops in and
around Dumfries on the
Burns trail*

here in 1296. In 1650, the Covenanting army met the same
fate at the hands of Oliver Cromwell.

Today, the townscape owes its origins partly to funds
generated by intense trading activities in the 18th
century, which included, briefly, whaling. The handsome
17th-century town house predates these times, though
Dunbar or Lauderdale House, blocking the eastward
High Street view, was built by one of the powerful trading
families in the town. There are other elegant buildings to
be admired, but a stroll will inevitably lead seaward, past
the Cromwellian Old Harbour to the New or Victoria
harbour, dating from 1842. In spring, gulls nest on the old
castle and other harbor-front buildings.

Dunbar lies adjacent to the John Muir Country Park►►,
175 acres of excellent coastal habitat, varying from salt
marsh to sea buckthorn, around the Tyne estuary. It offers
plenty of walks at all seasons, and has the further attraction of completely altering its character at high tide.

► Eyemouth Museum 99E3

*Open: Apr–Jun and Sep, Mon–Sat 10–5, Sun 1–3; Jul–Aug,
Mon–Sat 10–6, Sun 11:30–4:30; Oct, Mon–Sat 10–4.
Admission charge*

A converted Georgian church in the fishing port of
Eyemouth is the setting for this successful
community venture. Eyemouth Museum
was set up in 1981 to record the cente-
nary of the Great East Coast Fishing
Disaster of October 1881, when 189
fishermen lost their lives in a sudden
hurricane. The tale of the disaster is
commemorated in a magnificent
tapestry, and the museum also
touches on other aspects of folk life
in the area, including agricultural
developments. A visit here could be
combined   with   bird-watching
around St. Abbs' Head.

AN UNFORTUNATE NAME
The former county town of
Duns is recalled in the
uncomplimentary "dunce."
This is ironic, as it refers
to John Duns Scotus
(1266–1308), a philoso-
pher and leading divine
said to have been born in
the town. The modern
usage came about
through later criticism of
his teachings.

TOURIST INFORMATION
Dumfries: 64 Whitesands
(tel: 01387-253862).
Eyemouth: Auld Kirk,
Market Place (tel: 01890-
750678).

Lochcarron Woollen Mill

HISTORY IN STONE
Haddington's picturesque Nungate Bridge is a bridge with a past. Referred to as early as the 13th century, it has seen many alterations over the years, as the different colors of its stonework suggest.

THE QUEEN'S WAY
A712 between Newton Stewart and New Galloway, as it passes through the Galloway Forest Park, is known as the Queen's Way. The original Queen's Way was the old pilgrim road used by Mary, Queen of Scots, among many other monarchs, which led down to Whithorn (see page 120).

Outdoor refreshments by the Tyne, Haddington

The South

► Galashiels   99D3

A sturdy, respectable mill town, rather than a picturesque place, "Gala" has lots of shops to browse in for knitwear bargains. In fact, the textile theme is inescapable, notably at **Lochcarron Cashmere Woollen Mill**►► (*Open* Mon–Sat 9–5; Jun–Sep, Sun 12–5. Tours Mon–Fri only. *Admission charge*). The museum there, with its traditional spinning and weaving artifacts, tells the story of the town's development as an important textile-manufacturing center. There is also a factory tour and a mill shop.

►► Galloway Forest Park   98B2

Between the Rivers Cree and Ken, the open moors below the gray hills of Galloway lost their original tree cover long ago. From 1922 onward, the Forestry Commission reclothed many of the slopes using alien species, designating the area a forest park in 1943, and leaving a third of its 240 square miles as open land. Like all Forestry Commission properties, it offers unlimited access to the public unless areas are closed for tree felling. There are numerous marked forest trails and opportunities to fish or camp, and the park is also bisected by the Southern Upland Way (a long-distance footpath). Among the many points of interest are the 10-mile forest drive near Clatteringshaws Loch; the Raider's Road, linking A712 and A762; and the peerless views from the road end at Glen Trool. The Bruce's Stone, commemorating the first victory in the Independence Wars, can also be found here.

►► Gatehouse of Fleet   98B1

Peaceful in pastel colors, Gatehouse of Fleet, on the edge of the hills, was founded in the 1760s as a mill community competing with others in the English counties of Yorkshire and Lancashire. Looming over the access road (A75) just southwest is the 15th-century **Cardoness Castle**, a typically austere tower house (*Open* Apr–Sep, daily 9:30–6; Oct–Mar, Sat 9:30–4, Sun 2–4. *Admission charge*). B796 north out of Gatehouse offers a flavor of the empty hinterland and high hills of Galloway, as well as a long view to the viaduct over the Big Water of Fleet. Use this road if you are visiting the Gem Rock Museum at

Creetown; it is a much more attractive drive than A75. **Mill on the Fleet▶▶▶** (*Open* Easter–Oct, daily 10–5:30. *Admission charge*). A visitor center in a former bobbin mill tells the tale of Gatehouse's cotton spinning, offering a high-tech interpretation. Visitors are given hard hats, inside which are tiny speakers activated at various points in the displays to provide commentary. This can be a little disconcerting.

TWEED OR TWILL?
The traditional explanation for the name "tweed" is that a merchant in London received a consignment of Scottish cloth and misread the word "tweel" (twill). Because of the River Tweed, the name stuck. This is probably a myth, though at least two Scottish tweed mills claim they sent the consignment. There is a written reference from Aberdeen in 1541 to "small twedlyne"— tweedling. According to philologists, the words tweel and tweeling, tweed and tweedling have been around a long time, and have nothing to do with rivers. Besides, the traditional version does not explain Harris tweed, given that Harris in the Outer Hebrides islands in the northwest is so far away.

115

A gentle corner of the Galloway landscape in Scotland's south-western corner

▶▶▶ Haddington 99D4

One of the most pleasing towns of the Lothians, the counties surrounding Edinburgh, Haddington was the former administrative headquarters of the old county, and for centuries played an important part in Lothian affairs. A 12th-century royal burgh (town), it also lay at the center of one of the most favored agricultural regions of Scotland and had Continental trade through the now silted-up port of Aberlady to the north.

Today, it retains its triangular medieval street plan, and the fine, mainly Georgian, buildings in the center of town have been preserved and carefully painted to create a coordinated and harmonious façade along High Street rivaled by few other Scottish towns. The air of a prosperous old community is enhanced by other trappings of a Scottish burgh: the impressive town house originally built by William Adam, the market cross, the courthouse, and the 14th- to 15th-century St. Mary's Church, with its warm, red stones reflected in the river. This is a town to study at a slow pace, admiring the detailing of wrought-iron balconies, ornamental urns, cornice decoration, and so on. Note also the small passageways running off the main thoroughfares. Tucked around a corner on Sidegate, a plaque at eye level records the exact heights of the River Tyne floods: the last big one was in 1948.

TOURIST INFORMATION
Galashiels (Apr–Oct): 3 St. John's Street (tel: 01896-755551). Gatehouse of Fleet (Apr–Oct): Car park (tel: 01557-814212).

The South

A LONG RIDE

Mary, Queen of Scots rode from Jedburgh to Hermitage Castle and back in a day, just over 50 miles, to visit the wounded Earl of Bothwell trusted lieutenant on border matters. Though this is sometimes romantically described as a foolhardy venture undertaken on her own, it was not in fact unusual to cover such a distance in a day, and besides, the queen was in company with many members of her court and a squad of soldiers.

TOURIST INFORMATION

Hawick (Apr–Oct): Drumlanrig's Tower, Tower Knowe (tel: 01450-372547).

► Hawick   99D2

Hawick is the largest of the Borders towns. Its long and bustling main street is worth a browse for woolen shops with keenly priced cashmeres. At one end is **Drumlanrig's Tower**, which portrays the local history of the area. A few minutes' walk away, **Wilton Lodge Park** is also attractive, with Victorian walled gardens and its own museum and art gallery.

► Hermitage Castle   99D2

Open: Apr–Sep, daily 9:30–6. Admission charge
Off B6399 in bleak and lonely Borders country, the grimness of Hermitage Castle echoes the emptiness around. High in atmosphere, reeking of the violence of the medieval Borderlands, Hermitage is particularly impressive if the clouds are low on the hills. One of the tales about this 14th-century keep, or fortress, concerns the wicked Lord Soulis, who was so cruel that the locals eventually revolted, wrapped him in lead, and boiled him to death in a cauldron.

► Innerleithen   99D3

A compact mill town by the confluence of the Leithen Water with the mighty Tweed, Innerleithen is home to some famous knitwear names, notably Ballantynes. Sir Walter Scott used it as the setting for his novel St. *Ronan's Well* (1821).

Robert Smail's Printing Works►►►, run by the National Trust for Scotland, is perhaps the main attraction within the town (*Open Easter, May–Sep, Mon–Sat 10–1, 2–5, Sun 2–5; Oct, Sat and Sun only. Admission charge*). The local printing firm, which served the community for over a hundred years, remained in the original family's hands until purchased by the Trust in 1986. The Victorian office,

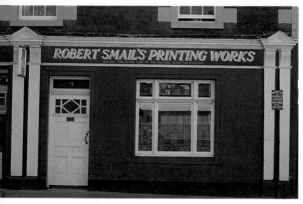

A Borders time capsule

paper store, composing room, and machine room all survived as a unique time capsule. Most importantly, so did 50 "guard books"—a record of every item ever printed at the works, as well as endless ephemera from the past. There are now print demonstrations.

Just minutes away to the south is one of the most interesting grand homes in the Borders. **Traquair House►►►** (*Open Jun–Aug, daily 10:30–5:30; Apr–May and Sep, daily 12:30–5:30; Oct, Fri–Sun 12:30–5:30, last entry 5. Admission charge*) boasts that it is the oldest continuously inhabited house in Scotland, and that it has been associated with the Stuarts or Maxwell-Stuarts, the Lairds (lords) of Traquair, since 1491. Before that it was a hunting lodge used by Scottish monarchs. Over the centuries it has been transformed from a grim Borders keep to a stately mansion, and has remained practically unchanged since the end of the 17th century. Curiously, a record for a house occupied by frequent holders of high

ST. RONAN'S WELL

The sulfurous waters of St. Ronan's Well were said to be particularly effective for "ladies desirous of becoming in an interesting condition." According to local legend, the sulfur content is the result of the local holy man, St. Ronan, catching the Deil (Devil) with his shepherd's crook and immersing him in the waters.

THE CLOSED GATE
Traquair House has two parallel drives, one of them ending at permanently closed gates. When Bonnie Prince Charlie rode out after a visit to Traquair in the fall of 1745, the 5th Earl wished him success and closed the gates behind him, vowing they would never be opened again until a Stuart was on the throne.

Traquair Castle, left, a fine fortified Borders castle, and below, the Traquair coat of arms

office during Scotland's troubled past, the mansion only once saw violence—in 1688, when a mob from Peebles stormed the building and destroyed religious artifacts.

The lairds were staunch Catholics, which is why the house has a secret staircase intended as a quick escape route for priests. As Catholics, they were also Jacobites. A total of 27 Scottish and English monarchs have been guests at Traquair, and Bonnie Prince Charlie is said to have visited. Family lore and the paraphernalia and treasures of generations, including notable relics of Mary, Queen of Scots, are further attractions of the house, which is also pleasantly unintimidating in scale. If there is only time for one Borders house, then make it Traquair.

▶ **Irvine** 98B3

Scattered around the riverside area of the New Town of Irvine, the **Scottish Maritime Museum**▶ has a variety of craft, including a lifeboat, a tug, and a puffer (an inshore supply boat) moored in the harbor by floating pontoons, an undercover exhibition, a typical shipyard worker's cottage, and a Victorian boat shed, the largest of its kind ever built. This latter used to be on the Clyde and was reconstructed here, brick by brick. (*Open* Apr–Oct, daily 10–5. *Admission charge*). A ferry runs from nearby Ardrossan to Brodick on the Isle of Arran (see page 230).

A HISTORIC HECKLER
In the old part of Irvine is the Glasgow Vennel, formerly the main road out of town. Robert Burns came here to learn to dress flax, a process known as heckling. (Hecklers tended to be politically argumentative types, hence the modern usage.) The venture came to an end when Burns's partner's wife dropped a candle during a drunken Hogmanay party. The dried flax caught fire and the business was burned down. The thatched Heckling Shop has been restored, along with Burns's lodgings nearby.

Above: Jedburgh's mercat (market) cross, symbol that the town enjoyed certain trading rights. Right: Kelso Abbey, at the heart of the town Sir Walter Scott described as the most beautiful in Scotland

TOURIST INFORMATION
Jedburgh: Murray's Green (tel: 01835-863435). Kelso (Apr–Oct): Town House, The Square (tel: 01573-223464). Kirkcudbright: Harbour Square (tel: 01557-330494).

A FLATTERING DESCRIPTION
With its long waterfront, Lord Cockburn described Kirkcudbright as "the Venice of Scotland." Clearly, he never saw it with the tide out.

THE UNION CANAL
Linlithgow is a good place to discover the Union Canal, ideal for strolls along the towpath. There is an impressive aqueduct about 2 miles to the west. Linlithgow has a canal museum and cruising opportunities. Inquire on weekends in summer.

▶ **Jedburgh**   99D3

Jedburgh, on A68, is a typical Borders town, with a history of tweed making. The local weavers were the first to combine two colors in their weave, thus inventing tweed. Even the tourist information center and parking lot are on the site of a former mill. The original woolen developments were centered around the activities of the monks in the Borders' abbeys, of which Jedburgh's abbey is the best preserved.

The shell of the once great building of **Jedburgh Abbey**▶▶▶ still dominates the town skyline, though it was destroyed by English forces during the "rough wooing" (see page 30). The Abbey Visitor Centre makes an excellent introduction to the vanished monastic life of the Borders (*Open* Apr–Sep, daily 9:30–6; Oct–Mar, Mon–Sat 9:30–4, Sun 2–4. *Admission charge*). Also of note is Mary, Queen of Scots' House, a near-contemporary fortified or "bastel" (like the French *bastille*) house, now a museum (Open Mar–Nov, Mon–Sat 10–5, Sun 12–4:30 (10–4:30 Jun–Sep). *Admission charge*). The former prison, on the site of the vanished castle (Castle Jail), was once a Georgian model prison, but is now another museum. The town has further associations with Sir Walter Scott and Bonnie Prince Charlie.

▶▶ **Kelso**   99E3

When the writer H.V. Morton passed this way in the 1920s, he was struck by the appearance of the main square in Kelso. "Surely I was in France! An enormous *grande place* paved with whinstone forms the heart of the town. Round it rise those tall, demure, many-storied houses, which seem to know almost as many stories as a concierge." Little has changed, except the traffic. Stroll from the square past the poignant fragment of **Kelso Abbey**, which was severely damaged by the Earl of Hertford's forces in 1545. All 112 inhabitants were slaughtered. The tourist information center is almost opposite. Rennie's handsome bridge of 1803 spans the Tweed just a little farther on. From the parapet there is a fine view to

Floors Castle▶ (*Open* Easter–Sep, daily 10–4. *Admission charge*), the largest inhabited house in Scotland. It offers glittering excesses of fine French furniture, porcelain, paintings, and tapestries, as well as extensive parkland and walks.

Mellerstain House▶▶, an attractive Robert Adam mansion with fine views, to the northwest of Kelso, has typically ornate Adam plasterwork and decoration (*Open* Easter, May–Sep, Sun–Fri 12:30–5. *Admission charge*).

▶▶▶ Kirkcudbright   98B1

Pronounced "kir-*coo*-bree," Kirkcudbright has a typically spacious Galloway layout, and its genteel, brightly painted Georgian streetscapes give it a dignified and harmonious air. The 16th-century **Maclellan's Castle** is a ruined turreted mansion conspicuous on the skyline, and an exception to the prevailing 18th-century work (*Open* Apr–Sep, daily 9:30–6. *Admission charge*). There are a few antiques shops to browse around, as well as the Harbour Gallery, though the main artistic connection is **Broughton House** (*Open* Apr–Oct, daily 1–5:30. *Admission charge*), with its collection of the works of Edward Hornel (1864–1933) of the artistic set known as the "Glasgow Boys." The picturesque tolbooth and mercat (market) cross complete the harmonious groupings within this Solway town, which has one other pleasing feature. **The Stewartry Museum▶▶** is a traditional museum with no high-tech embellishments (*Open* May, Mon–Sat 11–5; Jun and Sep, Mon–Sat 11–5, Sun 2–5; Jul–Aug, Mon–Sat 10–6, Sun 2–5; Oct–Apr, Mon–Sat 11–4. *Admission charge*). Visitors can discover the Dorothy L. Sayers connection (see panel) and find out why the founder of the American navy was once locked in the local tolbooth.

▶ **Linlithgow Palace**   98C4

Open: Apr–Sep, daily 9:30–6; Oct–Mar, Mon–Sat 9:30–4, Sun 2–4. Admission charge

Birthplace of Mary, Queen of Scots, this once magnificent royal palace is now a cold shell. It was burned, probably accidentally, during the last Jacobite rebellion in 1745. A visit can be combined with a look at St. Michael's Church.

119

FIVE RED HERRINGS
The renowned English detective novelist Dorothy L. Sayers had two aunts and an uncle in Kirkcudbright. She used the local area as a setting for one of her Lord Peter Wimsey novels, *Five Red Herrings*, published in 1931. Another and more famous work set in Galloway—at least in part—is John Buchan's *The Thirty-Nine Steps* (published in 1915).

The Scottish Parliament met in the 15th-century Linlithgow Palace on several occasions, most "recently" in 1646

Logan Botanic Garden where many species from the southern hemisphere enjoy some of Scotland's mildest air

A RECORD CLAIM
The Whithorn excavation team reconstructed a Viking Age house on the site of their dig for the benefit of visitors. It was built of poles and brushwood, and unfortunately it burned down. Seeking compensation through their insurers, the team made the very first Viking Age insurance claim.

▶▶ Logan Botanic Garden   98A1

Open: Mar–Oct, daily 9:30–6. Admission charge

Galloway trumpets its prevailing mildness to persuade visitors to stay. Nowhere is the benign influence of the North Atlantic Drift more apparent than in Logan Botanic Garden. This specialist garden of the Royal Botanic Garden in Edinburgh specializes in tender plants that would not survive in other parts of Scotland. It has a great deal of success with the arrestingly exotic Australasian tree ferns, as well as cabbage palms and a whole range of temperamental Southern Hemisphere species.

▶▶ The Machars   98B1

Lush green is the key color of the Machars, to which are added the black and white of cattle in the pasture and the yellow splash of gorse on the little rough hillocks. This is gentle, rolling countryside, with the big hills of Galloway receding to the north. A triangle lying between Wigtown Bay and Luce Bay, the Machars are sometimes overlooked but have a curious serenity. Perhaps this echoes their early religious links. Here, at Whithorn, not at Iona, is the cradle of Christianity in Britain.

Whithorn Dig and Visitor Centre▶▶ This archeological attraction (*Open* Apr–Oct, daily 10:30–5, last tour 4:30. *Admission charge*) is on the site of the first Christian community in Scotland, and displays material dating from ad 400 that was dug up on the site. The ruined Whithorn Priory and a museum are adjacent. Whithorn became a place of pilgrimage for the Scottish kings and is associated with St. Ninian. His chapel on a grassy headland at Isle of Whithorn (not actually an island) is an anticlimax, though his cave makes a worthwhile walk down a lane and along the pebbly shore.

The town of Wigtown is also attractive, with a wide main street. It is associated with the drowning of two Covenanter martyrs, tied to a stake before the incoming tide in 1685. You can visit the site, down by the endless mudflats of the shore.

▶▶▶ Melrose   99D3

Melrose is cozy and handsomely rustic, almost too neat to be true. It has an abbey, romantically ruined in red sandstone, visible from the road (*Open* Apr–Sep, daily, 9:30–6:30; Oct–Mar Mon–Sat 9:30–4:30, Sun 2–4:30). Next door, the National Trust for Scotland sells various gifts and dried flowers grown in Priorwood Garden. There are also plenty of gift and clothes shops. Melrose is overshadowed by the beautiful Eildon Hills, where an energetic walk (starting across the golf course) offers outstanding views.

Trimontium Exhibition▶▶ This is a fascinating account of one of the Romans' main forts in Scotland, just a few fields away at Newstead (*Open* Apr–Oct, daily 10:30–4:30. Closed 12:30–1:30 on Sat, Sun. *Admission charge*). Alternatively, there are a number of excursions from Melrose, including Dryburgh Abbey and Scott's View (see page 126).

A grim reminder of the Covenanters at Wigtown

The River Bladnoch as it reaches the sea near Wigtown; it rises high on the Galloway moors

▶ Moffat   98C2

The ram statue on the Colvin Fountain in the middle of the town square is a reminder of Moffat's origins in the wool trade, though it also had a reputation in the 18th century as a spa town. The woolen bargains at Moffat Weavers at the southern end of town are popular with tourists.

Moffat is on A701, a scenic route to Edinburgh known as "the Beeftub road." In addition to the **Devil's Beeftub**, a hollow carved out by a glacier at the head of the valley, there are more glaciation features to the northeast, up the Moffat Water by A708. This passes the Grey Mare's Tail, a geologically classic waterfall pouring over the lip of a hanging valley. Hardy walkers can penetrate beyond the waterfall, either to circle around Loch Skeen or to reach the broad, rounded summit of **White Coomb**, which at 2,550 feet is one of the highest hills in the Southern Uplands.

A CANNY LOCATION
Why did the Romans build their main fort at Trimontium? According to the Trimontium Exhibition in Melrose, when the legions came over the Cheviot Hills, they made for the most conspicuous landmark, the triple-peaked Eildon Hills, instantly recognizable from any angle, and right in the center of southern Scotland.

121

**AN AMERICAN
CONNECTION**
Arbigland Garden can be combined with a visit to Sweetheart Abbey. The garden is attractively sheltered by mature trees, and has a pleasantly tinkling creek, a Japanese Garden, poolside prim-roses, and sea views. However, its claim to fame is its connection with John Paul Jones, the founder of the American navy. He was born in a cottage on the estate, and worked in the gardens as a boy. A museum tells the story (*Open* May–Sep, Tue–Sun 2–6).

TOURIST INFORMATION
Lanark: Horsemarket, Ladyacre Road (tel: 01555-661661).

*Shambellie House
Museum of Costume*

The corn mill at New Abbey, which, along with a picturesque abbey and a museum of costume, make the vil-lage worth seeing

▶▶ New Abbey   98C1

New Abbey is a little village on A710, dominated by the red ruins of *Sweetheart Abbey*. This religious seat was founded in 1273 by Devorgilla, wife of John Balliol (see page 28). On his death she had his heart embalmed in an ivory and silver casket, hence the abbey's name. The abbey suffered from

its proximity to the border in the Wars of Independence. During the Protestant Reformation its riches were disposed of, and the building gradually deterio-rated. Today, visitors can enjoy a peaceful stroll through the pointed gothic ruins. The 18th-century **New Abbey Corn Mill▶** is moments away from the abbey (*Open* abbey and mill Apr–Sep, daily 9:30–6; Oct–Mar, Mon–Wed and Sat 9:30–4, Thu 9:30–12, Sun 2–4. *Admission charge*). The great grinding stones, powered by water via an impressive set of gearing, produce oatmeal of various grades. Walk a bit farther to reach the **Shambellie House Museum of Costume**, an outstation of the Royal Museum of Scotland. It shows material from the National Costume Collection (*Open* Apr–Oct, daily 11–5. *Admission charge*).

▶▶▶ New Lanark and the Falls of Clyde   98C3

The River Clyde seems a world away from its downstream industry here amid the farms and orchards of Lanarkshire, on the edge of the hills. It roars through a wooded gorge over spectacular waterfalls ("linns") in a setting unique in Scotland. This alone would justify the detour, but it is only one part of the experience. The river was harnessed to power cotton mills in an unusual experiment in workers' welfare. The model village of New Lanark has survived intact, and there is a visitor center within the mill complex (*Open* daily 11–5. *Admission charge*).

A remarkable industrial and social experiment, embodying the principles of welfare and worker care, took place in the upper reaches of the River Clyde in the late 18th and early 19th centuries. Two hundred years later, there is still a great deal to see.

In 1783, a successful Glasgow businessman, David Dale, bought this wooded bowl with its roaring river as a potential site for a spinning mill. Before the end of the century, New Lanark had become the single largest industrial enterprise in Scotland. Some of the river's force was diverted, a little way downstream, to turn giant waterwheels that, with belts and drives, powered noisy cotton looms housed in vast mill buildings. In 1793, over 1,100 employees tended these machines, of whom 800 were young boys and girls.

Social benefits Dale the master was no despotic employer. Hours were long, but substantial housing was provided as well as educational facilities. Many of his child workers were orphans who were, by the standards of the day, well fed and cared for. Another source of workers was Highland emigration: New Lanark employed people who would otherwise have headed for the New World because of repression and depressed economic conditions in their native lands to the north.

Robert Owen This Welshman was born in 1771 (32 years after Dale) and also made his way in the spinning industry. He had strong ideas about equality and social welfare. In 1799, he married David Dale's daughter. Along with two partners, he then bought New Lanark and assumed management in 1800. Already embodying principles of welfare and worker care, the model village became the setting for Owen's own social experiments and even more benevolent management style.

After some business vicissitudes in the early years of the 19th century, Owen was able to put his principles into practice with new Quaker backers. To the four great mills and blocks of workers' houses were added the New Institute for the Formation of Character (1816) and Robert Owen's School (1817), as the first steps in the creation of his vision of a society without crime, poverty, or misery —the fundamentals of "Owenism."

THE FALLS OF CLYDE
The waterfalls that comprise the Falls of Clyde are in a delightful wooded river gorge, and well reward the walk upstream. (Go through the gap in the wall at the far end of the village.) Some of the water is diverted through tunnels to run a hydroelectric power station. When this is not operating, for example during station maintenance work, the falls are at their best.

123

Bell tower on New Buildings, New Lanark

Robert Owen, an entrepreneur of vision who transformed the banks of the Clyde at New Lanark with his model working village

▶ Newton Stewart 98B1

A kind of gateway between the Machars and the Galloway Forest Park, Newton Stewart has a good range of shops (including antiques). Nearby, the Wood of Cree is a Royal Society for the Protection of Birds nature reserve. Species include several summer warblers, plus dippers and gray wagtails. The scenically outstanding Glen Trool road (see page 114) is easily reached from the town.

▶▶ North Berwick 99D4

Within easy commuting range of Edinburgh, North Berwick has developed from a small fishing port into a resort. Its little harbor is jammed with pleasure craft, its harbor-front granary is converted to apartments, and its Victorian and Edwardian architecture likewise suggests prosperity. The golf course reaches almost to the center of town. Behind the town is the conspicuous cone of the North **Berwick Law**, a 580-foot volcanic plug. Views from the top are excellent and take in the Bell Rock Lighthouse, off the fishing port of Arbroath in Angus, east Scotland. North Berwick gives easy access to some fine coastline, notably westward along the sands toward Yellowcraigs (see page 111). East of the town, on the way to Tantallon, is another good beach at Seacliff. Other nearby attractions include the historic aircraft collection at the **Museum of Flight** at East Fortune (*Open* Jul–Aug, daily 10:15–6:16; mid-Mar–Jun, Sep–mid-Nov, daily 10:30–5; mid-Nov–mid-Mar, Mon–Fri 11–3. *Admission charge*, free in winter).

Tantallon Castle▶▶▶ This 14th-century former Douglas stronghold straddles a headland, a grim, fortified wall of eroded red sandstone, with the Bass Rock (see panel) as a backdrop beyond. (*Open* Apr–Sep, daily 9:30–6; Oct–Mar, Mon–Wed and Sat 9:30–4, Thu 9:30–12, Sun 2–4. *Admission charge*).

▶▶ Peebles 99D3

Respectable, well-scrubbed Peebles is well within day-trip range of Edinburgh, and is accordingly busy throughout

124

WEALTHY VANDAL
Neidpath Castle came into the hands of the Douglas Earls of March. The 3rd Earl cared little for this country property, leading a spendthrift life in London. He even sold for timber a fine stand of ornamental trees planted by his father and grandfather. This vandalism earned William Wordsworth's scorn in his *Sonnet Composed at Neidpath Castle.*
"Degenerate Douglas! oh the unworthy Lord!"

Pride of Peebles

the year. There is a good choice of shops for antiques and fashions, and probably the best old-fashioned ironmonger (hardware store) in Scotland. Famous sons, William and Robert Chambers, compilers of *Chambers Dictionaries*, after making their fortune in Edinburgh, endowed their home-town with the impressive municipal buildings on the main street, now housing a library and museum.

Neidpath Castle▶▶ (*Open* Easter–Sep, Mon–Sat 11–5, Sun 1–5. *Admission charge*). A few minutes west of the town, this stronghold can be reached on foot along the River Tweed as a pleasant alternative to going by car. An L-plan tower house, originally built by the Hayes family, Neidpath has survived remarkably intact. It was "modernized" for comfort in the 17th century, though retaining its medieval outward appearance, but fell into decay by the early 19th century. It was restored by the present owners, the Earls of Wemyss .

▶▶ Rosslyn Chapel 99D3

Open: Mon–Sat 10–5, Sun 12–4:45. Admission charge
The best example of medieval stone carving in Scotland (if not Britain) can be found a few minutes' stroll beyond the former mining village of Roslin. Perched above the wooded Roslin Glen, Rosslyn Chapel was founded in 1446 by William Sinclair, 3rd Earl of Orkney. The church, still used as a place of worship, is really only the choir of a much larger design, which was never completed. It is associated with Scott's romantic poem *The Lay of the Last Minstrel*. There are fine wooded walks from the site, with both Rosslyn Castle and Hawthornden (both private) hidden in the glen below.

"Maude" (former Class J36) at Bo'ness

▶▶ Scottish Railway Preservation Society (Bo'ness and Kinneil Railway) 98C4

Open: Jul–Aug, Tue–Sun 10:30–4:30 (6 trains); Apr–Jun and Sep–mid-Oct, Sat–Sun 11:20–4:30 (5 trains). Admission charge.
At Bo'ness on the River Forth, a typical Scottish branch line has been re-created, offering a 4-mile trip uphill to Birkhill (with extensions likely) where a former clay mine can be visited. It captures the feel of a vanished age, and could be tied in with a trip to Linlithgow.

LITERARY VISITORS
Rosslyn Inn (now a private house), adjacent to the chapel, was the main lodging for many famous folk who came to see the wonders of the place. The Wordsworths stayed here, leaving very early to visit Sir Walter Scott at his first marital home at nearby Lasswade (the Scotts were still in bed when they arrived). Before that, Robert Burns stayed, and English lexicographer Dr. Samuel Johnson and his biographer James Boswell took lunch and tea here.

A branch line— re-created

BASS ROCK BIRDS
The gannet's Latin name, Sula bassana, recalls its long association with the Bass Rock. Gannets occupy about 14,000 nest sites on the Bass. There are smaller numbers of kittiwakes, guillemots, razorbills, and puffins. Boat trips go from North Berwick.

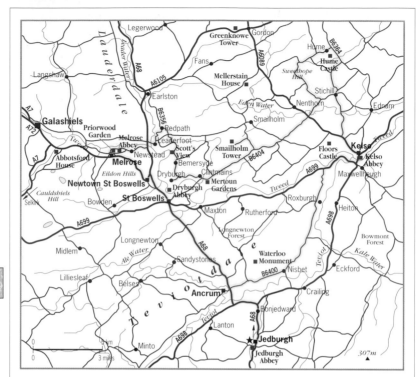

Drive

Border views and abbeys

Smailholm Tower for Borders views

The river valleys and rounded hills of the Borders make rewarding country for touring. This route is 40 miles long, and easily driven in a day if no diversions are taken.

Take A68 north from Jedburgh, then B6400 heading east. The unmistakable high tower of the **Waterloo Monument**, which can be seen on an ancient earthwork, was raised in 1815 on the instructions of William Kerr, 6th Marquis of Lothian.

Continue past the modern village of Roxburgh, to reach **Kelso** with its ruined abbey.

Take B6364 northward, and soon you will see a dark square of battlements rising ahead. Take a minor road to Hume. Built by Lord Hume in the 1790s on the site of the original **Hume Castle**, the site offers one of Scotland's best views.

Travel west to cross A6089 at a staggered crossroads for the view from **Smailholm Tower**, a 16th-century fortified Borders keep (fortress) associated with Sir Walter Scott. Then drop gently down westward to find signs for the peaceful riverside **Dryburgh Abbey**.

Scott's View, Scott's favorite viewpoint for the Eildon Hills, is signposted. The minor road leads to A68 and Melrose, with its abbey. You can either detour to Selkirk, or return to Jedburgh on A68.

▶ Scottish Mining Museum 99D3

The former Lady Victoria Colliery (coal-mining works) in the former mining village of Newtongrange was once the largest of its kind in Scotland. Pit and village were under the sway of domineering pit managers, a story told by tableaux that follow the career of a typical miner. There is also an impressive steam winding engine.

Industrial-heritage enthusiasts can also take a coal trail down to Prestongrange on the coast near Musselburgh, where there are other mining artifacts. (*Open* Mar–Oct, daily 10–4. *Admission charge*).

▶▶ Selkirk 99D3

Sir Walter Scott presided as sheriff in Selkirk, and his **Courtroom** (*Open* Apr–Sep, Mon–Sat 10–4, also Sun 2–4; Jul–Aug, Oct, Mon–Sat 1–4. *Admission charge*) tells of his life, writings, and time as a judge. **Halliwell's House▶ ▶** is now a museum with plenty to be learned. Ask to see the excellent videos about the Common Ridings (*Open* Jul–Aug, daily 10–6; Apr–Jun and Sep–Oct, Mon–Sat 10–5, Sun 2–4. *Admission free*). **Abbotsford House** is nearby (see page 102).

▶ South Queensferry 98C4

South Queensferry makes a pleasant evening excursion from Edinburgh to view the great bridges both upriver and down. Alternatively, tie it in with a day visit to **Hopetoun House▶** to the west, where architects William and John Adam created a spectacular mansion that is now filled with valuables (*Open* Apr–Sep, daily 10–5:30, last entry 4:30. *Admission charge*). Also nearby is **Dalmeny House**, where fine porcelain from the Rothschild Mentmore collection is among an impressive range of items on display (*Open* Jul–early Sep, Sun 1–5:30, Mon–Tue 12–5:30, last entry at 4:45. *Admission charge*).

QUEEN MARGARET
The queen in the name South (or North) Queensferry refers to Queen (and Saint) Margaret, the Saxon wife of the uncouth King Malcolm. She is associated with the ancient ferry-crossing here, which connected the old capital at Dunfermline with the counties of Lothian.

TOURIST INFORMATION
Selkirk (Apr–Oct): Halliwell's House (tel: 01750-20054).

A vanished way of life at Newtongrange

DESIGNED TO FAIL
Commenting on the flimsiness of an 1818 design for a chain bridge across the mighty Forth near South Queensferry, a later Victorian engineer noted: "It would hardly have been visible on a dull day, and after a heavy gale it would no longer be seen on a clear day either."

"King Coal" now a museum within easy reach of Edinburgh

The estuary of the Forth was the last great challenge of the Victorian railroad age. In 1873, the railroad companies of the east coast trunk route oversaw the laying of a foundation stone for a Forth Bridge designed by Sir Thomas Bouch. But then the Tay Bridge—which he had designed— fell, and his plans for the Forth were abandoned.

MAINTENANCE COSTS
The phrase "painting the Forth bridge" has passed into common usage to describe a never-ending job. The painting area has been estimated as 146 acres, and 8,403 gallons of Forth Bridge oxide of iron brushing paint are needed to coat it from end to end. Originally, many of the bridge painters were ex-sailing ship crew, accustomed to shinning up and down holding only a rope. Today, hydraulic lifts and cradles are used.

128

A new Forth design was supplied by Benjamin Baker of the engineering company Fowler and Baker. This was based on the cantilever principle, invented in the Far East, and used steel instead of the treacherous cast iron of the first Tay Bridge. The contract for the work was signed in 1882, with William Arrol as the main contractor.

Building progress The next four years were taken up with building the cofferdams, sinking the caissons (watertight chambers used for laying foundations underwater), and building the piers on which the immense weight of steel would rest. The superstructure was built in the following four years. While the first Tay Bridge has sometimes been described as an optimist's bridge, the Forth is a pessimist's bridge. The engineers were all too aware of the effects of lateral wind pressure, which had been the downfall of the Tay design. Exhaustive scale-model tests were carried out, and all the various calculations were based on a "worst-case scenario"—the freakish situation in which a hurricane blew its way up one side of the Forth and down the other.

Facts and figures The bridge cost 57 lives during construction before it was opened in March 1890—and still proves an endless source of astonishing statistics, not the least curious of which is the fact that the bridge is almost a yard longer on a hot summer day than in mid-winter. It had consumed 60,346 tons of steel, 194,273 cubic yards of granite (on the approach viaducts), 23,463 tons of cement, and almost 7 million rivets. The last one was banged into place by the Prince of Wales at a spot marked by a plaque. It was the monument of the age.

The Forth Bridge, impressive from every angle

▶▶▶ St. Abbs 99E4

The great seabird colonies of northern Scotland, particularly Shetland, are justly famous. But there is one place in southern Scotland where, for very little effort, in May and June in particular, a spectacular "bird city" can be seen that rivals anything the north can offer. The cliffs and stacks of St. Abbs Head are favored by 10,000 guillemots alone. This portly, penguin-like auk is just one of the many species that make the experience a cacophony of noise, sound, and, not least, smell (a distinctly fishy one). Razorbills, fulmars, and kittiwakes add to the din. The cliffs can be viewed with relative ease, as some of them are offshore stacks. If time permits, walk the whole length of the path from the Northfield Farm parking lot to the lighthouse, starting at the eastern end to walk counterclockwise around the reserve. There are magnificent sea views all the way, with the biggest seabird colonies bursting into view by the lighthouse itself. Bird-watchers haunt the spot at fall migration time as well. There are lots of rare birds—ask the warden for details.

▶ Wanlockhead 98C2

Wanlockhead is Scotland's highest village, though it is a considerable distance from the Highlands. It stands among the bald, bleak domes of the Lowther Hills, a strange, almost claustrophobic, gathering of steep-sided glaciated hills buffering Strathclyde and Galloway. The Lowthers are cut by impressive road passes, notably the Dalveen and the Mennock, the latter leading to Wanlockhead and its neighbor, Leadhills.

Britain's most important nonferrous metal mining area used to be there, in the endless winds and open moors. Gold was found in the reign of King James IV, but lead made fortunes for local landowners. The mine closed in the 1930s, a story told in the **Museum of the Scottish Lead Mining Industry** (*Open* Apr–Oct, daily 11–4:30, last tour 4; Nov–Mar by appointment. *Admission charge*). There are several other historical threads to follow, ranging from the vanished branch line, once Britain's highest railway, to the Covenanters, whose strongholds were here.

EARLY CHARITY
More than one grand duke made money from the lead mines at Wanlockhead. The Hopetoun estates were involved at nearby Leadhills. In the early 19th century, the Wanlockhead proprietor, the Duke of Buccleuch and Queensberry (owner of Drumlanrig Castle), passed through and gave £5 ($7.50) to the miners to drink to his health. Instead they "considered they should testify their respect and gratitude by making the £5 the commencement of a charitable fund for the relief of miners when sick, or rendered unfit for work by age, as also for the benefit of their widows." Whether or not this gave the duke food for thought is not recorded.

St. Abbs, where clear waters and a diverse underwater flora create a marine paradise for divers

Gulls on offshore rocks, St. Abbs

Central Scotland

130

*Nicoll Moncrief's
gratitude seems to be as
much to King James (VI
of Scotland, I of England)
as to God. This carving is
in the village of Falkland*

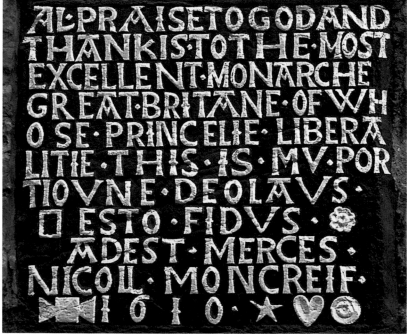

A MEETING OF TWO CULTURES This region has two distinct characters because it bridges the Highland Line, or, more accurately, the Highland Boundary Fault. This is not just a geological distinction but a real divide between two cultures, Highland and Lowland, separated by a mountain barrier and, formerly, also by language and traditions.

It was in the Highland part of Central Scotland that the cult of the picturesque first took root. From the cities of the central belt, the first tourists admired the beauties of the Trossachs and Loch Lomond—not just because they were attractive, but also because they were the first bit of wild Scotland that was accessible from the Lowlands. This led to the growth of resort towns that still cater to visitors today: places such as Callander, Crieff, Dunkeld, and Pitlochry, all of which have long-established reputations as vacation spots in or near the Highlands.

The feeling of entering or leaving different cultures is an important element in the Central Scottish "experience." Ben Ledi looms at the end of Callander's main street as a reminder that there is real grandeur beyond the cut-rate woolen mill sales. At Dunkeld, there is a strong sense of passing between the Highland portals. Alternatively, drive up any of the Angus glens—or follow back roads beyond Alyth—for a full flavor of the openness in the silent, rounded hills of the Grampian edge. From the unexpected drama of the Reekie Linn waterfall near Kirriemuir, Scotland's mini-Niagara smoking its way over a high ledge, to the heights of Ben Lawers, Central

Central Scotland

ROMANTIC PROSPECTS

Though Sir Walter Scott is often said to have put the Trossachs on the tourist map, he was certainly not the first to discover them. As early as 1794, the Statistical Account of Scotland noted under the heading "Romantic Prospects" that "The Trossachs are often visited by persons of taste, who are desirous of seeing nature in her rudest and most unpolished state."

THE HEART OF SCOTLAND

Breadalbane is an ancient name for the heart of Scotland in central Perthshire. Crianlarich, Killin, and, farther east, Aberfeldy, with all the high hills around, are considered to be within it. The name is derived from two Gaelic words: *braghaid*, the upper part, and *Alban*, Scotland, hence Breadalbane means "the uplands of Alban," an appropriate enough name for this wild country.

VIEWING THE FAULT LINE

Perhaps the best vantage point for viewing the Highland Boundary Fault is from the top of Conic Hill behind Balmaha on the shores of Loch Lomond. The climb can be made along a bit of the West Highland Way. From the hilltop, the fault line runs out and through the main Loch Lomond islands to the west, while it disappears eastward toward Callander. The pink and pebbly conglomerate rock is characteristic of the geology of the edge of the Highlands.

Scotland's much trampled-upon highest mountain, scenic drama can be found in abundance.

Yet Central Scotland is not without a very attractive Lowland character. Northeast Fife, with its long beaches backed by finely trimmed golf courses, seems a long way both from the Highlands and from the legacy of the Industrial Revolution. This portion of Fife missed out on the effects of industry, so plain in other parts of the Lowlands. Instead, it kept its essentially rural character. Its European heritage from its early trading links with the Low Countries is seen today in architecture, especially on the coast. Thus St. Andrews and the East Neuk of Fife have very distinct personalities, being Scottish without being either tartan or grimy. Angus is almost wholly rural, though here the Grampian hills are always a backdrop, forming one side of Strathmore, the long rural corridor that leads northeastward from Perth up to the Mearns on the edge of the former county of Kincardineshire.

Central Scotland's industrial background includes linoleum at Kirkcaldy, Dunfermline's specialized damask ware, and also industries based on the city of Dundee, still

noted for its jam and its journalism. Brewing is still associated with Alloa in the former county of Clackmannan below the Ochil Hills. Perhaps the most interesting chunk of industrial heritage can be found at Culross overlooking the Forth, where a small Scottish burgh (town) seemed to be passed over by progress for more than two centuries until restoration.

Just as the shipyard workers of the industrial Glasgow of old would escape on weekends to the mountainous beauty of the Trossachs, and the mill workers of Dundee would go northwest to the long Angus glens, so it is still the hills and mountains that inevitably call to visitors today. To take in the essence of Central Scotland, find a high point near the Highland edge: Callander Crags behind Callander, the highest section of the Duke's Road in the Trossachs, Dumyat (pronounced "De-my-att") behind Stirling, the delectable Duncryne Hill on the southern edge of Loch Lomond, or the Caterthun hill forts on a Grampian shoulder in Angus. Northward, waves of hills roll on to the end of Scotland. Southward is all the grit and liveliness of the Lowland towns. That is the essence of Central Scotland.

Rural Perthshire

THE SIGNAL TOWER

The Bell Rock lighthouse by Robert Stevenson was built on the Inchcape Rock, a reef submerged at high tide, about 11 miles southeast of Arbroath. It was first lit in 1811 and was a magnificent achievement for its day. To facilitate rock-to-shore communication when the lighthouse was under construction, a signal tower was built, which was also the shore base for the light. This is today's Signal Tower Museum, where the story is told in full.

▶▶ Aberfeldy   130B2

The largest settlement in the area known as Breadalbane, Aberfeldy is a pleasantly peaceful place. It makes a good center for exploring the local walks and trails, notably along the Moness Burn (Creek) to view the **"Birks of Aberfeldy"** in the wooded den. These birch woods were made famous by Robert Burns, who penned the lyrics of the Scottish song of the same name. Aberfeldy itself has a water mill and a distillery to visit. **Castle Menzies** is nearby to the northwest on B846 (*Open* Apr–mid-Oct, Mon–Sat 10:30–5, Sun 2–5, last entry 4:30. *Admission charge*). This 16th-century fortified Z-plan tower is in the care of the Clan Menzies. To reach it by road means crossing the River Tay by the finest of General Wade's bridges (see panel). This handsome, five-arched, humpbacked structure was designed by the architect William Adam and built in 1733.

▶ Arbroath   131D2

A salty, seagull-strafed seacoast town, Arbroath in Angus gave its name to the Arbroath smokie—a smoked, split   haddock. Smokies can be bought from

Blair Castle

WADE'S BRIDGES

General Wade, the military road builder, built many fine bridges in Scotland, but none were so grand as his work at Aberfeldy. It was not to everyone's taste. Dorothy Wordsworth toured with her brother William in 1803 and, among many carping comments on things Scottish in her journal, she described how the party "crossed the Tay by a bridge of ambitious and ugly architecture. Many of the bridges in Scotland are so...."

several merchants in the narrow streets of the "fishing quarter." Arbroath mixes its fishing activities with the slightly time-warped air of a 1950s traditional Scottish vacation resort. There is fine coastline to explore north of the town, as well as the hinterland of Angus within easy reach. In the center of the town stand the red sandstone walls of the 12th-century **Arbroath Abbey▶**, (*Open* Apr–Sep, daily 9:30–6; Oct–Mar, Mon–Sat 9:30–4, Sun 2–4. *Admission charge*), scene of important events in Scotland's history (see panel, page 135). Other aspects of the town's history are portrayed in the curious **Signal Tower Museum▶**, close to the harbor. By way of a change from maritime themes, the museum has a display on one of Arbroath's specialist industries: the manufacture of lawn-mowers (*Open* May–Sep, Mon–Sat 10–5, also Sun 2–5 in Jul–Aug. *Admission free*). Contributing to the town's vacation atmosphere is **Kerr's Miniature Railway▶▶**. This ride-on track, running parallel to the high embankment of the adjacent main Edinburgh–Aberdeen railroad, has delighted generations, as photographs on the entrance kiosk reveal (*Open* Easter–Sep, Sat–Sun 2–5, also Mon–Fri 2–5 in Jul–mid-Aug. *Admission charge*).

▶ Balquhidder   130B2

The Braes (slopes) of Balquhidder and Balquhidder Glen, in which lie the long reaches of Loch Voil, are often missed by those rushing north on A84 from Callander. Once a place in which desperate men from broken clans chose to settle—though it was also the stronghold of the MacLarens and the Macgregors—the area around Balquhidder has glorious scenery that is worth exploring. Many people visit the **grave of Rob Roy** (see pages 136–137), in Balquhidder churchyard, something of an anticlimax, while others make their way to the end of the public road, in order to climb the choice of **Munros** (see panel, page 149 for definition) within easy reach. Another worthwhile walk is to hike up through the trees to the windy heights of Kirkton Glen (start by the church) where the little jewel of **Lochan nan Eireannaich** (Loch of the Irish) sits below the crags of an old hill pass to Glen Dochart. Listen for the ring ouzel (the mountain blackbird), which sings here in summer.

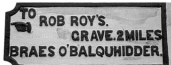

DECLARATION OF ARBROATH
In the Scots Wars of Independence, the country's leading churchmen were firmly nationalist. In 1320, they met in Arbroath Abbey to write the famous Declaration of Arbroath. Its most widely quoted passage is: "For so long as a hundred of us shall remain alive we shall never accept subjection to the domination of the English. For we fight not for glory, or riches or honour, but for freedom alone which no good man will consent to lose but with his life."

135

TOURIST INFORMATION
Aberfeldy: The Square (tel: 01887-820276). Arbroath: Market Place (tel: 01241-872609)

▶ Blair Atholl and Blair Castle   130B3

Blair Atholl is famed chiefly for **Blair Castle▶ ▶** whose white-painted turrets are conspicuous from A9. The old established settlement that grew up near the castle also has a mill and a folk museum to visit. Blair Castle itself (*Open* Apr–late Oct, daily 10–6, last entry 5. *Admission charge*), the ancestral seat of the earls, then the dukes of Atholl, dates from at least 1269. There are many stories associated with it, in particular its role in the 1745 Jacobite rebellion, and many rooms filled with possessions accumulated over centuries of occupation. It is the archetypal Scottish castle, though you may tire of hearing that the Duke of Atholl was the only person in Britain allowed to keep a private army.

THE FALLS OF BRUAR
North of Blair Castle, accessible from the old A9, these falls are within the extensive landholding of the Blair Charitable Trust. Robert Burns visited on his Highland tour and suggested that the Duke plant more trees to beautify the falls further. The idea was taken up and the falls today are noted for their mature larch trees.

Near Aberfeldy: fishing the River Tay, and Castle Menzies (detail)

Central Scotland

▶ **Blairgowrie**   *131C2*

A busy center with a good range of stores, Blairgowrie first prospered from the River Ericht as it powered its way out of the Highlands. Flax mills were built on its bank, and by the early 19th century the town was booming. A second wave of prosperity followed after raspberry-growing on a commercial scale was introduced. Today, the berry crop is still important, with the long rows of raspberry canes in the surrounding fields looking a little like vineyards.

The old Keathbank Mill▶▶ (on the north side of town off A93) has been converted into a visitor center. The waterwheel and machinery still turn to impress visitors with their awesome scale. Also on display is the largest model railroad in Britain—a complete "O-gauge" model of Norton Fitzwarren junction on the old Great Western Railway. There is a heraldry workshop, too, carving huge coats of arms. (*Open* Easter, May–Oct, daily 10–5. *Admission charge*).

En route to the town, A93 is bordered for 1,700 feet just beyond the River Isla by the 100-foot-high *Meikleour Beech Hedge*.

Keathbank Mill

▶▶ **Callander**   *130A2*

Right on the Highland edge, with Ben Ledi looming at the end of the main street, Callander seems busy throughout the year. The town's bustle is a reminder of its role as a gateway not just to the Highlands but specifically to the Trossachs. The old village of Callander was rebuilt and extended—an example of early town planning—after 1763, when the authorities took over the land of the Drummonds, the previous owners who forfeited them after the 1745 Jacobite rebellion. Callander soon took on its role of serving visitors, which it has had ever since. Escape from the tartan wares of the shopping street to discover picturesque **Bracklinn Falls**▶▶, signposted from

Walk

The Bracklinn Falls

Only minutes from Callander's busy main street lies an escape on the very edge of the Highlands. Allow one hour to the Falls, or three hours for the Callander Crags circuit.

The Bracklinn Falls are signed north (right if coming from Stirling) up a street near the Roman Camp Hotel sign. If traveling by car, drive up this road, soon entering attractive mixed woodland for a short way until the Falls parking lot is seen on the right.

Take the level path running east from the parking area. Soon the pines flanking the path end, revealing a pleasing green vista back across the Lowlands. Continue through a double kissing gate, with the falls sounding close at hand. Descend steps to a bridge over the white water. The path peters out on the far side, among the oak trees.

Retrace your steps. The energetic can walk uphill along the road from the parking lot, into open country with views north of an attractive glen. It is possible to circle back to Callander via the Callander Crags on the skyline, but you will need good walking shoes.

137

the east side of the town (see the walk above). Slightly more demanding (for pedestrians) are **Callander Crags►►**, overlooking a dense bowl of woodland immediately behind the town and threaded by sheltered paths. Waterfall and woodland can be combined in a single excursion by continuing farther up the signposted road into an attractive Highland glen.

Rob Roy and the Trossachs Visitor Centre►►, a modern tourist orientation center, interprets the life of Rob Roy Macgregor, Scotland's Robin Hood, by means of audiovisuals and fairly high-tech displays (including a talking cow). It also sets the folk hero firmly in the Trossachs landscapes (see page 160). (*Open* Jul–Aug, daily 9–7; Jun and Sep, daily 9:30–6; Mar–May and Oct–Dec, daily 10–5; Jan and Feb, weekends 10–4. *Admission charge*).

►► The Caterthuns *131D3*
These 2,000-year-old ramparts are Scotland's prehistory at its best. To stand in the center of a great ring of broken stone with only a curlew call for company is certainly atmospheric. It is well worth the effort of seeking out this breezy high place on the shoulders of the Grampians near Edzell in Angus, with superb views to the Lowlands. The builders of the White and the Brown Catherthun hill forts must have been capable of organizing manpower in plenty to quarry and build such defenses, impressive even in ruin.

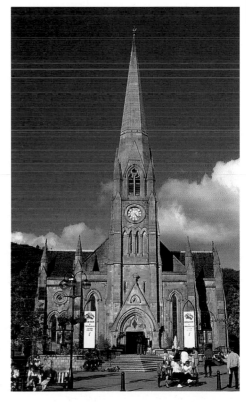

Callander's Rob Roy and the Trossachs Visitor Centre makes good use of a redundant church

Crieff's paperweights

EARLY INDUSTRY
Throughout the 17th century, Culross was the sole maker of baking girdles (griddles). It is said the local smiths invented them after Robert the Bruce ordered them to provide iron plates so that his soldiers could cook their oatcakes.

The Palace, Culross

▶▶ Crieff 130B2

A town on the edge of the Highlands, Crieff seems all hills. Until 1970 it was an important cattle market. It has also been a spa. Down by the River Earn is **The Crieff Visitor Centre▶** offering on-site manufacture and sale of glass paperweights and pottery (*Open* daily 9–5:30. Restricted winter hours. *Admission free;* factory tour charge). Opposite, **Stuart Crystal▶** glitters with Stuart, Waterford, and Wedgwood wares. Just down the road is the sunken Italian garden of **Drummond Castle▶**, with formal terracing ideal for strolling in summer (*Open* Easter, May–Oct, daily 2–6, last entry 5. *Admission charge*). North of the town the **Glenturret Distillery▶**, one of Scotland's oldest, offers a tour, audiovisual program, and shop (*Open* Mar–Dec, Mon–Sat 9:30–6, Sun 12–6; Jan–Feb, Mon–Fri 11:30–4, last tour 2:30. *Admission charge;* free in Jan).

▶▶▶ Culross 130B1

Because of its very early involvement in coal mining and salt pans, Culross ought to have been just another nondescript industrial community on the banks of the Forth. Instead, after the town's early economic prosperity, the Industrial Revolution bypassed the town for a variety of economic reasons, and it was all but forgotten. Thus Culross entered the 20th century with many 17th- and 18th-century domestic buildings intact. The streetscapes have been preserved, and the attractive dwellings with their red pantiled roofs restored. Cobbled streets and the old mercat (market) cross give the place the air of a movie set (which indeed it is on occasion), but this is a lived-in community. There are some interiors to see, notably the Culross **Palace** (really the town house) of Sir George Bruce, Culross's 16th-century entrepreneur. (*Open* palace Apr–Sep, daily 11–5 (last entry 4); study and town house Apr–Sep, daily 1:30–5; Oct, weekends 11–5. *Admission charge*).

▶ Cupar
131C2

Cupar is a handsome enough, typical Lowland Scottish town in the center of a rural and agricultural area, the Howe (hollow) of Fife. Cupar once made money with its linen manufacture and still maintains its role as the administrative headquarters of the old county of Fife. A network of pleasantly out-of-the-way rural roads includes a fine ridge route to Falkland (see page 145). It is also worth visiting **Hill of Tarvit House▶▶**, an Edwardian mansion, in the care of the National Trust of Scotland. (*Open* house Easter, May–Sep, daily 1:30–5:30; Oct, weekends only. Gardens Apr–Oct daily 9:30–9, Nov–Mar 9:30–4:30. *Admission charge*).

▶▶ Deep Sea World
131C1

In this fishy panorama of a visitor center in North Queensferry, a moving walkway carries you unnervingly along an underwater viewing tunnel as large sharks swim by—you feel like a fish in an aquarium. There are also coral reef displays, rock pools to fumble in, and a variety of other marine exhibits. (*Open* Apr–Jun and Sep–Oct, daily 10–6; Jul–Aug, daily 10–6:30; Nov–Mar, Mon–Fri 11–5, Sat–Sun 10–6. *Admission charge*).

139

Doune Motor Museum houses the world's second-oldest Rolls Royce

▶▶ Doune
130B1

Doune was once the Scottish center for manufacturing pistols. Today, this little place with winding streets is chiefly visited by those going to **Doune Castle▶▶▶**, the finest surviving medieval castle in Scotland (*Open* Apr–Sep, daily 9:30–6; Oct–Mar, Mon–Wed and Sat 9:30–4, Thu 9:30–12, Sun 2–4. *Admission charge*). The 14th-century fortress is built to a simple and strong plan: a formidable range of buildings surrounding an inner courtyard. Note the security features, such as a separate stairway for each main hallway and the duke's bedroom's emergency exit. In addition to allowing the main quarters to be sealed off if intruders gained entry to the courtyard, the design acknowledges the need for some comfort: the guest bedrooms are built directly above the kitchen with its 18-foot-wide fireplace.

Central Scotland

AN ANCIENT WALK
The Darn Road is an
ancient route (used by the
Romans) that links
Dunblane with Bridge of
Allan for foot traffic. It
makes a pleasant
afternoon's walk. On the
way, the path passes a
cave overlooking the Allan
Water, which is asso-
ciated with Robert Louis
Stevenson. He used to
vacation nearby as a boy.

*Though now surrounded
by the urban
development of Dundee,
Claypotts Castle is one of
the most complete exam-
ples of a 16th-century
Z-plan tower house*

▶ Dumbarton 130A1

This town on the Clyde estuary is associated with shipbuilding, but is worth visiting for two very different
features. The first of these, **Dumbarton Castle▶**, is built
on the natural defensive site of Dumbarton Rock, a volcanic plug (*Open* Apr–Sep, daily 9:30–6; Oct–Mar,
Mon–Wed and Sat 9:30–4, Thu 9:30–12, Sun 2–4.
Admission charge). Though little remains from its early
pre-Viking defensive days, the fortress is associated with
Mary, Queen of Scots. She was held there in safety before
her departure for France at the age of five. The **Denny Ship
Model Experiment Tank▶▶** was the world's first commercial experimental tank for shipbuilders' scale models,
built in 1882 by the local firm of William Denny. The hulls
of many famous vessels were designed and tested here,
including P & O's *Canberra*. (*Open* Mon–Sat 10–4.
Admission charge).

▶ Dunblane 130B1

The little city of Dunblane on the Allan Water has winding streets and little shops and, thanks to a bypass, it is a
peaceful kind of place, especially around the
cathedral▶▶. The seat of the bishop of the Diocese of
Dunblane since the 13th century, this place of worship is
the usual Scottish mix of very early architecture and more
recent restoration work. (The nave was roofless for 300
years until 1893.) It demands a slow walk around to
examine the 15th-century misericords, early effigies, and
other points of interest (*Open* Apr–Sep, daily 9:30–6;
Oct–Mar, Mon–Sat 9:30–4, Sun 2–4 and for services.
Admission free). The 14th-century **Doune Castle** (see page
139) is a few minutes to the west.

Dundee 131C2

Dundee sits on slopes facing south over the estuary of the
River Tay, which is spanned by road and rail bridges. Its
center is an uneasy mix of Victorian edifices, slashed by
new roads and partly overshadowed by a covered shopping mall. Scotland's fourth city promotes itself under the
banner "City of Discovery," yet it is not a natural visitor

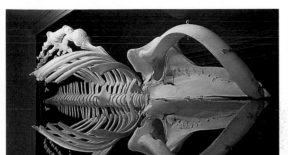

THE DOGGEREL POET
William McGonagall (1830–1902), the Scottish doggerel poet, is strongly associated with Dundee. His uniformly bad verse soon met with acclaim, notably from the student and legal fraternity. His eulogies to the Tay Bridge and the stranding of the great Tay whale are just two occasions when his special talents (a complete disregard for meter in particular) were brought to bear.

magnet. The "Discovery" part of its slogan is a reference to RRS (Royal Research Ship) **Discovery**▶ ▶, berthed permanently at the Discovery Point floating exhibition (*Open* Apr–Oct, Mon–Sat 10–5, Sun 11–5; Nov–Mar, Mon–Sat 10–4, Sun 11–4. *Admission charge*). This was the vessel used by Captain Scott (of Antarctic fame) and built in Dundee in 1901 because of that city's expertise in building whaling vessels. The nearby frigate **Unicorn** is the oldest British warship still afloat. (She was built in Chatham, England in 1824.) Then there are Dundee's museums to investigate: the **Barrack Street Museum**▶ (*Open* Mon 11–5, Tue–Sat 10–5. *Admission free*) with its natural history collection including the famous Tay Whale eulogized by the notorious William McGonagall, and the **McManus Galleries**▶ (*Open* Mon 11–5, Tue–Sat 10–5. *Admission free*), the city's municipal museum and art gallery focusing on local history. A newer attraction is the **Verdant Works**▶ ▶, which brings the story of jute to life in a former jute mill (*Open* Apr Oct, Mon Sat 10–5, Sun 11–5; Nov–Mar, Mon–Sat 10–4, Sun 11–4. *Admission charge*).

Within the endless coastal suburbia that ends at the golf courses at Carnoustie is **Broughty Castle Museum**▶ (*Open* Mon 11–1, 2–5, Tue–Thu and Sat 10–1, 2–5, Jul–Sep only Sun 2–5 *Admission free*), with more tales to tell about whales and other local historical matters. Then there are the **Mills Observatory** (*Open* daily except Sun), opened in 1935, a candy factory in the style of the 1940s, also open to visitors, and country parks in the attractive Angus hinterlands.

Andrew Carnegie in Pittencrieff Park

INDUSTRIAL ESPIONAGE
Dunfermline was already engaged in spinning when, in the early 18th century, Huguenot master weavers set up in Edinburgh using a secret process to make attractive patterns on plain linen cloth. The new damask was a huge success. Dunfermline weaver James Blake got himself a job cleaning the Huguenot looms, memorized the process, then built his own loom. Thus began Dunfermline's damask linen industry.

Dunkeld "Little Houses" (private)

▶ **Dunfermline** *131C1*

"What Benares is to the Hindu, Mecca to the Mohammedan, Jerusalem to the Christian, all that Dunfermline is to me." Thus eulogized Dunfermline's most famous son, Andrew Carnegie. The Dunfermline of today is still full of Carnegie associations—it even has a Carnegie Hall—but this "auld grey toun" above the Forth goes much further back. It was the capital of Scotland in the time of the 11th-century king, Malcolm Canmore (the Gaelic *ceann mohr* means great head or chief). This Celtic warlord married Margaret of the English royal house after she was shipwrecked nearby while fleeing the Norman Conquest in 1070. Margaret was later canonized and under her good influence, Dunfermline became the religious center of Scotland.

Dunfermline Abbey▶, with its adjoining monastery and the royal palace, still survive, though they have been rebuilt over the centuries. Today, there is a strong sense of layers of history around the historic heart of the town, though sorting them out takes time. There are plenty of explanatory panels and models within the palace complex to clarify matters. (*Open* Apr–Sep, daily 9:30–6; Oct–Mar, Mon–Wed and Sat 9:30–4, Thu 9:30–12, Sun 2–4. *Admission charge*). The 12th-century work in the abbey church may be the finest surviving Scottish-Norman architecture in Scotland. King Robert the Bruce is buried here: his name is written on great stone blocks on the church tower.

Andrew Carnegie Birthplace Museum▶▶ Dunfermline soon turned to commercial matters: brewing and weaving. Andrew Carnegie (1835–1919) was the son of a weaver who emigrated to the United States in 1848. In due course, Carnegie's business acumen in the steel industry made him rich enough to give away $350 million. Exactly how is told in this museum, which starts off modestly enough in the cottage of his birth. The adjacent Memorial Hall is filled with an extraordinary assemblage of Carnegie memorabilia, including a whole display case filled with "freedom caskets"—the ornate boxes in which grateful communities gave him the metaphorical keys to their towns and cities. (*Open* Apr–May and Sep–Oct, Mon–Sat 11–5, Sun 2–5; Jun–Aug, Mon–Sat 10–5, Sun 2–5; Nov–Mar, daily 2–4. *Admission charge*).

Dunfermline's Carnegie Library was the first of nearly 3,000 worldwide. This and other amenities, including the local museum, the Music Institute, the Carnegie Center (complete with ornate Turkish baths), and the substantial Pittencrieff Park all indicate the generosity of this extraordinary "local boy made good" who transformed his hometown from a gray workaday place into a well-resourced community. Dunfermline may not be the most picturesque of Scotland's towns, but it has an interesting story to tell.

► Dunkeld   131C2

A classic Highland-edge community, Dunkeld has benefited environmentally (if not commercially) from the A9 bypass. In addition to shopping (including antiques) and the picturesque 18th-century "Little Houses," it also has Thomas Telford's handsome bridge, opened in 1809. This was a toll bridge, and the imposition of the toll caused riots in 1868. Downstream by a footpath is the Birnam oak, last

relic of Birnam Wood ("Macbeth shall never vanquished be until/Great Birnam wood to high Dunsinane hill/Shall come against him," prophesy the witches in Shakespeare's *Macbeth*). Dunkeld also has a cathedral, founded in the 12th century and wrecked at the Reformation. Its choir has been restored as the parish church. Walk up the wooded valley of the River Braan (on the opposite side of A9 to Dunkeld) to **the Hermitage►►**, the pleasure grounds of the dukes of Atholl. On the way, what might be the tallest tree in Scotland can be seen, a 200-foot-high Douglas fir. It grows in a hollow by the river at the foot of a slope. The Hermitage is open at all times.

    Loch of the Lowes►► Accessible off a minor road on A923 above Dunkeld, this Scottish Wildlife Trust reserve is a gem of Highland-edge scenery and has ospreys in summer. The visitor center is open in summer only (Apr–Sep, daily 10–5), but the observation blind is open all year.

Carnegie's initials on Pittencrieff Park gates, Dunfermline

LITERARY INSPIRATION

It was while vacationing in the Dunkeld area in 1893 and studying fungi that Beatrix Potter wrote an illustrated letter about a naughty and adventurous bunny to a young friend. The bunny became the famous Peter Rabbit, and an expert local amateur naturalist, Charles Mackintosh, the retired postman, is suspected of being the prototype for Mr. McGregor the gardener.

143

Dunkeld Cathedral and "Little Houses"

THE HERMITAGE FOLLY

Also known as Ossian's Hall, this was built in 1758 by the 2nd Duke of Atholl's nephew. The curious belvedere overlooks the roaring waters of the River Braan. By 1783, it had acquired a set of mirrors within: a pulley slid back a partition (a painting of Ossian) to reveal them and give the illusion of water pouring in from all directions. This aristocratic toy was not to everyone's taste. William Wordsworth visited and was appalled, and the place was vandalized in 1821 and again in 1869. The restored shell survives to this day.

Maintaining the fishing fleet, Pittenweem

▶▶▶ East Neuk of Fife 131D1

The chief attraction of the East Neuk of Fife, a land of well-manicured golf courses, lush hedgerows, and rich barley fields and woods all set by a glittering sea, is its little string of coastal communities. The area can easily be reached from Edinburgh, and it makes a very worthwhile day's excursion from St. Andrews (see page 154).

The eastern tip of Fife, Fife Ness, is not one of Scotland's most dramatic headlands, though bird-watchers enjoy it at migration time. However, nearby **Crail▶**, easternmost of the villages, is a pretty place with one of the most frequently photographed harbors in Scotland (wait for high tide). Old trading links with the Low Countries are echoed in the architecture, with crow-stepped gables and a Dutch-style town house whose bell, cast in 1520, has a Dutch inscription. There is also a good local museum.

Moving west, next comes **Anstruther▶**, with its seafront stores selling colorful fishing nets and beach balls as a reminder of the traditional vacation trade. The **Scottish Fisheries Museum▶▶▶** (*Open* Apr–Oct, Mon–Sat 10–5:30, Sun 11–5; Nov–Mar, Mon–Sat 10– 4:30, Sun 2–4:30. *Admission charge*) overlooks the harbor, with a comprehensive presentation on the development of fishing in Scotland, from open boats right through to the most awesome modern catching machines. There are plenty of ship models, as well as the real thing (historic vessels float in the harbor). Children should enjoy the marine aquariums and tableaux full of authentic details, right down to the smell of tarry rope. This museum gives a very strong sense of the endless struggle, frequent tragedy, and foundations of prosperity of many east coast communities.

Pittenweem▶▶ also offers plenty of challenge to the photographer torn between bright-hulled fishing boats and red-pantiled houses. Up a lane near the harbor, the cave-shrine of St. Fillan can be found. The damp abode of an ancient saint is referred to in the name Pittenweem ("place of the cave").

Continuing west, you reach **St. Monance**, another community tied to the sea—its kirk could not stand any closer to the waves. In between these communities is a varied coastline of sand and rock.

Kellie Castle▶▶ is a short way inland. This National Trust for Scotland property dates mainly from the 16th and 17th centuries and was restored in Victorian times. Its walled garden is a peaceful scented haven in high summer and is worked organically (*Open* castle Easter May–Sep, daily 1:30–5:30; Oct, weekends only, last entry 4:45; grounds daily 9:30–sunset. *Admission charge*).

The East Neuk's heritage is firmly bound up with the sea

TOURIST INFORMATION
Anstruther: Scottish
Fisheries Museum (tel:
01333-311073).
Crail: 62–64 Marketgate
(tel: 01333-450869).
Dunfermline: 13/15
Maygate (tel: 01383-
720999).
Dunkeld: The Cross
(tel: 01350-727688

► Edzell 131D3

Edzell slumbers happily behind its ornate arch commemorating Queen Victoria's visit, and is one of those out-of-the-way places where little ever seems to stir along the wide main street. However, there are a number of points of interest nearby. **Fasque House►**, home of the family of the 19th-century prime minister W.E. Gladstone, is within easy reach (see page 176), as are the **Caterthuns** (see page 137). **Edzell Castle►►** is also worth exploring, and is sign-posted from Edzell along a minor road. The early 16th-century red-stoned tower was a former Lindsay strong-hold and features an unusual pleasance, or walled garden, with unique heraldic and symbolic sculptures. (*Open* Apr–Sep, daily 9:30–6; Oct–Mar, Mon–Wed and Sat 9:30–4, Thu 9:30–12, Sun 2–4. *Admission charge*).

SCOTS NAMES
Howe in "Howe of Fife" means hollow. *Neuk*, as in East Neuk, is the Scots for corner (hence nook).

AN EDUCATIONAL VISIT
Visit the Scottish Fisheries Museum and learn the difference between fifies, zulus, and scaffies (they are all different kinds of early fishing craft).

145

►► Falkland Palace 131C1

Open: Apr–Oct, Mon–Sat 11–4:30, Sun 1:30–4:30. Admission charge
The façade of this Renaissance-style former hunting lodge (1501–1541) dominates the village of Falkland, tucked below the Lomond Hills. Behind the castle are small but attractive gardens and a real (royal) tennis court dating from 1539, said to be the oldest in Britain.

Pittenweem, one of the most picturesque of Fife's many coastal villages

► Fife Folk Museum 131C2

Open: Easter, mid-May–Oct, Sat–Thu 2–5. Admission charge
Set in Ceres, the very essence of a rural northeast Fife village, this collection of artifacts showing Fife's rural past is housed in a 17th century weigh house and adjoining former weavers' cottages. In the village watch for "The Provost," a curious "toby-jug" carving, set in a niche in a gable wall by the crossroads.

A simple plaque over a cottage door in Crail, Fife

The devil on this Helensburgh dormer stares directly at a church opposite

▶ Glamis Castle and Angus Folk Museum *131C2*

Glamis (pronounced "Glahms") is an ancient castle site. Its present appearance dates from the 17th century, but the main tower is in part much older. It has fine collections of china, tapestry, painting, and furniture (*Open* Apr–Oct, daily 10:30–5:30, from 10 AM Jul–Aug, last tour 4:45. *Admission charge*). Illustrating life at the other end of the social scale is the **Angus Folk Museum▶**, a National Trust for Scotland property (*Open* Easter, May–Sep, daily 11–5; Oct, weekends only, last entry 4:30. *Admission charge*). A row of 19th-century cottages has been converted into a continuous passage with rooms, tableaux, and display cases covering everyday rural life (suitably sanitized).

▶ Helensburgh *130A1*

Sir James Colquhoun, eighth baronet of Colquhoun and Luss, had plans for the little *clachan* (the Gaelic for "village") near his castle, since it was the fashion of the Georgian age to improve. He bought the land and advertised for weavers but failed to attract any. Then he went upscale, promoting the new town of Helensburgh (named after his wife) as a residential place. This plan worked, thanks in part to the later improved communications by rail and sea. Ever since, Helensburgh has retained its properous character, its wide streets and grand properties (built by well-to-do Glasgow commuters), earning it a reputation as a "museum of villas."

Hill House▶▶ (*Open* Apr–Oct, daily 1:30–5:30, last entry 5. *Admission charge*). Finest of all the villas is Charles Rennie Mackintosh's masterpiece, now in the care of the National Trust for Scotland. His design was so comprehensive that he even included details for light fixtures, carpet patterns, and window snibs (Scots for "catches"). It was built in 1904 as the family home of the wealthy Glasgow publisher Walter Blackie.

▶ Hillfoots Towns *130B1*

The Hillfoots towns of Menstrie, Alva, Tillicoultry, and Dollar are strung out below the steep scarp face of the Ochil Hills east of Stirling. They formed the second-largest textile manufacturing area in Scotland, using the streams running steeply off the Ochils to power the mills, and the high, green, open pastures on the heights to raise the sheep whose wool was processed. Most (but not all) of the manufacturing has gone now, leaving impressive mill architecture at places such as Alva. The hill country above the towns is quite unspoiled and offers a good selection of walks into the Ochils, notably from the **Ochil Hills Woodland Park** between Alva and Tillicoultry.

Dollar▶▶, to the east, is the most attractive of the towns, while Blairlogie, to the west, is a pleasant village. (The others are rather dour, their attraction lying in the countryside of the Ochils above them.) Behind Dollar, on a high shoulder

Castle Campbell above Dollar

TOURIST INFORMATION
Alva: Mill Trail Visitor Center, West Stirling Street (tel: 01259-769696).
Kirkcaldy: 19 Whytes-causeway (tel: 01592-267775)

BEN CLEUGH
The highest point in the Ochil Hills is Ben Cleuch (2,362 feet). If the clouds are high its summit offers superb views of the hills of the Central Highlands. But do not underestimate these exposed broad slopes, especially in winter: use proper footwear and walking equipment. The Ben Cleuch path starts from Tillicoultry or Alva.

ADAM SMITH
The Adam Smith Centre, Kirkcaldy's civic center and theater (built in 1889 and refurbished in 1973), is named for the economist, who was born in the town in 1723. A plaque near Kirk Wynd marks the site where he wrote his influential treatise *An Inquiry into the Nature and Causes of the Wealth of Nations*.

Typical Wemyss ware cats

above a darkly wooded glen, is **Castle Campbell**▶▶▶ (*Open* Apr–Sep, daily 9:30–6; Oct–Mar, Mon–Wed and Sat 9:30–4, Thu 9:30–12, Sun 2–4. *Admission charge*). This impressive stronghold is accessible by car or by a very picturesque (and quite dramatic) walk, at one stage through a narrow gorge. The fortress was owned by the first Earl of Argyll, Chancellor of Scotland to King James IV, and comprises a basic 15th-century tower house with later additions, including a notable loggia—an arcade with arches. Rearing above the trees at the head of the valley, it is impressively situated and well worth a visit—especially on a clear day, for the views from the ramparts. It could be tied in with a trip to Culross, an easy distance away.

▶ Kirkcaldy   131C1

Kirkcaldy (pronounced "Kir-coddy") may not be the most scenic of Scottish towns, but it has good amenities, including a fine park and a theater. Visit its art gallery and museum, both for a fine collection of Scottish artists (notably Peploe) and its displays of local Wemyss ware pottery (*Open* Mon–Sat 10:30–5, Sun 2–5. *Admission free*). Nearby **Ravenscraig Castle** is an austere ruined fortress overlooking the Firth, founded by King James II in 1460 and later owned by the Sinclair earls of Orkney. Also close at hand is the picturesque **Dysart**, with attractively restored properties around a tiny harbor.

One of Scotland's most famous stretches of inland water is the result of a glacier dumping its gouged-out gravels, thus creating a dam at the southern end of the deep trench it had dug. This took place 10,000 years ago, leaving Loch Lomond 26 feet above sea level, in contrast to the long narrow sea loch of Loch Long immediately to the west.

THE BANKS OF LOCH LOMOND

By yon bonnie banks and
    by yon bonnie braes,
Where the sun shines
    bright on Loch Lomond
Where me and my true
    love were ever wont to
    gae
On the bonnie bonnie
    banks o Loch Lomond.

Chorus
Ye'll tak the high road and
    I'll tak the low road
And I'll be in Scotland
    afore ye
But me and my true love
    will never meet again
On the bonnie, bonnie
    banks o Loch Lomond

MUSICAL CONNECTIONS

The song "The Banks of Loch Lomond" is thought to have been written by a condemned Jacobite prisoner while in jail in Carlisle, England, after the 1745 rebellion. His lines about "yon bonnie banks" have gone round the world, though the unknown lyricist is not the only one to make reference to the loch. Alan Jay Lerner's 1947 hit "Almost Like Being in Love" has the lines:
"Maybe the sun gave me the pow'r,
But I could swim Loch Lomond and be home in half an hour.
Maybe the air gave me the drive
For I'm all aglow and alive."

Accessibility Loch Lomond is Scotland's largest loch in surface area. Famed in song, it has exerted its pull on visitors since the late 18th century. The "bonnie banks" are indisputably bonnie—but probably no more so than those of many a Highland loch lying farther north. Loch Lomond's attraction really lies in its accessibility, a characteristic it shares with the Trossachs.

Its Lowland southern end is only half an hour (sometimes less) from central Glasgow by road. This makes it commuter and also weekend-cottage country, as a stroll around neat little Drymen, with its exclusive shops, will confirm. The nearest point of the loch to Glasgow is at Balloch, at the head of the surprisingly industrialized Vale of Leven. Though Balloch is hardly

picturesque, **Balloch Castle Country Park** (open all year) has a visitor center at the castle (which is also the ranger service headquarters).

To grasp how this loch was made, climb little **Duncryne Hill** south of Gartocharn, for a sublime view of the receding loch, narrowing northward and squeezed by the hard shoulders of Highland hills. The Highland Boundary Fault with its tough rocks confined the land-shaping glacier. When it reached the soft rocks of the Lowland edge, it widened out, just as Loch Lomond's waters do today.

The eastern side Take B837 (no through road) up the eastern bank of the loch. **Balmaha**, with humpy Conic Hill behind it marking the geological line where the Highlands begin, is the stepping-off point for boat excursions around

Loch Lomond's islands. These come in various shapes and sizes, though **Inchcailloch** (Scottish Natural Heritage), with its ruined 13th-century chapel and fine woodlands, is particularly outstanding. Cruises land there from Balmaha.

Rowardennan is the end of the road for car explorers, though it is pleasant to continue eastward on foot up the track that forms part of the **West Highland Way**. This officially signposted 98-mile long-distance footpath from Milngavie, by Glasgow, to Fort William drops to the lochside at Balmaha for its journey northward. The parking lot at Rowardennan is also the favored starting-off point for the climb up Ben Lomond, Scotland's most southerly (and probably most popular) "Munro" (see panel).

Tourists in cars can also sneak up on the loch via Aberfoyle to reach Inversnaid, where the road drops steeply out of the "hanging valley" of **Glen Arklet** and down to the water. This scantily populated place with its ferny banks and waterfalls is recalled in a poem by Gerard Manley Hopkins. The northern tip of Loch Lomond tails away in the marshy fields at the end of Glen Falloch.

The western side The main A82 road takes the west side of the loch, slicing away at the bonnie banks with road improvements in order to carry the tourists north at ever higher speeds. Thus many visitors miss tiny Inveruglas, from where a private road (walkers only) leads to **Loch Sloy**, the old homelands of the Clan MacFarlane, tucked behind the high hills known as the Arrochar Alps. Farther south is **Tarbet**, its name meaning a place of portage: the Vikings once carried their longships from the head of Loch Long and pillaged Loch Lomond's settlements. Also on A82 is **Luss**, its pretty cottages part of the planned estate village originally built by the Colquhouns.

MUNROS
A Munro is a mountain in Scotland over 3,000 feet high. Munro-bagging is a popular sport north of the border. The name recalls the first compiler of Scotland's heights, Sir Hugh Munro, who published a list of 277 peaks in 1891. The actual number of Munros in Scotland changes sometimes as surveys add or eliminate certain peaks. In addition, there can be problems of definition of what qualifies as a discrete mountain. For example, when does a subsidiary top of a Munro become a separate Munro? However, the current agreed figure is 284.

149

LUSS
The village name Luss is explained by a charming legend concerning the death of a local girl married to a high-ranking French officer during the 14th-century Anglo-French wars. She died in France but was buried by Loch Lomond. Fleurs-de-lis (a species of iris and a heraldic device of the Bourbons) were scattered on her grave and, it is said, grew there ever afterward. Though the story is romantic, it is equally likely that Luss is from the Gaelic word lios, meaning "garden."

THE STONE OF SCONE

The Stone of Scone, or Stone of Destiny, was the traditional coronation throne of the Scottish monarchs until it was stolen by King Edward I of England in 1297 (and only returned to Scotland in 1996). Controversy still surrounds this stone. Some Scots believe it is a fake, and that the real Stone of Destiny was hidden before Edward's arrival and briefly found again in the early 19th century, though it subsequently vanished. Whatever the truth, the Stone of Scone remains a powerful nationalist symbol in Scotland. It can be seen in Edinburgh Castle.

TOURIST INFORMATION

Montrose (Apr–Sep): Bridge Street (tel: 01674-672000).
Perth: 45 High Street (tel: 01738-638353).

Scone Palace, one of the very grandest of Scotland's stately piles, is largely an early 19th-century design

▶ Montrose 131D2

A typical east coast Lowland town, Montrose looks both to land and sea, with a maritime past, an involvement in North Sea oil, and one of Angus's main livestock markets. It is also something of a resort, with long beaches and a choice of old-established golf courses. Bird-watchers flock to the basin of the River Esk, which hems in the town to the west, as this Scottish Wildlife Trust reserve is an important and decidedly muddy habitat for waders and wildfowl.

Coastal scenery is impressive, with further natural history interest at **St. Cyrus** (Scottish Natural Heritage) to the north. A visitor center here interprets the formerly important local activity of salmon netting, as well as the nearby bird and plant life. Close by to the south are the long sands of **Lunan Bay**, guarded by the ruined Red Castle above the dunes—an idyllic spot for beach strollers.

The House of Dun▶▶▶ (*Open* Easter, May–Sep, daily 1:30–5:30; Oct, weekends only. Grounds daily 9:30–sunset. *Admission charge*). Close to the town, this National Trust for Scotland property was originally built in 1730 to a William Adam design, and has seen extensive restoration work, especially to its spectacular plasterwork. In a courtyard building, Angus weavers create real linen napery (table linen) on traditional hand looms—a rare survivor of an industry once widespread in the area.

▶▶ Perth 131C2

Though known as a site still prone to flooding, Perth's strategic position as a major Lowland town with easy access to the Highlands has always given it an important role. It was the cradle of the Reformation in Scotland, after John Knox's preaching sparked off a riot in the town—and it also had bleaching and dyeing industries because of the softness and power of the River Tay's waters.

Rebuilding and renewal mean that very little is left of the ancient town. Instead, there is a grid of handsome streets completed by the early 19th century. They

Branklyn Garden, Perth

151

obliterated much of the earlier medieval plan, but include
neo-classical buildings such as Perth Academy (1807), the
County Buildings (1815–1819)—Perth is the county town—
and the unique waterworks (1832), now a picture gallery.
Meanwhile, amid these stately civic surroundings, Perth
gets on with its role as a center for a mainly rural, well-off
hinterland. It has a wide range of specialist shops for
antiques, crafts, jewelry, outdoor and sports equipment, a
museum, an art gallery (George Street. *Open* Mon–Sat 10–5.
Admission free), and a thriving repertory theater. The
Regimental Museum of the Black Watch at Balhousie
Castle on the North inch tells the story of the Highland regiment, founded in 1740. (*Open* May–Sep, Mon–Sat 10–4:30;
Oct–Apr, Mon–Fri 10–3:30. *Admission free*).

On the edge of town, the small scale **Branklyn
Garden►►►** has outstanding late spring color from
azaleas, blue poppies, and other horticultural treasures
(*Open* Easter–Oct, daily 9:30–sunset *Admission charge*).
Fairways Heavy Horse Center is another popular
excursion only a few minutes farther on the Dundee road.
This center has working Clydesdales, with dray rides,
vintage horse implements, and video shows (*Open* daily
10–5. *Admission charge*).

Off the Blairgowrie Road, **Scone Palace►►** is one of
Scotland's grandest stately homes (*Open* Easter–Oct, daily
9:30–5:15, last entry 4:45. *Admission charge*). Scone
(pronounced "skoon") was the traditional crowning place
of Scottish monarchs. The
site was actually the Moot
Hill, within the palace
grounds. Scone Palace as
seen today dates mainly
from the early years of
the 19th century. It has
splendid collections
of porcelain, furni-
ture, 18th-century
clocks, and 16th-
century needlework
as well as fine gardens.

*Shopping for antiques,
Perth*

Gates at Scone Palace

Clan skirmish re-enactment by Loch Achray, Trossachs

TOURIST INFORMATION
Pitlochry: 22 Atholl Road
(tel: 01796-472215).

THE SOLDIER'S LEAP
The Battle of Killiecrankie in 1689 was the first attempt by the Jacobites to restore the exiled king, James VII. They won after the government forces were unable to resist the wild charge of the Highland clans. However, in his victory, the Jacobite leader, John Graham of Claverhouse, Viscount Dundee, was killed by a stray bullet. Without "Bonnie Dundee's" charismatic leadership, the rebellion fizzled out. Also in this battle, a certain Donald MacBean, a government soldier, leapt 20 feet across the River Garry to avoid being impaled on a Highland claymore sword. The spot is known as the Soldier's Leap.

▶▶ Pitlochry   130B2

Pitlochry claims to be the geographical center of Scotland. Its situation among the Perthshire hills was noted by Queen Victoria's personal physician when she stayed along the road at Blair Castle. His recommendations on the wholesome air led to many of the well-to-do subsequently building large mansions in this previously quiet weaving village. The Perth-to-Inverness railroad's arrival in 1863 accelerated the growth of the fledgling resort. New hotels were built, including the Pitlochry Hydropathic, and Pitlochry developed a popularity it has retained ever since. Statistics suggest that the population of 2,500 offers 6,700 beds and plays host to nearly a million visitors a year.

Not as dull as it sounds, the **Hydro-Electric Visitor Centre** (*Open* Apr–Oct, daily 10–5:30), overlooking Loch Faskally, only moments from the main street, has a fish ladder—a stepped series of pools enabling fish to get upriver—and an explanation of the complex Tummel Valley hydroelectric project. You can see the fish jumping or swimming past the viewing chamber—if you are lucky. Another highlight of the town is the Pitlochry Festival Theatre, which features popular productions right through the main season.

Killiecrankie ▶▶▶ is a dramatic battle site set amid a very scenic river gorge with woodlands and steep rocks. The National Trust for Scotland visitor center tells the story of both the battle and the gorge itself, where there are superb walks among the tall pines and larches planted by the dukes of Atholl. Combine a trip here with the Queen's View of Loch Tummel, to the west. (*Open* site all year; visitor center Apr–Oct, daily 10–5:30. *Admission charge*).

▶▶ Queen Elizabeth Forest Park   130A1

The poorly drained, infertile uplands of Scotland have defeated many a landowner. After World War I, many of these unprofitable areas, for example, around the Trossachs and Loch Lomond, were bought by the state for forestry. In 1953, the 65 square miles (approximately) owned by the Forestry Commission in some of the most attractive landscapes of the Central Highlands became the Queen Elizabeth Forest Park. At least 60 miles of forest roads are open to foot traffic. The starting point is the

Queen Elizabeth Forest Park Visitor Centre above Aberfoyle, with its magnificent views back to the Lowlands. In addition to a profusion of well-marked trails for walkers, right across the area, there is a forest drive by Loch Achray for those who cannot bear to leave their cars, as well as bicycle routes. The amenity value of the forests around Loch Lomond and the Trossachs is heavily emphasized, and even though this is Scotland's best-known tourist area, it is perfectly possible to escape from people.

▶ **Rumbling Bridge** 130B2

Rumbling Bridge is a geological curiosity. The phenomenon that brought generations of tourists was the sinister rumbling of boulders grinding in a deep pot called the Devil's Mill, in a gorge that the River Devon has cut into the soft rock of the Lowland edge. The place even had its own train station (though the railroad has long vanished), and excursionists would picnic by the steep and ferny banks and wander the narrow footpaths and viewing points. They also admired the quaint little bridge of 1713, which spans the gorge and is spanned in turn by a later, higher bridge of 1816, which carries today's A823. These days, there are fewer visitors, as the Rumbling Bridge gorge lies in a kind of tourist no-man's land, bypassed by travelers rushing up M90 for Perth or M9 for Stirling, but it is a curious spot and makes a pleasant extension to, say, an excursion to Castle Campbell or the Hilltoots towns.

Loch Faskally, near Pitlochry, is part of the complex of lochs used for the generation of hydro-electric power

153

Loch Venachar is the most easterly of the Trossachs lochs, and supplies "compensation water" to the River Forth, replacing the water taken from Loch Katrine to quench Glasgow's thirst

TREE TYPES
The dominant tree species in the Queen Elizabeth Forest Park, in common with most other commercial forests in Scotland, are the alien sitka and Norway spruce, with some Scots and lodgepole pines in the drier areas. There are also some oak and beech plantings, supplementing the seminatural oakwoods (whose bark was once harvested for tannin) as well as birch scrub—a reminder of the natural regeneration that would take place if there were fewer sheep and deer.

Not only is St. Andrews famed as the home of golf and of Scotland's oldest university, but it is also a decidedly handsome east coast town. This is the view from the top of St. Rules Tower, near the ruined cathedral

TOURIST INFORMATION
St. Andrews: 70 Market Street (tel: 01334-472021).

SCOTLAND'S LARGEST CHURCH
Some say that the design of St. Andrews Cathedral was in advance of the building technology of its age. It was by far the largest church in Scotland and one of the longest ever built anywhere in the U.K., with a length of about 350 feet.

A BEACH WALK
For a change from the town, take a stroll along the beach at Tentsmuir, north of Leuchars near St. Andrews, where the pinewood-backed sandy beach goes on forever. En route, admire the fine Norman architecture of the parish church at Leuchars. Craigtoun Country Park, also near the town, is great for children.

▶▶▶ **St. Andrews** *131D2*

St. Andrews is unique: an ancient ecclesiastical capital, the oldest Scottish university town, and a world golfing mecca. According to legend, a Greek monk, Regulus (or Rule), carrying relics of St. Andrew, one of Christ's disciples, was shipwrecked here and founded a church. Thereafter the cult of St. Andrew was focused on this part of Fife. The monk's name survives as St. Rule's Church (or tower), still standing near the ruined cathedral and probably from the early 12th century. Its topmost point makes a good place to view the town's medieval street plan.

Founded in 1160, **St. Andrews Cathedral▶** is today a mere ruined fragment of what must once have been awesome architecture. It was damaged by natural disasters and then laid low by the Reformers. The cathedral's stonework was ultimately pillaged for use elsewhere in the town. Its on-site museum (*Open* daily) is well worth a visit for the glimpses of vanished magnificence. The ruins are open any time.

Teetering on the sea's brink, **St. Andrews Castle▶▶** tells a tale of drama and religious conflict, and boasts an impressive bottle dungeon. A claustrophobic underground experience can be had following the route of sappers as they counter-mined during an attempt to tunnel under the castle during a 16th-century siege. The tunnel is electrically lit now. (*Open* Apr–Sep, daily 9:30–6; Oct–Mar, Mon–Sat 9:30–4, Sun 2–4. *Admission charge*).

There are other local museums and the **Sea Life Centre** (*Open* daily 10–5; Jul–Aug 10–7. *Admission charge*) to visit, plus a golfing museum and excellent long beaches on either side of the town. Visitors can stroll around the many college precincts of Scotland's oldest university (founded in 1411), before sampling some of the finest shopping of any provincial town in Scotland. (The combination of university, visitors, and a prosperous farming hinterland ensures that high-quality wares are for sale.)

Scotland is often called "the home of golf" and, brushing aside any suggestion that the game probably originated in the Low Countries, claims it for her own. Certainly, Scotland has a number of very old, established courses, often lying close to town centers, where, had it not been for the early rights of golfers, the land would have been swallowed up by developments long ago. Nowhere is this better seen than in St. Andrews.

Seaside pastime It is quite possible that golf came over when the medieval trading links with the Low Countries were strong. By the time of the early Stuart monarchs, a game with sticks and balls was taking up the time of both king and commoner alike. In 1457, King James II decreed that soldiers should not play golf. In 1503, King James IV treated himself to a new set of clubs.

Some say the sport originated with a piece of driftwood, a sea-washed pebble, and a rabbit burrow—all three are found on the Fife coast among the turf, links, and dunes. In the days before mowing machines were invented, golf had to be played where grass was naturally short. Usually only on seaside links did the exposure, poor soil, and nibbling rabbits all combine to keep the turf close-cropped. Bunkers developed from natural hollows into which a golf ball would frequently roll. Wind erosion on the thin grassy skin already damaged by players' efforts to hit out would soon create a sandy hazard.

The Old Course All this substantiates St. Andrews Old Course's claims to 15th-century origins. The Old Course is still the ultimate dream of many, which may explain why, for instance, Japanese visitors have acquired a reputation for slow play over it—they want to savor every moment. It represents traditional design at its very best. However, remember that there are other courses, both adjacent to the Old Course and right along the Fife coast.

A GOLFING HAZARD
One of the former hazards of the Old Course was the storage shed of the nearby railroad yard on the Fife coastline from Leuchars. This demanded a high approach shot on the 17th to clear the roof. Though the railroad has gone in one of the more short-sighted closures of the 1960s, the outline of the old shed has been preserved as the golf school of the nearby luxury hotel, which now occupies the site of the former sidings. Meanwhile, a campaign continues to reopen the line.

155

St. Andrews, the Old Course

A JACOBITE BATTLE
The Battle of Sheriffmuir, on the open slopes of the Ochil Hills above Stirling, was fought in 1715 between the rebellious Jacobite forces under the Earl of Mar and the government army under the Duke of Argyll. Unusually, it ended in a draw, with each of the opposing wings pushing back the other but neither side gaining overwhelming advantage. Argyll took his forces off to Dunblane, while Mar's men withdrew to Perth. As it was November, many of the Highland rebels wanted to go back home for the winter, and the rebellion fizzled out.

▶▶▶ Stirling   130B1

Whoever controlled Stirling controlled the Scotland of old. It was the lowest bridging point of the River Forth running east, with marshes to the west, the Campsie Hills to the south, and the Ochil Hills (and the Highlands) northward. Stirling Castle preserves its impregnable air, rising out of the former marshlands. Downhill from the castle, the Old Town has the air of an old Scottish burgh (town), with its mercat cross, tolbooth (town jail), and Church of the Holy Rude (ca1456) as the ancient symbols of commerce, the law, and the church. Farther down, Victorian developments begin with handsome shopping streets and a railroad station.

Stirling Castle▶▶▶ (*Open* Apr–Sep, daily 9:30–5:15; Oct–Mar, daily 9:30–4:15. *Admission charge*). Everyone who comes to Stirling gets at least as far as the Esplanade with its breathtaking panorama, but it is well worth entering the castle complex itself. This former royal court with its fine Renaissance work was sadly misused after Scotland's James VI deserted it to become King of England as well. Much has been restored, including the Renaissance palace of James V and the Chapel Royal of 1594.

The story of one of Scotland's few victories against the English is told at the **Bannockburn Visitor Centre**▶ (*Open*

Walk

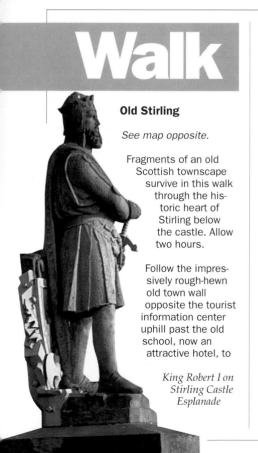

King Robert I on Stirling Castle Esplanade

Old Stirling

See map opposite.

Fragments of an old Scottish townscape survive in this walk through the historic heart of Stirling below the castle. Allow two hours.

Follow the impressively rough-hewn old town wall opposite the tourist information center uphill past the old school, now an attractive hotel, to the historic buildings of St. John Street. These include the **Erskine Marykirk**, a classical church (1842–1846), now fronting a modern youth hostel; and the old **Detention Barracks** (1847), now the Old Town Jail museum.

The **Church of the Holy Rude** lies beyond, with Cowane's Hospital (the Guildhall, used as a summer ceilidh venue) nearby. A gate between the two buildings leads to the cemetery, which provides a fine view of the castle from the Ladies Rock. Steps and a gate lead to the Esplanade, running next to the castle. The distant views from the Esplanade include the Arrochar Alps to the west, Ben Chonzie northward, and the Pentland Hills behind Edinburgh.

After visiting the **castle**, go downhill past **Argyll's Ludging**, Scotland's finest surviving Renaissance mansion (open to the general public), and pass the façade of **Mar's Wark**, a Renaissance palace damaged during the '45 rebellion. Broad Street, complete with cannon and tall 18th- and 19th-century tenement buildings, gives way to Victorian developments and the main shopping streets of the city.

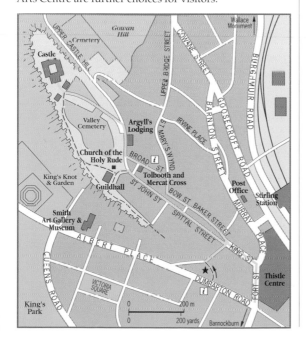

Apr–Oct, daily 10–5:30; Mar, Nov–Dec, daily 11–3. *Admission charge*) 2½ miles southeast of Stirling.

The National Wallace Monument▶▶ recalls Scotland's first freedom fighter (William Wallace), and has an audio-visual presentation as well as views from the top of the tower after a climb up 246 steps. (*Open* Mar–May and Oct, daily 10–5, Jun, Sep, daily 10–6; Jul–Aug, daily 9.30–6:30; Feb and Nov, weekends 10–4. *Admission charge*).

The summer program of costume drama set in the castle and in the atmospheric streets, changing exhibitions at the Smith Art Gallery, and performances at the MacRobert Arts Centre are further choices for visitors.

The view from the ramparts of Stirling Castle toward the Church of the Holy Rude

TOURIST INFORMATION
Stirling: 41 Dumbarton Road (tel: 01786-475019).

THE REASONS FOR BANNOCKBURN
The Battle of Bannockburn was not what King Robert I (the Bruce) wanted. He was forced into this confrontation with the might of the English knights after his brother, Edward, besieging Stirling Castle, accepted an offer from its English governor that "if by midsummer a year thence he was not rescued by battle, he would yield the castle freely." This committed King Edward II of England to rescue his governor and fight the Scottish forces in a pitched battle.

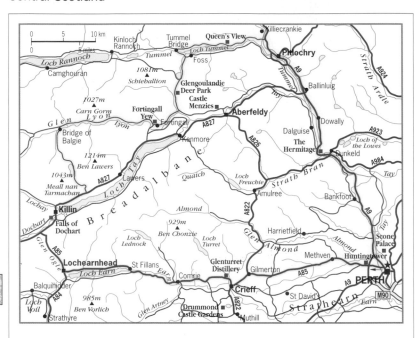

Drive

Perthshire's glens

A drive around some typical Highland glens with ribbon lochs and characteristic glaciated U-shaped profiles. This

The Queen's View, Loch Tummel

is a good autumn drive, when the roads are quiet and the colors spectacular. The trip totals 114 miles via Glen Lyon but not including the Loch Tummel extension. Allow one long day, or alternatively stop overnight in the Kenmore area.

Take A85 west from Perth, noting 15th-century Huntingtower on the outskirts of the town. On this section, south of the Highland Boundary Fault, the green landscape of well-worked farmland and woods rolls out across

Falls of Dochart, Killin

the shallow bowl of Strathearn, the valley of the River Earn, as far south as the Ochil Hills.

Continue through **Crieff**, keeping on A85. The town has plenty of stores, and a cluster of visitor attractions on the edge of town (see page 138).

Because of its position on the Highland Boundary Fault, the village of **Comrie** farther along A85 is known as the earthquake center of Scotland. **Earthquake House**, built as a recording station in 1874, lies just west of the town. The hills close in toward St. Fillans, on the eastern end of **Loch Earn**, a popular loch for water sports. There is a major water-sports center at Lochearnhead. Note, en route, the fine views south to the bulk of Ben Vorlich.

At Lochearnhead, turn north up **Glen Ogle**. This grand glen, according to Queen Victoria's diaries, reminded her of a print of the Khyber Pass. The old railroad (closed 1965), with its decaying viaduct, is now a walkway, though not totally peaceful because of the roar of peak-season traffic in the confines of the hills. Try the turnoff at the head of the pass for views of the **Meall nan Tarmachan** and **Ben Lawers** ranges.

After turning right at Lix Toll, on reaching Killin, watch out for pedestrians peering into cameras on the narrow bridge over the **Falls of Dochart**. There are friendly little shops in this attractive community, which, during winter, has an alpine flavor when there is snow on the slopes above.

Continue eastward, then take the unclassified road north toward Glen Lyon, unless it has recently snowed on the tops—this road traverses high ground. The National Trust for Scotland's visitor center blights the bright green flanks of **Ben Lawers**. The Trust is a conservation body, but ironically Ben Lawers' mountain flora is threatened by too many visitors, so pass on into Glen Lyon.

Turn east down this typical Highland glen, with a "big hoose" behind its wall, warning notices to keep off the hills during stalking, forestry on the slopes, farming on the river flats, and a hydroelectric project at the head of the glen. Note the Fortingall Yew where Glen Lyon opens out. This is reputed to be more than 3,000 years old, possibly the oldest tree in Europe. The Fortingall Yew is said to be the birthplace of Pontius Pilate, whose father is supposed to have been a legionnaire stationed in Scotland. Victorian

Schiehallion and Loch Rannoch

guide book writers were notoriously imaginative.

Continue the tour by going north to **Loch Tummel** and then circling back by way of Pitlochry, or rejoin A9 east of Aberfeldy to return to Perth.

H. V. Morton, in In Search of Scotland, sums up the Trossachs. He complains how a traveler can wander around for months looking for essential Scotland "enduring heat, cold, fatigue, high teas, Sabbaths, kirks, and at the end comes suddenly on the whole thing in concentrated form, boiled down to the very essence..." Even more exasperating, as he points out, the place is conveniently near Edinburgh and Glasgow.

160

WORDSWORTH IN THE TROSSACHS

Among the many poems inspired by his Trossachs visits, Wordsworth composed *Stepping Westward* after exploring Loch Katrine. *The Solitary Reaper*, with its lines "Breaking the silence of the seas/Among the farthest Hebrides," owes its origins not to some west coast lass, but to a field-worker the poet heard singing as she worked near Balquhidder.

SS Sir Walter Scott, *steam power on popular and beautiful Loch Katrine (pronounced "Kattren")*

Definitions The Trossachs phenomenon is a curious one. For a start, nobody can quite agree on where it is. It certainly centers on the narrow pass that leads from Loch Achray through to the huge parking lot at the east end of **Loch Katrine**. Usually it encompasses the hills and knolls southward to take in **Aberfoyle** and **Loch Ard**. **Ben Ledi** is a part of it to the east. Sometimes the Trossachs is taken to mean all of this area as far as the **Braes of Balquhidder** and the banks of **Loch Lomond** at Inversnaid.

Then nobody can agree on what the word Trossachs means. Generations of writers have accepted an early explanation that it means "the bristly country" in Gaelic—yet no Gaelic word in current use supports this theory. The standard work for Victorian travelers, *Murray's Handbook* of 1894, dismisses it as the rugged country. Possibly the name derives from an obsolete Gaelic word *trasdaichean* meaning a transverse glen joining two others.

Popularity in the Romantic age Wherever it is and whatever it means, it was firmly on the tourist trail before the end of the 18th century, thanks to the Romantic

movement with its cult of the picturesque. A Callander minister, writing in the **Old Statistical Account** for 1794, states that "The Trossachs are often visited by persons of taste, who are desirous of seeing nature in her rudest and unpolished state." Before then, shaggy landscapes were considered uncouth and vulgar, without order or harmony—as well as being downright dangerous and probably filled with savages as well.

The Romantic poets came to admire the wooded peaks mirrored in shimmering lochs. William and Dorothy Wordsworth, accompanied by Samuel Taylor Coleridge, passed through in 1803. Though the scenery hardly needed the extra attention, Sir Walter Scott took the landscapes around Ben Ledi and Loch Katrine (as well as Stirling Castle) for *The Lady of the Lake* (1810), and peopled them with heroes, knights, hermits, and fair ladies. This dramatic verse-narrative was an overnight sensation and helped propel the Trossachs toward becoming the very byword for Scottish scenery. New inns were built, and roads opened up. At the eastern gateway, Callander's shopkeepers prospered.

Modern visitors The Trossachs are just as popular today, and a few new visitor attractions have opened. The **Rob Roy and Trossachs Visitor Centre** in Callander (see page 137) tells the Trossachs story through the eyes of the local hero and popular rogue Rob Roy Macgregor, who knew these Highland-edge landscapes well. (His clan found them convenient for hiding cattle stolen from Lowland farms.)

At Aberfoyle, the **Scottish Wool Center** offers a worthwhile variation on the Scottish combination of large giftware shop with attractions attached. The "Story of Scottish Wool" from prehistoric times to the present is told through a presentation in a 150-seat arena, and in summer there are live demonstrations of shearing and working sheepdogs, as well as a chance to try carding and spinning (*Open* Apr–Sep, daily 9:30–6; Oct–Mar, daily 10–5). These modern developments add a wet-weather dimension to the attractions of the Trossachs.

However, the best way to understand the place is to walk—up **Ben Aon** overlooking Loch Achray; around the head of Loch Katrine in Glen Gyle to discover the old Macgregor graveyard; up Ben Ledi in the heart of the Trossachs. After all, visitors have had so much enjoyment doing just that for two centuries.

HILLTOP RITUALS
Ben Ledi, tallest of the Trossachs hills, is associated with Beltane rites, ancient fire ceremonies on hilltops formerly practiced by the Celts. The coming of their summer was May 1. A folk memory of this lingers on but has attached itself to Midsummer Eve instead, when the uphill path to this 2,883-foot-high hill can be quite busy as people gather to watch the sunset at its most northerly point.

161

The ferryman who takes visitors to the atmospheric Inchmahome Priory, on an island in the Lake of Menteith, near Callander

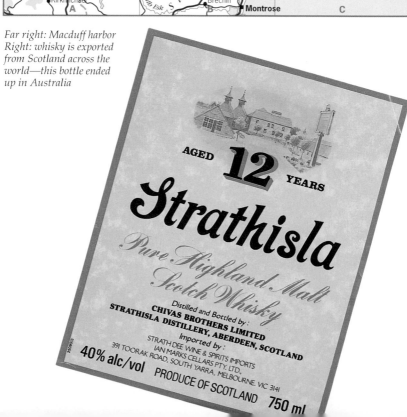

Far right: Macduff harbor
Right: whisky is exported
from Scotland across the
world—this bottle ended
up in Australia

AGED **12** YEARS

Strathisla

Pure Highland Malt
Scotch Whisky

Distilled and Bottled by :
CHIVAS BROTHERS LIMITED
STRATHISLA DISTILLERY, ABERDEEN, SCOTLAND
Imported by :
STRATH DEE WINE & SPIRITS IMPORTS
IAN MARKS CELLARS PTY. LTD.
391 TOORAK ROAD, SOUTH YARRA, MELBOURNE. VIC 3141

40% alc/vol   PRODUCE OF SCOTLAND   750 ml

BEYOND THE GRAMPIAN HILLS The northeast region, strictly speaking, lies north of the Highland Line, the geological fault that runs from Helensburgh in the west to Stonehaven in the east. Yet the region has good Lowland farmlands and the densest forms of the Lowland Scots tongue. It used to be described as "the Grampian cocoon"—the land beyond the Grampians, isolated from developments in Central Scotland. This may explain the vigorous survival of its old tongue, as well as a kind of independent spirit and attitude among many of the locals. But modern communications, as well as new settlers and the impact of North Sea oil, have made their mark in this essentially rural area.

The Northeast is different: not like the empty, wet, and rugged deserts of the Highlands with their original inhabitants in exile; nor even like the brisk and busy central corridor of Scotland, which spawned the industrial revolution. It is a community tied together by the twin bonds of its seagoing and its farming heritage. Its main center, Aberdeen, the third largest city in Scotland, sometimes seems to operate like a very large market town, in spite of all the peripheral industrial estates that grew up in the wake of the oil finds in the shallow seas to the east and north.

Geographically, the Northeast can be seen as a series of shelves, running down from the frost-shattered granite heights of the Cairngorm Mountains to the gently rolling, well-farmed Lowlands. These descending steps end

Oil supply vessels in Aberdeen harbor

164

spectacularly in a coastline whose beauty is hardly matched in the United Kingdom—preserved partly by remoteness, partly by the unglamorous workaday fields behind it, and also because it is usually very chilly.

CASTLES The "cocoon" effect means that many great castles have survived, away from the destructive mainstream of Scotland warfare and safely tucked out of sight behind their stone walls and woodland "policies" (grounds). Some still control farms and grand estates; others are now in the care of bodies such as the National Trust for Scotland and open to the public. If you travel in the Northeast, there seem to be signposts with castle logos at every turn.

DISTINCT AREAS The Northeast splits into a number of areas. There is the city of Aberdeen itself, with its wide commuter belt, taking in places from Ellon in the north, Inverurie, Alford, Banchory, and other little country towns that expanded in the oil boom. North from this area to Kinnaird Head, the northeast tip, is Buchan, built on fishing and farming, with granite towns and villages tucked into the folds of open farmland. The old county of Banff, at least in its lowland stretches, is transitional, softening the bleak edges of Buchan and merging in turn with the softer airs of Moray, in the rain shadow of the high hills in the inner Moray Firth.

Running west of Aberdeen is the valley of the River Dee, given royal approval by Queen Victoria and still, at least in part, a playground for the wealthy, not just aristocrats on hillground and forested estates, but also the occasional foreign millionaire. Deeside eventually runs into the great whalebacks of the Cairngorms, whose northwestern slopes face Speyside and the upper reaches of Moray. North and northeast of the Cairngorm plateau are the

THE TURRA COO
One tale of Northeast thrawnness (stubbornness) is that of the (locally) famous Turra Coo. Turra is Turriff, a small market town, and a coo is a cow. In 1912, a local farmer refused to cooperate with the new National Insurance Act. He was fined but refused to pay. The Sheriff Officer poinded (seized) a cow. After a failed attempt to auction it in Turriff—before a crowd of 1,500 intent on merriment—it was sold in Aberdeen, but bought by sympathizers. The coo was taken back home to its first owner, watched by another large crowd and the local brass band. This spawned a minor industry in Turra Coo commemorative postcards, pottery, glassware, etc. A memorial was erected in 1971.

lonely glens of former upper Banffshire, once hazy with the smoke from illicit stills.

WHISKY Today the whisky (note the Scots spelling) industry, centered on the River Spey, is big business. Grand malt whisky names—Macallan, Glenlivet, Glenfiddich, Glenfarclas, and so on—stretch all the way to the sea, sounding every bit as distinguished as the famous wines noted as place-names in France's Rhône valley.

Provost Skene's House, Aberdeen

King's College, Old Aberdeen

The Northeast

THE NORTHERN LIGHTS

"The Northern Lights of Old Aberdeen" is a Scottish anthem sung worldwide by Aberdonians. However, the Northern Lights are certainly not confined to the city. The *aurora borealis* (to give the Northern Lights their proper name) is a not an uncommon phenomenon in the north of Scotland, illuminating the sky with (usually) greenish waving curtains and beams of light at any time of year when there is enough darkness to view it.

Granite detail from the entrance to St. Nicholas's churchyard

TOURIST INFORMATION

Aberdeen: St. Nicholas House, Broad Street (tel: 01224-632727)

▶▶▶ Aberdeen

162C2

With its population of well over 200,000 and its glittering granite and spacious streets, the United Kingdom's most northerly city makes an impact on first-time visitors. Built between the river mouths of the Dee and the Don, this old-established place—a royal burgh (town) since 1124— once had strong trading links with Europe, while serving its agricultural hinterland and developing other industries such as textiles.

Before the end of the 18th century, it was exporting its characteristic silver-gray granite to London among other places and also building the distinctive townscape that is still seen today around Union Street (the main shopping thoroughfare).

Unlike the soft sandstones of Edinburgh and Glasgow, tough granite does not suit ornate carving. Instead it was used boldly in buildings, parapets, and spires. In sunshine, the mica chips become a million mirrors; in rain, the stones reflect only the gray sky.

Many of Aberdeen's places of interest are within walking distance of each other. The east end of Union Street is the former center of the early settlement, indicated by the **mercat cross**. Aberdeen's is one of the most splendid in Scotland, dating from 1686, and arcaded with heraldic

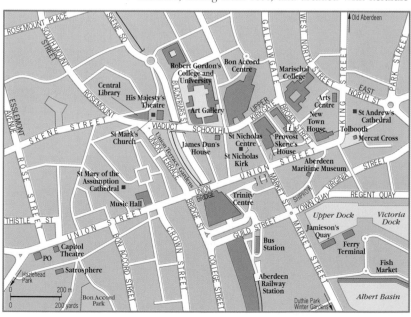

panels and portraits. Opposite is the 17th-century **Tolbooth** or **Old Town House**. (It once held prisoners before trial, and tours of the old cells are available.) Note the Flemish medieval-style turrets on the adjacent **New Town House**, a reminder of old trading links. The Shiprow opposite, one of the oldest streets in the city, leads down to the harbor.

Aberdeen Maritime Museum▶ The 16th-century **Provost Ross's House** is a unique survivor on the old Shiprow, between the marketplace and quayside. The museum portrays the city's seagoing past, from early times via fishing boats and tea clippers right up to the oil boom (*Open* Mon–Sat 10–5, Sun 11–5. *Admission free*).

Marischal College▶ ▶ was founded in 1593 by the Earl Marischal as a Protestant alternative to the Catholic King's College in Old Aberdeen (see page 168). The two combined to form Aberdeen University in 1860. Marischal's arresting façade was built from 1891 onward, breaking all rules about granite and its severity. The spectacularly ornate work is set off by gilded flags, and this giant granite wedding cake is still the second-largest granite building in the world. (Only El Escorial, near Madrid, Spain, is larger.) The Marischal Museum (*Open* Mon–Fri 10–5, Sun 2–5. *Admission free*) is within.

Provost Skene's House▶ Past the eye-catching façade of Marischal College and almost underneath the ugly modern building of St. Nicholas House, this steeply gabled rubble built structure is the remnant of a once closely packed area of town houses. It dates in part from 1545. It is now a museum of civic life with restored furnished period rooms and a painted chapel, as well as a café (good for afternoon tea). (*Open* Mon–Sat 10–5. *Admission free*).

167

168

A TRAVELER'S TALE
Thomas Pennant, the Welsh traveler, visited Aberdeen in 1769 and took in St. Machar's. He describes how the Reformers took the lead off the roof of St. Machar's and stole the bells. Then they "shipped their sacrilegious booty with an intention of exposing it to sale in Holland; but the vessel had scarcely gone out of port, but it perished in a storm with all its ill-gained lading." Others tell the same story of Elgin Cathedral.

Right: an exhibit of character in the Aberdeen Maritime Museum

Old Aberdeen

Aberdeen Art Gallery▶▶ has excellent collections of 18th- to 20th-century work (*Open* Mon–Sat 10–5, Sun 2–5. *Admission free*). Close by is **St. Nicholas Kirk▶**, the first place of worship in Aberdeen, founded in the 12th century.

Old Aberdeen▶▶, once a separate community near the River Don, lies north of the main city near the precincts of **King's College▶**. The university was founded in 1494: and its cobbled streets and artisans' cottages make it an atmospheric campus. **King's College Chapel▶▶**, with its crown spire, is a very fine example of an early collegiate chapel (ca1500). The tall oak screen, ribbed ceiling, and stalls have ornate medieval wood carving. The Visitor Centre (*Open* Mon–Sat 10–5, Sun 12–5. *Admission free*) is a good starting point for a tour.

Beyond the handsome Georgian **Old Aberdeen Town House▶▶** is the Chanonry, leading to St. Machar's Cathedral and Seaton Park. The River Don curves around this park, then flows under the picturesque 14th-century Brig o'Balgownie.

St. Machar's Cathedral▶ St. Columba sent St. Machar to build this church near the sea, where a river flowed in the shape of a shepherd's crook. The nave was possibly rebuilt in red sandstone by around 1370, then finished in granite by the mid-15th century. The building was damaged during the Reformation and in the 17th century, but extensively restored in the 19th century (*Open* daily 9–5. *Admission free*).

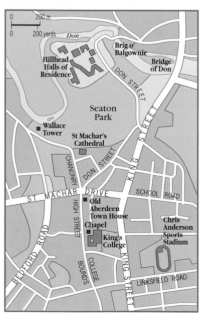

Aberdeen has sandy beaches, an amusement park, leisure centers, swimming pools, and spacious parks—in short, many of the trappings of a resort town. It also has a large number of indoor sights specifically geared for children. If all else fails, you can always lose them for awhile in the large maze in the city's Hazlehead Park.

The Satrosphere, signposted from the west end of Union Street, is undoubtedly Aberdeen's top children's attraction (*Open* Apr–early Oct, Mon–Sat 10–5, Sun 1:30–5; mid-Oct–Mar, Mon, Wed–Fri 10–4, Sat 10–5, Sun 1:30–5. *Admission charge*). Do not be put off by the "interactive science and technology exhibition center" description: it is a hands-on, absorbing experience for any child with imagination. There are endless experiments and demonstrations for children. They can play with mirrors and light, create a giant bubble a yard wide, play tunes on 6-foot pan pipes, whisper into a parabolic reflector and be heard across the hall, become a TV newscaster, balance balls in streams of hot air, build a waterwheel, and become involved in dozens of other activities. Allow plenty of time to make the most of it.

Other Aberdeen attractions Jonah's Journey in Rosemount Place takes its theme from life in Bible times—here children can visit a nomad's tent, dress up, and grind grain (*Open* Mon–Sat 10–12, Sun 2.30–4.30). **James Dun's House**, just by the art gallery in Schoolhill, sometimes has special exhibitions with children's themes, so is worth checking out. Older children will enjoy the interactive computers at the Maritime Museum (*Open* Mon–Sat 10–5, Sun 11–5. *Admission free*) and some of the exhibits (probably the shrunken heads!) at the Marischal College Museum (*Open* Mon–Fri 10–5, Sun 2–5. *Admission free*).

The Winter Gardens at the **Duthie Park** are popular with families. **Hazlehead Park** also has a domestic animal zoo, as has **Doonies Farm**. Most of Aberdeen's parks have good playgrounds—try the one on the Beach Esplanade, where there is also a traditional amusement park in summer. Out of town, **Storybook Glen** near Maryculter is a sheltered valley where fiberglass models of cartoon and fairy-tale characters loom disconcertingly out of the undergrowth. (*Open* Mar–Oct, daily 10–6, Nov–Feb, Sat–Sun 11–4. *Admission charge*).

FLORAL FACTS
Seaton Park is only one of the city's open spaces. Aberdeen puts special emphasis on flowers and is a frequent winner of the "Britain in Bloom" award. Aberdeen's flower displays were initiated using 60 tons of daffodil bulbs and 600,000 crocuses in one phase alone. Rosebushes outnumber the locals by nine to one.

169

A ghoulish exhibit from the Marischal College Museum

The Northeast

TOURIST INFORMATION
Ballater: Albert Hall,
Station Square (tel:
01339-753306).
Banff: Collie Lodge
(tel: 01261-812419).
Braemar: The Mews, Mar
Road (tel: 01339-
741600).

Braemar holds the record for the lowest temperature recorded in Britain: -17°F

BALMORAL
Balmoral Castle is the private vacation home of the Royal Family and only opens its grounds and ballroom to the public for a short time each year (*Open* Easter–May, Mon–Sat 10–5; Jun–Jul, daily 10–5, last entry 4). Usually the ballroom houses a painting exhibition from the Royal Family's private collections. In August, when the Royals are in residence, the castle serves as a high-security playground.

Lonely Corgarff Castle

▶▶ Ballater
162A1

Well-scrubbed and handsome Ballater has profited greatly from the needs of the royals at Balmoral for everything from bread to rubber boots. With Balmoral just westward, there are more "By Royal Appointment" signs here than anywhere else in Scotland.

Local excursions include the not-to-be-missed **Glen Muick** (pronounced Mick), with red deer sightings all but guaranteed. Also worth exploring are the birch woods around Dinnet, notably **Loch Kinord** and the **Burn o Vat**, and a good network of trails around **Glen Tanar**, near Aboyne. Hardy walkers can explore the **Mounth passes**— a series of high-level ancient trails leading across the massif of The Mounth. Northward is 16th-century **Corgarff Castle**, with its star-shaped defenses added in 1748.

▶ Banff
162B3

Pressure from a local conservation group saved some of Banff's attractive Georgian domestic architecture from redevelopment into the retail anonymity that blighted so many other Scottish towns. So this old seacoast town is worth a stroll in its own right. However, its main attraction is **Duff House▶▶**, a restored Adam mansion, now the principal outstation of the National Galleries of Scotland with displays of Scottish portraiture of the 18th and 19th centuries, and fine period furniture (*Open* Apr–Sep, daily 11–4; Oct–Mar, Thu–Sun 11–4. *Admission charge*).

▶▶ Braemar
162A1

A93, coming west up Deeside, climbs out of the Dee valley and turns southward, seeking a pass over the Grampians. Braemar sits on the turn. It can feel a little transitory, yet it is an old established resort, benefiting like Ballater from the royal presence at Balmoral. The **Highland Heritage Centre** (*Open* daily 9–5. *Admission free*), takes up the theme of the royal connection and the Braemar Highland Gathering. There is an excellent selection of local excursions, including the **Linn of Dee**, a picturesque rocky cleft, west of Inverey. Also nearby is the **Devil's Punchbowl**, a water-worn rock feature among pines at the Linn of Quoich. The **Colonel's Bed** is yet more rock and water: a narrow gorge with slippery shelves in Glen Ey. For the ambitious walker, **Glen Derry** gives access to the eastern end of the Cairngorms, as well as the pass of the Lairig Ghru leading through to the Spey. But beware—these are hills on a large scale.

The northern Picts lived in and around the Grampians between the 4th and 9th centuries ad. The Mounth, the hill ground between Deeside and Angus, was an important barrier. Moray was their final stronghold before defeat and gradual absorption by the ascendant Scots, whose union with them formed the first kingdom of Scotland, known as Alba (see page 27).

Burghead The most important Pictish center was Burghead, on the coast near Elgin. A great promontory fort survived until a "new" town of Burghead was built on a grid plan in 1805–1809, destroying much of the Pictish ramparts, and timber-laced walling that had stood there for more than a millennium. Six Pictish bull carvings survive from that time, outlined boldly in stone.

The bull is just one of the symbols that tantalize modern archeologists and historians. The Picts left earthworks such as coastal headland forts in the northeast and inland sites like Bennachie, a hill near Inverurie, but it is their symbol stones that are the most vivid evidence of this long-gone culture. A few stones are still in their original locations, some have been re-erected or placed in museums, others have been built into walls or lost entirely.

Standing stones The **Picardy Stone** near Insch is typical, a whinstone pillar with, among other subjects, a clearly executed double-disk and Z-rod (a recurring symbol in Pictish art), serpent, and mirror. The **Malden Stone** near Pitcaple is an impressive red granite monolith of considerable presence, especially when slanting light highlights the curious so-called "Pictish elephant," one of the most mysterious of the designs. This is a late (9th-century) work.

Most magnificent of all is **Sueno's Stone** on the outskirts of Forres, with its many figures galloping on the face of an 8-foot monolith. Theories abound on the meaning of this and other stones. Some suggest that Sueno's Stone is war reporting on a grand scale—recording, ironically, the Scots' victory over the Picts. Some see particular stones as monuments, others as proclamations. Nobody knows, but the designs have both power and inspiration. Tracking them down can make for interesting excursions in this northern corner.

THE MEANING OF THE STONES
The Picts were divided into two realms, northern and southern. Many of the finest symbol stones belong to the northern grouping. Their language was ousted by the arrival of the Scots from Ireland, and they left no written records. It is known that inheritance was through the female line—though Pictish kings reigned, their sons did not succeed them. Do the symbols carved on the stones indicate lineages, alliances, and power within the leading Pictish families?

Left and below: the Maiden Stone, near Pitcaple

Whisky is one of Scotland's top exports, worth £2.1 billion in 1993, and is important in the economy of many communities. There are more than 40 distilleries in Moray alone, the greatest concentration anywhere in Scotland. More than just distinctive plumes of steam in the attractive wooded river valley, these distilleries sustain engineers, coppersmiths, painters, plumbers, maltsters, and specialists in many more trades.

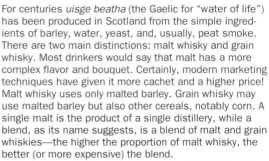

DALLAS DHU

Amid all the live distilleries, busy bubbling, frothing, and producing odd aromas, you can also visit a distillery of the past. In the care of Historic Scotland, Dallas Dhu near Forres is a time capsule and allows a more intimate inspection than working distilleries. (*Open* Apr–Sep 9:30–6; Oct–Mar, Mon–Wed and Sat 9:30–4, Thu 9:30–12, Sun 2–4. *Admission charge*).

172

Copper stills at the Glen Garioch Distillery, Oldmeldrum

For centuries *uisge beatha* (the Gaelic for "water of life") has been produced in Scotland from the simple ingredients of barley, water, yeast, and, usually, peat smoke. There are two main distinctions: malt whisky and grain whisky. Most drinkers would say that malt has a more complex flavor and bouquet. Certainly, modern marketing techniques have given it more cachet and a higher price! Malt whisky uses only malted barley. Grain whisky may use malted barley but also other cereals, notably corn. A single malt is the product of a single distillery, while a blend, as its name suggests, is a blend of malt and grain whiskies—the higher the proportion of malt whisky, the better (or more expensive) the blend.

Experts broadly classify malt whiskies into Highland, Lowland, Islay, and Campbeltown types. This can be generalized into eastern, notably from Speyside, and western, from the islands, mainly Islay. Of the two, the western malts are noticeably "peaty." The malt, which is the basis of malt whisky, has usually (but not necessarily) been bought from local maltings. Malt is germinated barley that has been killed off and then dried (sometimes with peat smoke).

The whisky-making process To make whisky, grind a large quantity of malted barley and add hot water to it in a large circular vat of several thousand quarts capacity called a mash tun. Eventually, the result will be wort, a sweet-smelling liquid. Hold this in a worts receiver or underback below the mash tun. Use the solids in the mash tun, called draff, for winter cattle food.

Take the wort and add it with yeast to another enormous vessel, known as a wash-back, where it will ferment. Then pump this liquid, called the wash, via a wash charger into a wash still, which is a large copper container. Heat it, using gas if available. Condense the vapors in a worm—

a coiled copper, water-cooled tube. Repeat this process at least twice. Then run the distillate into a spirit safe. This is the part that needs most expertise. Both the beginning and end of the distilling process produce impurities. The whisky is, so to speak, in the middle.

Next, procure casks. Old sherry casks are particularly recommended. Add water to the whisky and place in the casks. Leave for several years before bottling as a single malt. Then sell worldwide as a prestige product!

THE ANGELS' SHARE
This is the term used to describe the whisky that was definitely there when the distillery staff put it into the cask but has gone, five or more years later, when the casks are broached for bottling or blending. Nothing untoward has taken place. There is a natural evaporation through the wood of the casks.

173

Casks—and their contents—maturing at the Glenfiddich Distillery, Dufftown

Distillery tours The process of producing whisky is closely monitored by the British government. It is strictly commercially licensed and takes place only in Scotland's distilleries (and, in Scotland, the product is most definitely spelled "whisky," without an "e"). Many distilleries place strong emphasis on visitor facilities and attempt to inject some drama and excitement into a process that is visually undramatic but nevertheless requires skill, method, and large-scale investment.

A typical visit includes some kind of audiovisual presentation, with the malt whisky company describing its brand as the "true taste of Scotland" and laying great store on historical roots. (Awkward facts detracting from "Scottishness," such as the owning company being an overseas-based multinational, are skipped over.) Then there is a tour, of varying degrees of liveliness, depending on the guide; and afterward a return to the hospitality area where a dram is usually offered. There will often be some kind of historic exhibition and nearly always a shop. No tour of Speyside is complete without taking in at least one distillery.

The Northeast

DOLPHINS
The Moray Firth contains the largest inshore colony of bottle-nosed dolphins in Britain. (The species otherwise tends to favor offshore waters.) Leaping dolphins can be seen anywhere at any time in the Firth. The entrances to the inner firths can be rewarding for dolphin watchers, as can the mouths of the Rivers Findhorn and Spey (Spey Bay is particularly good for seals as well.) The bottle-nosed dolphin can be recognized by its uniform gray with a paler underbelly and a tall dorsal fin.

Painted ceiling in Crathes Castle; the original castle was built in 1323 on land granted to the Burnett family by Robert the Bruce

▶ **Craigellachie**   *162A2*

A typical Speyside community dependent on the whisky industry and visiting anglers, Craigellachie is noted for its cooperage, now the **Speyside Cooperage Visitor Centre▶▶**, where the skills of barrel making are demonstrated (*Open* Easter–Sep, Mon–Sat 9:30–4:30; Oct–Easter, weekdays only. *Admission charge*). Also nearby is **Craigellachie Bridge▶**, designed by Thomas Telford, which crosses the Spey with an iron span cast in Wales.

▶▶ **Crathes Castle**   *162B1*

Open: castle Apr–Oct, daily 11–5:30, last entry 4:45; grounds daily 9–dusk. Admission charge
This 16th-century L-plan tower house has many rare original features, notably four rooms with painted ceilings, as well as a ghost of a green lady and fine old furniture, locally made. Crathes is also noted for its gardens, made into compartments by close-clipped yew hedges and containing many unusual species.

▶ **Dufftown**   *162A2*

A planned town founded in 1817, Dufftown has wide streets which center on a square and a landmark **clock tower** (which houses the local museum). The little town is bound up with distilleries, including famous malt whisky names such as Glenfiddich, which is overlooked by the ruins of the 13th-century Balvenie Castle (itself a malt whisky name). **The Glenfiddich Distillery Visitor Centre▶▶▶** offers one of the very best audiovisuals and tours, showing all of the stages from malting through to bottling (*Open* Mon–Fri all year, 9:30–4:30, also Sat 9:30–4:30, Sun 12–4:30 from Easter–mid-Oct. *Admission*

free.) Though a planned town, Dufftown has a pedigree as a settlement that goes as far back as AD 566, when Mortlach Church was founded, one of the earliest religious sites in Scotland. There are Pictish stones and a "leper's squint," a hole through which lepers could observe proceedings inside the church

▶ **Elgin**   *162A3*

Elgin has rebuilt its townscape over the centuries yet retained fragments of early times. A medieval street plan

TOURIST INFORMATION
Dufftown: The Clock Tower, The Square (tel: 01340-820501).
Elgin: 17 High Street (tel: 01343-542666).

can still be made out, with narrow alleyways leading off the broad main street, and some arcaded façades from 18th-century shops also survive. Take in the view from the top of the Lady Hill at its west end. This was the site of the castle—a little of the wall remains—occupied by Edward I of England in the Wars of Independence.

Elgin Cathedral▶ ("The Lantern of the North") was founded in 1224 and burned in 1390 by the notorious Wolf of Badenoch, the black sheep of the royal Stewart family (following excommunication by the local bishop). The cathedral was rebuilt and in use till the Reformation, when it suffered the usual fate of great religious seats in Scotland. Much of its stonework was pillaged and used elsewhere, though the historic structure was taken into the care of the nation in 1825. (*Open* Apr–Sep, daily 9:30–6; Oct–Mar, Mon–Wed and Sat 9:30–4, Thu 9:30–12, Sun 2–4. *Admission charge*).

"Acorn to Cask," the story of whisky barrels at Craigellachie

Elgin Cathedral adds distinction to the skyline of the "capital" of Moray. Much of the surviving work dates from the 13th century

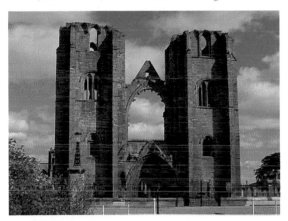

Elgin Museum▶ is reckoned to be one of the finest museums in the north. Among other exhibits it features the oldest dinosaurs found in Britain—though, like the museum itself, they are quite small. (*Open* Apr–Oct, daily 10–5. *Admission charge*).

Other attractions in town include **Johnstons of Elgin▶**, a woolen mill specializing in cashmere, with a visitor center and mill tours. The town also has a motor museum and a preserved meal mill. Nearby, out on the levels of the Laich of Moray, is **Duffus Castle▶**, the impressive remains of a medieval castle with a 14th-century tower. Unusually for Scotland the moat is still water-filled.

Spynie Palace▶, the ruin of a former bishop's mansion with good views from the tower, is to the east.

Elgin's former port is **Lossiemouth▶**, now a resort and fishing town, with a busy airbase nearby. A beautiful coastline stretches out to east and west. Also nearby is **Pluscarden Abbey▶▶**, originally a 13th-century foundation, suppressed at the Reformation. In 1948, monks from Prinknash Abbey, in Gloucester, started restoration (*Open* daily 5 AM–8:30 PM. *Admission free*).

THE BATTLE OF MONS GRAUPIUS
The Roman historian Tacitus tells how Agricola's forces, ranging north in the summer of AD 83, finally brought to battle and defeated the Caledonian warriors by a hill within sight of the sea in the north of Scotland. This was the Battle of Mons Graupius, which also gave the name Grampian, possibly due to a 1470s printing error when "m" was substituted for "u." Many historians favor a Grampian location for the battle, possibly Bennachie near Inverurie. The real battle site has never been found.

THE MOUNTH
The Mounth, from the Gaelic *monadh* ("moorland" or "mountain"), is the name given to the hill-mass south of Deeside. The Mounth passes were once important through-routes to the north. Today, they survive as hill tracks marked on maps: the Capel Mounth, the Firmouth, the Fungle, and many more, now mainly the haunt of leisure-time walkers and mountain bikers. Motorable passes include A93 over Glen Shee and B974 Cairn o Mount.

TOURIST INFORMATION
Forres: 116 High Street (tel: 01309-672938). Fraserburgh: 3 Salton Square (tel: 01346-518315).

One of Fyvie Castle's main attractions is its outstanding art collection: portraits by Batoni, Raeburn, Gainsborough, Ramsay, and others

▶ **Fettercairn**   *162B1*

Car travelers who tire of the fast A90 divided highway should try an interesting route to the Northeast via Fettercairn, a little place on the southern edge of the Grampian Hills. Fettercairn has an 1861 Gothic arch recalling the visit of Queen Victoria, and a malt whisky visitor center (*Open* May–Sep, except Sun). The Fettercairn diversion leads on to the start of a scenic hill road, B974 to Banchory, which reaches its highest point at the **Cairn o Mount**. This hilltop cairn gives excellent views southward over Angus and is typical of skyline cairns (heaps of stones) that have been altered by generations of travelers. It dates from the 2nd millennium bc.

Fasque House▶ near Fettercairn has been the home of the Gladstone family for six generations (none of whom seem to have thrown very much out). The most famous of them was William Gladstone, Victorian prime minister. Fasque (1809) is a castellated mansion in Georgian Gothic style, with a pleasingly mellowed, lived-in air (*Open* May–Sep, daily 11–5:30, last entry 5. *Admission charge*).

▶▶ **Fochabers**   *162A3*

Worth visiting for its choice of antiques shops, this handsome little planned town was built by the Duke of Gordon in 1776. He thought the old village was too near his castle, so he knocked it down. He did not think of building a bypass for the A96, which makes the main street very noisy today. Fochabers is the home of Baxters, whose canned-food factory dominates the western approaches. There is an excellent view of the River Spey from a viewpoint south of the town, signposted **The Earth Pillars**, where eroded columns of red conglomerate rock form the foreground to a striking river panorama seen through the pinewood.

Fochabers Folk Museum▶▶▶ is housed in a converted church and is filled with artifacts of a bygone rural life, from horse-drawn carts to a turnip-chopping machine (*Open* daily 9:30–1 and 2–5, 2–6 in summer. *Admission free*).

AN EARLY NAME
Some think that the
"Varris" on the map of
Ptolemy, the 1st-century
ad geographer, refers to
today's Forres.

RANDOLPH'S LEAP
Randolph's Leap, a
beauty spot on the River
Findhorn where the river
narrows among rocks and
woodlands, is unfairly
named. The Randolph was
Thomas Randolph, Earl of
Moray. He was in hot pur-
suit of one Alastair
Cumming who had just
raided his Darnaway
Castle. It was Cumming
who escaped by leaping
the river at this point.
Judge for yourself the relative ease of choosing
between a downward leap
of around 10 feet or being
skewered on a 14th-
century broadsword.

▶ Forres   162A3

Like Elgin, farther east, Forres also maintains its medieval
street plan in part. The main street bulges out at the
former marketplace in the town center, though the build
ings are mainly Victorian. The **Falconer Museum** (*Open*
Apr–Oct, Mon–Sat 10–5; Nov–Mar, Mon–Fri 10–5.
Admission free) explores local history.

Brodie Castle▶, a National Trust for Scotland property,
to the east of Forres, houses fine French furniture, porcelain, and a painting collection (*Open* Apr–Sep, Mon–Sat
11–5:30, Sun 1:30–5:30; Oct, weekends only. *Admission
charge*). Well worth visiting is the **Califer Braes** viewpoint, with a broad view of the Moray Firth to the east
and meeting the Highland Hills westward.

▶ Fraserburgh   162C3

Fraserburgh in itself is a fishing port with little merit in its
townscape. However, it has a superb beach and a most
interesting visitor attraction. Scotland's Lighthouse
Museum▶▶▶ portrays the story of lighthouse service,
now ending with automation. there are fascinating displays as well as a tour of Kinnaird Head lighthouse itself
(Open Apr–Oct, Mon–Sat 10–6, Sun 12:30–6; Nov–Mar,
Mon–Sat 10–4, Sun 12:30–4. Admission charge).

▶▶ Fyvie Castle   162B2

*Open: Apr–Jun and Sep, daily 1:30–5:30; Jul–Aug daily
11–5:30; Oct, weekends 1.30–5:30. Last entry 4:45. Admission
charge*

Five-towered Fyvie Castle epitomizes northeast castles: a
rambling pile, imposing yet hidden away behind its endless walls and tall trees. The original 13th-century quad-
rangular fortress evolved over the centuries into a
magnificent stately home. Famous families in the northeast, the Prestons, Meldrums, Setons, and Gordons, held
it in turn, each adding to the building. Then it was bought
by Alexander Forbes Leith, a local boy made good in
America. He refurbished it in parts, adding Edwardian
opulence to the mix. The castle has sumptuous interiors
and fine furniture, and displays a magnificent painting
collection, including a dozen Raeburns.

AN UNUSUAL VEHICLE
One of the exhibits in the Grampian Museum of Transport is the Craigievar Express. This is a steam-powered tricycle, and was one of Scotland's pioneering road vehicles. It was built in 1895 by the local mailman to help him on his rounds. The one-cylindered, coal-fired, vertical boiler contraption competed in the 1971 London to Brighton Car Rally—and completed the course.

Pastoral land near Inverurie

PITMEDDEN GARDEN
About 4 miles from Haddo House, Pitmedden Garden, another National Trust for Scotland property, is at its best in high summer, thanks to 40,000 annual plants and 3 miles of box hedging. This is the re-creation of a formal garden originally laid out in 1675 (*Open* May–Sep, daily 10–5:30, last entry 5. *Admission charge*).

▶▶ **Glen Shee**   162A1

Climbing to over 2,000 feet at the Cairnwell, the A93 between Bridge of Cally and Braemar is the highest main road in the United Kingdom (though not the highest drivable road). Surrounded on both sides by Munros (see panel, page 149), it has been a prey to ski developers and is very popular when snow conditions are right. The solitude of the high tops in the immediate vicinity has been invaded by vast parking lots, snow fencing, chairlifts, tows, and catering facilities. With the highest hills just under 3,000 feet, the downhill runs are not very long, however. The chairlift operates outside the winter season. On the steep south side of the pass is the Devil's Elbow, a once fearsome hairpin bend now bypassed, but still visible.

▶ **Grampian Transport Museum**   162B2

Open: Apr–Oct, daily 10–5. Admission charge
Alford (pronounced Ah-furd) offers plenty for children, in particular the Grampian Transport Museum with its extensive collection of historic vehicles and the adjoining narrow-gauge railroad—built on the site of the long-vanished "real" railroad—which runs to Haughton Country Park. Take the road north to **Suie Hill** for a peerless view over rural Aberdeenshire. If it is a summer weekend, continue over to the community hall of the enterprising village of Clatt, where the locals serve a real afternoon tea.

▶▶ **Haddo House**   162C2

Open: Easter, May–Sep, daily 1:30–5:30; Oct weekends only. Last entry 4:45. Admission charge
There is quite a concentration of National Trust for Scotland properties in the Northeast. Haddo House, with its country park, is on the **Castle Trail,** the signposted

route that takes in the best of them, though this William Adam design of 1731 has an elegance far removed from the bold and battered fortresses typical of the trail. Haddo's interiors are mostly "Adam revival" from about 1880, and the overall impression is light and cheerful, inside and out, with curving wings on either side of a harmonious façade. Combine this excursion with a visit to Pitmedden Garden (see panel, page 178).

▶ Huntly 162B2

A substantial (for Grampian) town serving a rural hinterland, Huntly was the power base of the influential Gordons, who built their castle here on a defensive site between the rivers Bogie and Deveron. Today, **Huntly Castle** stands as an imposing ruin, with heraldic adornments on its walls. (*Open* Apr–Sep, daily 9:30–6; Oct–Mar, Mon–Wed and Sat 9:30–4, Thu 9:30–12, Sun 2–4. *Admission charge*). Huntly also has an all-weather cross-country ski track, with equipment for rent.

▶ Inverurie 162B2

Now bypassed by the busy A96, Inverurie is a locally important administrative center in the prosperous farming area known as the Garioch (pronounced "geerie"). It is overlooked by one of the Northeast's landmark hills: Bennachie, with its hilltop vitrified Pictish fort. There are other prehistoric sites in the vicinity (see page 171), including the enigmatic Loanhead Stone Circle, near Daviot, 5 miles to the northwest. At Oyne, 8 miles northwest, the displays at Archeolink▶▶ will tell you much about the mysterious prehistoric peoples who built these monuments (Open Mar–Oct, daily 9:30–5; Nov–Feb, Mon–Fri 11–4, Sat–Sun 10–4. Admission charge).

▶ Keith 162B3

Another planned town on the main Aberdeen–Inverness road, Keith is also the gateway to the *Malt Whisky Trail.* This is a signposted drive around seven malt whisky distilleries, one of which, Strathisla, is in Keith, though the others lie in more picturesque settings in the attractive hinterland of the River Spey and around Ben Rinnes.

Grampian Transport Museum, Alford

TOURIST INFORMATION
Huntly: 9a The Square (tel: 01466-792255).

GORDON BENNETT
Few places can claim to be the hometown of an expletive, but Keith was the birthplace of "Gordon Bennett." This mild British oath refers to James Gordon Bennett, born in the town in 1795. He was the founder and editor of the *New York Herald*, and is sometimes described as the father of lurid journalism because of his innovative sensationalist style.

Drive

The northeast coast

The section of coast between the mouths of the rivers Don and Spey remains comparatively unexplored. Aberdeen to Sandend is 86 miles, the return along the main road 50 miles. Allow a full day.

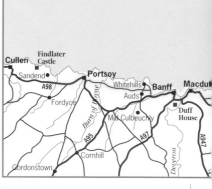

Starting from Aberdeen, A92 is set back from the coast until the Ythan (pronounced <u>Eye</u>-than) estuary at Newburgh on A975. The northern bank of the estuary is a wild habitat of dune and coastal heath, which is explained at the **Forvie Nature Reserve Visitor Centre** (run by Scottish Natural Heritage).

Continue north, diverting to tiny Whinnyfold, which has a view of the Bay of Cruden and the village of Cruden Bay. Bram Stoker used to vacation here, and the nearby ruin of Slains Castle reputedly inspired his *Dracula*.

At the gloomy **Bullers of Buchan**, the sea has burst through the cliff in a deep, tide-filled, kittiwake-haunted hollow. Beyond, **Peterhead**, the largest whitefish landing port in Europe, and also a North Sea oil servicing center,

Peterhead's harbor—busy with fishing boats

has a maritime museum.

After St. Fergus comes the austere and lonely coastline around **Rattray Head**. **The Loch of Strathbeg**, Scotland's largest landlocked coastal lagoon, is an important wintering ground for thousands of wildfowl.

Off B9033 the fishing villages of St. Combs and Cairnbulg huddle, with gable ends to the sea. **Fraserburgh**, dour in gray granite, has **Scotland's Lighthouse Museum** on Kinnaird Head and a fine beach (see page 177).

Turning west to leave the sands behind for gray rocks which rear up beyond Rosehearty and reach impressive heights around Pennan. Seabird colonies are spectacular around the fearsomely precipitous **Troup Head** (not suitable for young children). **Gardenstown** has an attractive little harbor, as well as a fine walk to the

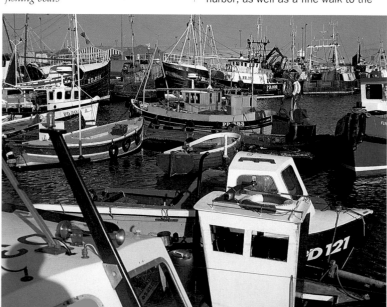

180

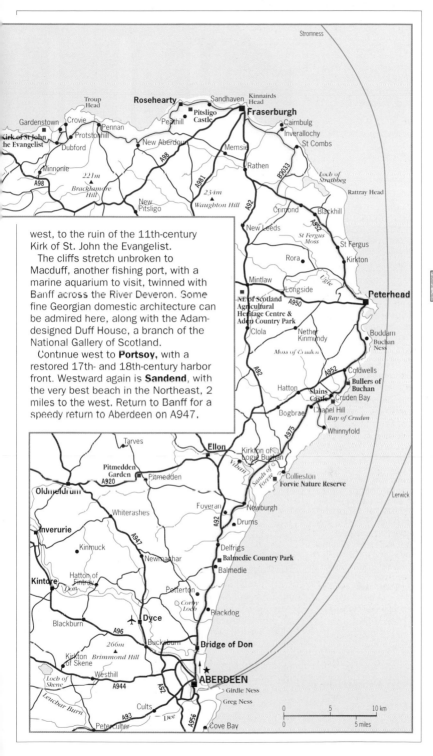

west, to the ruin of the 11th-century Kirk of St. John the Evangelist.

The cliffs stretch unbroken to Macduff, another fishing port, with a marine aquarium to visit, twinned with Banff across the River Deveron. Some fine Georgian domestic architecture can be admired here, along with the Adam-designed Duff House, a branch of the National Gallery of Scotland.

Continue west to **Portsoy,** with a restored 17th- and 18th-century harbor front. Westward again is **Sandend**, with the very best beach in the Northeast, 2 miles to the west. Return to Banff for a speedy return to Aberdeen on A947.

Kildrummy Castle, seat of the Earls of Mar; this is the great triple window of the chapel

A TRAITOR'S REWARD
Kildrummy was besieged by the English in 1306. Sir Nigel Bruce (King Robert's brother) held out but was betrayed by Osbarn the smith, who had been promised gold by the besiegers. After the castle fell he got his reward—poured molten down his throat. Or so the story goes.

AN ECCENTRIC BIRD
Among the Leith Hall soldiers was Colonel Alexander Sebastian Leith Hay, who became laird in 1862. He was in the Thin Red Line at Balaclava and also helped crush the Indian Mutiny. He returned home with a white cockatoo named Cocky, which spoke Hindustani and lived for 50 years at Leith Hall. On its death it was given a burial with full military honors.

TOURIST INFORMATION
Stonehaven: 66 Allardice Street (tel: 01569-762806).
Tomintoul: The Square (tel: 01807-580285).

▶▶ Kildrummy Castle and Gardens   *162B2*
Open: castle Apr–Sep, daily 9:30–6; gardens Apr–Oct, daily 10–5. Admission charge
Kildrummy is one of the best-preserved medieval castles in Scotland—though far from complete, as one glance at the shattered walls will confirm. Built to an unusual shield-shape plan and echoing the fortresses at Caernarvon and Harlech in Wales, Kildrummy controlled the routes through Donside to the north. It withstood many sieges and was finally dismantled after its role as Jacobite headquarters in the 1715 rebellion.

Kildrummy Castle Gardens are a separate concern from the castle, though the two make a good combined visit. They occupy the adjacent quarry from which the castle rock was cut. In this sheltered bowl are many unusual varieties of rock plant and shrubs, as well as a water garden designed by a Japanese engineer. There is often a chance to buy surplus plants.

▶▶ Leith Hall   *162B2*
Open: Easter, May–Sep, daily 1:30–5:30; Oct, weekends only. Last entry 4:45. Grounds daily 9:30–sunset. Admission charge
The archetypal "big hoose," Leith Hall was occupied by the Leiths, later the Leith Hays, for 300 years. They were a military family, and the National Trust for Scotland, which has been here since 1945, has made the most of this with an exhibition inside the grand mansion. There are fine walks within the grounds and a pleasant garden.

▶▶ North East of Scotland Agricultural Heritage Centre   *162C2*
Open: May–Sep, daily 11–4:30; Apr and Oct, weekends 12–4:30. Admission free
Anyone navigating the bleak hinterland of the old county of Aberdeenshire will realize that the forefathers of today's rural communities must have been a hardworking lot. They were the ones who turned a poorly drained, boulder-strewn, exposed shoulder into a fertile and prosperous landscape. Their story is told in this heritage centre, housed in the old home farm of the former Aden (pronounced "*Ah*-din") estate. The center's displays include a fine exhibition "*Weel Vrocht Grun*," defiantly entitled in the Northeast's own speech and meaning "the well-worked ground." The estate is now a 232-acre country park.

▶ Stonehaven

162C1

While Aberdeen's growth has turned many nearby places into dormitories, the center of Stonehaven appears to have retained its character. Originally a fishing settlement, it was extended in 1795 by the local laird (lord) who built spacious streets around a main square a short distance from the old harbor. Today, there are only a few working boats. The local museum is housed in the old town's 16th-century tolbooth, close to the harbor edge (*Open* Jun–Sep, Mon, Thu–Sat 10–12 and 2–5, Wed and Sun 2–5. *Admission free*).

Dunnottar Castle▶▶▶ (*Open* Mar–Oct, Mon–Sat 9–6, Sun 2–5; Nov–Feb, Mon–Fri 9–dusk. *Admission charge*). A few minutes down the coast, this 14th-century fortress is worth visiting for its spectacular setting on a rocky headland. Dunnottar was a stronghold of the Earls Marischal of Scotland. In the wars of the Commonwealth, the Scottish crown jewels were hidden here from Cromwell's army.

THE EARLS MARISCHAL
The title of Marischal originally meant "the keeper of the king's mares." The Keith family of Dunnottar were the hereditary Earls Marischal until their extinction in the 18th century.

Stonehaven harbor. This former fishing port used to have a seaside vacation trade, though this is now diminished

▶ Tomintoul

162A2

Near the southern end of the Malt Whisky Trail, Tomintoul lies among the uplands of Moray, with the Cairngorms on the far horizon. It was founded by the Duke of Gordon in 1779. The village makes a good base for exploring the Glenlivet Estate (part of the Crown Estate), which offers a variety of outdoor activities among the high moors and forests. Tomintoul also has a local museum, part of the tourist information center (closed in winter). It lies on the A939 to Cockbridge, which rises to 2,000 feet, giving access to the Lecht skiing area, and has gained a certain notoriety as it is usually the first road in Scotland to be blocked by snow. However, it is an important link for tourists between Speyside and Deeside.

SCOTTISH HEIGHTS
Tomintoul is the highest village in the Highlands at 1,161 feet; the highest village in Scotland is Wanlockhead (1,381 feet) in Dumfries and Galloway.

The Great Glen & Western Highlands

184

Carrbridge: the arch across the River Dulnain dates from 1715

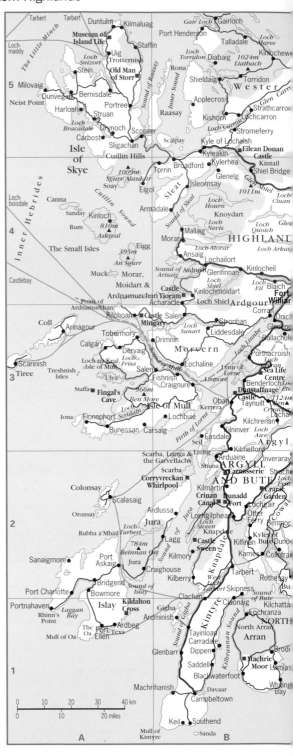

THE GREAT GLEN

The wrenching and sliding of the earth's crust formed this coast-to-coast fault line from the sea roads of Loch Linnhe to the inner Moray Firth. Granite from Foyers above Loch Ness on its eastern side matches granite around Strontian, nearly 60 miles away to the west, in the hills of Ardgour.

WESTERN HIGHLAND CONTRASTS

One example of the interplay between loch and high ground that typifies the Western Highlands is the summit of Ben Nevis. Though it is the highest point anywhere in the U.K., it is only 5 miles from the salt waters of Loch Linnhe.

186

THE GREAT GLEN The area surrounding this coast-to-coast fault line that splits the Highlands takes in Scotland's highest mountains and greatest lochs. With the exception of the gentler landscape around Nairn on the inner Moray Firth, and the greenness of the far end of Kintyre, reminiscent of pastoral Ayrshire, most of this terrain is rugged. Though the central Cairngorms have been almost tamed in recent years by ski lifts, which spill visitors all year round on the fragile arctic plateau, the western Cairngorms remain the province only of the hardy hill-walker. West of the Great Glen, the big glens of Cannich and Affric have hydroelectric dams, but emptiness still lies beyond. Loch Morar, deepest of all in the far west, still leads in to the trackless reaches of the Rough Bounds of Knoydart. Even some of the shores of Loch Linnhe are roadless.

As for the Great Glen itself, its hills just fail to reach truly magnificent proportions: it is large without being impressive. Yet it remains firmly on the touring route of those determined to "do" the Highlands in a day or two and especially of those who hope to find the essence of the Highlands in the busy town of Inverness. Excursions off this main through-route are rewarding, to places such as Glen Roy with its curious Parallel Roads, or to the far reaches of Loch Arkaig and the mysteries of hidden Jacobite treasure.

SPEYSIDE This region, among the old pinewoods, is subtly different. The blue shadows on the Cairngorm backdrop change as the sun goes around, first highlighting, then casting shadows deep into the Larig Ghru, the ancient mountain pass that links Speyside with Deeside. Adding to the enticements of birch and Scots pine, lochs with ospreys and other unusual birds, long hill passes and high level excursions, are the commercial developments which range from steam railroads to Highland estate safaris.

THE WESTERN HIGHLANDS The Argyll area, taking in Loch Linnhe, is different again. Here is the picture-postcard interplay of sea loch and wooded hill slope. The mountains diminish in height the farther south you travel, yet the landscape still retains a ruggedness, among the drowned valleys of Knapdale, for example. It is only toward the far end of Kintyre that a sense of the Highlands is lost almost entirely.

Most of the main population centers in the area have been involved with catering to the needs of generations of tourists. Inverness is a large commercial center serving all of the Northern Highlands. Aviemore was a custom-built 1960s development. Re-development seems always just around the corner: it is looking seedy and is a definite culture shock for those expecting quaint little cottages on the road north. Fort William is an all but unavoidable natural route center in the West Highlands. It has no pretensions toward the picturesque but is practical in terms of its services.

Farther south, Oban is a gateway to the Hebrides and an old-established resort. The often overlooked Campbeltown at the south end of Kintyre is a self-contained working community.

Away from the main towns, there are plenty of smaller places but the essence of this area is definitely rural and rugged, with extensive forestry plantings and a sense of mossy green lushness. When the cloud is down on the hills and the prevailing southwesterlies are dumping their moist contents on campgrounds and luxury hotels alike, consider it only to be an interlude in the ever-changing pattern of western weather (though it has to be admitted that some of the wettest parts of Scotland lie around the Great Glen). When the sun returns, the colors of hill and loch shine out with breathtaking clarity and the West Highlands can be forgiven for everything (except perhaps the midges). This is picture-postcard Scotland, if you time it right.

Ben Nevis from Corpach; this view of Britain's highest mountain hints at the great corries and cliffs hidden when looking up from Fort William

The true Highland cattle of old were wiry black beasts—unlike the modern cuddly version such as this calf

188

▶▶▶ (Aviemore) and Strathspey 185D4

The transformation of **Aviemore**▶ from sleepy Highland railroad junction to upscale St. Moritz-type ski resort never quite worked. Concrete shoe boxes among birches failed to appeal to the desired clientele who, unaccountably, still preferred the Alps. Skiing is very popular here, however, although a combination of gale-force winds and the icy upper slopes of the Cairngorm might deter those who just want to pose in fashionable skiwear. Aviemore bustles all year round with tourists and skiers, but is fortunately a very small blot on a very large and impressive landscape. **Strathspey**▶▶▶ itself is magnificent. Use Aviemore as a good *après-ski* base or at other times of the year for its shops and variety of leisure facilities: ice rink, theater, movie theater, restaurants, discos, amusements, snooker, and so on, all within the Aviemore Centre itself, plus a range of activities and places to visit within easy reach.

The innovative **Landmark Visitor Centre**▶▶▶ at Carrbridge was the first of its kind and portrays many aspects of Scotland, from history to wildlife, by means of audiovisuals and displays. There are also outdoor attractions: mazes, water slides, and adventure playgrounds (*Open* Apr–mid-Jul, Sep, Oct, daily 10–6; mid-Jul–Aug, daily 10–7:30; Nov–Mar, daily 10–5. *Admission charge*).

Rothiemurchus Estate▶▶ This working Highland estate, just southeast of Aviemore, offers estate and farm tours by tractor and trailer, Land Rover safari-type excursions, guided walks, a trout farm, fishing lochs, and other activities. Its visitor center opens daily all year.

Highland Wildlife Park (*Open* daily 10–4, extended hours in summer. *Admission charge*). Not just today's wildlife, but fauna such as wolves (now extinct in Scotland) can be seen safely fenced off at the Highland Wildlife Park at Kincraig.

Loch an Eilean▶▶▶ There is a good walk right around this inspiring loch close to Aviemore amid ancient pinewood, a low-level option well within the capabilities of most visitors. Crested tits and crossbills are a specialty. Watch your head on the door lintel of the visitor center beside the loch (*Open* daily).

TOURIST INFORMATION
Aviemore: Grampian Road (tel: 01479-810363).

CONTROVERSIAL NAME
The area around the River Spey is sometimes known as Speyside and sometimes Strathspey. The local tourist board's introduction of "Spey Valley" to its name provoked fierce correspondence in Scotland's serious press from numerous partisan Scots decrying the "anglicizing" of Scotland's place-names. Even road signs, at one stage, had the new name unofficially blanked out.

The Great Wood of Caledon—natural pine forest on Speyside

Inshriach Nursery▶▶ (Open Mon–Sat). This wonderful specialist nursery on B970, west of Loch an Eilean, is popular with rock garden enthusiasts. It has a good range of arctic alpine species—and if it grows at Inshriach, it will probably survive in your garden.

▶▶ Boat of Garten   185D4

Though singling out just one little community from the many in Speyside seems arbitrary, Boat of Garten is typical. A peaceful base for exploring the area, it has an excellent golf course and a choice of walks through sheltered pine-woods. It is also a steam railroad base.

Offering the best view (the Cairngorms) of any preserved steam railroad line in Britain, the **Strathspey Railway**▶▶▶ is pure nostalgia, especially at the original Boat of Garten Station, near the Boat Hotel. There is a small museum here as well. The line runs to Aviemore. Check the opening hours in advance, but it operates most of the season.

Loch Garten▶▶▶ Another gem lies within easy reach. This is where you can spy upon the domestic arrangements of Scotland's most famous pair of ospreys. They get on with the serious business of first catching fish and then feeding it to their voracious offspring, all before the relentless gaze of closed-circuit television cameras, large telescopes, and terribly earnest wardens. Ospreys are again becoming almost common in quite a few lochs and rivers hereabouts, though they were extinct in Scotland by the early years of this century, persecuted by gamekeepers guarding fish stocks, and returned only in 1959. Look for large, hovering, broad-winged birds, a little like giant lapwings at first glance. The visitor blind is open daily (ospreys permitting) in the breeding season (May to August); the reserve opens daily all year.

Speyside steam trains link Aviemore and Boat of Garten. There are plans to extend the tracks to Broomhill and eventually on to Grantown-on-Spey. Outstanding Cairngorm views are guaranteed

Cairngorm chairlift

A CAIRNGORM GHOST
Few Scottish ghosts are rugged enough for life on top of the Cairngorms plateau, except for one: the Gray Man of Ben Macdhui. He first terrified the life out of a respectable professor who was walking on the plateau in mist when he became aware of something that followed him, taking one step for every three of his. In 1943, another walker, who happened to be armed, fired his revolver at a "thing" that loomed at him out of the mist. Other tales are told by climbers and local stalkers around the fireside—especially after a dram or two.

Skiing in the Cairngorms—big business for Aviemore

▶▶ Cairngorms   185D4

The Cairngorms contain four of the five highest mountains in Britain, some of the finest hill passes and arguably the best ice, snow, and rock climbing. They represent the country's largest continuous stretch of high ground—an arctic tundra plateau. They are flanked by foothills whose slopes carry Britain's largest surviving fragments of natural pine forest. There are endless opportunities for ski touring, walking, climbing, and other activities that respect the fragile environment. The area is under threat from intrusive skiing and tourism developments (see page 188), excessive deer numbers, the proliferation of bulldozed tracks, and commercial afforestation, but still remains magnificent.

▶ Caledonian Canal   185C4

The Caledonian Canal, linking east and west coasts, was started in 1803 under the engineer Thomas Telford. It took 19 years to complete and is about 65 miles long. Approximately 45 miles is along the natural passage formed by three lochs: Lochy, Oich, and Ness, which lie in the Great Glen fault line. The canal has 29 locks, the most famous being the series of eight near Banavie (2 miles north of Fort William), known as Neptune's Staircase. The project received priority as it was considered to have strategic importance for Britain's navy, but was never wide enough to accommodate large naval craft. Today its chief use is recreational. One good place for watching canal activity is at Fort Augustus, with its series of locks through the center of the village.

▶▶▶ Cawdor Castle   185D5

Open: May–mid-Oct, daily 10–5. Admission charge
Some castles in private hands impress with their opulence, others display stuffy collections while the owner lives elsewhere. Cawdor Castle, the romantic family home of the earls of Cawdor, does neither of these things, but instead combines the appearance of a fortified stronghold with an air of friendliness.

Though it has a legendary association with Shakespeare's *Macbeth*, it postdates the historical events around which Shakespeare wrote the well-known tragedy. Most of Cawdor is 16th- or 17th-century, though the central tower dates from around 1370, with 15th-century fortifications. Unoccupied for about 100 years after the last Jacobite uprising in 1745, the castle owes much of its charm to its unaltered appearance since those days.

Generations of the family have accumulated a variety of artifacts: portraits, Flemish tapestries, Venetian bed hangings, and so on, as well as historical material, including the iron gate or yett from Lochindorb Castle (see page 195) which the sixth Thane of Cawdor was ordered to destroy. But Cawdor is much more about the overall effect than individual display items.

Best of all are the room notes. Far from silently tiptoeing past objects, visitors can be heard laughing out loud at the witty captions—a scenario unique in a Scottish castle which makes it well worth visiting for that reason alone. There are also attractive gardens.

▶ Cowal and the Kyles of Bute   184B2

Cowal reaches down toward the island of Bute and is bounded by the long fjord-like sea lochs of Loch Long and Loch Fyne. It is sometimes overlooked in the head-long dash for the west coast but is a most attractive part of Argyll. It is also easy to reach from the south via the Gourock-to-Dunoon ferry crossing. The Arrochar Alps guard its northern approaches, and it has a number of scenically spectacular roads, of which the Rest and Be Thankful (A83 west of Arrochar) is the best known.

Much of this area is contained within the **Argyll Forest Park**, with its diversity of walking and pony-trekking routes. There are more exotic trees to see in the **Younger Botanic Garden** at Benmore. This outstation of Edinburgh's Royal Botanic Garden features some of the largest trees anywhere in Scotland and a world-famous rhododendron collection. It is closed in winter.

Cowal's outstretched fingers on either side of Bute form the **Kyles of Bute** (from the Gaelic *caolas*, a strait). These peerless stretches of coastal scenery can be enjoyed from the A886, en route to or from the Bute ferry at Colintraive.

191

BRODIE CASTLE
After Cawdor, castle enthusiasts can travel eastward, just into Moray, to enjoy Brodie Castle (see page 177). The long and unbroken line of Brodies (they were here by 1160) has allowed a unique continuity in its acquisitions. Cawdor and Brodie could be fitted into a morning and afternoon, with lunch at Brodie Country Fayre en route.

One of the most entertaining of Scotland's castles, Cawdor also has attractive gardens and nature trails

▶▶▶ Crarae Garden   184B2

Open: daily 9–6, or sunset if earlier. Admission charge

If there is time for only one Argyll garden, then Crarae should be chosen. All the natural advantages of topography and climate have been used to create this woodland garden on a hillside with a tumbling brook. Snow does not linger, rainfall is copious, and these soft conditions are appreciated by many tender shrubs, acer and eucryphia, and a range of Himalayan species. Particularly arresting are the large-leaved rhododendrons, including *R. macabeanum*. There is good color here in spring and fall, too. Be prepared to walk a little way uphill to take it all in— that way you will see why Crarae has been described as being like a wild corner of some Himalayan gorge.

▶▶ Crinan Canal   184B2

Designed so that ships could avoid the long haul around the Mull of Kintyre, the 9-mile Crinan Canal was begun in 1794. After many construction problems and the help of

Crarae Garden, of interest throughout the year, but perhaps best in late spring

troubleshooting engineer Thomas Telford, it was pronounced satisfactory in 1817. Once used by the Loch Fyne herring fleet seeking new grounds, the canal is mainly used now by yachts, picturesque concentrations of which can be found at the Crinan end, where there is a good hotel and a coffee shop.

▶▶▶ Fort George   185D5

Open: Apr–Sep, daily 9:30–6; Oct–Mar, Mon–Sat 9:30–4, Sun 2–4. Admission charge

Fort George is one of the most vivid experiences of Scotland's history available today. It is also Europe's finest surviving piece of 18th-century military architecture—a huge Georgian fort on a headland jutting out into the Moray Firth like a vast battleship forever anchored to the land.

It was built as a response to the Jacobite rebellion of 1745, to ensure that the Highlands never rose again in rebellion. It has never fired a shot in anger. Weapon development soon made it redundant. Yet, oddly, it still has a military presence. You can stroll along the great walls with their sentry boxes and embrasures, noting that

Crinan Canal, west end, at Crinan

the whole design is in the form of a pentagon with a bastion at each angle. This is the place to learn a whole new military language: ravelin, casemate, counterscarp, firing step, and so on. There is a visitor center, period rooms of soldiers' quarters, and the regimental museum of the Queen's Own Highlanders.

▶ Fort William   184B4

Fort William is famed for its proximity to **Ben Nevis**, though Britain's highest mountain, at 4,407 feet, hides its best profile from the town itself (there are good views from both the Mallaig road and B8004).

The fort that was founded here in 1690 was named after William, Prince of Orange. It was finally demolished in the 1880s to make way for the railroad. Fort William is a natural route center in Lochaber, all but unavoidable for touring traffic heading for the Great Glen. Like Inverness at the northern end, Fort William is far from picturesque but has an excellent selection of services and shops for books, outdoor wear, tartans, tweeds, woolens, and so on.

The West Highland Museum▶▶ has an exhibition on tartan and touches upon the area's Jacobite connections; there is a fascinating hidden portrait of Prince Charles Edward Stuart (Bonnie Prince Charlie), painted on a cylinder and viewed with a mirror. (*Open* Jul–Aug, Mon–Sat 10–5, Sun 2–5; Jun and Sep, closed Mon; Oct–May, Tue–Sat 10–4, Sun 2–5. *Admission charge*).

A trip into Glen Nevis is worthwhile for its spectacular hill scenery. Look for the signpost from the roundabout (traffic circle) at the north end of the town.

Parallel Roads of **Glen Roy▶▶** These curious parallel lines etched on the sides of the glen are the shorelines of an Ice Age loch, dammed by a glacier at the mouth of the glen, which melted in stages, hence the parallel shorelines, the highest being the oldest.

Perhaps the toughest of various hill races throughout Scotland, the Ben Nevis race has a summit checkpoint at 4,407 feet

TOURIST INFORMATION
Fort William: Cameron Centre, Cameron Square (tel: 01397-703781).

THE GLEN COE MASSACRE

Of the massacres in the bloody history of clan warfare none has convulsed Scotland as much as the killing of around 38 members of the MacIan MacDonalds of Glen Coe on February 13, 1692 by a force of Campbell militia (that is, government troops). The official line was that the clan chief had been late in taking an oath of allegiance to King William (of Orange) so his clan was taught a lesson. But the king's troops had been billeted with their MacDonald hosts, observing an old Highland custom of hospitality even to bitter enemies. The breaking of this code and the resulting "murder under trust" shocked Scotland. The king had blood on his hands—and, besides, the job was botched.

TOURIST INFORMATION
Grantown-on-Spey:
54 High Street (tel:
01479-872773).

A Highlander, not Bonnie Prince Charlie, tops the Glenfinnan Monument

▶▶▶ Glen Affric   185C5

Glen Affric has a reputation as one of the most beautiful glens in all of Scotland—and this even with a hydroelectric dam. As a way of getting into the excellent hill and, in some places, natural pinewood scenery, there is a choice of Forestry Commission walks. The best known is around the **Dog Falls**, themselves close to the twisty road up the glen. This trip could also take in the **Aigas Dam Fish Lift▶**, on scenic A831 through Strathglass to the northwest, a facility for viewing migrating salmon. (*Open* Jun–Oct daily, 10 AM and 3 PM).

▶▶ Glen Coe   185C3

Glen Coe is probably the most famous glen in Scotland, partly because it carries a main road that allows some of the finest hill scenery in the central Highlands to be viewed with no effort whatsoever. This includes the impressive view of Buchaille Etive Mor guarding the eastern approaches to the glen, and the "Three Sisters," the three long spurs running off Bidean nam Bian, the highest peak in Argyll. Matching these south-side features is the long wall of the Aonach Eagach ridge enclosing Glen Coe to the north. This is the most spectacular ridge walk on the Scottish mainland—but definitely not for the fainthearted, the unfit, or the novice.

The National Trust for Scotland is in charge of much of the glen, hence the obtrusive visitor center (*Open* Apr–mid-May and Sep–Oct, daily 10–5; mid-May–Aug, daily 9:30–5:30. Last entry 30 mins before closing. *Admission charge*). These hills are awesome and high—but certainly not lonely. Also worth exploring is Glen Etive, a road down to the head of a sea loch with a fine, wild flavor.

At Ballachulish, a former slate-quarrying village west of Glen Coe, **Highland Mystery World** explores the myths and spirits believed in by the Highlanders of old (*Open* Apr–Oct, daily 10–5. *Admission charge*).

▶▶ Glenfinnan   184B4

The view down Glenfinnan is of a typical Western Highlands landscape, and is an image reproduced on

many a picture postcard. The rash adventurer, Bonnie Prince Charlie, hardly chose this location for scenery alone when he raised the flag of rebellion in August 1745. However, the subsequent Glenfinnan Monument, recalling the escapade, adds interest to the foreground in the view from the main Mallaig road. There is a National Trust for Scotland visitor center here, which tells the story of the prince's campaign (*Open* Apr–mid-May and Sep–Oct, daily 10–5; mid-May–Aug, daily 9:30–6. *Admission charge*).

Equally photogenic is the nearby **Glenfinnan Viaduct▶▶▶** on the "Mallaig Extension" of the West Highland Railway of 1901. The engineer Robert MacAlpine ("Concrete Bob") pioneered the use of mass concrete for such large works while building the line. Unlike Bonnie Prince Charlie's excursion here, this brought only benefit to the Western Highlands.

195

Glenfinnan Station and Museum

▶ Grantown-on-Spey 185D5

James Grant of Castle Grant planned his new town in 1766, intending to get some return on the poor moorland site. Handsome buildings of local silver granite soon sprang up, and local trades such as weaving, developed. The town became popular with tourists and is still a handsome place, well worth strolling around, especially for a complete contrast to Aviemore. It has interesting shops, if quality souvenirs and gifts are on your list, and a good café or two.

The **Speyside Heather Garden Centre▶▶** (*Open* Mon–Sat 9–6, Sun 10–6, for winter hours). Within easy reach of Grantown, this center sells a huge variety of

heather species; the centre will also inform you at its Heather Heritage Centre of the many different and remarkable uses of heather in the Highland economy of old, from folk remedies to rope-making.

Another excursion north of Grantown leads across endless moors to Lochindorb Castle, a shattered remnant on an island, once the lair of the Wolf of Badenoch (see page 175).

THE RAILROAD VIADUCT
Concrete Bob's railroad viaduct at Glenfinnan has 21 spans and is 1,280 feet long. It receives much attention from photographers when it is carrying one of the steam locomotives running a regular summer service between Fort William and Mallaig.

THE "LONE ROWAN"
On the way to Glen Coe from the south, on the left-hand side beyond Loch Tulla, look for the "Lone Rowan" on the approaches to the empty stretches of Rannoch Moor. This single tree grows from a crack on a large boulder. It has survived for years and as such has become a kind of symbol among conservationists seeking to restore Scotland's natural tree cover.

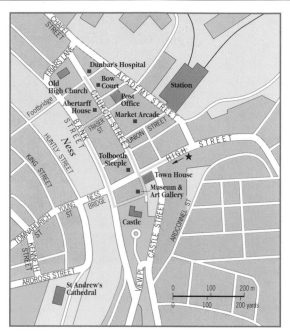

Walk

Around Inverness

Ancient Inverness was regularly burned by marauding clansmen, so little remains. Today, downtown Inverness is a noisy and bustling gateway town serving the north of Scotland. Allow one hour for this walk.

West along High Street, the **Tolbooth Steeple's** spire dates from 1791, and was damaged and repaired after an earth tremor in 1816. Opposite is Inverness **Town House**, where Prime Minister Lloyd George had the first Cabinet meeting ever held outside London in 1921.

Walk up Castle Wynd to **Inverness Castle**. Though its site is ancient, the present building only dates from 1834–47 and is the Sheriff Court. Note the nearby statue of Flora MacDonald, helpmate of Bonnie Prince Charlie.

Go down steps and follow the River Ness north to Fraser Street. **Abertarff House**, one of the oldest houses in the town, is on Church Street. Farther down Church Street is the much restored Dunbar's Hospital. The plaque on the side of the nearby Bow Court dates from the 17th century.

Turning south, the best shopping is on Church Street and in the fine Market Arcade to the east of Church Street. Return to High Street.

Inverness Castle and the River Ness

Culloden was the last major battle on British soil, fought two and a half centuries ago in order to decide a civil war between the ruling House of Hanover and the Jacobites, who wished to return the exiled House of Stuart—in the guise of Bonnie Prince Charlie—to power. The battle, which took place just to the east of Inverness, accelerated the final demise of a way of life already beginning to disintegrate in the Highlands: the Scottish clan system had become something of an anachronism in an increasingly mercantile age.

Anti-Jacobites Only 5,000–6,000 of the estimated 30,000 Highlands fighting men rose to support young Stuart prince Charles Edward, known as Bonnie Prince Charlie or the Young Pretender. Anti-Jacobite sentiment prevailed in many parts of Scotland. On his way north from his expedition into England, the prince had no help from Dumfries; and Glasgow was reluctant to supply him with the provisions he demanded. Edinburgh gave the Freedom of the City to the Duke of Cumberland as he took government troops north to confront the Jacobite forces.

BUTCHER CUMBERLAND
Butcher Cumberland acquired his unsavory nickname due to the conduct of his army after Culloden. Because the rebels were judged to be beyond the law and also because London was a long way off, no mercy was shown, a state of affairs made easier by the fact that the victims were perceived as being racially different in dress and language. This may explain the slaughter that took place on the road to Inverness where bystanders, including women, who had come to watch, were sabered. Wounded rebels were dispatched wherever they were found. Military looting was legalized throughout the Highlands, irrespective of the sympathies of the victims.

The battle On a sleety day in April 1746, about 5,000 Jacobites, exhausted after marching for an aborted surprise attack on the Hanoverians, faced 9,000 regular soldiers, including 15 infantry regiments. Through a tactical blunder by the prince's Irish adviser, the Highlanders were lined up at perfect shooting range for the superior government artillery.

The Jacobites were blown away in less than an hour. The Highland charge, when it finally came, was ragged and ineffective. The government troops then went on to commit, with their commander's blessing, the worst series of atrocities ever carried out by the British Army.

Today, the episode is graphically described in an excellent audiovisual in the **Culloden Visitor Centre**. This does much to counter the myth that this was a simple Scottish–English conflict. (Some say there were more Scots on the government side than with the rebels.) Whatever the truth, Culloden Moor is a strange and poignant place, the scene of much waste and little glory.

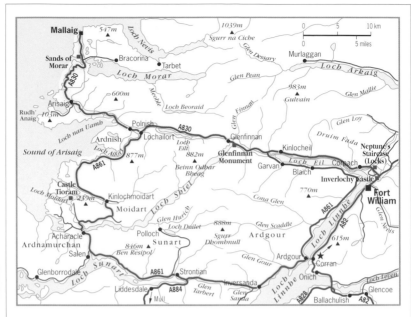

Drive

A loop to the isles

Castle Tioram, destroyed by its owners to prevent it falling to the Campbells

You could use part of this drive to reach Skye via the Mallaig-to-Armadale ferry link, or to make an excursion to the Small Isles from Arisaig—but, if the weather is good, the stupendous island views from Moidart alone make the trip enormously worthwhile. Without the Ardnamurchan option (an extra 41-mile round trip) the drive is 115 miles: it can be driven in three hours or so, using the Corran ferry, but it is best to allow a whole day.

If you are approaching from the south, note the Corran Ferry off A82, useful for your return. Go through Fort William to take A830 along the shores of Loch Eil. You climb away from the seaweedy levels of Loch Eil to reach the **Glenfinnan Monument** by Loch Shiel. Though the hills on either side of the loch are not especially high, their steeply tilting slopes receding down the loch into a blue haze make them the very distillation of Scottish scenery. The National Trust for Scotland Center outlines the story of (Bonnie) Prince Charles Edward Stuart's rebellious escapade here.

Rail buffs will doubtless admire the **Glenfinnan Viaduct** (see page 195). Take care: the train enthusiasts traveling by car are occasionally inclined to chase the locomotive—and it's quite possible that you may be passed several times along this stretch.

Continue to Lochailort, then keep right on A830 for Mallaig. Do not expect to have the dazzling **Sands of Morar** all to yourself in high season. You could also drive down for a close up view of **Loch Morar**, though its reputed resident, a monster named Morag, has been extremely quiet in recent years. Back on the main road, the approach to the town of **Mallaig** is picturesque, with plenty of interest.

chief of the MacDonalds of Clan Ranald, who burned it in order to prevent the Campbells getting their hands on it after the 1715 Jacobite rebellion. It has a grand setting on a bracken-covered islet barely attached to the mainland by a sandy beach.

Continue through Acharacle and Salen to Loch Sunart to decide on the Ardnamurchan option. If taking B8007 across the peninsula to the most

Mallaig harbor

Actually being there, at the end of the road (and railroad), is, however, something of an anticlimax. The **Mallaig Marine World** has fishing displays on the local fleet, a marine aquarium, and exhibition. (*Open* Jun–Aug, daily 9:30–9; Sep–May, daily 9:30–5:30. For winter hours tel: 01687-462292. *Admission charge*).

Return to take A861 loop at Lochailort. Here are the classic Scottish views of islands set in ultramarine—over the Sound of Arisaig to Eigg, Muck, and Rum—unless it is raining, which is statistically and regrettably very probable. Beyond Kinlochmoidart, **Castle Tioram** is a worthwhile diversion. It was the home of the

westerly point on mainland Scotland at the lighthouse, then allow plenty of time as the road is single-lane and winding. Otherwise, continue east to **Strontian**, the community that gave its name to the element strontium, formerly mined nearby. If you go up the road that led to the mining area, you will see a variety of craft businesses on the way.

Continue on A861 through **Glen Sanda**, joining the faster double-lane section and, unless returning to Fort William, exit via the Corran Ferry. Alternatively, note the two roads going south into Morven. Both are attractive ways to reach Mull, via the backdoor short ferry crossing at Lochaline.

Inveraray Jail with live jailer

BRIDGES
Some 18th-century town planning is seen at its best at Inveraray. The stylishness even extends to its bridges, a notable feature on its northern approaches by A83. One of the best examples is the Garron Bridge of 1747–9, reminiscent of those seen on willow pattern plates.

Kilmartin grave slabs

▶▶▶ Inveraray   184B2

Inveraray is one of the handsomest of Scottish towns and owes its appearance to the mighty chiefs of the Clan Campbell. One of them, Archibald, third Duke of Argyll, planned his grand new town in 1743 at a little distance from his castle. Churches and courthouse, bell tower, and Georgian façades all stand together in harmony. Sadly, Inveraray is one of the wettest places in the Highlands. However, it has some indoor attractions. These include **Inveraray Castle**, the stately pile of the present duke. (*Open* Jul–Aug, Mon–Sat 10–5:45, Sun 1–5:45; Apr–Jun and Sep–mid-Oct, Mon–Thu and Sat 10–1 and 2–5:45, Sun 1–5:45. *Admission charge*). There are fine interiors and valuable portraits to admire.

Inveraray Jail▶▶▶ (*Open* Apr–Oct, daily 9:30–6; Nov–Mar, daily 10–5, last entry 1 hour before closing. *Admission charge*). This is a re-creation of a 19th-century county prison, complete with courtroom and cells with live prisoner and jailer. It is more enticing than it sounds. Beware, the prisoner can be extremely talkative—do not mistake him for a wax figure!

Auchindrain Old Highland Township▶▶▶ (*Open* Apr–Sep, daily 10–5. *Admission charge*). This fascinating relic from an earlier age and authentic glimpse of Highland rural life of the past is the last communal tenancy farm township to have survived on its original site in something like its original form. Many of the buildings have been restored and there is an on-site museum.

▶▶ Kilmartin and Dunadd   184B2

Argyll has plenty of early sites and there is a profusion around Kilmartin, a small village on the main Oban–Lochgilphead road. The youngest are the medieval grave slabs in the churchyard at Kilmartin, the work of craftsmen from the so-called Loch Awe school of carving. The prehistoric monuments of the valley to the south of Kilmartin are also curious: 3,000-year-old cairns at **Nether Largie**, one with ax head and cup and ring decoration on the slabs of the cist (burial place) within. Among other early sites, the **Templewood Stone Circles** are close by, and the **Ri Cruin Cairn** farther south is in a group of five cairns in a straight line.

Dating from around AD 500, on a rocky hillock dominating the mossy flatland all around, **Dunadd Fort▶▶** was a stronghold or capital of the first kingdom of the Scots after they arrived from Ireland. Some early walling survives, but the chief point of interest of this hill fort is

Shopping choice in Inveraray: for a small loch-side town, the range is fairly wide

the carvings: a boar, an outline of a footprint, and a hollowed-out basin can be seen, as well as several lines of inscription in the ancient ogham system of writing (see panel). These features have been linked to the early kingship rituals of the embryonic Scotland. Altogether, it is a mysterious place, with superb views across the levels toward the Crinan Canal. Access at all times.

▶Kingussie   185D4

Kingussie (pronounced "kin-*yoo*-see") is a typical Speyside tourism community which benefits from the visitor trade year-round. Nearby **Ruthven Barracks▶**, destroyed by retreating Jacobites after Culloden, still dominate the valley floor near Kingussie. They can be visited en route to the Royal Society for the Protection of Birds' **Insh Marshes▶▶▶**, Scotland's largest inland marsh. Goosander and red-breasted merganser breed here; spotted crake and water rail are often heard; and there are wood and common sandpipers in summer, with hen harriers and buzzards all year. In winter, 10 percent of the United Kingdom's population of whooper swans is found here, along with greylag geese and goldeneyes.

Highland Folk Museum▶▶▶ (*Open* Apr–Oct, Mon–Sat 10–6, Sun 2–6; Nov–Mar, Mon–Fri 10–3. *Admission charge*). Not just a passive show of half-forgotten artifacts, this museum recaptures the past with a program of events and activities: you smell bannocks (oatmeal cakes) toasting or hear a horse being shod if you choose the right day. Costumes, musical instruments, and everyday bits and pieces can be seen, as can authentically reconstructed buildings such as a "black house" from Lewis.

HIGHLAND WILDLIFE PARK
KINCRAIG

►► **Kintyre**   *184B1*

This is the longest peninsula in Scotland, with the Mull of Kintyre at its tip. Kintyre's gateway is Tarbert on the isthmus, where there is a heritage center. Some visitors get no farther, which is a pity, as Kintyre offers splendid sea views from both its east- and west-facing coasts, as well as an unexpectedly Lowland air in places. (The Campbell Dukes of Argyll once settled the area with Lowland farmers.) The raised beaches backed by ancient sea cliffs, typical west-side landscapes, are bright pasture lands, echoing Ayrshire over on the "mainland."

Near Southend on the southern tip of the Mull of Kintyre, an area neither Highland nor Lowland in character, but with an ambience all its own

COLUMBA'S FOOTSTEPS
This is the name given to two footprint-shaped impressions on a flat-topped rock near an ancient chapel site. By tradition, this is where Columba first stepped ashore on Scottish soil. As he could still see Ireland, his home, he took to the sea again before ending up on the island of Iona.

With the impressive outlines of Islay, Jura, and Gigha parading along the horizon, the main road leads down to Campbeltown, a substantial town, busy with whisky, creameries, and fishing. It seems a lot farther than 12 miles down the narrow roads to the Mull of Kintyre itself. Facing west from this spot is very romantic at sunset. The best views are from the moorland before the road drops to the lighthouse, which is built well down the steep slope. This trip can also be combined with the loop which goes past **Columba's Footsteps**, on top of a flat-topped rock at Keil, moments from the road. Return north from Campbeltown by B842 (on the east side of the peninsula), which is narrow but scenically rewarding.

►► **Knapdale**   *184B2*

Knapdale is an area defined by the Crinan Canal to the north and West Loch Tarbert to the south. Without high mountains or overwhelming scenery, Knapdale nevertheless has a special charm. The woods that drop to the salty tidelines of the sea lochs clothe rugged hills. There are primroses in spring and, later, twining honeysuckle. Extensive plantings supplement the natural oakwoods, and there is some farming (the area was once noted for its beef cattle). There are no large towns; instead the small villages have often grown up around natural anchorages.

The stone walls of **Castle Sween**► overlook the loch of the same name. Possibly dating from the mid-12th century, the ancient fortress is one of the oldest in Scotland, and can be viewed at any time. There are also finely carved medieval grave slabs and crosses of the Knapdale School to be viewed at Kilmory and farther south at Kilberry, with the further advantage of a good pub near the latter. Knapdale is a spot for an unhurried visit. Choose a fine day for the sea views.

▶▶ Loch Awe   184B3

Loch Awe is Scotland's longest loch. Once it drained southward, until with the last Ice Age a breach was made in a fault line. The loch now empties by the Pass of Brander westward to Loch Etive. Loch Awe is most often seen from A85, the main Perth-to-Oban road, where its length is not appreciated. However, there are numerous points of interest along this stretch.

At the **Cruachan Dam Visitor Center▶▶▶** there are displays about the impressive hydroelectric project, which generates 400 MW of electricity by running water from a dam high on Ben Cruachan down into Loch Awe (and pumping it back at off-peak times). Minibuses take visitors half a mile into the mountain to see the turbine hall (*Open* Apr–mid-Nov, daily 9–4:30. *Admission charge*).

The former 15th-century Campbell stronghold of **Kilchurn Castle▶▶▶** is just a short walk across the flats by the loch. Interpretative boards help identify features in the extensive panorama. (*Open* Apr–Sep, daily 9:30–6; Oct–Mar, Mon–Sat 9·30–4, Sun 2–4. *Admission charge*).

Duncan Ban McIntyre Monument▶▶▶ Take the road behind Dalmally for one of the very finest vistas in the Western Highlands—an even better view than from Kilchurn. Also worth a look are **Ardanaiseig Gardens▶** (*Open* daily in season) and, farther west by Loch Etive, the **Bonawe Iron Furnace▶** (*Open* Apr–Sep, daily 9:30–6. *Admission charge*). Here Historic Scotland looks after the well-preserved remains of a charcoal furnace for iron-smelting founded in 1753, a reminder that industry reached even these peaceful Highland shores 250 years ago.

LONG LOCHS
Loch Awe is Scotland's longest loch at 25.4 miles, compared to 24.2 miles for Loch Ness and 22.3 miles for Loch Lomond.

"BURNS OF THE HIGHLANDS"
Duncan Ban McIntyre (1724–1812) was a Gaelic gamekeeper turned poet who was born in Glenorchy. He is commemorated by a large granite monument, like a temple, on the old Inveraray road, signposted from Dalmally. It offers superb views toward the ridges of Ben Cruachan and its high neighbors beyond Loch Awe.

Kilchurn Castle on the shores of Loch Awe offers outstanding views from its battlements toward Ben Cruachan and its satellite peaks

TOURIST INFORMATION
Fort Augustus (Apr–Oct):
Car Park (tel: 01320-366367).

204

Although very ruinous, Castle Urquhart, on the side of Loch Ness, remains popular in the summer months—perhaps with those hoping to see the loch's famous resident

▶ Loch Ness   185C5

Loch Ness has a larger volume of water than any other Scottish loch. It is around 825 feet deep in places, and the water in this great glacier-gouged trench is said never to freeze. Because of its mysterious reputation, it is very popular with tourists. Take time to explore the area away from the main loch itself, particularly the big glens to the west around Strathglass and also peaceful Stratherrick eastward. Though Loch Ness ends up on most people's touring list, like Inverness, Loch Lomond, and the Trossachs, the loch itself can be a mild anticlimax—a big sheet of water, certainly, yet lacking in real grandeur.

The west-bank road, the busy main A82, goes through Drumnadrochit with its "Official Loch Ness Monster Exhibition" and "Original Loch Ness Monster Visitor Centre," among other enticements. With souvenir shops and cafés as well, it is all-year monster marketing here. Nearby **Urquhart Castle** was once one of the largest castles in Scotland but was blown up in 1692 lest it fall into Jacobite hands. The castle viewpoint is popular with fast-moving tour buses "doing" Scotland in a day. It is a relief to escape to the gentler and more subtle attractions of the east-side road. These include **Loch Tarff**, north of Fort Augustus on B862, and the superb viewpoint beyond (toward Inverness) with its panorama of the Monadhliath and waves of northern Highland hills. The route here follows the old military road, completed by General Wade's men in 1726. The road runs to Whitebridge, with a handsome preserved Wade bridge, then on to Foyers, where the **Falls of Foyers**▶▶ are worth a visit. (Park beside the post office, but take care with young children on the slippery paths). Inverfarigaig is lower down. Starting from the Forest Centre, a forest walk leads up to a fine view of the loch.

Scottish folklore has plenty of references to water spirits, which lurk in and around lochs and burns (brooks), often with evil intent. The water kelpie is blended with Gaelic each-uisge, the water horse, and other beasts in a fantastic menagerie of the Celtic imagination.

The start of the story One quiet week on the *Inverness Courier* in May 1933, there was space for a report that had come from a local correspondent and water bailiff. He had heard of a couple who had seen a strange animal disporting itself in the dark waters of the loch. The couple was thought to be running one of the hotels in Drumnadrochit.

Soon other sightings flooded in. National papers took up the story, and "monster mania" hit the headlines. A prewar patrolman from a motorists' organization reported that he could create pandemonium among the lines of cars parked at the loch merely by pointing over the water. Meanwhile, Inverness Town Council voted to reduce its publicity expenditure substantially for 1934.

The story has refused to go away. It has spawned books, supported a variety of tourism-related businesses both by the loch and in Inverness, and attracted scientists, dedicated amateurs, and hoaxers. It has generated dubious movie sequences and still photographs, echo soundings, and sincere testimony from dozens of eyewitnesses who have seen something.

There is undoubtedly a strange phenomenon to be witnessed here, whose manifestation is of great importance to the local economy. Its appearance is in inverse proportion to the number of cameras trained on the loch at any given moment. Loch Ness is a very large body of water, prone to mirages in still, calm conditions—ideal visitor and monster-spotting weather.

In the Scottish legal system there is a verdict "not proven." Without enough evidence for a conviction, Nessie has to remain a modern myth—the water kelpie with an excellent publicity machine.

SUNDAY OBSERVANCE
A Free Church minister in Fort Augustus wrote of the 1930s monster craze: "...the word 'monster' is really not applicable to the Loch Ness animal, but is truly applicable to those who deliberately sin against the light of law and revelation." He was objecting to visitors going monster-spotting on a Sunday.

205

SOME EXPLANATIONS
Swimming red deer, diving otters, floating logs or vegetation, cormorants, boats' wakes, seals, and many more everyday things have been suggested as explanations.

Not the real thing at Drumnadrochit

ROAD-BUILDING EXPECTATIONS
One explanation often given for the sudden flurry of sightings in the 1930s was the new road, which gave better views of the loch. Some even said the beast or beasts had been disturbed by the blasting. Yet General Wade and his men built a military road down the east side of the loch to supersede the first high level road of 1726. They also blasted out rock above Inverfarigaig and must therefore have created quite a disturbance. Perhaps Wade's forces were too busy keeping a sharp lookout for Jacobites to notice long-necked creatures.

Busy ferry port and yachting haven, Oban's harbor also has room for more traditional commercial fishing activities

TWO CULTURES
It was once the boast of the Stuart monarchs that they had a town in their realm so large that the inhabitants spoke different languages at either end. This was a reference to Nairn, where the Lowland fishers at the sea end of town used the Scots tongue (still heard eastward along the Moray Firth today). At the landward end of the town, the farmers spoke Gaelic. Thus Nairn has for long been on the dividing line between Highland and Lowland cultures.

TOURIST INFORMATION
Nairn (Apr–Oct): 62 King Street (tel: 01667-452753).
Oban: Argyll Square (tel: 01631-563122).

THE ATLANTIC BRIDGE
The Clachan Bridge is a single-arched bridge of 1792 linking the island of Seil with the mainland. Seil is one of the so-called slate islands, recalling an industry that lasted for 200 years until a violent storm in 1881 flooded the quarry workings and closed down the industry overnight. The Clachan Bridge is often called the Atlantic Bridge, because it spans an arm of that ocean. Other bridges on the western seaboard do likewise, but only the Clachan Bridge is so labeled.

►► Nairn   185D5
More Lowland than Highland, Nairn, with its resort air and famous golf courses, always seems to have had a split personality. The former fisher town by the harbor is separated by the main road from the main shopping streets of a center once dependent on agricultural activities. Both lie apart from the mansions and hotels of the seaside resort development that benefited from the arrival of the Highland Railway in the mid-19th century. The resort atmosphere is doubtless helped by the low rainfall—a mere 22 inches annually.
Nairn Fishertown Museum►► (*Open* Jun–Sep, Mon–Sat 2:30–4:30, also Wed and Fri 6:30–8:30. *Admission charge*). This pleasingly informal museum, staffed by helpful enthusiasts, tells the story of how the harbor was built by Thomas Telford in the 1820s and how, about a hundred years later, the herring fishery business declined. The harbor is now mainly used by pleasure craft.
The **Nairn Museum** is a classic, slightly old-fashioned museum which includes relics from Culloden (*Open* mid-May–Sep, Mon–Sat 10–4:30. *Admission charge*). Then there are golf courses and miles of beach backed by dunes, stretching east to Culbin Forest. Fort George and Cawdor and Brodie castles are also within easy reach.

► Newtonmore   185D4
Newtonmore is a Speyside community made more peaceful by the A9 bypass. The old Celtic game of shinty (like a boisterous form of field hockey) has quite a hold here and at nearby Kingussie. The village is also home to the **Clan Macpherson Museum►** (*Open* Apr–Oct, Mon–Sat 10–5, Sun 2:30–5. *Admission free*) with its display of clan

artifacts. Within easy reach of Newtonmore, along A86, west of Laggan, a track leads to the **Corrieyairack Pass▶**, completed by General Wade's men in 1732. This high-level military route from Speyside to the Great Glen, which zigzags up to about 2,500 feet, fell into disuse because of the severe Scottish winters. Now it is disintegrating due to the attentions of four-wheel-drive enthusiasts.

▶▶ Oban   184B3

When the railroad arrived in 1880, Oban was described as the new "Charing Cross of the Highlands"—a reference to London's busiest train station. The rail company initiated trips to the islands and the sea lochs around. Today most of Oban's visitors come by road rather than rail.

On the way from the east, A82 passes the **Falls of Lora** at Connel Bridge. This curious turbulence at the mouth of Loch Etive can be seen below the bridge when the tide runs strongly. Even nearer to Oban is the 13th-century **Dunstaffnage Castle** (*Open* Apr–Sep, daily 9:30–6. *Admission charge*), an old MacDougall stronghold that once controlled the sea roads of Argyll.

Oban is built around a sheltered bay. Unashamedly visitor-centered, many of the well-built solid houses have "B & B" signs outside, and there is a wide choice of hotels. Oban is both a transit point for the ferry connections and a resort. Within the town is a good choice of commercial attractions with long main-season opening hours, including a distillery, audiovisual shows, plus other summer entertainments.

McCaig's Tower▶ is prominent above the harbor. Sometimes called McCaig's Folly, it recalls a local banker who had it built as a family memorial to ease local unemployment. It is open at all times. Both the tower and **Pulpit Hill▶** make excellent viewpoints over this quite handsome town. There are numerous excursions by boat—on spectacular Loch Etive, for example.

Sea Life Centre▶▶▶ (*Open* Jan–mid-Feb, weekends 10–5; mid-Feb–Jun and Sep–Nov, daily 10–6; Jul–Aug, daily 9–7; 1st 2 weeks Dec, weekends 10–5; Christmas and New Year, daily 10–5. *Admission charge*). This is at Barcaldine, 10 miles north of Oban, and makes a popular and rewarding excursion. Britain's marine life is revealed to be every bit as flourishing and exotic as anything in the tropics.

207

A world in miniature—½-scale exhibition, at Kilninver, south of Oban

Feeding seals at the Sea Life Centre, Barcaldine

The Northern Highlands

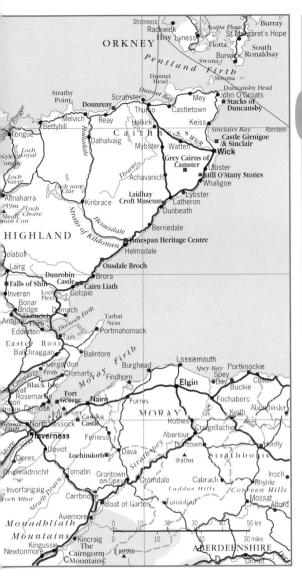

THE JOURNEY NORTH From a southern viewpoint, it is easy to assume that Scotland shrinks as you go north. But take care when route-planning in this area, as there is still a lot of ground to cover. Inverness to Thurso, for example, is farther than Carlisle to Glasgow, and the divided highway sections of A9 come to an end not very far over the Kessock Bridge beyond the Highland capital.

However, this is an area that has seen many road improvements in recent years. Ullapool is no longer a single-lane crawl made hazardous by southbound fish trucks. Instead, it is an easy hour from Inverness. Scourie and Laxford Bridge, far north on the western seaboard, are another two places that can be reached without resorting to single-lane driving.

All of this means there is more time to look at the scenery, the chief attraction of the north. The eastern side continues to resemble a Lowland farming strip most of the time. Look for the use of lines of Caithness flagstones set on edge as field boundaries, highly characteristic of the sparse wind-honed pastures of the north. Yet the moors with their attendant sense of wildness reach down to the eastern seaboard in places—around Helmsdale, for example. There are also spectacular sea cliffs.

Traveling westward, away from the coastal cultivation,

Destitution Road and the shoulders of An Teallach, near Ullapool

210

WEATHERBEATEN HILLS
Some mountains are disappearing fast. The popular Stac Polly in Coigach has lost a few pinnacles in recent years, and its red sandstone is powdering and strewing great screes down its flanks. Meanwhile, it is said that on Foinaven, a northern peak just below the magic Munro mark (see page 149), you can hear erosion—the gentle tinkle of chips of Cambrian quartzite intermittently falling from its fast-weathering gray rock summits. So visit soon!

you soon reach uplands—the boggy flows of Caithness, for instance, with their long open vistas ending in blue hills beyond the blocks of alien and controversial conifers. In the far north, the transition westward into uncultivated landscape is gradual. In the old county of Ross-shire it can be more abrupt. One point that typifies this transition is on the main A832 west of Contin, near the Falls of Rogie (see page 223). Quite suddenly, the last of the Lowland barley, woods, and pasture drops back eastward and its vivid greenness is replaced, at a single bend, by enveloping Highland pinewoods, gray hills, and a choppy loch.

EMPTY SPACES Beyond, you enter the empty quarter. Settlement in the north is mainly, though not exclusively, coastal. The interior conforms to the pattern of much of Highland Scotland. Generally, it is a network of privately owned estates, with vast areas given over to deer stalking, often bought as an investment by absentee landlords. It is the owners of these exclusive sanctuaries, determined to make their land pay, who feel threatened by the increasing numbers of other countryside users, notably hill walkers intent on "bagging" not a stag, but another Munro.

Fortunately, some of the very best chunks of landscape, such as the Torridons, Kintail, and parts of Coigach, are owned or managed by conservation agencies determined to compromise with all parties.

Beyond the backbone of Scotland in Wester Ross and particularly in Sutherland, the old sandstone peaks sit on their plinth of ancient glacier-scoured rock. It is this spare and empty landscape of a thousand lochans (tiny lakes) scratched out of the Lewisian gneiss (granite-like rock), overlooked by cliffs, rock terraces, and shattered hills that is the essence of the far north.

Summer daylight hours lengthen noticeably hereabouts—it is perfectly possible to read outdoors at 11 PM around midsummer (if the midges will let you) and it never seems to get dark. However, the climate does not alter in a uniform way. The far north sometimes has periods of a curious flat calm, especially away from the hills and out on the headlands. Golfers can be enjoying a round at Gairloch in good conditions while climbers in the Torridons are taking compass bearings and extracting rain jackets from rucksacks. Even at low level, for example, walking by Loch Clair, admiring the profile of Liathach in Glen Torridon, you may well experience four seasons within an hour.

It is all too easy to be hopelessly beguiled by the northwest landscapes, especially in the Torridon hills or, farther north, around Inverpolly. Certainly, the Northern Highlands have attracted lots of permanent newcomers from other parts of the United Kingdom throughout the 1980s, with a noticeable improvement in eating-out options, compared with 20 years ago. Though many visitors want to make their way north and west, do not forget the gentler attractions of Easter Ross and Caithness with their old communities such as Cromarty and Dornoch, just two of the handsome little places on the eastern seaboard.

In this northern region, all roads seem to lead to the "Capital of the Highlands." Inverness is now bypassed but is still a natural route center, with roads to the north and west leading out like the spokes of a wheel. And though caution is advised when planning touring routes—it may be farther than you think—it is also true that no matter how great the sense of emptiness, of remoteness and spare beauty in these lands of ancient rock, if it all becomes a little too intimidating, then you can always rush back in a few hours to Inverness with its supermarkets, traffic lights, and other comforting signs of civilization…

Durness schoolchildren's wallhanging of the Highland Clearances

AN OVERVIEW OF THE NORTH

From the summit of Ben More Assynt, one of Sutherland's Munros (see page 149), on a clear day it is possible to see not only a great sweep of the Northern Highlands but simultaneously Orkney and the Western Isles.

Duncansby Stacks, near John o Groats, Caithness

Remembering Queen Victoria's Diamond Jubilee, Dingwall

HIGH-LEVEL GROUSE
There are few places in Scotland where you can see ptarmigan from the car, but this sometimes absurdly tame high-altitude grouse makes its home among the frost-shattered boulders on the exposed plateau at the top of the Bealach-na-Ba (Gaelic, meaning the cattle pass). This is the spectacular way to Applecross, reaching 2,050 feet with magnificent views to Skye.

FOSSIL FISH
Cromarty-born Hugh Miller (1802–1856) was a pioneering self-taught geologist, who started work as a stonemason. He developed an interest in the fossils he found in the local sandstone quarries, and eventually achieved an international reputation for his discoveries and classification of primitive fishes. His birthplace cottage is in the care of the National Trust for Scotland and may be visited in Cromarty.

The road to Applecross, toward the Bealach-na-Ba

▶▶▶ Achiltibuie and the Summer Isles   *208B3*

A side road through Coigach beyond Ullapool offers spectacular views of the impossible crenellations of Stac Polly on the skyline. The single-track road eventually runs through the 3-mile straggle of homesteads that is Achiltibuie. The Summer Isles make up part of the peerless sea views. This bleak group off the mainland of Wester Ross hold a strange fascination for some. Cruises go from Ullapool (inquire at the tourist information center there) and from Achiltibuie (ask at the post office).

▶▶ Applecross   *208A1*

Access to Applecross used to be easiest by sea, especially when the high-level Bealach-na-Ba was closed by snow. Since the 1970s, the settlement has had a low-level road built from Shieldaig. Applecross is associated with St. Maelrubha, who established a monastery here in AD 673. Only a few fragments of early crosses survive from its ancient religious past, but the place still has the air of a remote sanctuary.

▶▶▶ Cromarty   *209C2*

Well worth the Black Isle diversion, this is one of the most satisfying of Scottish towns: full of character, a place that has seen its fortunes rise and fall, with herring and coastal trading, and rise again with oil.

   Cromarty Courthouse▶▶▶ is perhaps the best place to start a tour of the town. Now a visitor center, it portrays the development of Cromarty into a prosperous 18th-century trading burgh (town). If time permits, take the "personal tape tour" of the town's fine buildings. (*Open* Apr–Oct, daily 10–5; Nov, Dec, Mar, daily 12–4; Jan–Feb by appointment. *Admission charge*).

▶ Dingwall   *209C2*

The former county town of Easter Ross has long been an administrative center—its name, from the Norse *thing-vollr*, place of assembly, is a reminder that it was an important settlement in 11th-century Viking times. Within easy reach is the little-known **Black Rock Gorge**▶▶ above Evanton. The River Glass runs through a gorge, about 100 feet deep in parts, yet hemmed in by black and mossy rocks only 13 feet apart at their narrowest. The spot has a decidedly sinister atmosphere.

Brahan is an estate near Dingwall whose name is now strongly associated with the most famous of Highland prophets, the Brahan Seer. Various stories and legends have become attached to him, and fact and fiction interwoven. The Brahan Seer is thought to have been a certain Coinneach Odhar (the Gaelic for "Brown Kenneth," pronounced "co-in-yach oar") who came to work on the estate in the late 17th century.

His prophecies The Brahan Seer predicted the railroads: "long lines of carriages without horses will run between Inverness and Dingwall and Skye." The rise of Strathpeffer as a spa was likewise noted. Of the well he said: "Uninviting and disagreeable as it now is...the day will come when it shall be under lock and key." Some prophesies are eerie, especially one curious prediction concerning the terrible disaster that would befall the world when the River Ness in Inverness was spanned by five bridges. A fifth bridge was opened on the river a few days before the outbreak of World War II.

The most unsettling of his prophesies has already partly come to pass. In it he saw the 19th century coming of the sheep and the emptying of the glens of people. Complete fulfillment of the ending has yet to happen: "the deer and other wild animals in the huge wilderness will be exterminated and browned by horrid black rains. The people will then return and take undisturbed possession of the lands of their ancestors." This meaning is still discussed in the Highlands, with oil pollution and nuclear fallout as two unpleasant alternatives.

An unforeseen end Brown Kenneth came to an unfortunate end when, at an aristocratic gathering to which he had been invited, perhaps as a novelty act, he reported what the husband of Lady Seaforth was doing at the time (being unfaithful while on a visit to Paris). For such an insult in front of her assembled guests, the furious Lady Seaforth had him burned in a tar barrel—or at least that's how the story goes.

BURNED IN A BRAHAN TUB
On the orders of Lady Seaforth, the Brahan Seer was rolled down a hill in a burning tar barrel at Chanonry Point near Fortrose in the Black Isle. A memorial can be seen there to this day. However, this may not have happened to the 17th-century seer but to another Brown Kenneth accused of witchcraft a century earlier. It seems unlikely that someone with a gift for foretelling the future could not have foreseen the consequences of insulting his hostess.

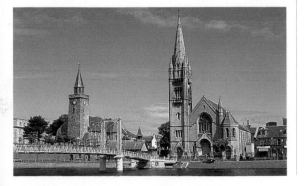

Inverness, where the fifth bridge over the Ness turned out to be "a bridge too far"

[Map showing the northern coast of Scotland from Cape Wrath to Farr, including locations: Cape Wrath, Faraid Head, Balnakeil, Durness, Smoo Cave, Keoldale, The Parph, 485m, Strath Shinary, Portnancon, Kinlochbervie, Rhiconich, 908m Foinaven, Whiten Head, Loch Eriboll, A838, Strath More, Talmine, Eilean Nan Ròn, Skerray, Torrisdale, Farr, Bettyhill, Coldbackie, Tongue, Kyle of Tongue, Borgie, Loch Craggie, Loch Loyal, 927m Ben Hope]

Dunnet Head to Durness, along the north coast

Drive

By traveling in an east–west direction on this north coast drive, you can see the open, flagstone-bordered fields of the edge of Caithness gradually giving way to the moors and mountains of wild Sutherland. This

Crossing the Kyle of Durness, for the Cape Wrath minibus

route (in all 82 miles long) could be driven in two hours or so, but to get the best from it you might wish to

arrange an overnight stay in either the Durness or Tongue area.

Dunnet Head is the most northerly point in Scotland and makes a worthwhile short excursion from **Thurso**. Heading west from the town, you will see the unmistakable profile of **Dounreay**, which became the world's first fast reactor to produce commercial electricity, on a site about as far from the Houses of Parliament as it could possibly be. It is now being decommissioned.

At **Melvich**, the landscapes start to become more rugged. If time permits, divert to lighthouse-tipped **Strathy Point**, with the dunes and coastal grasslands en route harboring some rare plants, notably the tiny Scots primrose in May and June. (The more conspicuous blue among the grass is spring squill.) Back on the main road, **Bettyhill** is a post-clearance settlement. The name refers to Elizabeth, Countess of Sutherland, whose husband ordered the removal of 1,200 people from their dwellings to the coast during the shameful Highland Clearances (see page 38), as the **Strathnaver Museum** relates. More cheerfully, little coastal loops lead down to empty and beautiful, if windswept, pale sand beaches.

The A836/838 leads on to the **Kyle of Tongue**, with its breathtaking view of spiky Ben Loyal from the causeway that shortens the route around the sea loch. Across the empty moors,

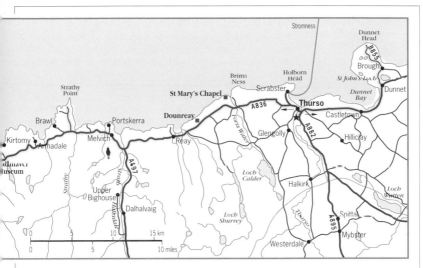

with vast and remote seascapes around Whiten Head to the north, lies the next great sea inlet. **Loch Eriboll** was a former wartime convoy assembly point, known to mariners as Loch 'orrible. There is a well-preserved prehistoric wheelhouse, among other barely acknowledged sites in the vicinity, just a walk across the moorlands—but you should take a map.

Smoo Cave by Durness is a popular spot, a series of caverns by the shore, cut into the limestone by water action. The other Durness attraction is the excursion to **Cape Wrath**, the north westernmost tip of mainland Scotland. Note that you cannot take your car. A small ferry crosses the Kyle of Durness and then a minibus goes to the lighthouse. The tallest mainland cliffs are nearby as well, with the whole area carrying a faintly sinister air, thanks partly to the military range that lies between the Kyle and the Cape. A calmer option is puffin-watching at Faraid Head, a very pleasant walk from Durness: leave the car near the beach at Balnakeil.

Smoo Cave, Durness

THE DESTITUTION ROAD

The roads from Gairloch to Poolewe and northward were built in a poverty-relief program following the famine after the failure of the 1840s potato crops. Government boards put up half the cash on the understanding that local landowners would match the funds. The lairds benefited from the improved communications, their estates increasing in value. Instead of wages, the half-starved locals were paid in meal, as both government and landowners wished to avoid a "dependency culture" developing. Part of A832 is still known as the Destitution Road.

TOURIST INFORMATION

Dornoch: The Square
(tel: 01862-810400).
Gairloch: Achtercairn
(tel: 01445-712130).

►►► Dornoch   209C2

Were it not for its northerly location, Dornoch would be better known: a mellow sandstone burgh (town) with a handsome cathedral on its skyline, a picturesque setting by a great sweep of beach, and a famous golf course. The opening of the Dornoch road bridge on A9 has, however, been of benefit. It is one of the most pleasingly attractive of Scottish towns, also known as the "St. Andrews of the North" because of its reputation for great golf. Though much rebuilt and altered, **Dornoch Cathedral►** (*Open* daily), dates from the 13th century. The town was the seat of the Bishops of Caithness. As well as just strolling around, admiring how the yellow sandstone sets off the roses in the little gardens, things to do in Dornoch include visiting the town jail, now a craft and exhibition center (*Open* Easter–Sep, daily 9–5; Oct–Easter, Mon–Fri 10–1 and 2–4. *Admission free*). Another of the peaceful little town's delights is the golden beaches to the north and south. Ripple-patterned and unpolluted, the long shoals and banks at the mouth of Dornoch Firth are exposed at low tide.

Between Dornoch and Golspie stands **Beinn a Bhragaidh**, a hill west of A9 whose top is crowned by a massive statue. This colossus by Sir Francis Chantney is in memory of the first Duke of Sutherland (d. 1833), a prime mover in the Highland Clearances which resulted in mass emigration.

► Dunrobin Castle   209C2

Open: Apr, May, Sep, Oct, Mon–Sat 10:30–4, Sun 12–4; Jun–Aug, daily 10:30–5. Admission charge

On this sparsely populated and wild coastline, the settlement of Gairloch has a golf course, beaches, and a choice of accommodations

The largest house in the Northern Highlands, Dunrobin started as a 13th-century sandstone keep on a raised beach overlooking the Dornoch Firth. The original keep was progressively enveloped by newer work, the last and most spectacular being 1835–1850 extensions. These were by Sir Charles Barry, architect of the Houses of Parliament in London. He gave the structure its present French-style look with spires and elaborate stonework.

For centuries this has been the seat of the dukes and

earls of Sutherland. The third duke (d. 1892) was Western Europe's largest landowner—his holdings included most of the county of Sutherland. However, Dunrobin has also been an auxiliary naval hospital and a boys' school in the present century. Stuffed with the goods acquired by one of the wealthiest families in the land, it has a makeshift air, a series of rooms laid out to impress with displays of uniforms, trophies, medals, endless portraits, tapestries, and such eccentricities as the duke's own steam-powered fire engine.

The old summer house is a museum containing hunting trophies, from which you gain the impression that the Sutherlands must have kept a squad of taxidermists in work over the years. The attractive gardens laid out below the castle were inspired by Versailles.

▶ Fortrose   209C2

With its neighbors, Avoch and Rosemarkie, on either side, Fortrose is an attractive village by the shores of the Moray Firth. The community originally grew around the cathedral, completed in 1485 but now a red sandstone roofless ruin. Avoch, with its fishing heritage, is like the Lowland towns on the south side of the Firth. North of the three villages is Eathie beach, where pioneering 19th-century geologist Hugh Miller (see panel, page 212) made important discoveries about the origin of the local sandstones.

▶▶ Gairloch   208A2

Gairloch overlooks the safe anchorage of the Gair Loch. Largest of the settlements along this fine stretch of Wester Ross seaboard, Gairloch combines some sea fishing (and processing) activity with tourism, an industry that established itself here in mid-Victorian times. It is a small resort that relies on its own scenic charm. The local sandy beach helps attract families, as does the golf course. Also in the vicinity are **Inverewe Garden** (see page 221) and the beauties of **Loch Maree** (see page 218), as well as **Gairloch Heritage Museum**▶▶ (*Open* Apr–Oct, Mon–Sat 10–4).

Dunrobin Castle, grandest home in the Northern Highlands, is irrevocably associated with the Highland Clearances

GOLFING HISTORY
Many of the priests who came to Dornoch Cathedral had been trained in St. Andrews, where the close-cropped coastal turf was already being used for a curious game with a ball and stick. These religious men were soon exploiting the similar terrain around Dornoch. Thus golf took a very early hold here on the magnificent links, perhaps even as early as the 16th century.

In Fortrose

The mountains of Torridon are exactly to the taste of modern leisure travelers eager to escape from urban pressures. Austere and uncompromising, notched and carved into terraces and ridges, they have a beauty that has made an impact for as long as tourists have made their patient way over the long reaches of Strath Bran to Achnasheen, then the high pass over Glen Docherty.

218

A TRAIL WITH VIEWS
From a clearly marked parking area by the shore of Loch Maree, a hill path ascends the steep slopes leading to the flanks of Beinn Eighe. This Scottish National Heritage nature trail is for the well-shod walker, but gives excellent views over Slioch and Loch Maree as height is quickly gained and the ancient pinewoods peter out.

Far from being a long way off across the backbone of Scotland—now that the roads have been improved across the empty middle—the western seaboard and the Torridons are all too accessible. An easy excursion from Inverness will give a taste of the region, though the mountains deserve much more time.

The main mountains Glen Torridon runs from the sea toward the southern end of **Loch Maree**. A single-lane road runs through the glen, becoming double-lane by the shores of **Loch Torridon**. It is from the southern side of Loch Torridon, on the way to or from Shieldaig, that the best views of **Beinn Alligin** can be obtained. This is the most westerly of Torridon's peaks, a half-horseshoe ridge of red sandstone with a spectacular gash on its southern cliffs, casting a sinister shadow by late afternoon. Its equally lofty companion, Liathach, lies east of it. Rising precipitously from sea level, its quartzite-topped sandstone terraces and summit pinnacles are best appreciated from the east, by Loch Clair. Next is Beinn Eighe— several miles of summits on a quartzite ridge with gray-white rocks cascading down its flanks in long scree slopes. These three mountains are the main performers in the Torridon spectacular.

The National Trust for Scotland owns much of the land by the glen and above Loch Torridon—about 10,700 acres. The visitor center by the Diabaig road junction is the starting point for ranger-led walks, as well as giving an introduction to the unique geology and wildlife of the area. The east end of the glen and much of the west side of Loch Maree was Britain's first national nature reserve, now under Scottish Natural Heritage, which operates a visitor center by the loch (on A832).

Take your time—but do not delay the locals!

Walks in the area Though much can be seen from the roadside, the Torridons are best explored on foot. All the rules of Scottish mountain walking obviously apply: and even at lower level, the terrain is rough enough to make proper hiking boots a necessity. One popular but demanding low-level walk is the "circumnavigation" of the Liathach massif. This demands either two cars, extreme fitness, or a confident approach

Single track road Use passing places to permit overtaking

to hitchhiking. Start either at the waterfall parking lot beyond Torridon House on the Diabaig road or at the lot halfway along Glen Torridon. The off-road section of the walk is 7 miles. The views take in the northern slopes and corries (deep basins) of Liathach and, notably, the less well-known **Beinn Dearg** with its spectacular rock terraces.

Another popular excursion is to view the mighty triple buttresses of **Coire Mhic Fhearchair**. This diverges from the "round Liathach" path to circle into one of the most magnificent corries in the Scottish hills. Alternatively, take advantage of the nature trails on the Loch Maree side, though the mountain trail goes steeply up through the old pines and demands some particularly careful footwork. There are breathtaking views over the loch to Slioch, the peak on its eastern shore.

Fit hill walkers have many possible excursions. The pinnacles of Liathach are not for the vertigo-prone, though there is a path around them. The **Horns of Alligin**, on Beinn Alligin's eastern end, demand a little bit of hand work and need great respect. Meanwhile, the long ridge of Beinn Eighe should not be underestimated. If in doubt, stay at low level, explore the shore path by Diabaig, or the route to the headland near Shieldaig, or stroll by Loch Clair, admiring one of Scotland's finest views, with Liathach filling the skyline like an upturned boat.

NORSE PLACE-NAMES
Diabaig is derived from the Norse *deop-vik* (deep bay), while Shieldaig is *sild-vik* (herring bay). Both little villages are in attractive locations and both offer some accommodations, though Kinlochewe at the east end of the glen is a slightly larger center.

Beinn Eighe from Glen Torridon

Caithness craftsman

SPANIARD'S PEAK
Eilean Donan's destruction by naval gun-fire in 1719 came about because of its involvement in the Jacobite rebellion of that year. A force of 300 Spanish soldiers landed nearby to link up with local Jacobites, mainly Mackenzies and Camerons (plus Rob Roy and a few Macgregors). They joined battle in Glen Shiel with government forces, whose superior firepower made retreat or surrender inevitable. The Glen Shiel place-name Sgurr na Spainteach (Spaniards' Peak) recalls the incident.

Kintail sunset

▶ John o' Groats 209D4

"From Land's End to John o'Groats" is an expression denoting the length of Britain. Yet John o' Groats is not the most northerly point of mainland Scotland—that distinction belongs to **Dunnet Head▶▶** to the west. The seascapes here are, however, spectacular, notably around **Duncansby Head▶▶▶** with its rock stacks. There is a passenger-only summer ferry service from John o' Groats to Orkney.

▶▶▶ Kintail 208A1

Just how much landscape perceptions have changed is indicated by Dr. Johnson's remark, when traveling hereabouts. He described the main mountains west of the Great Glen as "...matter incapable of form or usefulness, dismissed by nature from her care and disinherited of her favours." Kintail today is highly prized for the same elemental qualities that so appalled the urban doctor. The National Trust for Scotland cares for much of the area, which includes the famously picturesque **Five Sisters of Kintail▶▶▶**. These five peaks are all Munros (see page 149), as indeed are many others farther east up Glen Shiel. Also within the National Trust for Scotland sphere are the spectacular **Falls of Glomach▶▶**, tumbling 370 feet in remote Glen Elchaig, accessible only by a 5-mile path over rough country—treat it as a hill walk and dress accordingly.

The best-known (and most photographed) low-level landmark is **Eilean Donan Castle▶** on its islet on Loch Duich. This was wrecked in 1719 (see panel) and rebuilt between 1913 and 1932 (*Open* Apr–Oct, daily 10–5:30. *Admission charge*). It includes a memorial to the Clan Macrae, whose seat it was.

A dead-end minor road heads off from the end of Glen Shiel to Glen Elg. This route is worth exploring, to view not only Skye and Knoydart but also the best preserved brochs (circular defensive structures) on the Scottish mainland. **Dun Telve** stands over 30 feet high. Also nearby are the ruins of the **Bernera Barracks**, originally built around 1722 to control Jacobite activities (see pages 34–35).

Inverewe Garden is on the same latitude as Labrador, but it has a cool and temperate climate because it is favored by the lapping waters of the North Atlantic Drift. The western seas blunt the keen edge of the winter frosts, and extensive shelter belts create the microclimate beloved of rhododendrons, mahonia, and other lovers of dappled shade and moisture. Plants from cool temperate zones all over the world can be found here.

History Until 1862, the garden site was a windy, bare headland with only the island of Lewis between it and northern Canada. But Osgood Mackenzie, whose father and grandfather had been lairds of Gairloch, started his lifetime's work to create a garden in this unpromising landscape. Some of the first trees were planted, not by digging a hole in soil (since often there was none), but by carving out solid rock.

Osgood Mackenzie died in 1922, with the now maturing garden appreciated by temperate eucalyptus trees from Tasmania, species rhododendrons from the Himalayas, and pernettyas, olearias, nothofagus, and other Southern Hemisphere plants that found this Highland home compatible with the Patagonian plains or the high forests of the Andes. By 1952, the garden was in the care of the National Trust for Scotland.

The garden today Inverewe is a late garden, which can mean that you might add a month to six weeks onto flowering times quoted in the gardening manuals—particularly in the early months. This cautious start also means that there is a running together of late spring- and early summer flowering plants into a more continuous display than in many southern gardens. Its most attractive feature is the sense of different "rooms" within the overall structure—turn a corner to reinvigorated plantings and geographically linked species, a deliberate management policy in which the team of gardeners is given comparatively free rein within their own patches.

EARTH MOVING
Osgood Mackenzie's labors in creating Inverewe did not only involve excavating holes in solid rock for trees. Soil by the basketload had to be moved in as even the thin blanket of peat that had originally overlaid the rock had been stripped off for fuel by previous crofting tenants.

OPENING TIMES
Daily mid-Mar–Oct 9:30–9; Nov–mid-Mar 9:30 5.
Guided walks with head gardener: Apr–Sep, Mon–Fri at 1:30.
Admission charge.

Inverewe Garden is a tribute to its determined founder, Osgood Mackenzie, as well as a reminder of the warming effect of the North Atlantic Drift on the western seaboard of Scotland

Guillemots, razorbills, and kittiwakes on Handa's cliffs

AN UNSIGHTLY SCAR
When a proposal was made to put a deep-water oil rig platform site near Drumbuie, close to the railhead at Kyle of Lochalsh, the National Trust for Scotland, which owns land nearby, fought hard for an alternative site. The yard was eventually built near Kishorn, arguably a more onspicuous spot, with its breathtaking mountain backdrop. In the boom years it had a workforce of 4,000 and was the birthplace of the largest mobile structure ever built, the Ninian Central rig.

TOURIST INFORMATION
Lochcarron (Apr–Oct): Main Street (tel: 01520-722357).
Lochinver (Apr–Oct): Kirk Lane (tel: 01571-844330).
Strathpeffer (Apr–Oct): The Square (tel: 01997-421415).

▶ **Lochcarron** *208A1*

Glen Carron seems mostly empty: its soaring hills are clothed with forestry. The blueness of Loch Carron, on the western seaboard, is almost a relief after the unpeopled wildness. The village of Lochcarron is a long ribbon of dwellings, shops, guest houses, hotels, and so on, without a real focal point (it even boasts a golf course). Across the loch, beyond the road and the rail-road with its avalanche shelter, is one of Scotland's larger virtually uninhabited areas. With the Applecross Hills and the Torridons to the north, Lochcarron is ideal for exploring wild country. A896 northward passes through Kishorn and then opens up breathtaking views of the series of corries on the Applecross hills. Also nearby is the **Rassal Ash Wood**▶ nature reserve (administered by Scottish Natural Heritage), where fenced grazing "exclosures" show a rich woodland fauna, contrasting with the overgrazed moors around.

▶▶ **Lochinver** *208B3*

Lochinver is the largest center in Assynt, and a busy little fishing port. Seen from across the sea loch, the blunt bows of Suilven (2,398 feet) rise end on in the rough lands behind the village, as a reminder of the eye-catching Assynt landscapes. Though far north on the map, Lochinver has double-lane road all the way, and also offers magnificent touring options on (single-lane) loops to both north and south. B869 goes around via Stoer and Drumbeg, giving fine views of **Quinag**. From this road at Stoer, there are unclassified roads leading out to the Stoer peninsula with its scattered crofts (small farms). Park near the lighthouse for a cliff-top walk to see the rock stack, the **Old Man of Stoer**▶▶. (It is farther than you think.)

For equally spectacular coastal scenery, a longer excursion (by car) goes via the Kylesku Bridge and on beyond Scourie to Tarbet, where a boatman can take you over the water to **Handa**▶▶▶. This R.S.P.B. (Royal Society for the Protection of Birds) reserve has impres-sive seabird colonies—including puffins—on awesome cliffs, as well as skuas in the interior which alarmingly dive-bomb intruders near their nests. Southward, there is more wildlife interest to be found by taking the unclassified road leading toward the **Inverpolly National Nature Reserve**▶▶ (look for wildcats and golden eagles) There is an information center at Knockan Cliff, by A835.

▶▶ Plockton   208A1

Too impossibly neat to be true, Plockton was a fishing settlement but now has a number of vacation properties. Complete with rambling roses and hardy palm trees, the trimly painted coastal village makes the most of its sheltered east-facing position—unusual in Wester Ross—and turns its back on the prevailing westerly winds. Other points of interest on the Lochalsh peninsula include the **Lochalsh Woodland Garden**▶, a National Trust for Scotland woodland garden with pleasant sheltered walks by the lochside (open throughout the year). Many of the trees are over 100 years old, but the garden is still being developed.

▶▶ Strathpeffer   208B2

The mineral springs in this spa town were described in print by 1772. The first pump room was built in 1819. The local lairds gave the town their blessing and further development took place, assisted by the arrival of the

railroad, which conveyed a regular clientele to take the sulfurous waters. The spa attracted royalty and even George Bernard Shaw. The great Victorian heyday lives on in the town's confident and solid architecture. The waters can still be sampled. Though the railroad has gone, the station remains as an attractive craft complex with a small **Highland Museum of Childhood**▶ (*Open* mid-Mar–Oct, Mon–Sat 10–5, plus 7–9 Mon–Fri Jul–Aug, Sun 2–5. *Admission charge*).

Nearby are a number of points of interest, including the vitrified walling of the fortified hilltop of **Knock Farril** (as yet unexcavated), which can be reached on foot from Strathpeffer. **Strathconon** is also worth exploring, as this long glen often offers good views of red deer. The **Falls of Rogie** are signed from the main road west of Contin and also make an enjoyable short stroll.

THE BATTLE OF STROME PIER
In May 1883, east coast fishermen started landing herring at Strome Pier for rail shipment seven days a week. The west coast fishermen opposed the Sunday activity. Along with the locals, they seized the pier, thus preventing the loading of fish onto London-bound trains. The protestors fought off six local constables and the loading crews. Matters escalated. The War Office in London was informed. Only a large police presence and a troop train on standby the following Sunday ensured that religious beliefs did not stand in the way of commerce. Sabbatarianism is still quite strong in certain parts of the Highland

223

Plockton, arguably Wester Ross's prettiest village

Inspiration by Loch Carron

Though the fishing industry was vital to Wick, no harbor existed here before 1803. Until then the 200 or so boats that sailed for herring had only the river mouth for shelter

AN UNSAFE SANCTUARY

Tain may have been a shrine and sanctuary of St. Duthac, but that did not stop it from being violated. In 1306, the wife and daughter of King Robert I (the Bruce) fled the tightening English siege of Kildrummy (see page 182) to find sanctuary at Tain. This proved no obstacle to the local Earl of Ross (who supported Balliol, not Bruce). He snatched them from the sanctuary and made them prisoners. In the next century, a MacNeil warrior pursued his foes to the chapel and set fire to it.

224

Whaligoe Steps near Ulbster—not for the vertigo-prone

▶ Tain   209C2

Some say Malcolm Canmore granted Tain's first charter in the 11th century. The little town has a fine tolbooth (jail) and steeple. The ruins of nearby **St. Duthac's Chapel** (built 1065–1256) mark the site of the birthplace of St. Duthac, an early missionary to the Picts. Tain was a place of pilgrimage for centuries, the chapel a sanctuary and shrine. **St. Duthus Church▶**, built in 1360, also served the many pilgrims, a story told in the **"Tain through Time" Pilgrimage Visitor Centre▶** and museum (*Open* Apr–Sep, 10–6; Oct–Mar, 12–4. *Admission charge*).

▶▶ Timespan Heritage Centre   209C3

Timespan, in Helmsdale, is the work of a local group of enthusiasts who wanted to preserve the area's heritage, and knew how to acquire funding. The center portrays many aspects of life in the Highlands of old, from Neolithic and Pictish times right up to the Clearances, with a mixture of tableaux, artifacts, and audiovisuals. It also has a fascinating account of the "gold rush" of 1869, which took place in the nearby Strath of Kildonan. What makes Timespan different is the thought-provoking way the exhibits tell the story. There is only one jarring note: the center also has a bizarre shrine to the romantic novelist Barbara Cartland, who has property nearby (*Open* Apr–Oct, Mon–Sat 9:30–5, Sun 2–5, until 6 in Jul–Aug. Last entry 1 hour before closing. *Admission charge*).

Farther up the Strath is the site of the gold rush town. At **Baile an Or** "gold town," 8 miles to the northwest, it is still possible to pan for gold, using equipment rented from a craft shop in Helmsdale. Do not expect to be able to subsidize your trip this way!

▶▶ Ullapool   208B2

In contrast to many ancient settlements with obscure origins, Ullapool can be dated precisely. The abundant herring in Loch Broom inspired the founding of a fishing station and village there soon after the formation of the

British Fisheries Society in 1786. This society paid for the infrastructure of curing sheds, storehouses, a pier, inn, and even a school and some of the dwelling houses. All was laid out on a regular grid plan and mostly completed by 1792. However, it soon became clear that the herring were not a reliable harvest. Ullapool's fortunes rose and fell, and many turned to the land for a living. Overall, however, Ullapool has maintained a strong fishing connection, rising into prominence in the 1980s with the arrival of the Eastern Bloc "klondykers"—vessels buying fish direct for onboard processing.

Two small museums in the town, plus a number of shops and a pottery factory, provide diversion for the strolling tourists, as this is one of the largest centers on this stretch of seaboard. Ullapool also has an important ferry link with Stornoway in the Outer Hebrides.

Corrieshalloch Gorge▶▶▶ On A835 south of Ullapool, this is just one of the area's many scenic attractions. Meltwater from a glacier at the end of the last Ice Age cut a 200-foot-deep gorge, into which the **Falls of Measach** now plunge, half hidden by trees and lush greenery. The falls can be viewed from a spindly, acrophobia-inducing suspension bridge.

▶ Wick

209D3

The workaday, east-wind-flavored town of Wick made a big contribution to the development of fishing. **Wick Heritage Centre**▶▶, with its wide-ranging displays of fishing artifacts, recalls the time when herring brought great prosperity to the town in spite of a dangerous and inadequate harbor (*Open* Jun–Sep, Mon–Sat 10–5, last entry 4:15. *Admission charge*).

North of the town, a pleasant walk along the coastal grazings from the signposted parking lot soon leads to **Castles Girnigoe** and **Sinclair**, perched on the cliffs above Sinclair's Bay. These adjacent gloomily ruined strongholds were the works of the Sinclair Earls of Caithness and can be visited any time—but take care, their situation is exposed.

CHEAP FOOD
Before slavery was abolished, Wick herring, salted in barrels and exported, was used as a source of cheap food for plantation slaves

ALONG A99
Diversions off A99 near Wick include trips to Whaligoe Steps, where a dizzying set of steps leads down the cliff to a former fishing station, and, inland from Whaligoe, to the Grey Cairns of Camster, Neolithic burial cairns of the area's first farmers. Nearby is the Hill of Many Stanes: 200 stones arranged in 22 rows, dating from the early Bronze Age. Their purpose is a mystery.

225

TOURIST INFORMATION
Helmsdale (Apr–Oct): Coupar Park (tel: 01431-021040).
Ullapool (Apr–Oct): Argyle Street (tel: 01854-612135).
Wick: Whitechapel Road (tel: 01955-602596).

On the Stornoway to Ullapool ferry

The Islands

226

*Changeable weather,
Cladach Chairinis, North
Uist, with Eaval beyond*

*The CalMac ferry making
the Ardrossan–Brodick
(Arran) run*

THE ISLANDS Scotland's western seaboard covers about 260 miles in a straight line, but, counting indentations and island shores, is around 2,000 miles long. On such a complicated and rocky coast, even counting islands can be difficult (it all depends on the definition), but it is usually said that Scotland has 790, of which 130 are inhabited.

Apart from the outliers like North Rona or St. Kilda, the island clusters fall into natural groupings: the islands of the Clyde which lie within the estuary between the mainland and the Kintyre peninsula; the Inner Hebrides, comprising the main islands of the western seaboard between Kintyre and Skye; the Outer Hebrides (now usually called, somewhat confusingly, the Western Isles) stretching in a long line from the Butt of Lewis to Barra and beyond; and finally Orkney and Shetland, utterly different in culture and outlook from anything western.

THE CLYDE ISLANDS Access has much to do with character. The Clyde islands were for generations an easy-to-reach vacation playground for the workforce of metropolitan Glasgow and, no matter how much the local authorities try to change this image, just a little of earlier days still hangs around. A 1950s air clings on in the occasional café in Arran or Bute—that is part of their charm. **Arran** is sometimes labeled "Scotland in miniature" because of its scenic attractions. The granites of the Goatfell ridges (the principal hill complex) have enticed generations of outdoor enthusiasts.

The Islands

FAIR ISLE

Sometimes the P & O ferry between Lerwick and Aberdeen sails close to Fair Isle to give passengers a glimpse of this isolated island midway between Orkney and Shetland. It is called the remotest inhabited island in the U.K., and has outstanding coastal scenery, bird colonies, and a bird observatory, as well as the George Waterston Memorial Centre, displaying the island's folklore and history. A ferry runs from Grutness, Sumburgh.

MENDELSSOHN AND THE HEBRIDES

The basalt columns carved by the sea into caves on the island of Staffa, west of Mull, inspired the composer Mendelssohn to write his overture The Hebrides, or Fingal's Cave. This little island has recorded a series of famous literary visitors: Scott, Tennyson, Keats, and Wordsworth, as well as the artist Turner, all came to admire the soaring cathedral-like symmetry. It can be visited from Iona or from Mull.

Orkney tractor

Bute, meanwhile, still echoes the old days of traditional vacations, with its seafront mansions built by wealthy industrialists in Victorian times. It is now a very peaceful place, with an attractive rural hinterland, to which the spectacular Victorian Gothic Mount Stuart House provides an unusual contrast.

THE INNER HEBRIDES Islay and Jura are often grouped together because of their proximity and ferry connections (the Jura ferry leaves from Islay). Yet they are completely different in character. Because of its farming and whisky, **Islay**, at least in part, still has a sense of a community held together without recourse to too many cute craftware ventures earnestly worked by urban refugees—the characteristic feature of all too many parts of the west.

Jura is simply empty—not literally devoid of people, perhaps, but there are few other places where depopulation has been so spectacular. The island has been divided up into a few sporting estates. Some come to the island because of its connection with George Orwell's *Nineteen Eighty–four*, which was written at Barnhill, a remote house well up the east coast. Neither this spot nor the famous but seldom seen Whirlpool of Corrievreckan, a tidal conflict at the tip of Jura, is accessible by ordinary car.

Mull boasts the only other island Munro (see page 149) apart from Skye: Ben More. There is also one highly attractive coastline. Like Skye, Mull has proved a magnet for a new breed of resident eager to escape the pressure of life in the south of the U.K.

As for the smaller Hebridean islands, **Colonsay** is the very distillation of Hebridean charm. With only 14 miles of roads it is hardly worth bringing a car. Colonsay is popular both as the ultimate in relaxing Scottish hideaways and as a good place for bird watchers, with its variety of habitats. These include sand, cliff, machair (see page 283), moor, and garden, and its own (stunted) woodland. Note that **Oronsay**, its companion to the south, with an interesting ruined priory, is only really a separate island at high tide—take your rubber boots for the walk. **Coll** and **Tiree** are also interesting Hebridean destinations, with machair and long beaches. The so-called Small Isles—**Rum**, **Eigg**, **Muck**, and **Canna**—also offer a true island experience, very definitely away from it all, with Rum the best for scenery.

SKYE AND THE WESTERN ISLES Skye—strictly part of the Inner Hebrides—is the most scenically spectacular island of the western seaboard, with glorious mountain landscapes. It is therefore very popular. However, the main ridge of the Cuillins (with the possible exception of Bruach na Frithe) is not a place for the inexperienced climber. The ascent of many of the Cuillins peaks demands rock-climbing skills or, at the very least, a good head for heights.

One way in which the **Outer Hebrides (Western Isles)** differs from most of the mainland is in the deeply felt Sabbatarianism. Once

SCOTTISH BROCHS
These are circular defensive structures, dry-stone walled and double skinned, of which the Broch of Mousa is the best preserved. There are about 400 of them scattered in Shetland, Orkney, Caithness, and Sutherland and farther down the western seaboard. Brochs are presumed to have been built for defensive purposes around the 1st century BC to 3rd century AD, probably against seaborne raiders in the turbulent Celtic world of the time.

Orkney Farm and Folk Museum, Kirbister, Orkney

widespread in the west, the setting aside of Sunday for almost exclusively religious pursuits has retreated to a stronghold here. All too easy for outsiders to dismiss as curiously joyless, the staunch faith must be a source of strength for those who choose to live among the bleak landscapes of the north end of the island. Visitors should respect it.

The lower end of the island chain is Catholic, with a more relaxed community to be found there. Beaches receding to infinity, corncrake-haunted hayfields, and outhouses tied down to escape the wind, are just a few of the far Hebridean images—as is the very real sense of a rhythm of life attached to tide and ferry times.

ORKNEY AND SHETLAND Orkney and Shetland look to their Scandinavian heritage. Orkney also looks further back, to a time when the climate was warmer and the ancient peoples who farmed here left more prehistoric monuments than anywhere else in Britain. These include Skara Brae, an ancient settlement where, amid the Stone Age furniture, an idea of the life of these shadowy ancestors can be gained.

Most northerly of all, **Shetland** is, from the average Briton's point of view, almost like a foreign destination—yet is still within Britain. Shetland's specialties include awesome seascapes—Esha Ness on Mainland, for example—and brochs (see panel).

Do not let the sea be any kind of barrier to visiting any of these islands. Access by the main ferry gateways—Oban, Mallaig, Ullapool, Scrabster, Aberdeen, and others—is straightforward. All of Scotland's main islands are viable communities, with reliable car-ferry links and, in the case of the Outer Hebrides, Islay, Orkney, and Shetland, with good air services as well. And if you want the island experience but do not like ferry travel, then the new bridge to Skye is the answer.

Trimming hooves on Shetland; on the poor pastures and brown moors of the islands only the hardy sheep survive

230

The Arran tapestry, Brodick, displays aspects of island life

Islands of the Clyde

▶▶ Arran   230A1

Arran has long enjoyed a reputation as an island for outdoor-lovers and walkers. The Highland Boundary Fault runs through the island: Arran's southern end is accordingly less hilly. Its largest township is Brodick, with a frontage spaciously set back from promenade and beach.

Brodick Castle and Country Park▶▶ is Arran's most famous attraction (*Open* Easter–Oct, daily 11:30–5, last entry 4:30; garden and park daily 9:30–dusk. *Admission charge*). On the north side of Brodick Bay and in the care of the National Trust for Scotland, the former seat of the dukes of Hamilton displays furniture, paintings, silver, and sporting trophies, but the real attractions are the rhododendrons, particularly in late spring and early summer. There is also a walled garden, and many other shrubs among the great-trunked trees.

Much of the settlement on Arran is clustered around the coast: pottery and crafts at **Corrie**, with its mountain backdrop; even better views at **Mid Sannox** with its bay of ground-down granite. **Lochranza**, where Loch Ranza spills in shallows up the flat-bottomed glacial glen, is yet another focus of crafts activity. Here, too, is **Lochranza Castle** where Robert the Bruce is said to have first landed in 1307 at the start of the independence campaign. Look for the "**Twelve Apostles**" at Catacol—a row of former fishermen's houses, identical except for differing window shapes, in order to be identified from offshore.

On the west side, around Machrie Moor, are

Evening calm on Bute

atmospheric standing stones, chambered cairns, and hut circles. On the east shore, cheerful Lamlash has views to Holy Island (now a religious settlement) and a sobering boulder memorial to the Highland Clearances (see pages 38–39).

► Bute   230B3

The old traditional waterfront resort of Rothesay contrasts with the pasture, peace, and brackeny woodland on the rest of this little island. The resort was popular in the heyday of the steamer network on the Clyde, a story told at the **Bute Museum** in Rothesay (*Open* Apr–Sep, Mon–Sat 10.30–4.30, Sun 2.30–4.30 May–Sep, Oct–Mar, Tue–Sat 2.30–4.30. *Admission charge*).

Rothesay Castle►► This fortress in the town center is built around a circular courtyard. The Norse assailed it in 1230, breaching the wall. (*Open* Apr–Sep, daily 9.30–6, Oct–Mar, Mon–Wed and Sat 9:30–4, Thu 9:30–12, Sun 2–4. *Admission charge*).

Just outside Rothesay is **Mount Stuart House►►►**, ancestral home of the marquesses of Bute. A splendid Victorian Gothic palace, it has plenty to admire inside, from the Marble Hall's galleries, stained glass, and painted vault, to outstanding furniture, paintings, and tapestries (*Open* gardens May–mid-Oct, Mon, Wed, Fri–Sun 10–5; house 11–4:30, last entry 4. *Admission charge*).

Bute has beaches and interesting walks up the west coast overlooking the Kyles of Bute. There are also ancient hill forts and faint echoes of neolithic folk, but the most peaceful place is **St. Blane's Chapel**, a 6th-century religious foundation with a 12th-century ruined chapel, set amid the hushed trees and sheltering mossy rocks.

MEDICAL SUPPLIES
The soft and mossy woods of Bute once provided an unusual harvest. During World War I, cotton became scarce and sphagnum moss, with its antiseptic and absorbent properties, was used instead for dressing wounds. It was gathered from the Balnakeilly Woods, dried, sorted, and packed for hospitals and field units.

THE CUMBRAES
Often overlooked, these are the smallest of the main Clyde islands. Like Arran they are fondly regarded by many visitors, who come for the beaches, sailing, biking, gentle walks, and traditional entertainment. Great Cumbrae and its even smaller neighbor are only a few minutes off Largs on the Ayrshire coast, to which they are linked by ferry.

Cart decoration, Arran & Argyll Transport Museum, Brodick

The Islands

CHOUGHS

These very rare crows (pronounced "chuffs") are a Colonsay (and Islay) specialty. From a distance, they look black, in common with most of their cousins. If you observe choughs closely as they poke about for insects in old cowpats, you may glimpse their bright red beaks and feet. In flight they look like square and ragged-winged jet-black jackdaws. Their survival, research shows, seems to be dependent on the overwintering of cattle outside. Hence the cowpats.

232

Spectacular coastline on Colonsay, an island that offers rocky coastline, sandy beaches, and dunes

JURA

Jura has one road, one distillery, one hotel, six sporting estates, and 5,000 red deer—outnumbering the people by at least 20 to one. Jura's human population was cleared to make the island into a deer forest and sheep pasture. It is a haunting kind of place, with a few traces of the vanished villages—the faint shapes of the "lazybeds" (cultivated strips) still show through the heather. Otherwise, especially near the road end, the bracken and yellow flag-irises, mossy woods, and strands of seaweed crisping on the salty grass form idyllic pictures of summer on the Hebrides.

The Inner Hebrides

▶ Coll and Tiree   233A4/A3

Coll and Tiree duck low on the Hebridean horizon to let the Atlantic weather systems pass over, thus boasting good sunshine records. Tiree looks friendlier in cream and green, while Coll is rockier, with more acid moorland. Tiree has long been famed for its fertile, sandy soil, and the crofting way of life is still followed, more so than in Coll with its cattle-rearing. Both islands were cleared, at least in part, with Ayrshire dairy farmers the new tenants in Coll in the 1850s. In Tiree the clearances were less severe: even today its population, around 750, is five times that of Coll.

Long beaches with crashing Atlantic waves are popular with surfers. Tiree has reliable conditions almost all year. Visit these islands if wide skies, open seas, wildflowers on windy dunes, and a pace of life governed by the tide and the ferry are your idea of Hebridean bliss.

▶▶ Colonsay   233B2

Two hours from Oban lies 8-mile-long Colonsay, its gray rock rubbing through threadbare moorland. If you only have time for one Hebridean island, this is the one to choose. Colonsay's farms raise sheep and cattle, the rabbit-cropped coastal strip is shadowed by hunting buzzards, while wild goats browse around the edges of protected patches of unusual Hebridean natural woodlands of oak, hazel, and willow. Bird habitats include gleaming sandy beaches and extensive tidal sand flats as well as impressive sea cliffs and a loch. Colonsay's most famous (and scarcest) bird is the chough (see panel, page 232).

Lord Strathcona's family owns Colonsay, residing at Colonsay House. The grounds of this rambling pink mansion, **Kiloran Gardens**, with their tender rhododendrons, thickets of rampant escallonia, and many much rarer species, are open to the public all year.

▶▶ Gigha   233C1

Tucked out of the weather off Kintyre, 5-mile-long Gigha has a mild climate. Its main attraction is **Achamore House Gardens**. These 325-acre gardens were originally created by Sir James Horlick in 1944, who saw the place as ideal for exotic shrubs. Within the wooded windbreaks he created one of Scotland's finest woodland gardens. There are thickets of camellias, azaleas hoary with lichen, heather banks, and damp places as well as a superb viewpoint revealing Jura's spectacular profile. The gardens are open all year, and it is possible to visit them by ferry from the mainland in a long morning or afternoon.

ORONSAY

Oronsay is separated from Colonsay at low tide by 1.2 miles of sand flats, a splashy cockle-strewn haunt of plover. Bring waterproof boots to visit Oronsay Priory, an abandoned 14th-century Augustinian foundation with impressive grave slabs and a magnificent early 16th-century cross. Keep an eye on the tide to avoid being cut off.

233

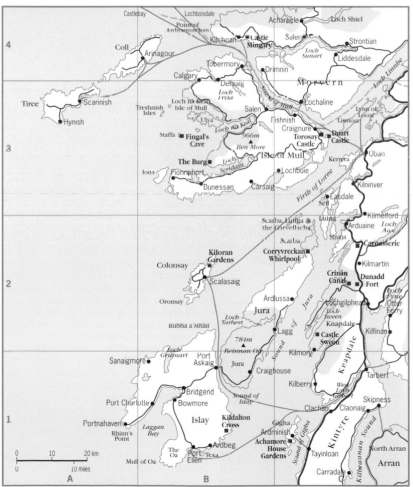

Map of Islay

Rubh a Mhail · Colonsay · Rubha Bholsa · *364m* · *785m* · Nave Island · Gortantaoid · Bunnahabhainn · Ardnave · Tayovullin · Killinallan · Ardnahoe · *Pass of Jura* · Sanaigmore · Kilnave · **Loch Gruinart Nature Reserve** · Port Askaig · **Jura** · Braigo · Leckgruinart · Kilchoman · Aoradh · Craigens · **Finlaggan Centre** · *Loch Gruinart* · Feolin Ferry · Daimh-sgeir · Ballinaby · *Saligo Bay* · *Loch Gorm* · Ballygrant · *Sound of Islay* · Coul Point · Aruadh · Gruinart Flats · Moin a choire · Machir · Kilchoman · Blackrock · Redhouses · Ardfin · *Machir Bay* · Bruichladdich · Bridgend · Kilchiaran · **Museum of Islay Life** · *Loch Indaal* · Barr · Kennacraig · Tormisdale · Port Charlotte · Gartbreck · *Kilennan* · McArthur's Head · *Rinns of Islay 232m* · **Bowmore** · *Laggan* · *Islay* · *191m* · Rubha Liath · Lossit · Nereabolls · Laggan · *Duich* · *Beinn Bheigeir* · Ardtalla · *454m* · Trudernish · *Claggain Bay* · Portnahaven · Easter Ellister · Ardmore Point · Orsay · Port Wemyss · *Rinns Point* · *Laggan Bay* · Glenegedale · Kintour · **Kildalton Cross** · Machrie Kintra · Rubha Mor · *165m* · Ardbeg · Rubha na Gainmhich · Kennacraig · Glenastle · Carnmore · Lagavulin · Lower Killeyan · Port Ellen · Laphroaig · *Texa* · *Mull of Oa* · Inerval · Rubha nan Leacan

0 2 4 6 km
0 2 4 miles

Drive

Around Islay

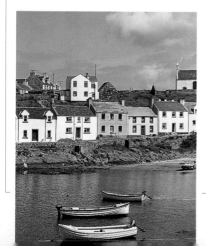

Portnahaven, Islay

Islay has a quite different feel from the rest of the Hebrides. In the western half in particular, it is a place of large farms rather than crofts, and a number of distilleries provide work for the local community. For both the 56-mile round trip from Bowmore and the southern excursion via the Mull of Oa (52 miles), make sure you allow plenty of time for short walks and sea views.

Bowmore is a tidy little town which gives its name to the whisky made in the distillery (founded 1779) by the shore. The dominating parish church of 1767 was built to an unusual circular design so that the devil could not find a corner to hide in.

Take A846 north out of Bowmore to Bridgend, then A847 to skirt the sand flats at the head of Loch

Indaal, following its shores to **Bruichladdich**, a village with a distillery and another malt whisky name. Continuing south for a few minutes you reach Port Charlotte. On the right of the road, in a converted church, is the **Museum of Islay Life** (*Open* Apr–Oct, Mon–Sat 10–5, Sun 2–5. *Admission charge*).

Return north to turn onto B8018, then take a minor road that ends close to **Machir Bay** with its superb sandy beach. The nearby derelict church of Kilchoman has some interesting grave slabs and two late medieval crosses. Circle **Loch Gorm**, pausing to enjoy the fine seascapes at Saligo Bay beyond the former wartime camp.

Return east, turning right onto B8018, then left on B8017. Take a left for **Kilnave**, where the chapel is associated with the massacre of Maclean clansman after a skirmish with the Macdonalds in 1598. In the graveyard is a weathered 8th-century carved cross.

The Royal Society for the Protection of Birds has several farms here, including **Aoradh Farm**, a visitor center with full information on its nature reserve. The low-lying lands are still farmed, the extensive acreage providing a wintering ground for geese around the splendidly wild dunes and endless beaches of **Loch Gruinart**. Drive up its east shore and park before a gate, where the road deteriorates. Walk as far as the

The Paps of Jura from Kintyre; George Orwell wrote 1984 *while staying on the island*

headland—Killinallan Point—on this peerless and lonely coast before returning to Bowmore.

To the south of the island is the southern peninsula of **The Oa**, a region of caves, cliffs, and smuggling tales. At the tip, the **Mull of Oa**, a monument recalls 650 men who lost their lives when the troopships *Tuscania* and *Otranto* went down nearby in 1918. Farther east near Ardmore Point is the highly wrought 8th-century Kildalton Cross, carved from a single slab of epidiorite rock.

En route for the Jura ferry take in the **Islay Woollen Mill** and, a little farther, **Loch Finlaggan**, former power base of the Macdonalds, the Lords of the Isles. Their story is told in a small visitor center overlooking the loch with its little island on which their headquarters stood.

The magnificent Kildalton Cross

The Islands

Torosay Castle, Mull

SUNKEN TREASURE
After England's defeat of the Spanish Armada, several vessels were driven into northern waters. The *San Juan de Sicilia* put into Tobermory for supplies. Rumors spread that it was carrying £300,000 in gold. Donald Maclean of Duart sneaked on board and fired the ship's magazine, though how this would have helped him acquire a fortune is unclear. The ship blew up and sank in 11 fathoms, just offshore, with the loss of over 300 lives. Since then, every so often, salvage attempts have been made but with little success.

In Torosay Castle Gardens, Mull

TOURIST INFORMATION
Mull: Tobermory (tel: 01688 302182)

►► Mull   *233B3*

Eilean Moula, Isle of Mull, is an island of great beauty and emptiness. It has a history of emigration and eviction. Today, it is sometimes called "The Officers' Mess," from its popularity with retired military men.

You can take the ferry from Oban to Craignure, though it is more interesting to use the short (summer-only) ferry crossing from Lochaline to Fishnish. Both ferries are within easy reach of Torosay and Duart Castles.

Torosay Castle►►► Scottish baronial-style Torosay (*Open* Easter–mid-Oct, daily 10:30–5:30, last entry 5; gardens summer, daily 9–7; winter, dawn–dusk. *Admission charge*) is full of interest and humor with its information boards and family albums. The energetic can walk along the shore from Torosay to **Duart Castle►**, otherwise reached off the A849. This ancient Maclean seat was restored by Sir Fitzroy Maclean in 1911 (*Open* May–mid-Oct, daily 10:30–6. *Admission charge*).

Tobermory is the largest settlement, and, like Ullapool was founded as a fishing station. Its gradual decline was hastened by the arrival of the railhead at Oban, which took away fish traffic. However, the brightly painted crescent of mainly 18th-century buildings give Tobermory a faintly Mediterranean air. A museum and a distillery stand on the waterfront, both opening weekdays all season.

Mull's attractions tend to the ruggedly scenic. Near the tip of the dramatic cliff ramparts of Ardmeanach is **The Burg►**, with its fossil tree reached by a rough walk. There is more coastal spectacle at Carsaig, where a very rough path leads west, below lava cliffs, to the impressive **Carsaig Arches►►**.

Even from the road, there is plenty of dramatic scenery, notably on the west coast loops. North of Loch Scridain, B8035 breaches stepped cliffs and drops to the shore with fine views of the island of Ulva. This is a remote stretch with unnervingly fresh-looking rock splinters strewn on it.

Isle of Mull Weavers

Although St. Ninian, the first named mission-ary to Scotland, is said to have built a church at Whithorn in Galloway around AD 397 (see pages 120–121), it is the tiny island of Iona that is called the cradle of Scottish Christianity, because of its association with St. Columba.

Foundation of the monastery The fiery and argumenta-tive Irish monk Columba chose Iona for the setting up of a monastery in AD 563 because it was the first place he reached from which Ireland could not be seen—or so the tale is told. The word of St. Columba's church was spread widely among the northern Picts, these early missionaries being regarded as some kind of superior "medicine men." Such was the importance of this religious community that it eventually became the burial place of the kings of Scotland.

It also suffered dreadful atrocities during repeated Norse sackings which finally caused the evacuation of the community to Kells in Ireland. Even after this it was not abandoned entirely, and many monks were martyred here. It became a Benedictine foundation around 1203, finally falling into ruin by the Reformation. Restoration work began at the turn of the present century, the Iona Community was founded in 1938, and today the restored buildings are a spiritual center under the jurisdiction of the Church of Scotland.

Iona today Today the ambience within the complex is a curious mix of the ancient and the earnest, but beyond the restored cloisters the most mystifying aspect of all is the little island's ability to absorb its visitors and still feel peaceful. Most people only make the short walk from the ferry pier via the nunnery to the abbey. They miss the beautiful white shell beaches and the machair with its undisturbed rich insect and bird life beyond the bare rocks and the thin pasture of the interior. The best place to see the shape of the island is from the top of a certain low hill, the oddly named Dun I (see panel).

A LITERARY LOCATION
From Dun I (a low hill), look for Erraid island, lying close inshore to the south, and difficult to see separately from Mull. Robert Louis Stevenson came from a famous light-house engineering family and knew the area well, as there was a shore base and quarry on Erraid in 1867 for the building of the Dhu Heartach light-house, on an outlying tooth of rock 11 miles southwest. In *Kidnapped*, Stevenson set the wreck of the brig *Covenant* on the reefs offshore, the treacherous Torran Rocks.

The 15th-century MacLean's Cross, Iona

237

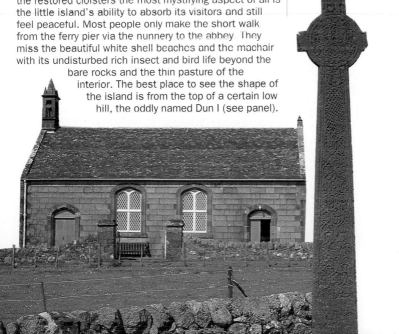

Stromness garage

Orkney

►► Mainland   238A2

Orkney is an ancient archipelago of gently contoured islands, with place-names identifiable from the rich Norse heritage of the Viking sagas. It has the greatest concentration of prehistoric sites anywhere in Western Europe. Mainland is the largest island, and quite a lot of visitors never venture beyond it. **Kirkwall** is the largest town and island capital, built by a natural harbor. This early Christian settlement took its name from the Old Norse kirkjuvagr, "church bay," and has several attractions.

Earl Patrick's Palace and the **Bishop's Palace►►** The Bishop's Palace dates originally from the mid-12th century as accommodations, close to the then new cathedral. Earl Patrick's Palace, Scotland's finest example of French Renaissance architecture, was built in 1600 for Patrick Stuart, ruler of the islands, executed for treason soon after (*Open* Apr–Sep, daily 9:30–6. *Admission charge*).

The **Orkney Wireless Museum►►** (*Open* Apr–Sep. *Admission charge*). Crammed together are numerous examples of wartime communications equipment, including some tiny radio sets used by spies.

St. Magnus Cathedral►►► This magnificent church's harmonious proportions belie its smallness. Founded in 1137 by Earl Rognvald Kolsson and dedicated to his uncle St. Magnus, the red sandstone structure took three centuries to complete. Visit any day to admire its Romanesque, Transitional, and Gothic styles.

Tankerness House►► This 16th-century merchant-laird's mansion is now a museum of Orkney life from prehistoric times to the present. (*Open* Mon–Sat 10:30–12:30, 1:30–5, May–Sep also Sun 2–5. *Admission charge*).

Maes Howe►►► Off A965 8 miles from Kirkwall; this huge burial chamber dates from around 2500 BC and has

workmanship unsurpassed in Western Europe. It was almost 3,500 years old when Vikings scratched graffiti on the walls. (*Open* Apr–Sep, daily 9:30–6; Oct–Mar, Mon–Wed and Sat 9:30–4, Thu 9:30–12, Sun 2–4. *Admission charge*).

Marwick Head Nature Reserve►► Orkney has a wealth of wildlife, notably seabird colonies. These easily reached great red cliffs are stacked with 35,000 guillemots, among other species.

The Ring of Brogar►►► Orkney's best-known stone circle, has 36 surviving stones and other mounds and standing stones all add to the mystery of these monoliths. The **Stenness Standing Stones** are also in the vicinity in this extraordinarily rich area. (*Open* daily).

Skara Brae►►► At this unforgettable prehistoric site, 5,000 year-old stone dressers, beds, and cupboards have survived as furnishings to the snug circular dwellings built before the pyramids. (*Open* Apr–Sep, daily 9:30–6; Oct–Mar, Mon–Sat 9:30–4, Sun 2–4. *Admission charge*).

Stromness is the main ferry port for mainland Scotland connections. The little town became important in the 18th century as a watering place for shipping. Whalers, Hudson's Bay traders, and round-the-world explorers all stopped off here. Today, with its own fishing fleet and boatyards, its narrow lanes and old traders' houses, it has a decidedly period feel. Visit the **Pier Arts Center** (*Open* Tue–Sat 10:30–12:30, 1·30–5; Jul–Aug 10·30–5) for exhibitions and a permanent 20th-century collection.

A FAMOUS MARINER
Captain Bligh (of later *Bounty* fame) was one of many well–known mariners who called at Stromness. This was in 1780 when he was with the *Discovery* and *Resolution*, returning home from the South Seas after Captain Cook's death. He dined at the Whitehouse of 1680, which can still be seen today.

VIKING INSCRIPTIONS
The party of Vikings who came into the Maes Howe tomb in the winter of 1153 not only contributed to one of the largest surviving collections of runic inscriptions, but also executed some fine animal drawings on a buttress. These include the Maes Howe Dragon (though some say it looks like a lion) which has inspired artists and jewelry designers ever since its rediscovery in 1861.

Skara Brae, on Mainland Orkney, is perhaps the most spectacular of the island's prehistoric sights. This extra-ordinary slice of Stone Age life lay buried beneath the sands until a storm revealed it in 1850

A SCUTTLED FLEET

It was off the islands of Cava and Flotta that the interned German High Seas Fleet scuttled itself on Midsummer Day in 1919. In doing so, they not only created a massive amount of scrap metal that was salvaged for years after, but they also became what is now rated as Britain's best amateur diving site, as not all of the German ships were cut up.

Many of Orkney's landscape features come together at St. Margaret's Hope, South Ronaldsay: the prevailing greenness of the pasture, the sturdy, gray-slated dwellings, and the ever-present sea

A WALK ON HOY

Naturalists who want to explore the rugged Hoy hinterland can reach Rackwick on foot by a well-marked track that goes around the north side of Ward Hill, the highest point on Orkney at 1,571 feet. Look for great skuas bathing at the Sandy Loch on the way.

▶▶ **Hoy**   *238A1*

Hoy, the second-largest island in the group, is the exception to Orkney's prevailing low-lying greenness, its north and west being high and craggy. Here the red sandstone has weathered into almost Highland scenery, with a west coast of spectacular natural beauty glimpsed from the ferry en route to Stromness. With the most northerly natural woodland in Britain, glacial features such as small corries (hollows) at comparatively low levels, and U-shaped valleys, plus an arctic-alpine flora (and mountain hares), Hoy has a very distinct character.

The eerily deserted **Lyness Naval Base** on the east coast was the shore base that served the key anchorage for the Royal Navy in two world wars. The former Pump House is an interpretation center. Here, too, is the cemetery as an inevitable epilogue to warfare, with sailors' graves from many famous ships, including H.M.S. *Hampshire*, mined and sunk in 1916, H.M.S. *Vanguard*, accidentally blown up off Flotta in 1916, and H.M.S. *Royal Oak*, torpedoed at anchor here in 1939. Also nearby are the **Martello Towers**, on either side of Longhope Bay, first built in 1813–15 as protection for Baltic-bound British convoys against American privateers.

A road leads west to **Rackwick**, a crofting township gradually coming back to life after a period of decline. This is one of the most attractive parts of all of Orkney, amid the heathery hills with steep shoreward cliffs nearby. From here a footpath leads to the **Old Man of Hoy**, a spectacular sea stack.

North Hoy Nature Reserve▶▶▶ This area takes in the Old Man of Hoy and is noted not only for its seabird colonies, but also species such as the piratical great skua, of which 1,500 pairs breed on the island. It is administered by the Royal Society for the Protection of Birds.

Dwarfie Stane▶ Yet another curiosity, reached on foot from the Rackwick Road, is the so-called Dwarfie Stane, the only rock-cut tomb in Britain. Quite why its 3rd millennium bc excavators should have bothered to chip away at this natural block of red sandstone in its windy valley is a mystery. The tomb has been empty since recorded time.

SEBAY FARM

▶ South Ronaldsay

Though strictly speaking a separate island, this can be easily visited from Mainland by the road link over the Churchill Causeway, formed by lines of tipped concrete blocks. Sir Winston Churchill ordered its construction during World War II in order to close off the eastern arm of the Scapa Flow anchorage after a German U-boat slipped in and torpedoed H.M.S. *Royal Oak* with great loss of life. Rusty shipwrecks, previously scuttled as part of the navy defenses, still line part of the route, adding a surreal quality to the scene.

Italian Chapel▶▶ Starting with a Nissen hut, Italian P.O.W.s in 1943 built this extraordinary *trompe l'oeil* building (even the windows are painted on), creating an intricate embellishment with only scrap metal, cement, and other scrounged bits and pieces. Years after World War II had ended, the Italians' labor of love began to fall into decay. By this time the local Orcadians had become so fond of it that they used the Italian media to find the original builders, who then returned to Orkney to restore it. It stands on Lamb Holm, half-way along the Churchill Causeway, and is open at all times.

The road continues to **St. Margaret's Hope**, gray houses tucked next to a seaweedy harbor, and on to Burwick on the southern tip.

OTHER ORKNEY ISLANDS Among the farther-flung Orkney islands are **Papa Westray**, where two 5,000-year-old dwellings (believed to be the oldest houses in Europe) at Knap of Howar can be seen; **Sanday**, where a tomb of the Maes Howe type—and many other remains—suggests that this was a burial place of great importance in the 2nd millennium bc; and **Westray**, with its ancient church and **Noltland Castle**, a very impressive 16th-century Z-plan edifice, guarding the natural harbor at Pierowall. These and almost all of the other northern outliers of Orkney are well served by the interisland airplane and ferry network from Kirkwall.

241

The Old Man of Hoy, an amazing sand-stone sea stack

Many-layered Jarlshof near Sumburgh Head on the southern tip of Shetland

SUMBURGH HEAD
With its cluster of attractions, South Mainland alone needs a couple of trips from Lerwick, particularly if you are interested in the bird life. Though there are plenty of other places to see puffins, the Sumburgh Head colony is particularly convenient. Park before the wall that marks the lighthouse area, go through the gap in the wall, and walk up the road to the first hairpin bend. Look over the cliff to the right for the puffins.

A fairly quiet day at Esha Ness

Shetland

With its ever-changing seascapes, its Norse heritage, and the sheer challenge of its ocean-girt northerly setting, Shetland confounds any stereotypes of tartans and glinting lochs. Nowhere is more than 5 miles from the sea, thanks to the voes and (smaller) geos, the long fingers of sea that find their way far inland. The ocean is a glittering or grim backdrop to every view, and has historically made Shetland into a surprisingly cosmopolitan place.

The islands themselves are subtly different, with a prevailing inland landscape of crofts and small fields or eroded peatland vegetation, and virtually no trees. The biggest island, Mainland, has the island "capital" Lerwick, the only town of any size, and also some excellent seascapes and nature interest as well as historic sites.

▶ ▶ ▶ Mainland
243A2

Esha Ness ▶ ▶ ▶ Here the sea has hammered away at the cliffs and quarried out awesome rock features: the Holes of Scraada, the Heads of Grocken, and the Grind of the Navir. South of B9078, **The Drongs**, sea stacks in the bay, resemble a Norse galley under sail. North of Ronas Voe, the scoured hump of Ronas Hill can be seen. Though only 1,476 feet high, its exposed northerly situation has created a low-altitude arctic environment, with a variety of interesting arctic and alpine plants on its boulder fields.

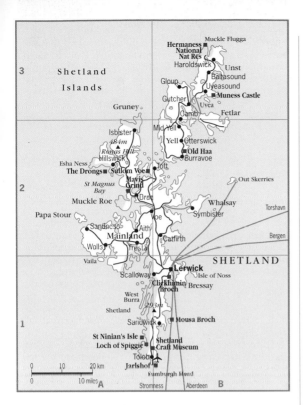

Explanatory panels at the Jarlshof site help unravel the complex pattern of settlement

Minutes from Sumburgh Airport, the important archeological site of **Jarlshof**► ► (in the care of Historic Scotland) represents waves of settlement from the Bronze Age right through to medieval times. Among the earliest huts was a bronze smiddy (blacksmith's). The buildings were then covered by an Iron Age broch (see panel, page 229) whose walls still stand about 6 feet high. This in turn became a wheelhouse, and there are examples of others on site.Then there are traces of possible Pictish occupation, probably between the 6th and 8th centuries AD, before the Viking farm was built over them. A series of medieval homesteads and finally a late 16th-century house of the Earls Patrick and Robert Stuart were built. The latter's ruins dominate the site today. (*Open* Apr–Sep, daily 9:30–6. *Admission charge*).

Nearby look for puffins and otters on **Sumburgh Head** and bonxies (great skuas) loafing around the Loch of Spiggie before their next spot of air piracy. Also within easy reach is **St. Ninian's Isle**, where a treasure was discovered in 1951 near an ancient chapel site. St. Ninian's Isle is a tomboloan—an island joined to Mainland by a spit of dazzling cream sand.

The Shetland Croft House Museum► ► ► is a 19th-century thatched building once typical of the style of croft house found throughout the islands (*Open* May–Sep, daily 10–1 and 2–5. *Admission charge*). The museum provides an excellent way of understanding rural life in Shetland and the helpful attendant answers any questions. Walk down to the fascinating "click mill"—a miniaturized horizontal water mill powered by a tiny burn.

MAVIS GRIND
Mavis Grind is the appealing name given to a point on the A970, west of Brae, where Mainland all but splits in two, except for a narrow rocky waist that carries the road. It is said to be the only place in Scotland where it is possible to throw a stone from the North Sea to the Atlantic, though you still need a strong arm.

The Islands

TOURIST INFORMATION
Lerwick: Market Cross
(tel: 01595-693434).

A NORSE LEGEND
The Orkneyinga Saga tells how Mousa Broch, or Moseyjarborg, already a thousand years old, was used as a refuge in 1153 by a wayward Orkney earl who had abducted the woman of his dreams (a rival earl's mother, hence the complications).

244

▶ Lerwick
243B1

This is by far the largest town in Shetland. No settlement existed here before the 17th century, as the area was not considered very fertile. The Norsemen named the area *leir vik*—mud bay—but muddy or not, the sheltered stretch of water between modern Lerwick and the island of Bressay was a safe anchorage for enterprising Dutch fishermen. Lerwick started as a fishing season trading post, then in the Anglo-Dutch wars of the mid-17th century, it became a permanent town, built around Fort Charlotte, whose walls still survive. Now it has around 8,000 people, one third of the total Shetland population.

Today, "downtown" Lerwick is full of character, especially the waterfront, with the older buildings hard against the sea still retaining their "lodberries" built out over the water. These were shops/houses/storage areas with their own private loading and unloading areas. The main commercial street is at least partly for pedestrians only, with as good a range of shops as you will find anywhere else in Scotland. There are also fine and sturdy Victorian buildings as well as the housing boom on the

Lerwick and its harbor are inseparable, always busy with ferries, fishing boats, and oil-supply vessels

Exclusive knitwear labels, Lerwick Museum

edge of town prompted by the oil developments. The **Shetland Museum** (*Open* Mon, Wed, Fri 10–7, Tue, Thu, Sat 10–5. *Admission free*) covers the principal Shetland themes of folk life, shipping, art, and archeology.

Once solitary on the edge of a boggy loch, now with lots of new housing nearby, **Clickhimin Broch▶▶** has the complication of being a broch built within an Iron Age fort. Open any time, it makes a good preamble to an excursion to Mousa Broch.

Mousa Broch▶▶▶ is the most complete example of a broch anywhere in Scotland, with 40-foot walls. As it is on the island of Mousa, the visit involves taking a boat, which runs daily in summer—check with the tourist information center in Lerwick. Mousa Broch is impressive because it is eerily complete. Boats can be rented on summer afternoons, also weekend mornings and some evenings.

THE SHETLAND BUS
This was the name given to the small craft that maintained the highly dangerous sea connection from Shetland to Norway during World War II. It was used by the Norwegian Resistance for taking in saboteurs and taking out refugees.

Scalloway Castle adds a sense of drama to the skyline of the little town

Another very worthwhile Lerwick excursion is across the neighboring island of Bressay to visit the nature reserve of **Noss▶▶▶**, a much smaller island looked after by Scottish Natural Heritage. Though its vertiginous seabird colonies are not for the fainthearted, the puffins and rapier-beaked gannets offer spectacle on a grand scale. Take the regular Lerwick-Bressay ferry, then walk, cycle, drive, or take a taxi 3 miles across Bressay for a small boat crossing to Noss, and walk all around the island.

Scalloway▶▶ The second-biggest settlement on Mainland (and in all of Shetland) is older than Lerwick. It lies in a more fertile area on the west coast and was the original main town. Dominating the roots of the town are the ruins of **Scalloway Castle**. After the demise of Norse power, Shetland gradually came under the sway of a particularly predatory breed of Scottish baron, of which Earl Patrick Stuart was a typical specimen. As the displays within the castle tell, he used forced labor from the surrounding area to build his fortress in 1600. He was executed in Edinburgh in 1615, the castle thereafter gradually falling into ruin. The key-keeper lives nearby and access is at any reasonable time.

Also nearby is the locally run **Scalloway Museum** (*Open May–Sep, Tue–Thu 2–5, Sat 10–1, 2–5*) which, among other maritime matters, tells the story of the Shetland Bus (see panel) which used Scalloway as a base. (The museum can be visited at other times by telephoning one of the numbers displayed outside). Access to the lesser islands of Trondra and East and West Burra is by B9074, also near Scalloway. All are linked to Mainland by bridges, and the road eventually ends at Papil. At the road end, walk through a little gate to find another fine beach, with views to distant Foula framed by rocky headlands.

By the Town House, Lerwick

CURIOUS ENCLOSURES
First-time visitors to "the bonnie isle" of Whalsay are often puzzled by the small circular stone-built enclosures that dot the landscape. The locals will inform you that they are "planticruives" (variously spelled). They were used to grow winter fodder of the brassica variety. The round wall kept the sheep out and provided shelter. The structure was usually covered with net to keep out birds.

FOULA
Foula (from a Norse word for bird island) offers spectacular coastal scenery even by Shetland standards. The Kame on the west coast is a sheer 1,197-foot cliff, the second highest in Britain. (Only the cliff by Conachair on St. Kilda is higher at 1,411 feet.) Foula is 27 miles west of Scalloway.

A variation on the theme of a boathouse at Gutcher, Yell

▶▶ Unst
243B3

Thanks to cheap prebookable interisland ferries, getting up to Unst is not a problem. It is worth going, if only to see the United Kingdom's most northerly just about everything, from post office to lighthouse.

Muness Castle▶ Scotland's most northerly stone castle was built on low ground by the sea for yet another tyrannous Shetland laird, Lawrence Bruce, half brother to Scalloway Castle's Earl Patrick Stuart. Muness shares approximately the same building date as Scalloway (1598) and the same architect, Adam Crawford. He created a handsome yet functional oblong fortress flanked by two towers on the diagonal, though the third floor and roof are now missing. His client's invocation in verse carved above the main entrance—"To help and not to hurt his work always"—did not impress the French privateers who burned the building within 30 years of its completion. Access is at all reasonable times, via a keykeeper, and the building can also be seen from the road.

Hermaness National Nature Reserve▶▶▶ At the other end of Unst from Muness, this is the very end of the United Kingdom. However, the R.A.F. community at Baltasound and the conspicuous radar station on top of Saxa Ford, one of the twin headlands on top of Unst, give the area a slightly sinister ambience. To make the most of the headland, climb the 660-foot-high Hermaness Hill. Strong shoes are advised on the rough moorland path. There is a good hilltop view of Muckle Flugga with its lighthouse. Take care if investigating the puffin-hollowed cliffs and gannet-plastered stacks on the west side, as the grassy edges slope away treacherously. Keep an eye out, too, for dive-bombing great and arctic skuas breeding on the moor, and keep on the path.

Other features of Unst to note are the most northerly post office at **Haroldswick**, as well as a number of broch sites and other prehistoric places; also, for the botanist, the **Keen of Hamar**, a low, domed hill near Baltasound with plant species from the arctic tundra (Scottish National Heritage permits access only—though the general terrain can be seen from the road).

▶ **Whalsay** 243B2

The Hanseatic League, the trading confederation of European cities that flourished until the 17th century, was important for Shetland. The most vivid reminder of those sea-trading days can be seen at Symbister on the island of Whalsay. The **Bremen Böd** (booth) is a curious little building by the harborside, a restored Hanseatic storage and trading booth, possibly dating from the 17th century. The key-keeper is nearby, so visiting is possible at reasonable times. Otherwise, Whalsay is an island for bird lovers, with several rarities recorded on migration here. It is also a wealthy island, as it is the home of many of the successful local skippers.

▶ **Yell** 243B2

Yell is a dark brown stepping stone between Mainland and Unst. It has more peat than any other part of Shetland, and this is commonly cut for fuel. **The Old Haa of Burravoe** is a 17th-century house (or hall) built by the local laird on the best spot to keep an eye on shipping entering Burra Voe. It has been restored as a local museum with extras such as genealogy, crafts, and a good cup of tea (*Open* late Apr–Sep, Tue, Wed, Thu, Sat 10–4, Sun 2–5).

Clickhimin Broch, Lerwick

VIKING QUARRIES
Among the variety of rock types in Shetland is steatite or soapstone, a soft, easily worked rock extensively used by the Vikings for making a variety of vessels including lamps. One source was near Clibberswick, east of Haroldswick on Unst, where traces of quarrying can still be seen. Sometimes the vessels were formed while still attached to the living rock. They were chiseled into shape, upside down, then removed and hollowed out.

Up at the north end of Yell, it's worth tracking down the **Gloup Fishermen's Memorial** in a field behind one of the crofts. Gloup Voe is long and narrow, and at one time had a large fishing community, which was devastated in July 1881 by the loss of 58 men from 10 "sixerenes," the native six-oared craft.

THE WHITE WIFE
On the way up Yell by B9081, look toward the sea edge for the White Wife near Otterswick and Queyon. She was the figurehead of the German sail training ship Bohus and now looks over the waters in which her ship was wrecked. The Old Haa at Burravoe has a copy of her, as well as details of the drama.

Skye and the Western Isles

▶ Barra   251A1

The seagoing Macneil clan owned Barra for centuries, and often practiced piracy. One chief sold the island to pay debts in 1838, and part of it was bought back in 1937 by the 45th chief, an American architect, who restored **Kisimul Castle▶** (also known as Kiessimul) in Castlebay (Open Apr–Sep, Mon, Wed, Sat 2–6). Castlebay itself was once a thriving fishing port.

In addition to the open shell-sand beaches (one of which achieved fame as the island's landing strip), and the rough inland walking, other points of interest on Barra include **Kilbarr Church**, a ruinous medieval church dedicated to the saint who gave his name to the island. The last thatched croft house on the island is at **Craigston**, northwest of Castlebay. It is now a little museum (*Open* Jun–Sep, Mon–Fri 11–5; other times contact tourist information center, Castlebay).

▶ Benbecula   251A2

Benbecula, joined to the Uists by causeways, is patterned and interlaced with inland waters. It presents great sweeps of sand to the Atlantic, with flowery machair beyond and attendant crofts. To the west, a missile range points into the ocean. To the east there is much rough bogland. The highest point, Rueval, is barely 393 feet above sea level and overlooks endless peaty lochans (small lochs) beloved of fishermen.

▶▶ Harris   251B3

Harris has austere rocky landscapes, except for some western machair and the highest hill in the Outer Hebrides, **Clisham**, at almost 2,598 feet. The "border" between Lewis and Harris runs east from Kinlochresort. Traditionally, the Macleods of Lewis held the island of their name, while Harris was under the sway of

LEVERBURGH
One odd chapter in Harris's story is encountered at Leverburgh, near Rodel, which recalls the efforts of one of Britain's most successful industrialists, the soap magnate Lord Leverhume, to spend some of his riches turning a tiny fishing village into a major fish-processing port. He owned most of Lewis and Harris at the time.

Stockinish post office and postmaster, on Harris

the Macleods of Dunvegan in Skye.

Hiking, fishing, bird-watching, and visiting beaches are the main activities. **St. Clement's Church**▶▶ at Rodel, on the southern tip, is a cruciform church built around 1500 by the eighth chief of the Macleods, sometimes known as Alasdair Crotach, who died 20 years after the construction of his magnificent tomb within the church. Visit it at any reasonable time.

Kisimul (Kiessimul)
Castle and Castlebay,
Barra

249

Above East Loch
Tarbert, Harris

If visiting Rodel from Tarbert, take in the endless empty sands of **Traigh Luskentyre**▶▶▶ and loop back toward Tarbert from Rodel by the east coast road, enjoying the wild and remote boulder country before a whole mountain is removed and a new sea loch is created. This gigantic feat of engineering will make way for a new superquarry which is planned here for the future. Another very twisty drive along B887, northwest of Tarbert toward uninhabited Scarp, passes the former whaling station at **Bunavoneadar** (which was abandoned in 1930—look for the sentinel chimney stack beside the road), and **Amhuinnsuidhe Castle** with its "no stopping" notices. This grand structure was built by the then owners of Harris, the earls of Dunmore, in the 1860s.

ERISKAY
This island between Barra and South Uist was the place where Bonnie Prince Charlie first landed on Scottish soil. Its other claim to fame is that the S.S. *Politician* was wrecked there in 1941 while carrying 20,000 cases of whisky. The subsequent events inspired Compton Mackenzie's *Whisky Galore*.

The Islands

Callanish Standing Stones

TOURIST INFORMATION
Lewis: 26 Cromwell Street
(tel: 01851-703088).

SCOTLAND'S OLDEST UNIVERSITY
Some historians maintain that the Teampuill na Trionaid (Trinity Temple) on North Uist is Scotland's oldest university. This monastery and college founded in the early 13th century lies in ruins, ransacked in the Reformation, its valuable books said to have been cast into the sea. A number of other historical sites are near this ancient seat of learning.

LORD LEVERHUME
Perhaps Lewis's owner, Lord Leverhume, with his English public school background and wealth, failed to understand the Gaelic mind. He became deeply involved in post–World War I politics on the island, in a complex confrontation with land raiders—ex-servicemen returning from war and eager to acquire crofts. Yet many on Lewis supported his vision of an industrialized island society. He eventually turned his attentions to Harris, his grand dreams for Lewis unfulfilled.

An abandoned croft at Barvas, Lewis

► **Lewis**   *251B4*

Most of Lewis's townships are close to the coast, forming a narrow green strip between the ocean and the inland brown sea of endless lochan-dotted peatlands. This initially unpromising landscape has a long history of settlement dating from neolithic and Norse times.

Callanish Standing Stones►►► This is the most famous of the prehistoric sites, possibly dating from 3000 bc, sometimes described as Scotland's Stonehenge. This is a cruciform setting of stones: 19 monoliths form an avenue running north–south from a circle of 13 other stones, with outliers adding to the inexplicable design. View any time.

Dun Carloway Broch► A fairly well-preserved structure visible from the main A858. The walling stands in part over 30 feet high. View any time.

Black House at Arnol►►► This once typical local dwelling is in the care of Historic Scotland. The byre (cow barn) is under the same roof. (*Open* Apr–Sep, Mon–Sat 9:30–6; Oct–Mar, Mon–Thu, Sat 9:30–4. *Admission charge*).

Callanish, Carloway, and Arnol are all on the west coast. It is worth continuing northeast on the A857, all the way to Port of Ness to see the **Butt of Lewis** and its lighthouse. Though the cliffs are not spectacularly high, the ambience is wild and windswept. There are streams of gannets, other seabirds, skuas, and sometimes dolphins or whales to be seen.

Lewis also offers good seascapes on the way to Great Bernera, an island joined to the "mainland" by a causeway: there are plenty of diving gannets and terns off the little beach at the road end at **Bosta**. Arguably the finest beach on Lewis is on the east coast: **Tràigh Mhór** (literally in Gaelic "big beach") can be seen toward the end of the Tolsta road.

Stornoway is the main administrative center for the Western Isles. It is not overtly picturesque and is very hushed on Sundays but has a fine asset in the **An Lanntair Gallery** with its changing exhibition program.

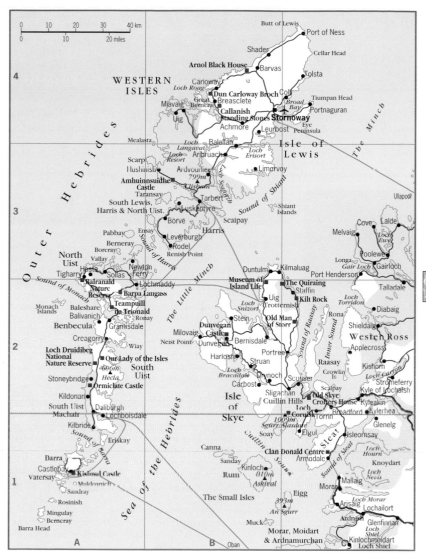

▶ North and South Uist

251A2

These are classic Hebridean islands of shell-sand and peaty lochans, golden beaches with crashing Atlantic surf, and a rocky, wild, and forbidding easterly coast. All of this provides a varied habitat for wildlife, hence the importance of the R.S.P.B.'s **Balranald Reserve** on North Uist. There is a reception cottage (for information on what to see on the reserve), which is open daily.

On South Uist **Loch Druidibeg** is another wildlife area under the care of Scottish Natural Heritage and noted for its breeding greylag geese, among many other species. Check with the warden's office for visiting details. There is access to machair land at several points on the Uists, where the full glory of wildflowers and bird life can be seen in late spring and early summer.

THE TALLEST MONOLITH

The Callanish stones may be tall, but tallest of all on the islands is the Clach an Trushal, a solitary monolith standing by the township of Ballantrushal (between Barvas and Shader) on A857 (north of the junction with A858). This gray, grizzled, lichen-covered tooth reaches a height of around 20 feet.

*Pony trekking at
Sligachan, Skye*

*Roadside shrine on the
predominantly Catholic
island of South Uist*

*A Gaelic welcome on a
Skye road*

FAILTE GU SGIRE
AN EILEIN SGITHEANAICH
AGUS LOCHAILLSE

WELCOME TO
SKYE & LOCHALSH

►►► Skye   251B2

Superlatives and Skye scenery go together. The big hill masses catch southwesterly weather systems, so it does rain a lot here, but when it is clear, the hills make the heart ache. Skye is unforgettable.

Though there is a Mallaig–Armadale ferry link, most people arrive via the new Skye Bridge near Kyle of Lochalsh, which replaced the ferry to Kyleakin. Among attractions on the way to Portree is the **Luib folk Museum►**, north of Broadford. (*Open* Apr–Oct, daily 10–6. *Admission charge*). This thatched, traditional period piece shows the kind of dwelling that the crofters of Skye once lived in.

En route for Portree, the **Cuillins** first show themselves around Sligachan and are still distantly in view from the "capital" of Skye itself. Fairly picturesque (depending on the angle of view) **Portree** has quite a good range of shops and services.

The **Skye Heritage Centre►►►** is a good starting point for understanding the island, particularly the struggles of the crofters. It tells Skye's story from the viewpoint of the ordinary folk who lived there in the fairly bad old days, rather than dwelling upon heroic tales of clans and chieftains. The center uses headphones to pick up and relay information, depending on where you are in the exhibition (*Open* Apr– May, Mon–Sat 9–6, Jun–Oct, Mon–Sat 9–9; Nov–Mar, 10–5, *Admission charge*).

The most interesting of Skye's scenic road loops is the **Trotternish** peninsula. Beyond the curious rock form of the **Old Man of Storr►►**, a popular stop is **Kilt Rock►►** at Elishader. Seen from a reassuringly safe viewing platform, the cliff edge has alternate bandings of sedimentary rock with dolerite, giving the strong impression of kilt pleats. Much of the coastline around here is scenically spectacular, including the 300-foot seaward vertical drop of the **Mealt Falls**.

Beyond the impressive **Quiraing**►►► with its rock towers and pinnacles, and around the top of the peninsula, the Skye **Museum of Island Life**►► by the main road at Kilmuir portrays crofting life as it was lived in a self-contained township. The staff are helpful and eager to tell you more. Flora Macdonald's grave is nearby. (*Open* Easter–Oct, Mon–Sat 9:30–5:30. *Admission charge*).

Though there are other places with Jacobite associations to track down on your way around Trotternish, **Dunvegan Castle**► is the big attraction in the northern half of Skye. For 700 years the chiefs of the Clan Macleod have inhabited this rock above the sea lake, and between the 19th-century front entrance and the 14th-century keep there is plenty of historic lumber to enjoy. Among the relics is the Fairy Flag. All true Macleods believe this ancient cloth has the power to save the clan one more time if waved in battle. (*Open* mid-Mar–Oct, daily 10–5:30, last entry 5. *Admission charge*).

Clan Donald Centre► The Sleat peninsula is sometimes overlooked by visitors heading for Trotternish and the Cuillins, unless they are traveling from the ferry port at Armadale. The area's principal attraction is this center in a restored portion of Armadale Castle. It tells the story of the MacDonalds when they held sway over the western seaboard and beyond as the Lords of the Isles. Around the castle are gardens and nature trails. (*Open* Apr–Oct, daily 9:30–6, last entry 5. *Admission charge*).

The Small Isles►► This is the collective name for Muck, Eigg, Rum, and Canna. Accommodations are very limited (though not impossible) on all of them, so these little green chunks are usually visited on a day trip from either Arisaig or Mallaig. Rum is the most spectacular and entirely in the care of Scottish Natural Heritage. Red deer are studied here, and there are also large numbers of breeding burrow-nesting shearwaters.

A VIEW OF THE CUILLINS
B8083 runs to Elgol and offers a close view of the Cuillins. Hardy walkers can get into the interior via a rough track, which leads to Camasunary. This starts some 4 miles from Elgol itself. There is also a coastal path from Elgol.

TOURIST INFORMATION
Skye: Bayfield House, Bayfield Road (tel: 01478-612137).

253

...AND ANOTHER CUILLINS VIEWPOINT
Follow the minor road, off B8009 near Drynoch, into Glen Brittle. An obvious path, starting from the large parking lot right at the end of the road by Loch Brittle, rises onto rough moorland for a closer view of the Cuillin ridges. Strong footwear is advised, otherwise enjoy the roadside views, especially from where the road descends into Glen Brittle.

Dunvegan Castle is on the itinerary of most visitors to Skye. It offers a wide range of historic artifacts with Clan Macleod connections

Skye's 50-mile length is the distilled essence of Scottish scenery. In geological terms it has a greater area of basaltic plateau than anywhere else in the United Kingdom. It also has what some writers claim to be the finest view: the view of the Cuillin Hills from Elgol. Sir Walter Scott was inspired by it, so was the painter Turner, who was one of many artists who journeyed here.

SKYE MARBLE

Among the many geological complexities of Skye, the island even has its own marble. This gray-, green-, and white-striped rock is not only found in lamp bases and paperweights in souvenir shops, but is also exported for decorative, building, and agricultural purposes from the Torrin Quarry on Loch Slapin (visible from the Elgol road). The marble has come about by "thermal metamorphosis" millions of years ago—limestone in contact with neighboring igneous rocks in their molten state has been converted and hardened into the attractive stone found here today.

254

Sgurr nan Gillean from the Old Bridge at Sligachan

South of the island Skye starts off gently enough, from a tourist's point of view, with the **Sleat** peninsula. Even the bulky granite flanks of the **Red Hills** (sometimes known as the Red Cuillin) give no hint of the spectacle just around the corner. Then the pinkish granite gives way to dark toothed gabbro, and the **Cuillins** reveal themselves at Sligachan with the spire of Sgurr nan Gillean, well over the 3,000-foot contour. More than 20 of its high companions also reach this magic Munro mark (see page 149), the highest being Sgurr Alasdair at 3,310 feet, on a spiky arête that eventually tumbles into **Loch Scavaig** in the west. Complicated volcanic geology has been further notched and splintered by more recent glaciation.

The Trotternish peninsula Yet even with the Cuillins, Skye has not finished with scenic spectacle. Most of the north of the island is basalt plateau, the ancient lavas suddenly ending in a long line of slipping cliffs, again the most spectacular of their kind in Britain. **The Old Man of Storr** on the horizon is a 161-foot pinnacle adrift from its parent cliff. It stands insecurely on a jumbled complication of clays and limestones unable to support the weight of the lava plateau above. The infinitesimally slow rotational slippage of great slabs of lava cliff has also created the extraordinary rock forms of the **Quiraing**, into whose confines only surefooted walkers should venture. Skye is unbeatable—when the sun shines.

Travel Facts

Communications map

Lerwick

Orkney Islands

A965
Kirkwall
Stromness
A964
A961
Burwick

Pentland Firth

Thurso
John O'Groats
A9
Wick
A99

A9

Helmsdale

Shetland Islands

Isbister

A970

Lerwick

Sumburgh

same scale
Stromness | Aberdeen
Lerwick

Firth
Elgin
Buckie
Macduff
Fraserburgh
A96
A941
A98
Peterhead
A95
Huntly
A96
Ellon
A90
Spey
Grantown-on-Spey
Inverurie
NORTH SEA
Ballater
Dee
Aberdeen
Braemar
A93
Stonehaven
Laurencekirk
A92
A90
Montrose
Blairgowrie
Forfar
A90
Tay
A9
Arbroath
A90
Dundee
A92
St Andrews
A91
Forth
A915
M90
Kinross
Dunfermline
A977
Firth of Forth
M9
Dunbar
Falkirk
M8
A71
EDINBURGH
A1
Eyemouth
A702
A7
A68
A721
Peebles
Carstairs
A72
Galashiels
Tweed
Abington
Jedburgh
Moffat
Hawick
A68
A74(M)
A7
Langholm
Dumfries
A75
Annan
Firth

ENGLAND

0   20   40   60   80 km
0   20   40 miles

In all, Scotland has about 790 offshore islands, most of which are uninhabited. Ferry routes between larger islands, and between them and the mainland, are shown on this map, as are other communication routes

Arriving

By air

All transatlantic scheduled services fly into Glasgow, though this option is under increasing pressure, particularly from London Heathrow, and there has been a reduction in the number of North American carriers serving Glasgow. There are direct, overnight services to Glasgow from Newark and Chicago, with journey times of six hours 30 minutes and 7 hours 30 minutes respectively. Visitors flying from San Francisco can travel either via Chicago or Toronto.

Transatlantic visitors can also fly to Frankfurt or Amsterdam, and connect with a wide choice of flights to Scotland. This can be a better option than journeying via London, with more direct connecting flights.

For visitors traveling from London, there are direct flights to Edinburgh, Glasgow, Aberdeen, and Inverness. There are also Scottish connections from other English airports. Main operators within Scotland are British Airways, British Midland (New York office call 203/661-8980, fax 203/661-9221) and KLM UK. British Airways flies many routes within Scotland as well as cross-border routes. Some carriers offer fly-drive deals; check with your travel agent for information.

There is a departure tax of £10 for flights within the European Union, and £20 for flights elsewhere.

By sea

From mainland Europe There are frequent ferries to the north of England within easy reach of the Scottish border. There are a variety of Scandinavian connections to Newcastle, within 90 minutes of the border, and Hull, three–four hours away, has ferry links with Rotterdam and Zeebrugge. From Northern Ireland There are frequent regular sailings from Larne to Stranraer and to Cairnryan. Complete details are available from Sealink or from P & O appointed travel agents. There is also a SeaCat service from Belfast to Stranraer.

By train

Rail services connect the main cities of Scotland with the south, though with privatization of the rail network, matters are in a state of flux. Fast electrified routes run from London Kings Cross to Edinburgh Waverley and between London Euston and Glasgow Central. Some Kings Cross services also run to Glasgow Central. In addition, there are some (nonelectrified) direct services from London to Aberdeen and Inverness. The travel time between Edinburgh and London is just under four hours (the fastest timing) with many services taking around four hours 30 minutes including stops. The fastest direct service between London Euston and Glasgow Central takes around five to five and a half hours, with services linking Glasgow and Kings Cross taking about the same time.

Rail services also connect main English cities and towns with Scottish destinations. For overnight travel, sleeping cars are available.

By bus

There are a number of companies in the United Kingdom that operate express service to Scotland. They offer direct service (often daily throughout the year) to a variety of destinations. Overnight travel is available on most major routes.

Many companies offer facilities such as steward or hostess service with hot and cold drinks and light refreshments, rest rooms, air-conditioning, and seating in smoking or no-smoking areas. Further details on all services and ticket prices can be obtained from appointed travel agents or main city bus stations.

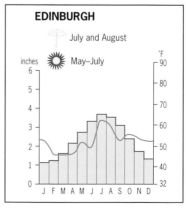

EDINBURGH

July and August

inches   May–July   °F

By car

Many travelers from the south use the M6 expressway, which becomes the M74 and A74 north of the border. Using this route to Glasgow, and then taking M80 and A/M90 north, it is possible to reach Aberdeen by expressway or divided highway all the way from London or even Bristol in the southwest of England.

Alternatively, M1, A1(M), and A1 is the main route in the eastern half of the country, though it is not possible as yet to reach Edinburgh, the capital, without encountering some undivided stretches of the A1 north of the border. Allow around seven or eight hours to reach Edinburgh comfortably from London, including stops and keeping reasonable average speeds.

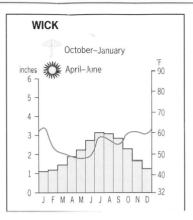

WICK

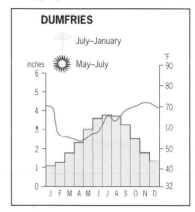

DUMFRIES

Customs

Transatlantic visitors flying direct to Glasgow will find the standard U.K. regulations apply with regard to quantities of duty-free tobacco, alcohol, and perfume. There are higher allowances for duty-paid goods bought in the E.U.

When to go

Most Scots would say that May and June are the best months. Peak vacation season is July and August, and accommodations may be scarce in some of the smaller, western places during this period. Festival time in Edinburgh (late

August to early September) is very busy. Scotland's indigenous biting insect, the midge, is active from the end of May–mid-September on the west coast and the islands. It can be an irritation but does not pose any real threat.

Most attractions belonging to the National Trust for Scotland are closed by the beginning of November and open again at Easter. However, the grounds of many of these properties stay open throughout the year. Many Historic Scotland properties are open throughout the year, though some opening times are quirky, with Thursday afternoon and all-day Friday closing between October and March. Many castles that are still in private hands also close between November and March.

Most municipal museums and art galleries in Scotland stay open in the winter, as do some nature reserve visitor centers, plus a surprising number of other types of attractions. For example, Cromarty Court House and Scotland's Lighthouse Museum are just two places of interest in the north that are open all year (but remember winter daylight hours are very short).

Rainfall, Edinburgh

Average rainfall in inches (1961–1990)

	Jan	Feb	Mar	Apr	May	Jun	Jul	Aug	Sep	Oct	Nov	Dec
inches	2.2	1.6	2	1.6	2	2	2.2	2.5	2.6	2.5	2.4	2.2

Essentials

Climate

The Scots say that Scotland does not have a climate: it only has weather. Scotland's position on the edge of Europe, surrounded by sea on three sides, means that the weather is very varied—though plenty of east-coast places have less rain than Rome.

The east coast of Scotland tends to be cool and dry, the west coast milder and wetter. Remember also that a short distance can make a great difference. The occasional outbreak of haar (summer sea mist) along the east coast is usually a sign of brilliant sunshine only a little way inland. Most important, if you do meet rain, with Scotland's ever-changing weather patterns, the chances are that it will not last for long. See also When to go on page 259.

Hours of daylight

There are longer summer daylight hours in the north of Scotland—up to an hour's difference on Midsummer Day (June 24) depending how far north from Edinburgh you go.

Public holidays

In Scotland, "bank holidays" apply only to banks and some other financial and commercial offices, although in England and Wales they are general public holidays. Christmas Day, Boxing Day (December 26), and New Year's Day (and January 2) are usually taken by everyone.

In place of the general holidays in England, Scottish towns and cities normally have a spring and a fall holiday. These holidays vary from place to place, but they are almost invariably on a Monday. In

There are five major banks with branches throughout Scotland: Bank of Scotland, Royal Bank of Scotland, Clydesdale Bank, TSB Scotland, and Girobank, three of which issue their own paper money ("bank notes").

Bank of England and Northern Ireland bank notes are legal tender in Scotland. Note also that, unlike England, there are £1 notes (issued by the Royal Bank of Scotland) as well as £1 coins.

The hours of Scottish banks are approximately 9:15–4:45, with some closing later on Thursdays. Very few banks are open on Saturday mornings.

In Scotland generally, banks give the best exchange rates for foreign currency. All banks offer this service. It is also possible to change money in airports, larger train stations, travel agents, and some of the larger hotels (if you are a guest). Traveler's checks can be used in some shops, and can be cashed in banks.

261

Several major English banks have branches in Edinburgh, Glasgow, and Aberdeen. There are also several foreign banks in Edinburgh and Glasgow. For details of these see the *Yellow Pages*, the *Phone Book*, or ask at local tourist information centers.

Credit Cards Most larger shops, stores, hotels, and restaurants in Scotland accept the majority of international credit cards, such as American Express, Diners Club, MasterCard, and Visa. Despite this widespread acceptance of credit cards, it is advisable to carry some cash. Many smaller establishments offering accommodations, such as bed-and-breakfasts, are unlikely to accept any form of credit card. American Express has offices in Glasgow, Edinburgh, and Aberdeen.

general, all visitor-oriented places, including restaurants, remain open, but a holiday in a small town means that local businesses and many stores will be closed for the whole day.

Time differences
Scotland observes the same time as the rest of the United Kingdom. Between the end of October and the end of March, Greenwich Mean Time operates: thus at 12 noon in Edinburgh it is 8–10 PM in Australia, 4–8:30 AM in Canada, 12 noon in Eire, midnight in New Zealand, and 4–7 AM in the U.S.A. From the end of March to the end of October, British Summer Time operates (one hour ahead).

Visas and vaccinations
Scotland's visa requirements are identical to those of the rest of the United Kingdom. U.S. citizens need a valid passport, though visas are not required for a stay of less than six months. No special vaccinations are required.

Money and banking
English currency is accepted in Scotland, and a sign to this effect can be seen decorating the till of many a Highland shop.

Near Aberfeldy in Tayside…

Driving

Car rental
Scotland has a selection of car rental firms. Major operators can often arrange in advance for a car to be available at your destination. Some hotels also offer this service. Away from the main cities , there may be only a few local firms.

Car rental companies at Scotland's major airports include:

Aberdeen Airport
Avis, tel: 01224-722282
Europcar, tel: 01224-770770
Hertz, tel: 01224-722373

A familiar sight—a CalMac ferry

Edinburgh Airport
Alamo, tel: 0131-344 3250
Avis, tel: 0131-333 1866
Europcar, tel: 0131-344 3114
Hertz, tel: 0131-333 1019
National, tel: 0131-333 1922

Glasgow Airport
Alamo, tel: 0141-848 1166
Avis, tel: 0141-887 2261
National, tel: 0141-887 7915
Europcar, tel: 0141-887 0414
Hertz, tel: 0141-887 2451

Inverness Airport
Avis, tel: 01667-462787
Hertz, tel: 01667-462652

At the smaller airports in Scotland, local car rental companies can often deliver and collect cars from the airport by prior arrangement.

Car rental companies can, in many instances, arrange for your rental car to be available at a ferry terminal.

You can also arrange to collect a Hertz car at any station on the rail network. Hertz has offices at many principal stations. If traveling during normal office hours, make your reservation just before starting your train journey and your car will be waiting on your arrival.

Hertz reservation centers
Aberdeen, tel: 01224-210748
Edinburgh, tel: 0131-557 5272
Glasgow, tel: 0141-248 7736

Driving in Scotland
As in the rest of the United Kingdom, cars drive on the left.

Unfamiliar British driving terms may include petrol (gas), car park (parking lot), motorway (freeway), dual carriageway (divided highway), roundabout (traffic circle), and overtaking (passing).

You may never turn on a red light anywhere in Britain; wait for green. In urban areas, honor marked bus lanes or you could get a ticket.

Many roads are numbered, and these are prefixed by an M (for motorway), an A (major road), or a B (minor road). Central Scotland has an efficient motorway network, with good roads to main cities farther north such as Aberdeen and Inverness.

Compared to America's freeways, British motorways have very few access points (numbered junctions at key places) and rare opportunities for fuel, meals, and restrooms. Look for the "Services" sign and take advantage of the facilities—it may be 50 miles before your next chance!

Radio Scotland (92.4–94.7 FM or 810 MW) broadcasts details of road conditions throughout the day, as do the many local stations.

Insurance Visitors bringing their own cars from overseas require appropriate insurance and should carry their car registration documents.

Driver's license Any holder of an overseas license may, for up to one

Rush hour in the Highlands

year, drive a motor vehicle in Britain, but only a class of vehicle authorized by that license.

Speed limits Unless signs state otherwise: on motorways and dual carriageways 70 mph; on undivided highways 60 mph; in residential, business, or commercially developed areas 30 mph.

Drinking and driving The police strongly advise overseas visitors (as well as U.K. citizens) not to drive at all after drinking even a small amount of alcohol. If breathalyzing indicates more alcohol than the legal limit, the driver is subject to prosecution.

Breakdowns If your car breaks down on the motorway, pull over and stop on the paved hard shoulder, where there are free emergency telephones placed every mile or less. Follow the arrows to the nearest one, which will connect you to the police. Return to your car and wait inside until help arrives (usually within an hour).

The hard shoulder is for emergency use only. You must never use it for a rest stop.

Single-lane roads In some of the more remote areas of Scotland there are still some single-lane roads. When two cars are approaching from opposite directions, the car that reaches a passing place first should pull over to allow safe passage. Note that passing places are not for parking. Also, it is an offence not to allow a vehicle that is following behind you to pass.

Parking On-street parking is difficult in Scotland's cities, and you are advised not to take chances. Parking tickets are diligently issued, and fines are high. Your car could even be clamped or towed away.

Double yellow lines painted on the road beside the curb mean no parking at any time; single yellow lines mean restricted parking (small signs give details). In marked parking zones, look for coin-operated meters or machines issuing pay-and-display tickets. Parking lots or multistory garages are run by city councils or National Car Parks (N.C.P.). These can be the best option, saving you the time and frustration of looking for a space on the street, and sparing you a parking ticket if you spend more time sightseeing than anticipated.

An unusual cast-iron milepost points the way in Fife

	MILES		MILES
Lawhead	½	Brewester Wells	½
Peat Inn	1	North Bank	1
Falfield	2½	Lathockar	2
New Gilston	4	Kinaldy	3
Teasses	6	Brighton	3
Montrave	7½	Stravithie	4
Crosscates	1½	Bonnytown	5
Wilkieston	2½	Boarhills	7
Drumcarro	4	Cameron	1½

Public transportation

By train

Scotland has a reasonable internal network, with fast connections to the four main Scottish cities and points between. In addition, there are 161 miles of track north of Inverness and west coast railheads such as Mallaig and Kyle of Lochalsh, with superb scenery on the way. Privatization of the service means changes to the current structure of tickets. Check with your travel agent, main train station, or the nearest tourist information center in Scotland.

Glasgow Underground

By bus

A network of operators covers the smaller towns and rural areas of Scotland. Local tourist information centers have complete details and timetables. Alternatively, for further information on getting around, contact the following:

Aberdeen & Grampian Tourist Board
27 Albyn Place
Aberdeen AB10 1YL
tel: 01224-288800
fax: 01224-581367

Angus & City of Dundee Tourist
Board
Market Place
Arbroath
Angus DD11 1HR
tel: 01241-872609
fax: 01241-878550

The Borders Council
Public Transport Unit
Newtown St. Boswells
Melrose TD6 0SA
tel: 01835-824000, ext. 5123

Dumfries & Galloway Council
Public Transport Unit
Council Offices, English Street
Dumfries DG1 2DD
tel: 0345-090510
fax: 01387-260111

Edinburgh & Scotland Information
Centre
3 Princes Street
Edinburgh EH2 2QP
tel: 0131-557 1700
fax: 0131-473 3881

Fife Council
Public Transport Unit
Fife House, North Street
Glenrothes, Fife KY7 5LT
tel: 01592-416060
fax: 01592-413061

Highland Council
Public Transport Unit
Glenurquhart Road
Inverness IV3 5NX
tel: 01463-234121
fax: 01463-702606

Orkney Tourist Board
6 Broad Street, Kirkwall
Orkney KW15 1DH
tel: 01856-872856
fax: 01856-875056

Shetland Islands Tourism
Market Cross, Lerwick
Shetland ZE1 0LU
tel: 01595-693434
fax: 01595-695807

Stirling Council
Public Transport Unit
Viewforth
Stirling FK8 2ET
tel: 01786-442707
fax: 01786-442707

Strathclyde Passenger Transport
Authority
Travel Centre, St. Enoch Square
Glasgow
tel: 0141-226 4826

Tourist Information Centre
Granada A1 Service Area
Oldcraighall, Musselburgh
East Lothian EH21 8RE
tel: 0131-653 6172
fax: 0131-653 2805

Western Isles Council
Public Transport Unit
Sandwick Road, Stornoway
Lewis, Western Isles HS1 2BW
tel: 01851-703773, ext. 319
fax: 01851-706426

Postbus Many remote areas are
served by Postbuses, small minibuses
that deliver mail and also have seats
for fare-paying passengers. Space is
limited, so do not plan an entire or a
tight itinerary around the Postbus
network, especially if you have a lot
of luggage. There are over 130 rural
routes throughout Scotland: timetables are available from:
Royal Mail
7 Strothers Lane
Inverness IV1 1AA
tel: 01463-256200
fax: 01463-256220

By ferry
Ferries are a major means of transportation on the western seaboard
and around Orkney and Shetland.
Caledonian MacBrayne Ltd.
(CalMac) operates the majority of
ferry services on the River Clyde and

tel: 01475-650100, fax: 01475-637607.
Car ferry reservations: tel: 0990-
650000, fax: 01475-635235

P & O Scottish Ferries sails
regularly to Orkney and Shetland
from Aberdeen and Scrabster (near
Thurso). The main Orkney crossing is
from Scrabster to Stromness. There
are also some sailings between the
islands of Orkney and Shetland,
although these are not as frequent as
the ferries to and from the Scottish
mainland. Make sure that you make
advance reservations for cars on all
sailings and also for passengers from
Aberdeen to Lerwick. Information is
available from:
P & O Scottish Ferries, P.O.Box 5,
Jamieson's Quay, Aberdeen AB9
8DL, tel: 01224-572615, fax: 01224-
574411

Western Ferries operates between
the mainland towns of Gourock and
Dunoon and between the islands of
Islay and Jura. Information is
available from:
Western Ferries (Clyde) Ltd., Head
Office, 16 Woodside Crescent,
Glasgow G3 7UT, tel: 0141-332 9766,
fax: 0141-332 0267

265

Kirkwall harbor

west coast of Scotland, sailing to 23
islands. Most ferries carry vehicles,
although some (to the Small Isles, for
instance) only convey passengers. On
many services, it is advisable to make
advance vehicle reservations, especially during the summer and at
other peak times. Caledonian
MacBrayne offers flexible tickets that
make island touring easier. Contact:
Caledonian MacBrayne Ltd.
The Ferry Terminal, Gourock,
Renfrewshire PA19 1QP,

Orkney Islands Shipping Co. Ltd.
has regular ferry services running
between the various Orkney
islands. Information is available
from:
Orkney Ferries Shipping Co. Ltd.,
Head Office, Shore Street, Kirkwall
KW15 1LG, tel: 01856-872044, fax:
01856-872921

The Shetland Isles Council operates
ferries within Shetland.
Information is available from:
Shetland Isles Tourism,
Market Cross, Lerwick, ZE1 0LU,
tel: 01595-693434, fax: 01595-695807

Media and communications

The Media There is a reasonably widespread circulation and availability of quality and tabloid newspapers printed in England, partly serving the many English people living in Scotland. Scotland also has its own indigenous media, again at both the serious and tabloid ends of the market. *The Scotsman*, based in Edinburgh, aspires to the crown as Scotland's national newspaper, though challenged by its Glasgow-based competitor, *The Herald*. Both are exceeded in circulation by the unashamedly regional, if not parochial, Aberdeen-based *Press and Journal*. (It is said that the *P & J* headlined the Titanic's sinking with "North-East Man Drowns at Sea.") All of these papers have their evening equivalents. Scotland's other popular daily is the tabloid *Daily Record*.

'ALL OF SCOTLAND'

Television), based in Glasgow, and Grampian Television from Aberdeen.

One anomaly of the 1990s is funding for the making of Gaelic programs, which both the BBC and independents beam out not just to the Gaels but to chunks of Scotland where the language has not been spoken since the 13th century (such as the Northeast), or even Orkney and Shetland, where it has never been spoken.

The Scotsman, *voice of Edinburgh*

The Sunday Post is a top-selling Scottish institution peddling its own unique brand of homespun, conservative, family-oriented journalism, while *Scotland on Sunday*, from the same stable as *The Scotsman*, is a heavyweight that sees off *The Sunday Times* north of the border. Scotland also has many local weekly papers that list entertainment opportunities. *The List* is excellent for Glasgow and Edinburgh options.

Scotland's television consists of what is broadcast from south of the border, with some home-based material slotted in. Both BBC1 and BBC2 have Scottish opt-ins, including, on BBC1, substantial Scottish news coverage and weather forecasts.

Commercial television networks north of the border include Border Television, the influential STV (Scottish

BBC Radio Scotland has a loyal following. Though also on FM, its medium-wave transmissions can easily be found by locating Radio 4 on long-wave (sometimes referred to as "Radio England" north of the border) and pressing the medium-wave button (not guaranteed to work on all radios!). Radio Scotland is very useful for *Scottish* (rather than English) weather forecasts. Otherwise, the station broadcasts a broadly based mix of news, discussion, travel, magazine format, and music programs.

There are also various local commercial radio stations, some good, with just one or two of startlingly amateurish quality.

Whatever the medium, do not expect to hear any but the most earthshaking, bizarre, or comical news items from America.

Post offices

Post offices in reasonably sized Scottish towns are sometimes housed in distinguished buildings. However, many are heavily disguised as pharmacies or small grocery stores, for example. Look for the sign "Post Office" in yellow lettering on red.

Some old-style red "phone kiosks" survive in Scotland

Smaller post offices close for an hour at lunch and tend to honor the weekly "half-day closing" and local holidays. Otherwise 9–5 is usual, plus Saturday mornings.

Telephones and fax facilities

Whether local or long-distance, all phone calls—except free calls to the operator (dial 100) or emergency services (dial 999)—are charged according to their duration. Rates vary; evenings and weekends are cheapest.

Pay phones display the amount inserted and count down during the conversation. Some pay phones accept prepaid **phone cards**, sold at post offices, convenience stores, and newsdealers; others accept the more commonly used **credit cards**.

Hotels often charge high rates from room phones and even pay phones; ask for rates beforehand.

Fax machines are often available at hotels, as well as at printing and photocopying shops in larger towns.

267

Language guide

English-speakers will be able to understand just about anyone north of the border unless people are using a dense form of Scots.

When dealing with non-natives, Scots speakers often adopt some form of "standard English." In case of difficulties, ask them to speak more slowly. See also page 283 for a select glossary of Scots terms and phrases.

Scottish post offices come in all shapes and sizes

Emergencies

In general, Scotland is extremely safe, though police advise common sense. Thefts from cars (and of cars) do occur, especially in major cities and at popular sights (you may want to be careful in the crowded parking lot at the Cairngorm chairlift, for example). It is not a good idea to keep valuable items of any sort in an unattended vehicle. If you must, then make sure they are hidden well out of sight.

As for personal safety, again, use common sense. You are probably perfectly safe late at night in any Scottish city center, but from time to time, muggings do occur, often alcohol-related.

One Scottish activity that all too often requires emergency action by the authorities is hiking. Scotland's hills are rugged and must be treated with respect. Snow can occur above 3,000 feet in any month, and hill conditions can change very rapidly. Proper water- and windproof clothing and equipment and—most important—properly soled hiking boots (definitely not with a cut-away heel) should be worn. Always take a good map and a compass with you, and know how to use them. Leave your proposed route and estimated time of return with your hotel. Despite the obvious security implications, it is also advisable to leave a similar note displayed on or in your car.

Embassies and consulates

As Scotland is part of the United Kingdom, the chief foreign embassies are in London. However, a number of representatives for other nations have consular offices within Scotland—phone numbers for these can be found in the *Yellow Pages*. They include:

The American Consulate General,
3 Regent Terrace,
Edinburgh,
tel: 0131-556 8315.

The Australian Consulate,
25 Bernard Street,
Leith
Edinburgh, EH6 6SH
tel: 0131-555 4500

Emergency telephone numbers

As in the rest of the United Kingdom, dial 999 to summon police, fire, and ambulance services, as well as coast guard and mountain rescue. These calls are free from all phones, including public pay phones.

Lost and found

The police operate an efficient lost and found service, as do the railroad companies and major bus operators. Broadly speaking, the Scots are fairly honest, and if an item is left behind in a restaurant or other establishment it is always worth going back or making inquiries about it by phone.

Health

Medical Insurance If you become ill in Scotland, unless you are a United Kingdom. or E.U. (European Union) citizen, you are eligible only for free emergency treatment at National Health Service (N.H.S.) Accident and Emergency departments of hospitals. If you are hospitalized, even from an Accident and Emergency department, or referred to an out-patient clinic, you will be asked to pay. Therefore you are strongly advised to make sure you have adequate insurance coverage before traveling to Scotland. Check your policy.

Pharmacies Except in remote areas, where some doctor's surgeries have their own dispensaries, you must take a doctor's prescription to a pharmacy. These part-dispensing, part-retail businesses are open normal shopping hours but also operate a system whereby one pharmacy in a given area stays open to cover half-day closings and other holidays.

In cities, there is usually a pharmacy that stays open at other times to deal with urgent prescriptions. In all cases, a notice—usually prominently displayed on the shop door—will tell you where you can get the prescription filled. In addition—but only in an emergency—police can contact a pharmacist and request his or her assistance.

Other information

Camping and "caravanning"
There are over 400 licensed and recognized camping and caravan (trailer) parks in Scotland, and upgrading is an ongoing process. All area tourist boards carry listings of campground parks within their own area, and the Scottish Tourist Board produces a annual guide called *Scotland: Caravan and Camping Parks*. This is available both direct from the Scottish Tourist Board (address on page 272) and from bookstores.

"Caravanning" is popular in Scotland. Any roads that are unsuitable for towed caravans are clearly marked. Towing a caravan on single-lane roads demands extra vigilance, and you should be careful not to hold up traffic behind you. Please note that most local authorities do not permit overnight parking of caravans in pull-offs and other parking lots, and in several places barriers of a suitable height prevent the entry of caravans.

So-called "wild camping" is still fairly popular in Scotland. In fact, Scotland is one of the last areas of the United Kingdom where camping away from recognized parks is still possible. Always seek permission from the landowner before camping in the countryside.

House rentals
The main source for house-rental listings is the Scottish Tourist Board's *Scotland. Self-Catering* guide, published annually and available direct from the S.T.B. (address on page 272) or from bookstores. There are also a number of agencies that specialize in short-term property rental.

Visitors with disabilities
Disability Scotland has a comprehensive vacation database with information on hotels, camping and caravanning, sports and leisure facilities, guest houses, and so on. A vacation directory is also published, covering all of Scotland. Information is available from: Disability Scotland, Princes House, 5 Shandwick Place, Edinburgh EH2 4RG, tel: 0131-229 8632, fax: 0131-229 5168.

A wide range of information for visitors with disabilities can also be found in the Scottish Tourist Board's *Practical Information for Visitors with Disabilities*, available directly from them or from tourist information centers.

Opening times
Times are given within the text for all main attractions and tourist sights. Information on opening times has been provided for guidance only. We have tried to ensure accuracy, but things do change, and we advise you to check locally before planning visits to avoid any possible disappointment.

Scotland's supermarkets and home improvement ("do-it-yourself" or D.I.Y.) centers often open on Sundays even in quite small towns, and in the main cities shopping malls may also be open. In popular tourist areas, most shops are open daily. Beware the local half-day, usually a Wednesday or Thursday, on which many little stores in small towns close. Evening hours for shopping are usually confined to Thursdays in the cities, though, certainly in Edinburgh, bookstores tend to stay open late in the evening. In addition, many superstores remain open most nights till around 8 pm.

Conservation and historic perservation
Historic Scotland,
Longmore House,
Salisbury Place, Edinburgh EH9 1SH (tel: 0131-668 8800).
The government agency that is responsible for the preservation of a huge range of monuments, from standing stones to castles and industrial buildings.
Many of its properties have standard hours: April–September, daily 9:30–6. October–March, Monday–Saturday 9:30–4, Sunday 2–4.

National Trust for Scotland
5 Charlotte Square, Edinburgh EH2 4DU (tel: 0131-226 5922).
The leading charitable organization that cares for castles and other grand properties, as well as a smaller range of humbler places, and also untouched land of great beauty.

Scottish Natural Heritage, 12 Hope Terrace, Edinburgh EH9 2AS (tel: 0131-447 4784, fax: 0131-446 2277). The main government agency with responsibility for environmental matters and nature conservation, it operates nature reserves in some of Scotland's finest unspoiled places.

Royal Society for the Protection of Birds (R.S.P.B.), 17 Regent Terrace, Edinburgh EH7 5BN (tel: 0131-557 3136, fax: 0131-557 6275). The leading charitable body in the preservation of habitat suitable for bird life, this operates a number of nature reserves of high ornithological interest.

Scottish Wildlife Trust, Cramond House, 16 Cramond Glebe Road, Edinburgh EH4 6NS (tel: 0131-312 7765, fax: 0131-312 8705). Scotland's own charitable conservation agency, concerned with the preservation of habitat for all kinds of wildlife, operates a number of nature reserves.

Places of worship
The most widespread Christian denomination is the (Presbyterian) Church of Scotland. Roman Catholics, Anglicans/Episcopallians, Baptists, and Free Presbyterians are also represented as well as a variety of nondenominational "chapels". Several major cities have Jewish synagogues.

Dunblane Cathedral

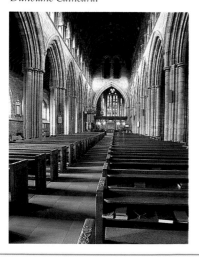

Because of liberal drinking laws and shopping hours, Sunday observance is fairly low-key, with the notable exception of Lewis and Harris and also Skye. The local press usually provides times of worship, and tourist information centers can also help.

Toilets/rest rooms
A rest room is commonly called a "loo," "W.C.,"or simply a toilet. Public rest rooms are fairly good but vary in standard from town to town. Some are free, but some attended facilities make a small charge. Petrol stations do not always offer rest rooms. If desperate, try a pub or fast food outlet.

Photography
With its spectacular scenery, Scotland is a great place for landscape photography. Even small towns have photography shops where a wide range of film can be obtained. Pharmacists and other stores, particularly in popular tourist areas, also carry film. Films of larger format than 35mm can sometimes be trickier to find.

Electricity
U.K. voltage is 240 volts, about twice that of the U.S. American appliances require a voltage converter as well as a socket adapter, as U.K. sockets take three flat pins. Buy these before leaving on your vacation.

Etiquette: dealing with the Scots
The Scots can be defined as an ethnic minority within the United Kingdom, but they differ from other groups only in subtle ways. However, the Scots have an intense dislike of being labeled English.

"National," within the Scottish media can mean either Scottish or U.K.-wide British, depending on the context. Radio Scotland, for instance, announces itself as "The National Network." Many of the subtle distinctions that mark the Scots are actually linguistic, and in everyday speech, there are opportunities for misunderstanding.

A number of minor points of etiquette apply to food and drink.

If invited to someone's house for coffee or tea, do not be surprised if they insist that you have biscuits or "Home-Bakes"—no matter what the hour of the day

When ordering beer in Scottish pubs listen for the local words "export," "heavy," and "special," rather than the English word "bitter." And, if your host offers you a dram (a glass of whisky) and suggests malt whisky rather than an everyday blend, make sure that you add only water, if anything, to it. Ginger ale or other soft drinks will be at least an irritation, if not an insult.

However, no one will mind if you put sugar instead of salt in your porridge; nobody will arrest you for wearing the "wrong" tartan (there is no such thing); and hardly anyone will notice if you get the words of "Auld Lang Syne" wrong at the end of the ceilidh (most Scots do as well).

Please note: For reasons unknown, Scots do not like to be called "Scotch" and much prefer "Scottish." See also below.

- ❑ **Scotch** a word for whisky never used by Scots people.

Scotch broth broth made with a meat stock, plenty of vegetables and lots of barley to give it a glutinous texture.

Scotch egg a boiled egg in sausage meat and bread crumbs.

Scotch mist a characteristic western weather condition of relentlessly damp misery, created to test cheap summer raincoats.

Scotch bluebell *Campanula rotundifolia*, called the harebell south of the border, and common on Scottish heaths.

Scotch thistle the national emblem of Scotland, sometimes called the cotton thistle, though not a native plant.

Scotch verdict "not proven," a peculiarity of Scotland's legal system. ❑

CONVERSION CHARTS

FROM	TO	MULTIPLY BY
Inches	Centimetres	2.54
Centimetres	Inches	0.3937
Feet	Metres	0.3048
Metres	Feet	3.2810
Yards	Metres	0.9144
Metres	Yards	1.0940
Miles	Kilometres	1.6090
Kilometres	Miles	0.6214
Acres	Hectares	0.4047
Hectares	Acres	2.4710
U.S. Gallons	U.K. Gallons	0.8
U.K. Gallons	U.S. Gallons	1:25
U.S. Gallons	Liters	3.7854
Liters	U.S. Gallons	0.2642
U.K. Gallons	Liters	4.5460
Liters	U.K. Gallons	0.2200
Ounces	Grams	28.35
Grams	Ounces	0.0353
Pounds	Grams	453.6
Grams	Pounds	0.0022
Pounds	Kilograms	0.4536
Kilograms	Pounds	2.205
Tons	Tonnes	1.0160
Tonnes	Tons	0.9842

MEN'S SUITS

U.K.	36	38	40	42	44	46	48
Rest of Europe	46	48	50	52	54	56	58
U.S.	36	38	40	42	44	46	48

DRESS SIZES

U.K.	8	10	12	14	16	18
France	36	38	40	42	44	46
Italy	38	40	42	44	46	48
Rest of Europe	34	36	38	40	42	44
U.S.	6	8	10	12	14	16

MEN'S SHIRTS

U.K.	14	14.5	15	15.5	16	16.5	17
Rest of Europe	36	37	38	39/40	41	42	43
U.S.	14	14.5	15	15.5	16	16.5	17

MEN'S SHOES

UK	7	7.5	8.5	9.5	10.5	11
Rest of Europe	41	42	43	44	45	46
US	8	8.5	9.5	10.5	11.5	12

WOMEN'S SHOES

UK	4.5	5	5.5	6	6.5	7
Rest of Europe	38	38	39	39	40	41
US	6	6.5	7	7.5	8	8.5

Tourist information centers

Tourism in Scotland is in the overall control of the Scottish Tourist Board (S.T.B.), 23 Ravelston Terrace, Edinburgh EH4 3EU, tel: 0131-332 2433, fax: 0131-343 1513. Visitors in Scotland are asked to use the Edinburgh and Scotland Information Centre (see below). There are two other S.T.B. offices for visitors heading for Scotland:
• Scottish Tourist Board, 19 Cockspur Street, London SW1Y 5BL, tel: 0171-930 8661-2/3, fax: 0171-930 1817
• Southwaite Tourist Information Centre, (Southwaite Service Area, M6, south of Carlisle), tel: 01697-473445

Within Scotland, there are a variety of area tourist boards. In addition to information services, they offer on-the-spot accommodation reservations both locally and in other areas. The main year-round "TICs" are given below.

• Edinburgh and Scotland Information Centre, Waverley Market, 3 Princes Street, Edinburgh EH2 2QP, tel: 0131-557 1700, fax: 0131-473 3881
• Greater Glasgow and Clyde Valley Tourist Board, 11 George Square, Glasgow G2 1DY, tel: 0141-204 4400, fax: 0141-221 3524

The South
• Burns House, Burns Statue Square, Ayr KA7 1UP, tel: 01292-262555, fax: 01292-269555
• Murray's Green, Jedburgh TD8 6BE, tel: 01835-863435, fax: 01835-864099
• Horsemarket, Ladyacre Road, Lanark ML11 7LQ, tel: 01555-661661, fax: 01555-666143
• Burgh Halls, The Cross, Linlithgow, EH49 7AH, tel: 01506-844600, fax: 01506-671373
• Granada Service Area, Oldcraighall, Musselburgh, East Lothian, EH21 8RE, tel: 0131-653 6172, fax: 0131-653 2805
• High Street, Peebles EH45 8AG, tel: 01721-720138, fax: 01721-724401
• Whitesands, Dumfries, tel: 01387-253862

Central Scotland
• 4 City Square, Dundee DD1 3BA, tel: 01382-434664, fax: 01382-434665

• 45 High Street, Perth PH1 5TJ, tel: 01738-638353
• 70 Market Street, St. Andrews KY16 9NU, tel: 01334-472021
• 41 Dumbarton Road, Stirling FK8 2QQ, tel: 01786-475019

The Northeast
• St. Nicholas House, Broad Street, Aberdeen AB9 1DE, tel: 01224-632727, fax: 01224-620415
• 17 High Street, Elgin Moray, IV30 1EG, tel: 01343-542666, fax: 01343-552982

The Great Glen and the Western Highlands
• Grampian Road, Aviemore, Inverness-shire, PH22 1PP, tel: 01479-810363, fax: 01479-811063
• 7 Alexandra Parade, Dunoon, Argyll, PA23 9AB, tel: 01369-703785, fax: 01369-706085
• Cameron Square, Fort William, Inverness-shire, PH33 6AJ, tel: 01397-703781, fax: 01397-705184
• Castle Wynd, Inverness IV2 3BJ, tel: 01463-234353, fax: 01463-710609
• Boswell House, Argyll Square, Oban, Argyll PA34 4NN, tel: 01631-563122, fax: 01631-564273

The Northern Highlands
• The Square, Dornoch, Sutherland IV25 3SD, tel: 01862-810400, fax: 01862-810644
• Auchtercairn, Gairloch, Wester Ross IV21 2DN, tel: 01445-712130, fax: 01445-712071
• Whitechapel Road, Wick, Caithness KW1 4EA, tel: 01955-602596, fax: 01955-604940

The Islands
• 6 Broad Street, Kirkwall, Orkney, KW15 1NX, tel: 01856-872856, fax: 01856-875056
• Market Cross, Lerwick, Shetland ZE1 0LU, tel: 01595-693434, fax: 01595-695807
• Bayfield House, Bayfield Road, Portree, Skye IV51 9EL, tel: 01478-612137, fax: 01478-612141
• 26 Cromwell Street, Stornoway, Lewis HS1 2DD, tel: 01851-703088, fax: 01851-705244
• Ferry Terminal Building, Stromness, Orkney, KW16 3AA, tel: 01856-850716

Hotels & Restaurants

ACCOMMODATIONS

Finding good accommodations is not a problem. (Use the Scottish Tourist Board's grading if in doubt.) Off-season rates vary, and may be negotiable.

As a rough guide in this listing $$$ is over £60 ($90) per person for dinner, bed, and breakfast; $$ is from £20 to £60 ($30 to $90); and $ is under £20 ($30) for bed and breakfast only.

EDINBURGH

Balmoral Hotel ($$$) Princes Street, Edinburgh EH2 2EQ (tel: 0131-556 2414). $23 million bought a total refurbishment of Edinburgh's landmark hotel in the early 1990s. High standards in 189 rooms.

Caledonian Hotel ($$$) Princes Street, Edinburgh EH1 2AB (tel: 0131-459 9988). Another old-established top-flight hotel: like the Balmoral, a former railroad hotel. 236 rooms.

Carlton Highland ($$$) North Bridge, Edinburgh EH1 1SD (tel: 0131-556 7277). Close to the Royal Mile, 197 rooms, and extensive leisure facilities. A popular business and tourist hotel.

Channings ($$) 12–16 South Learmonth Gardens, Edinburgh EH4 1EZ (tel: 0131-315 2226). A superbly stylish conversion of five Edwardian rowhouses. A place for comfort and indulgence. 48 rooms.

Edinburgh Grand Sheraton ($$$) 1 Festival Square, Edinburgh EH3 9SR (tel: 0131-229 9131). This opulent and stylish hotel adds a subtly Scottish stamp to Sheraton quality without resorting to clichés.

George Hotel Inter-Continental ($$$) George Street, Edinburgh EH2 2PB (tel: 0131-225 1251). Supremely convenient, luxury standard in elegant surroundings. 195 rooms.

Hilton National Edinburgh ($$$) 69 Belford Road, Edinburgh EH4 3DG (tel: 0131-332 2545). A modern hotel in a quiet West End location, yet convenient for Princes Street. 144 rooms.

Howard Hotel ($$$) 34 Great King Street, Edinburgh EH3 6QH (tel: 0131-557 3500). Ideal central location amid New Town refinement. Very comfortable. 15 rooms.

King James Thistle Hotel ($$) 107 Leith Street, Edinburgh EH1 3SW (tel: 0131-556 0111). Conveniently sited modern hotel, slightly anonymous in feel, with helpful staff. 143 rooms.

Malmaison ($$$) 1 Tower Place, Leith, Edinburgh EH6 7DB (tel: 0131-555 6868). Elegantly converted from a former seamen's mission, close to the waterfront and only 10 minutes from the city center. French-style brasserie. 60 rooms.

Norton House ($$$) Ingliston, Edinburgh EH28 8LX (tel: 0131-333 1275). In parkland setting on the western outskirts of the city, a country-house hotel close to airport and motorway system. 47 rooms.

Roslin Glen ($$) 2 Penicuik Road, Roslin, Midlothian EH25 9LH (tel: 0131-440 2029). Small hotel in center of quiet conservation village south of the city. Close to bypass and 20 minutes to city center.

Roxburghe ($$$) 38 Charlotte Square, Edinburgh EH2 4HG (tel: 0131-225 3921). The heart of the New Town, with 75 well-equipped bedrooms and a choice of restaurants.

Swallow Royal Scot ($$$) 111 Glasgow Road, Edinburgh EH12 8NF (tel: 0131-334 9191). Modern hotel on western outskirts, 259 bedrooms recently refurbished. Leisure center with swimming pool.

Thrums Private Hotel ($$) 14 Minto Street, Edinburgh EH9 1RQ. (tel: 0131-667 5545). 14 rooms in two adjoining Victorian town houses on the city's south side, with frequent bus service (5 minutes to city center).

GLASGOW

Cameron House Hotel ($$$) Balloch G83 8QZ (tel: 01389-755565). Top-notch hotel on banks of Loch Lomond, a 30-minute drive from city center. 96 luxurious bedrooms. Sports facilities.

The **Devonshire** ($$$) 5 Devonshire Gardens, Glasgow G12 0UX (tel: 0141- 339 7878). Note the correct address of this simply sumptuous town house. Superb throughout. 14 rooms.

Glasgow Hilton ($$$) 1 William Street, Glasgow G3 8HT (tel: 0141-204 5555). Hilton style hit Glasgow in 1992 with themed eating and drinking, wide-ranging leisure facilities, and 319 rooms.

Glasgow Marriott ($$$) 500 Argyle Street, Glasgow G3 8RR (tel: 0141-226 5577). Close to the Kingston Bridge and Scottish Exhibition Centre. Modern 300-bed hotel with sports facilities.

Glasgow Thistle ($$$) 36 Cambridge Street, Glasgow G2 3HN (tel: 0141-332 3311). Very central, with own parking lot. 302 recently refurbished bedrooms.

Holiday Inn Garden Court ($$) 161 West Nile Street, Glasgow G1 2RL (tel: 0141-332 0110). New city center hotel with 80 modern bedrooms, parking nearby.

Malmaison ($$$) 278 West George Street, Glasgow G2 4LL (tel: 0141-221 6400). Style-concious hotel with 73 rooms (CD players, minibars) and good French cuisine in brasserie restaurant.

Glasgow Moat House ($$$) Congress Road, Glasgow G3 8QT (tel: 0141- 306 9988). In what seems like an endless parking lot by the river, a stylish modern hotel. 282 rooms.

Kelvin Park Lorne Hotel ($$) 923 Sauchiehall Street, Glasgow G12 9LG (tel: 0141-314 9955). 99-room hotel, friendly staff, making excellent base for Kelvingrove and Hunterian or Transport Museums.

One Devonshire Gardens ($$$) 1 Devonshire Gardens, Glasgow G12 0UX (tel: 0141-339 2001). Adjoining elegantly furnished town houses. Very high reputation in all departments. 27 rooms.

THE SOUTH

Abbotsford
Woodlands House Hotel ($$) Windyknowe Road, Galashiels TD1 1RG (tel: 01896-754722). Gothic Revival-style hotel with stunning views over Tweeddale.

Ayr
Grange Hotel ($$) 37 Carrick Road, Ayr KA7 2RD (tel: 01292-265679). Small hotel in residential area, with 8 rooms. In walking distance of seafront.
Piersland House Hotel ($$$) Craigend Road, Troon, Ayrshire KA10 6HD (tel: 01292-314747). Fine Edwardian mansion with 15 rooms, originally built for whisky firm owner.

Castle Douglas
Balcary Bay Hotel ($$) Auchencairn, by Castle Douglas, Kirkcudbrightshire DG7 1QZ (tel: 01556-640217). Family-run hotel set on the shore with bay views.

Castle Kennedy Gardens
North West Castle Hotel ($$–$$$) Stranraer, Wigtownshire DG9 8EH (tel: 01776-704413). Excellent range of leisure facilities at this former home of Arctic explorer. 70 rooms.

Châtelherault
Strathaven Hotel ($$–$$$) Hamilton Road, Strathaven, Lanarkshire ML10 6SZ (tel: 01357-521778). Adam fireplace and stairway feature in this refurbished house, making ideal base for Glasgow. 22 rooms.

Culzean Castle
Turnberry Hotel ($$$) Turnberry KA26 9LT (tel: 01655-331000). Famous golfing hotel with spa, leisure suite, and every comfort.

Dalbeattie
Balcary Bay Hotel ($$) Auchencairn DG7 1QZ (tel: 01556-640217). Waterside hotel dating from 1625, 17 well-equipped rooms with 3 acres of gardens.

Dirleton (Castle)
Open Arms Hotel ($$–$$$) Dirleton, East Lothian EH39 5EG (tel: 01620-850241). Old-established, much-loved, comfortable hotel in attractive village, easy access to Edinburgh. 10 rooms.

Galloway Forest Park
Kirroughtree House ($$$) Minnigaff, Newton Stewart DG8 6AN (tel: 01671-402141). 17th-century mansion house set high above Wigtown Bay. Elegant decor, antiques, and stunning views. 17 rooms.

Gatehouse-of-Fleet
Cally Palace Hotel ($$) Gatehouse-of-Fleet, Kirkcudbrightshire DG7 2DL (tel: 01557-814341). Georgian mansion set in a large forested estate. Extensive leisure facilities. 56 rooms.

Kelso
Cross Keys ($$) 36–37 The Square, Kelso TD5 7HL (tel: 01573-223303). Former coaching inn in Kelso town center, 24 rooms, café bar.
Dryburgh Abbey Hotel ($$$) St. Boswells TD6 0RQ (tel: 01835-822261). Stone-built mansion set beside Dryburgh Abbey ruins on the banks of the River Tweed. Spacious, with 25 rooms and swimming pool.
Ednam House Hotel ($$) Bridge Street, Kelso TD5 7HT (tel: 01573-224168). Georgian mansion beside the River Tweed, with 32 rooms and a choice of public areas. Run in traditional style.
Sunlaws House Hotel ($$$) Heiton, Kelso, Roxburghshire TD5 8JZ (tel: 01573-450331). Luxurious country house of the highest standards, owned by the Duke of Roxburghe. 22 rooms.

Logan Botanic Garden
Fernhill Hotel ($$) Heugh Road, Portpatrick DG9 8TD (tel: 01776-810220). Family-run; elevated position on coastal site, excellent service. 19 rooms.

The Machars
Corsemalzie House Hotel ($$) Port William, by Newton Stuart, Wigtownshire, DG8 9RL (tel: 01988-860254). Welcoming country house in total seclusion.

Melrose
Bon Accord Hotel ($$) Market Square, Melrose TD6 9PN (tel: 01896-822645). Town center hotel with 10 cheerfully furnished bedrooms. Restaurant, and bar meals.
Burts Hotel ($$) Market Square, Melrose, Roxburghshire TD6 9PN (tel: 01896-822285). Friendly, family-run hotel of the kind that generates a loyal local clientele. Ideally placed for Borders touring.

Moffat
Moffat House Hotel ($$) High Street, Moffat, Dumfriesshire DG10 9HL (tel: 01683-220039). Elegant Adam house, near town center, strategically placed for north-bound travelers and Borders explorers. 20 rooms.

North Berwick
Greywalls ($$$) Muirfield, Gullane, East Lothian EH31 2EG (tel: 01620-842144). Architecturally exciting house by Edward Lutyens adjacent to some of Scotland's best golf. A hotel of much finesse.

Peebles
Cringletie House ($$$) Eddleston, Peebles-shire EH45 8PL (tel: 01721-730233) Plenty of personal and professional attention in rural, family-run, 13-room baronial mansion.
Park Hotel ($$$) Innerleithen Road, Peebles EH45 8BA (tel: 01721 720451). 24 room hotel with valley views; guests can use leisure facilities of sister hotel, the Hydro.

275

Hotels & Restaurants

CENTRAL SCOTLAND

Aberfeldy

Guinach House ($$) Urlar Road, Aberfeldy, Perthshire PH15 2ET (tel: 01887-820251). Small country house emphasizing great cuisine in peaceful, rural surroundings.
Weem Hotel ($$) Weem, by Aberfeldy, Perthshire PH15 2LD (tel: 01887-820381). Refurbished 17th-century inn with plenty of country pursuits close at hand in Perthshire countryside.

Arbroath

Letham Grange Resort Hotel ($$$) Colliston, Arbroath DD11 4RL (tel: 01241-890373). Country-house hotel with two golf courses and curling rink. With many original Victorian features and choice of traditional or modern style in the 41 bedrooms.

Balloch

Cameron House Hotel ($$$) Loch Lomond, by Alexandria, Dunbartonshire G83 8QZ (tel: 01389-755565). Luxury resort hotel by loch shore. Very wide range of leisure facilities. 96 rooms.

Blairgowrie

Kinloch House Hotel ($$$) by Blairgowrie, Perthshire PH10 6SG (tel: 01250-884237). Mid-19th-century oak-paneled country house with 21 rooms, fine antiques (and 130+ malt whiskies).
Moorfield House ($$) Myreriggs Road, Coupar Angus PH13 9HS (tel: 01828-627303). 12 spacious, handsomely furnished bedrooms. In a country setting, with a library lounge, restaurant, and bar.

Callander

Lubnaig Hotel ($$) Leny Feus, Callander FK17 8AS (tel: 01877-330376). Spotless hotel in pretty gardens, with 10 rooms, three lounges, and dining room.
Roman Camp Hotel ($$$) Callander, Perthshire FK17 8BG (tel: 01877-330003). Beautiful riverside site for this charming 17th-century house, like a small château. 14 rooms.

Dundee

Old Mansion House Hotel ($$$) Auchterhouse, by Dundee, Angus DD3 0QN (tel: 01382-320366). A 16th-century baronial house with original plasterwork and other features. Set in spacious grounds. 6 rooms.

East Neuk Villages

Old Manor Hotel ($$$) Leven Road, Lundin Links KY86 AJ (tel: 01333-320368). On village outskirts with sea views. 24 rooms with modern furnishings.

Forfar

Idvies House ($$) Letham, Forfar DD8 2QJ (tel: 01307-818787). In woodland setting, a Victorian country house with 11 rooms.

Perth

Auchterarder House ($$$) Auchterarder, Perthshire PH3 1DZ (tel: 01764-663646). A sumptuously furnished country house with notable conservatory. The "house guest in private home" approach makes for an interesting alternative to neighboring Gleneagles. 15 rooms.
Gleneagles Hotel ($$$) Auchterarder, Perthshire PH3 1NF (tel: 01764-662231). Arguably Scotland's best-known hotel, with the ambience of an oceangoing liner. 234 rooms and every need catered for—you will never need to step outside the grounds.
Green Hotel ($$) 2 The Muirs, Kinross, Perthshire KY13 7AS (tel: 01577-863467). An independent hotel, now refurbished with excellent range of leisure facilities. 47 rooms.

Pitlochry

Knockendarroch House ($$) Higher Oakfield, Pitlochry, Perthshire PH16 5HT (tel: 01796-473473). Victorian mansion, 12 rooms, of considerable charm and style.
Pine Trees Hotel ($$) Strathview Terrace, Pitlochry PH16 5QR (tel: 01796-472121). With marble staircase and ornate plasterwork, this 20-room mansion offers high standards in all areas.

St. Andrews

Rufflets Country House ($$$) Strathkinness Low Road, St. Andrews, Fife KY16 9TX (tel: 01334-472594). Country house in its own grounds; garden provides fresh produce for restaurant. 25 rooms.
The Old Course Hotel ($$$) Old Station Road KY16 9SP (tel: 01334 474371). Superb setting beside the 17th hole of the famous championship course. There is a choice of lounges and the bright conservatory provides an informal dining option. 125 rooms.
Russell Hotel ($$) 26 The Scores, St. Andrews KY16 9AS (tel: 01334-473447). Family-run hotel with 10 rooms, close to Old Course on seafront.
St. Andrews Golf Hotel ($$$) 40 The Scores, St. Andrews KY16 9AS (tel: 01334-472611). Close to the Old Course, large Victorian building with high standards throughout. 22 rooms.

Stirling

Stirling Highland Hotel ($$$) Spittal Street, Stirling FK8 1DU (tel: 01786-475444). Fascinating conversion of former high school, full of character and very comfortable. 78 rooms.
Terraces Hotel ($$) 4 Melville Terrace, Stirling FK8 2ND (tel: 01786-472268). Town center business hotel, with 18 modern bedrooms and good restaurant.

THE NORTHEAST

Aberdeen

Atholl Hotel ($$) 54 King's Gate, Aberdeen AB15 4YN (tel: 01224-323505).

Handsome building in residential area, close to city center. Personally run establishment, friendly staff.

Craighaar Hotel ($$) Waterton Road, Bucksburn, Aberdeen AB21 9HS (tel: 01224-712275). Behind a plain exterior there is plenty of design flair and a high level of comfort.

Marcliffe at Pitfodels ($$$) North Deeside Road, Pitfodels, Aberdeen AB15 9YA (tel: 01224-861000). Luxury hotel run by proprietors who have plenty of experience. 42 rooms.

Palm Court Hotel ($$) 81 Seafield Road, Aberdeen AB15 7YU (tel: 01224-310351). Close to ring road, a comfortable business hotel with 24 rooms and memorably decorated split-level restaurant.

Simpsons ($$) 59 Queens Road, Aberdeen AB15 4YP (tel. 01224 327777). The granite facade of two converted town houses hides a most exciting hotel development. One building contains the modern bedrooms, whilst the other contains a large split-level bar and Mediterranean brasserie. 38 rooms.

Thainstone House Hotel and Country Club ($$$) Thainstone Estate, Inverurie Road (N), Inverurie, Aberdeenshire AB15 5NT (tel: 01467-621431). Georgian mansion on large grounds. 48 rooms.

Ballater

Balgonie Country House ($$$) Braemar Place, Ballater AB35 5NQ (tel: 01339-755482). Creeper-clad Edwardian house with sweeping lawns, 9 bedrooms, and excellent modern Scottish cuisine.

Darroch Learg ($$) Braemar Road, Ballater AB35 5UX (tel: 013397-55443). Country-house-in-town hotel, with Deeside views.

Banff

Banff Springs Hotel ($$) Golden Knowes Road, Banff AB45 2JE (tel: 01261-812881). Recently refurbished modern business and leisure hotel with 31 rooms, sea views and gymnasium.

Craigellachie

Craigellachie Hotel ($$) Craigellachie, Banffshire AB38 9SR (tel: 01340-881204). Imposing fishing and shooting hotel with excellent food and 29 well-appointed rooms.

Elgin

Mansion House Hotel ($$$) The Haugh, Elgin, Moray IV30 1AW (tel: 01343-548811). Peacefully situated baronial mansion with excellent leisure facilities.

Fyvie Castle

Lodge Hotel ($$) Old Rayne AB52 6RY (tel: 01464-851205). Country setting beside A96, with 7 rooms (4 in annex). Family-run.

Meldrum Arms Hotel ($$) The Square, Oldmeldrum AB51 0DS (tel: 01651 872238). Family-run, traditional town-center hotel with 11 rooms, restaurant, and bar.

Huntly

Kildrummy Castle Hotel ($$$) Kildrummy, by Alford, Aberdeenshire AB33 8RA (tel: 019755-71288). Imposing mansion house close to ancient castle in rural setting. Very high standard of accommodations and cuisine. 16 rooms.

Old Manse of Marnoch ($$) Bridge of Marnoch, by Huntly, Banffshire AB54 7RS (tel: 01466-780873). 19th-century country house in secluded gardens. Fine food and high standards throughout. Five rooms.

THE GREAT GLEN & WESTERN HIGHLANDS

Aviemore

Boat Hotel ($$) Boat of Garten PH24 3BH (tel: 01479-831258). A vacation hotel right beside the Strathspey Steam Railway, with Cairngorm views. 32 rooms with modern furnishings.

Fairwinds ($$) Carrbridge PH23 3AA (tel: 01479-841240). A Victorian former manse with 5 rooms and extensive gardens. Conservatory lounge/dining room.

Muckrach Lodge ($$$) Dulnain Bridge PH26 3LY (tel: 01479-851257). A former shooting lodge with mountain views, conservatory dining room, and 10 bedrooms.

Cowal

Enmore Hotel ($$) Marine Parade, Kirn, Dunoon PA23 8HH (tel: 01369 702230). Sea views, squash courts, 10 traditionally furnished bedrooms, and a genuinely friendly welcome.

Crinan

The Stag ($$) Argyll Sreet, Lochgilphead PA31 8NE (tel: 01546-602496). Town-center hotel with live music in downstairs bar at weekends. 17 (small) bedrooms.

Fort William

Allt-nan-Ros ($$$) Onich, by Fort William PH33 6RY (tel: 01855 821210). Fine family-run hotel with superb Loch Linnhe views. 21 modern bedrooms.

Inverlochy Castle Hotel ($$$) Torlundy, by Fort William, Inverness-shire PH33 6SN (tel: 01397-702177). The byword for luxury country-house-style accommodations in Scotland. 17 rooms.

Kilcamb Lodge Hotel ($$$) Strontian, Argyll PH36 4HY (tel: 01967-402257). Sturdy Georgian house with private shoreline on Loch Sunart. 11 rooms.

Letterfinlay Lodge ($$) Letterfinlay PH34 4DZ (tel: 01397-712622). A family-run hotel with 13 rooms, 12 miles north of Fort William on A82. Views over Loch Lochy.

Moorings Hotel ($$) Banavie, Fort William, Inverness-shire PH33 7LY (tel: 01397-772797). Canal-side location with panoramic mountain views. Ideal touring base. 24 rooms.

Nevis Bank ($$) Belford Road, Fort William PH33 6BY (tel: 01397-705721). Situated on the town outskirts at entrance to Glen Nevis. 31 rooms plus 8 annex rooms. Gymnasium.

Hotels & Restaurants

Glen Coe
Ballachulish Hotel ($$) Ballachulish, Argyll PA39 4JY (tel: 01855-811606). An imposing old baronial hotel with 54 rooms, overlooking main road and Loch Linnhe.
Holly Tree ($$) Kentallen, by Appin, Argyll PA38 4BY (tel: 01631-740292). A comfortably converted Edwardian station, on superb loch-side location.

Grantown-on-Spey
Garth Hotel ($$) Castle Road, Grantown-on-Spey PH26 3HN (tel: 01479-872836). Relaxed and friendly town-center hotel with log fires. 17 modern bedrooms.

Inverness
Bunchrew House ($$$) Bunchrew, Inverness IV3 6TA (tel: 01463-234917). 17th-century mansion on shores of Beauly Firth, popular with sporting, business, and leisure guests. 11 luxurious bedrooms.
Dunain Park Hotel ($$) Inverness IV3 6JN (tel: 01463-230512). Georgian country house in secluded grounds, six bedrooms, eight suites, pool, and sauna.
Kingsmills Hotel ($$$) Calcabock Road, Inverness IV2 3LP (tel: 01463-237166). An 84-room hotel with good leisure facilities, catering for tourist and business clientele.
Travel Inn ($$) Millburn Road, Inverness IV2 3QX (tel: 01463-712010). Modern hotel with 40 spacious rooms. Good for families.
Windsor Hotel ($$) 22 Ness Bank, Inverness IV2 4SF (tel: 01463-715535). Riverside town house hotel with 18 pine-furnished bedrooms, lounge, and dining room.

Loch Ness
Knockie Lodge Hotel ($$$) Whitebridge, Inverness-shire IV1 2UP (tel: 01456-486276). A 10-room hotel with simple high quality.

Oban
Ardanaiseig Hotel ($$$) Kilchrennan, by Taynuilt, Argyll PA35 1HE (tel: 01866-833333). Romantically set country house with an outstandingly attractive garden.
Falls of Lora Hotel ($$) Connel, by Oban PA37 1PB (tel: 01631-710483). Popular vacation hotel, restaurant, and bistro bar. 30 rooms, ranging from luxury to basic.
Isle of Eriska ($$$) Ledaig, by Oban, Argyll, PA37 1SD (tel: 01631-720371). Family-owned baronial mansion offering the highest standards of comfort. 17 rooms.
Manor House Hotel ($$$) Gallanach Road, Oban PA34 4LS (tel: 01631-562087). First-rate hotel in Georgian mansion close to town center. Sea views. Excellent restaurant.

THE NORTHERN HIGHLANDS
Dornoch
Burghfield House ($$) Dornoch, Sutherland IV25 3HN (tel: 01862-810212). Victorian mansion in extensive gardens, with antiques and open fires. 14 rooms.

Dornoch Castle Hotel ($$) Castle Street, Dornoch, Sutherland IV25 3SD (tel: 01862-810216). Originally the local bishop's palace this pleasant, town-center hotel has plenty of ambience.
Royal Golf Hotel ($$$) The First Tee, Grange Road, Dornoch, Sutherland IV25 3LG (tel: 01862-810283). Old-established hotel with views over the famous golf course. Popular with golfers, non-golfers, and business people. 25 rooms, plus 8 annex rooms.

Gairloch
Aultbea Hotel ($$) Aultbea IV22 2HX (tel: 01445-731201). On the shores of Loch Ewe, a small family-run hotel with relaxed atmosphere. 11 rooms, lounge, bistro, and restaurant.
Creag Mor ($$) Charleston, Gairloch IV21 2AH (tel: 01445-712068). Comfortable vacation hotel with 17 rooms and harbor views.

Lochinver
Eddrachilles Hotel ($$) Badcall Bay, Scourie IV27 4TH (tel: 01971-502080). Spectacular island-studded views. 11 recently upgraded bedrooms.
Inver Lodge ($$$) Lochinver, Sutherland IV27 4LU (tel: 01571-844496.) Modern hotel with wide coastal views; 20 rooms with good facilities.
Kinlochbervie Hotel ($$$) Kinlochbervie, Sutherland IV27 4RP (tel: 01971-521275). Family-run hotel overlooking sea loch and fishing harbor. 14 rooms.

Thurso
Park Hotel ($$) Thurso KW14 8RE (tel: 01847-893251). Modern hotel with lounge bar and restaurant. 11 rooms.

Torridons
Loch Torridon Hotel ($$$) Torridon, by Achnasheen, Wester Ross IV22 2EY (tel: 01445-791242). Extensively refurbished hotel, now of very high standard and earning excellent reputation. 21 bedrooms.
Tigh an Eilean Hotel ($$$) Shieldaig, by Strathcarron, Wester Ross IV54 8XN (tel: 01520-755251). Personally run hotel, maintained to a high standard. Offering good seafood. 11 rooms.

Ullapool
Ceilidh Place ($$) West Argyle Street, Ullapool IV26 2TY (tel: 01854-612103). Unique hotel with relaxed style, live music, restaurant, coffee shop and bars, lounge, and 13 rooms (bunkhouse also available).
Dundonnell Hotel ($$) Dundonnell, by Garve, Wester Ross IV23 2QR (tel: 01854-633204). Family-run for over 30 years; popular haven in wild country. Admirable lodgings. 30 rooms.

THE ISLANDS
Arran
Auchrannie Country House Hotel ($$$) Brodick, Arran KA27 8BZ (tel: 01770-302234). Previously home to a dowager

278

duchess; 28 bedroom hotel with luxurious add-on leisure facilities.

Kilmichael Country House Hotel ($$$) Glen Cloy, Brodick KA27 8BY (tel: 01770-302219). Delightful small mansion close to Brodick, with flowers, books, and excellent food. 9 rooms.

Colonsay

Isle of Colonsay Hotel ($$–$$$) Colonsay, Argyll PA61 7YP (tel: 01951-200316). A superb location and a very well-equipped hideaway. (Try the fresh oysters.) 10 rooms.

Harris

Ardvourlie Castle ($$) Aird a Mhulaidh, Harris HS3 3AB (tel: 01859-502307). Impressive-looking castle situated on loch shore amid wild scenery. Excellent home cooking and personal attention. Four rooms.

Harris Hotel ($$) Tarbert, Isle of Harris HS3 3DL (tel: 01859-502154). Down-to-earth family-run hotel located close to ferry. 25 rooms.

Scarista House ($$$) Scarista, Isle of Harris HS3 3HX (tel: 01859-550238). Elegance and comfort are provided in this Georgian house overlooking an endless shell sand beach. The hotel has a high reputation for its cuisine. Five rooms.

Two Waters Guest House ($$) Lickisto, Harris, Western Isles PA85 3EL (tel: 01859-530246). Home cooking; own smokehouse set amid wild hill and loch setting. Four rooms.

Lewis

Caberfeidh Hotel ($$$) or ($$) Manor Park, Stornoway, Lewis HS1 2EU (tel: 01851-702604). A 46-room modern hotel thought to be Lewis's finest. Serving good local seafood.

Galston Farm Guest House ($$) South Galston, Lewis, Western Isles HS2 0SH (tel. 01851-850492). 18th-century restored working croft by the shore with Butt of Lewis views. Three rooms.

Mull

Western Isles Hotel ($$) Tobermory PA75 6PR (tel: 01688-302012). Traditional vacation hotel with extensive views. 26 rooms, and 2 restaurants.

Shetland (Mainland)

Busta House ($$$) Busta, Brae, Shetland ZE2 9QN (tel: 01806-522506). Scotland's most northerly top-flight, country-house-style establishment; considerable charm and elegance. 20 rooms.

Lerwick Hotel ($$$) 15 South Road, Lerwick ZE1 0RB (tel: 01595-692166). Recently refurbished hotel, near town center, with 35 rooms.

Shetland Hotel ($$) Holmsgarth Road, Lerwick ZE1 0PW (tel: 01595-695515). Modern 64-room hotel conveniently located for the ferry.

Unst (Shetland)

Baltasound Hotel ($$) Unst ZE2 9DS (tel: 01957-711334). Informal hotel with open-plan lounge/restaurant/bar, 10 rooms, and 17 log cabins.

Restaurants

It is possible to eat very well in Scotland, though sometimes the locals would argue that the very best of produce—the seafood, the prime beef, and so on—is sent south to market. This is not entirely true. In addition to Scottish cuisine, often influenced by the French, Scotland's cities are notably cosmopolitan in their offerings.

As a rough guide in this listing, $$$ is over £25 ($37) per person for a three-course meal excluding drinks, $$ is from £15 to £25 ($22 to $37), and $ is under £15 ($22).

Edinburgh

Atrium ($$$) 10 Cambridge Street, Edinburgh EH1 2ED (tel: 0131-228 8882). Fresh Scottish produce, with a strongly theatrical element. Very popular with locals.

L'Auberge ($$) 56 St. Mary's Street, Edinburgh EH1 1SX (tel: 0131-556 5888). French staff, excellent French food close to the Royal Mile.

Ducks at Le Marche Noir ($$) 2/4 Eyre Place, Edinburgh EH3 5EP (tel: 0131-558 1608). French country cuisine in a little New Town restaurant popular with locals.

The Grill Room ($$) Sheraton Grand Hotel, 1 Festival Square, Edinburgh EH3 9SR (tel: 0131 229 9131). Classic French cuisine served in elegant, tartan-clad surroundings.

Jackson's Restaurant ($) or ($$) 2 Jackson Close, 209–213 High Street, Edinburgh EH1 1PL (tel: 0131-225 1793). On a main tourist thoroughfare and achieving authentic Scottish tastes without resorting to "whisky sauce on everything."

Kalpna ($) 2–3 St. Patricks Square, Edinburgh EH8 9EZ (tel: 0131 667 9890). How do they manage these flavors at this price? One of the most distinctive Indian places in town. You'll not even notice it's vegetarian.

Malmaison Brasserie ($$) 1 Tower Place, Leith, Edinburgh EH6 7DB (tel: 0131-555 6868). Simple, Mediterranean-style food in dockside setting.

Martin's ($$$) 70 Rose Street North Lane, Edinburgh EH2 3DX (tel: 0131-225 3106). Tucked well away in a downtown service lane but of top quality. This is simply one of the very best restaurants anywhere in Scotland.

No. 1 The Restaurant ($$$) Balmoral Hotel, 1 Princes Street, Edinburgh EH2 2EQ (tel: 0131-556 2414). Deep-red decor, deep-cushioned seats, and top-notch modern Scottish cuisine, served in supreme style.

Pompadour ($$$) Caledonian Hotel, Princes Street, Edinburgh EH1 2AB (tel: 0131 459 9988). Gracious, old-established. Supremely high standards with a Scottish flavor.

279

Vintner's Room ($$$) The Vaults, 87 Giles Street, Leith EH6 6BZ (tel: 0131-554 6767). An eating place of high repute, housed in a 17th-century historic building in Edinburgh's port.

The Witchery by the Castle ($$) Castle Hill, Edinburgh EH2 1NE (tel: 0131-225 5613). Two atmospheric candlelit rooms in which to savor the latest cooking trends and a huge choice of wines.

Glasgow

The Buttery ($$$) 652 Argyle Street, Glasgow G3 8UF (tel: 0141-221 8188). An old-established restaurant with famously polite, unobtrusive service and great food.

Camerons Restaurant ($$$) Glasgow Hilton, 1 William Street, Glasgow G3 8HT (tel: 0141-204 5555). Highland hunting-lodge theme, but plenty of style and panache.

Drum and Monkey ($) 93–95 St. Vincent Street, Glasgow (tel: 0141-221 6636). Atmospheric pub with appetizing snacks, moving up a gear in backroom bistro.

Malmaison Café Bar and Brasserie ($) 278 West George Street, Glasgow (tel: 0141-221 6401). British favorites mix with classic French dishes in this booth-lined restaurant.

October Café ($) or ($$) Princes Square, 46 Buchanan Street, Glasgow (tel: 0141- 221 0303). Persevere—go to the roof of the modern shopping mall to find this 1930s-style café serving exciting but simple food.

One Devonshire Gardens ($$$) 1 Devonshire Gardens, Glasgow G12 0UX (tel: 0141-339 2001). Stylish cuisine in the most luxurious surroundings.

Papingo Restaurant ($$) 104 Bath Street, Glasgow G2 2EN (tel: 0141-332 6678). City-center café bar/restaurant serving modern Scottish dishes.

La Parmigiana ($) 447 Great Western Road, Glasgow G12 8HH (tel: 0141-334 0686). Deservedly popular local trattoria featuring regional Italian cooking.

Rogano Restaurant and Café Rogano ($$$) 11 Exchange Place, Glasgow G1 3AN (tel: 0141-248 4055). Remodeled in art-deco style in 1935, the long-established Rogano is a top-class restaurant.

Stravaigin ($$) 30 Gibson Street, Glasgow G12 8NX (tel: 0141-334 2665). Cheerful basement restaurant serving excellently prepared dishes from around the world (Hanoi, Chile, Mexico) using Scottish ingredients.

Ubiquitous Chip ($$) or ($$$) 12 Ashton Lane, Glasgow G12 8SJ (tel: 0141-334 5007). A sophisticated interpretation of Scotland's larder is guaranteed at "the Chip"—the discriminating Glaswegian's favorite restaurant.

Victoria and Albert ($) 159 Buchanan Street, Glasgow G1 2JX (tel: 0141-248 6329). Yet another bar-restaurant straddling the categories, depending on chosen menu.

Yes ($$$) 22 West Nile Street, Glasgow G1 2PW (tel: 0141-221 8044). A sophisticated city-center crowd enjoys the eclectic menu featuring Scottish seafood, lamb, and game cooked in modern style; paintings by Glasgow artists hang all around.

THE SOUTH

Ayr

Fouters Bistro Restaurant ($$) 2A Academy Street, Ayr KA7 1HS (tel: 01292-261391). A highly regarded establishment taking full advantage of Ayrshire's own produce. Exciting food and interesting ambience.

Biggar

Shieldhill Hotel ($$$) Quothquan, by Biggar ML12 6NA (tel: 01899-220035). In a fortified mansion built in 1199 enjoy superb innovative modern Scottish cuisine.

East Neuk Villages

Cellar Restaurant ($$$) 24 East Green, Anstruther, Fife KY10 3AA (tel: 01333-310378). Probably one of the best seafood restaurants in Scotland. Don't miss it if visiting Fife.

Gifford

Bonars Restaurant ($$) Main Street, Gifford EH41 4QH (tel: 01620-810264). This former country tearoom now offers an admirable menu of modern Scottish delights; leave room for the delicious desserts.

Girvan

Wildings ($) Montgomerie Street, Girvan KA26 9HE (tel: 01465-713481). Enjoy the cheerful enthusiasm of this busy restaurant. It majors in seafood, though meat-eaters will also be happy with the menu.

Logan Botanic Garden

Knockinaam Lodge ($$$) Portpatrick DG9 9AD, Galloway (tel: 01776-810471). A place of pilgrimage for food lovers in the far west, basically modern French and highly inventive.

North Berwick

La Potinière ($$$) Main Street, Gullane EH31 2AA (tel: 01620-843214). Near-legendary, sophisticated restaurant in golf resort.
Open Arms Hotel ($$) Dirleton, East Lothian EH39 5EG (tel: 01620-850241). Food with panache from very experienced hoteliers.

Swinton

Wheatsheaf Hotel ($$) Main Street, Swinton TD11 3JJ (tel: 01890-860257). Country inn by the village green, serving carefully cooked seasonal produce.

Troon

Highgrove House ($$) Old Loans Road, Troon KA10 7HL (tel: 01292-312511). Popular venue overlooking the Firth of Clyde, serving well-prepared food—country paté, roasts, and traditional desserts.

CENTRAL SCOTLAND
Arbroath
Gordon's Restaurant ($$) Homewood House, Main Street, Inverkeilor, by Arbroath, Angus DD11 5RN (tel: 01241-830364). Cozy village restaurant, decorated in cottage style.

Balloch
Grill Room ($$$) Cameron House Hotel, by Alexandria, Dunbartonshire G83 8QZ (tel: 01389-755565). Very sophisticated cuisine of the highest standards at this country club hotel over-looking Loch Lomond.

Blairgowrie
Kinloch House Hotel ($$$) Blairgowrie PH10 6SG (tel: 01250-884237). Fruit and vegetables from the 19th-century walled garden of this country house are married to the best Scottish meats and seafood, cooked with a light, precise touch.

Callander
Roman Camp Hotel ($$$) Callander, Perthshire FK17 8BG (tel: 01877-330003). Cooking with Scottish flair at the restaurant of this old, riverside country house.

Carnoustie
11 Park Avenue ($$) 11 Park Avenue, Carnoustie DD7 7JA (tel: 01241-853336). Unpretentious town-center restaurant offering good, simply cooked food like mussels in white wine and grilled salmon.

Dundee
Stakis Dundee ($$) Earl Grey Place, Dundee DD1 4DE (tel: 01382-229271). Quayside setting for a modern hotel with open-plan restaurant. The menu includes Highland game terrine, Finnan haddock, and other Scottish classics.

Killiecrankie
Killiecrankie Hotel ($$$) Killiecrankie, Pitlochry PH16 5LG (tel: 01796-473220). Enthusiastically run, with a great atmosphere and cuisine proving that modern trends do penetrate far beyond the cities.

Perth
Auchterarder House ($$$) Auchterarder, Perthshire PH3 1DZ (tel: 01764-663646). The style and flair of this opulent Victorian country house is reflected in the menus.
Let's Eat ($$) 77/79 Kinnoull Street, Perth (tel: 01738-643377). Housed in premises of the former theater and popular with locals, this restaurant offers an ideas-packed menu ranging from fashionable salsas to char-grilled ribeye steak with fries.
Number Thirty Three Seafood Restaurant ($$$) 33 George Street, Perth PH1 5LA (tel: 01738-633771). Café bar/restaurant majoring in fish, with adjoining oyster bar.

St. Andrews
Ostlers Close ($$) Bonnygate, Cupar, Fife KY15 4BU (tel: 01334-655574). Hidden up a "close" or alleyway is outstanding cuisine, consistent over the years.

Trossachs
Braeval ($$$) Braeval, Aberfoyle FK8 3UY (tel: 01877-382711). TV chef Nick Nairn's home base. Sample his unique style of cooking in this converted mill.

THE NORTHEAST
Aberdeen
Ardoe House Hotel ($$$) South Deeside Road, Blairs, Aberdeen AB1 5YP (tel: 01224-867355). Paneled dining room in a baronial mansion, featuring a menu of game, roasts, and seafood.
The Marcliffe at Pitfodels ($$$) North Deeside Road, Pitfodels, Aberdeen AB15 9YA (tel: 01224-861000). A team of chefs emphasizes local produce here: lobster, halibut, Aberdeen Angus beef, venison.
Patio Hotel ($$) Beach Boulevard, Aberdeen AB24 1EF (tel: 01224-633339). Specializing in seafood and appropriately sited on the seafront.
Q Brasserie ($$) 9 Alfred Place, Aberdeen AB1 1YD (tel: 01224-595001). A former church owned building is the slightly unexpected setting for innovative modern Scottish cuisine.

Ballater
Darroch Learg Hotel ($$$) Braemar Road, Ballater AB35 5UX (tel: 01339-755443). A Victorian mansion on Royal Deeside with a choice of two set-price menus offering Scottish produce cooked with great flair.
The Green Inn, 9 Victoria Road, Ballater, Aberdeenshire AB35 5QQ (tel: 013397-55701). Health-conscious, local dishes (and specialty Scottish cheeses).

Craigellachie
Archiestown Hotel ($$) Archiestown, Aberlour AB38 7QX (tel: 01340-810218). A popular angling hotel with informal bistro; the blackboard menu features casseroles, fish, steaks, and treacle pudding to follow.
Rib Room Craigellachie Hotel, ($$$) Craigellachie, Banffshire AB38 9SR (tel: 01340-881204). Thoroughly Scottish in ambience, with professional hotel cooking of the highest standard.
A Taste of Speyside ($) or ($$) 10 Balvenie Street, Dufftown, Banffshire AB55 4AB (tel: 01340-820860). Good home cooking with extra touches (plus a huge malt whisky selection).

Elgin
Old Monastery ($$$) or ($$) Drybridge, by Buckie, Banffshire AB56 2JB (tel: 01542-832660). The best for miles around. Sophisticated, honest cooking without pretension.

Kildrummy Castle
Kildrummy Castle Hotel ($$$) Kildrummy AB33 8RA (tel: 019755-71288). Victorian country-house hotel beside medieval castle

ruins, featuring the excellent local game, Aberdeen Angus beef, and salmon.

THE GREAT GLEN & WESTERN HIGHLANDS
Arduaine
Loch Melfort Hotel ($$) Arduaine, by Oban PA34 4XG (tel: 01852-200233). Set beside Arduaine Gardens and with sea views, a hotel restaurant emphasizing seafood.

Cowal
Beverley's Restaurant ($$) Ardfillayne Hotel, Bullwood Road, Dunoon, Argyll PA23 7QJ (tel: 01369-702267). Classical French cooking meets Scottish traditional amid high Victoriana.

Fort William
Arisaig House ($$$) Beasdale, by Arisaig, Inverness-shire PH39 4NR (tel: 01687-450622). Special country house in impressive location with food to match.
Crannog Seafood Restaurant ($$) Town Pier, Fort William, Inverness-shire PH33 7NG (tel: 01397-705589). Here the catch is unloaded directly into the kitchen. Good value.

Grantown-on-Spey
Garth Hotel ($$) Castle Road, Grantown-on-Spey PH26 3HN (tel: 01479-872836). A friendly hotel offering straightforward, French-influenced cooking.

Inverness
Dunain Park Hotel ($$$) Inverness IV3 6JN (tel: 01463-230512). Top-quality Scottish game and seafood, with home-grown vegetables and home-baking, are merged in Scottish-French cuisine.

Kingussie
The Cross ($$$) Tweed Mill Brae, Ardbroilach Road, Kingussie, Inverness-shire PH21 1TC (tel: 01540-661166). A mill conversion full of character, but do not be distracted from the high-quality food.

Oban
Airds Hotel ($$$) Port Appin, Argyll PA38 4DF (tel: 01631-730236). This elegant hotel, housed in a former ferry inn, offers creative food with great finesse.
Isle of Eriska Hotel ($$$) Isle of Eriska, Ledaig, by Oban, Argyll PA37 1SD (tel: 01631-720371). An island setting for a hotel dining room starring a daily roast, ably supported by Scottish game, fish and seafood.
Taychreggan Hotel ($$) Kilchrenan, Taynuilt PA35 1HQ (tel: 01866-833211). A 300-year-old drovers' inn on the tree-clad shores of Loch Awe offering an eclectic menu, stressing local produce.

THE NORTHERN HIGHLANDS
Cromarty
The Dower House ($$$) Highfield, Muir of Ord IV6 7XN (tel: 01463-870090). The sophisticated menu is served in elegant surroundings. Dishes include spinach tagliatelle with scallops or filet of beef with rosti.

Dundonnell
Dundonnell Hotel ($$) Dundonnell IV23 2QS (tel: 01854-633204). Highland hospitality beside Little Loch Broom. The chef excels at fish and seafood.

Kylesku
Kylesku Hotel ($$) Kylesku, Lairg, Sutherland IV27 4HW (tel: 01971-502231). Small waterside hotel offering seafood landed minutes earlier on the pier nearby.

Lochinver
Lochinver Larder's Riverside Bistro ($$) Main Street, Lochinver, Sutherland IV27 4JY (tel: 01571-844356). Panoramic bay views, with steaks and seafood prominent on the menu.

Timespan (Helmsdale)
Royal Marine Hotel ($$) Golf Road, Brora KW9 6QS (tel: 01408-621252). The dining room offers a wide-ranging menu making good use of local produce.

Tongue
Ben Loyal Hotel ($$) Tongue IV27 4XE (tel: 01847-611216). A family-run hotel offering traditional Scottish cooking, including leek and potato soup, cod in cheese sauce, with Atholl brose for dessert.

Ullapool
Altnaharrie Inn ($$$) Ullapool IV26 2SS (tel: 01854-633230). Guests talk in reverent tones about food here. It can only be reached by boat—so you will want to stay.

THE ISLANDS
Mull
Druimard Hotel ($$) Dervaig, Isle of Mull PA75 6QW (tel: 01688-400345). Enjoy potted wild salmon with oatcakes, game terrine, or saddle of venison for a pre-theater dinner (Mull Little Theatre is next door).

Orkney
Creel Restaurant ($$) Front Road, St. Margaret's Hope, South Ronaldsay, Orkney KW17 2SL (tel: 01856-831311). A very popular restaurant, which has won numerous awards, working wonders with seafoods, as well as Orkney beef and lamb.

Skye
Ardvasar Hotel ($$) Ardvasar, Skye IV45 8RS (tel: 01471-844223). Straight-forward cuisine using island produce: potted crab, roast chicken glazed with honey and mustard, and game pie are typical dishes.
Three Chimneys Restaurant ($$$) Colbost, nr. Dunvegan, Skye IV55 8ZT (tel: 01470-511258). Cuisine of the highest order at the most westerly point of Skye in a converted crofter's cottage.

Glossary

Entries with asterisks indicate words of Gaelic origin

bastel a characteristically Scottish fortified house (cf. French bastille)

ben* a mountain, hill (usually used as a prefix)

bonnie bonny, pretty, fine, handsome

brae* slope, road with steep gradient, hillside

broch a late-prehistoric round tower

burgess a citizen of a burgh (see below)

burgh Scottish town with special privileges granted by (royal) charter

burn a stream

byre a cowshed

cairn* a pile of stones, often now marking hilltops or landmarks, or a memorial

ceilidh* originally an informal gathering or visit to neighbors at which stories and songs were performed, now a concert or entertainment in a hall or hotel

clachan* a small Highland village

clan* a Highland family group or tribe, owing allegiance to a chief

claymore* a large double-edged sword, often a basket-hilted, single-edged sword

Clearances the economic reorganization of the Highland estates, mainly taking place from 1800 to 1850, which resulted in the suppression or discouragement of arable farming and the clearing and resettlement of tenants, either on less productive coastal ground or by forced emigration

corrie* a deep hollow on the face of a mountain, scooped out by glacial action

Covenanter a supporter of the National Covenant (1638), a manifesto drawn up in protest against King Charles I's religious reforms

craig* a crag, cliff

croft a small holding

dram a single drink (or "nip") of whisky; to drink whisky

factor a Scottish estate manager

firth a wide sea inlet or major river estuary

Gael* a Gaelic-speaking Highlander

Gaeltacht* the Gaelic-speaking community

geo in Orkney, Shetland, and Caithness, a narrow gully-like sea inlet

glen* a Highland valley, often U-shape in profile

haar coastal mist, often occurring in summer on the east coast

howe a hollow or low-lying piece of ground

Jacobite a (Catholic) supporter of the exiled King James VII (of Scotland), his son, and grandson (Bonnie Prince Charlie)

kirk church

kirk elder an ordained member of the Presbyterian Church, elected to hold office

kyle* either an inlet or strait between the mainland and an offshore island

laird the owner (or the landlord) of an estate

linn* a cataract or the pool below a cataract or waterfall

loch* a lake

lochan* a small lake

machair* grassland lying immediately behind a sandy beach

manse the house of the kirk minister

mercat cross a market cross, symbol of the trading rights of a Scottish burgh

Munro a Scottish peak over 3,000 ft (914 m) in height (named after Sir Hugh Munro, the first compiler of such mountains)

neuk corner, as in East Neuk, the eastern corner of Fife

ogham, ogaman ancient Celtic alphabet with 20 characters

policies the enclosed grounds or parkland of a large house

quaich* a shallow, two-handled drinking bowl, now usually ornamental

sassenach* a non-Gaelic speaking Lowlander—Scots or English —often now used simply to indicate a non-Scot

strath* a broad open valley

tolbooth the former administrative center of a Scottish burgh

tombolo a narrow sand strip joining an island to the mainland

voe a bay or creek in Orkney and Shetland

Index

Index

285

Index

Index

Picture Credits

The Automobile Association would like to thank the following photographers, libraries, and associations for their assistance in the preparation of this book.
ABERDEEN UNIVERSITY LIBRARY 42–43 Embarking at Broomielaw, Glasgow   MARY EVANS PICTURE LIBRARY 25 19th-century shipbuilding, 28 Bannockburn, 30–31 execution warrant, 30b Mary, Queen of Scots, 34–35 Battle of Prestonpans, 104–105 Robert Burns, 197a Culloden   D. HARDLEY 110 Culzean Castle, 120 Logan Gardens, 202 Mull of Kintyre, 231a Rothesay Harbor, 232 Colonsay, 234 Islay, 235a Ferry to Jura, 235b Kildaton Cross   HULTON DEUTSCH COLLECTION LTD. 205a Loch Ness Monster   CATHERINE KARNOW front cover silhouette   NATIONAL GALLERY OF SCOTLAND 33 Earl of Seafield   ROYAL GEOGRAPHICAL SOCIETY 37a map   SCONE PALACE 150 Scone Palace   SPECTRUM COLOUR LIBRARY 39 Dunrobin Castle   THE MANSELL COLLECTION LTD. 26a seal and coins of Alexander III, 28–29 Bannockburn Battle, 30a Mary, Queen of Scots, 36b Adam Smith, 41 Andrew Carnegie, 42 building of Queen Mary, 123a Lanark, 123c Robert Owen
The remaining photographs are held in the Automobile Association's own library (A.A. PHOTO LIBRARY) and were taken by the following photographers: M. ADLEMAN 38, M. ALEXANDER 6–7, 18–9, 23b, 40b, 76, 77, 78a, 81a, 81b, 82a, 82b, 83b, 83c, 86a, 86b, 87a, 90, 91, 94, 97, 98, 99, 100a, 100b, 101, 102, 106a, 106b, 107, 112a, 112b, 113a, 114a, 115, 118a, 124, 125a, 125b, 127a, 127b, A BAKER 17a, 131, 147a, 154, 155a, 155c, 172–173, 190a, 190b, J. BEAZLEY 5c, 9, 35a, 108b, 109a, 109b, 114b, 116a, 117, 118b, 121a, 121b, 122a, 122b, 128b, 192, 193a, 196, 200b, 213b, 216, 221a, 221b, P. & G. BOWATER 169b, J. CARNIE 2, 10a, 10b, 14, 15, 20b, 31, 34, 130, 138b, 151c, 184, 189, 191, 199, 200a, 204, 205b, 212a, 213a, 226, 230, 231b, D. CORRANCE 20a, 23a, 48a, 50, 51a, 51b, 55, 59a, 64, 67, 111, 119, 129a, 129b, S. L. DAY 11a, 13b, 18, 19, 21b, 22a, 22b, 24a, 29a, 29b, 35b, 128a, 132, 133a, 133b, 135a, 135b, 135c, 136, 137, 138a, 139, 140, 141a, 141b, 142b, 143a, 143b, 144a, 144b, 145a, 145b, 147b, 148–149, 148, 149, 151a, 151b, 152, 153a, 153b, 156, 157, 158, 159a, 159b, 160–161, 160, 161, 167b, 186, 187a, 187b, 188a, 193b, 194, 195a, 195b, 198, 203, 206, 207a, 207b, 260, 261b, 263a, 263b, 266a, 270, E. ELLINGTON 5a, 7, 16–17, 26b, 163, 164, 165a, 166, 167a, 168, 170b, 174, 175a, 176a, 176b, 177a, 177b, 179, 182a, 210, 211a, 212b, 214, 215, 217a, 217b, 218–219, 218, 220a, 223a, 223b, 224b, 228, 229a, 229b, 238, 239a, 239b, 240a, 240b, 242a, 242b, 243, 244a, 244b, 245, 245b, 246, 247a, 247b, 262, 265, 267a, R. G. ELLIOTT 49, 64–65, 68, 69, 70b, 95b, 96, 220b, 225, 226–227, 236a, 236b, 237a, 237b, 248, 249a, 249b, 250a, 252b, 252c, 254a, 254b, 255, 267b, 273, S. GIBSON PHOTOGRAPHY 43, 79b, 80, 83a, 85a, 88a, 88b, 89a, 92, 93a, 93b, 95a, 108a, 264, D. HARDLEY 27, 146, 219, A. J. HOPKINS 188b, 222, R. JOHNSON 241, S. & O. MATHEWS 126, K. PATERSON 3, 8, 11b, 12a, 12b, 13a, 16, 17b, 21a, 32a, 32b, 36a, 37b, 44, 46, 47, 48b, 52a, 52b, 53, 54a, 54b, 56a, 56b, 57, 58, 59b, 60a, 61a, 61b, 62, 63a, 63b, 65, 66, 70a, 71, 72a, 72b, 73, 74a, 74b, 75a, 261a, 266b, D. ROBERTSON 5b, P. SHARPE 84, 103a, 103b, 105, 170a, 201, M. TAYLOR 171a, 171b, 171c, 178, 180, 211b, 224a, R. WEIR 4, 24, 134, 165b, 169a, 172, 173, 175b, 182b, 197b, 252a, 253.

Contributors

Revision copy editor/Americanizer: Janet Tabinski   Original copy editor: Barbara Fuller
Revision verifier: Gilbert Summers